LONDON BOROUGH OF ENFIELD

CENTRAL LIBRARY
CECIL ROAD, ENFIELD

No. L81302

This book to be RETURNED on or before the latest date stamped below unless a renewal has been obtained by personal call, post or telephone, quoting the above number and the date due for return.

13. JUN 1974			
26. JUN. 1974			
-3. JAN 1975			
-3. JAN. 1976			
-7. FEB 1976			
-3. SEP. 1976			
-5 NOV. 1977			
23. APR. 1978			
13. AUG. 1979			

In the case of infectious illness, do not return books to the Library, but inform the Librarian.

ESSAYS IN ANALYSIS

BY BERTRAND RUSSELL

1896 *German Social Democracy*
1897 *An Essay on the Foundations of Geometry* (Constable)
1900 *The Philosophy of Leibniz*
1903 *The Principles of Mathematics*
1910 *Philosophical Essays*
1912 *Problems of Philosophy* (Oxford U.P.)
1910–13 *Principia Mathematics* 3 vols. (with A. N. Whitehead) (Cambridge U.P.)
1914 *Our Knowledge of the External World*
1916 *Justice in Wartime*
1916 *Principles of Social Reconstruction*
1917 *Political Ideals*
1918 *Roads to Freedom*
1918 *Mysticism and Logic*
1919 *Introduction to Mathematical Philosophy*
1920 *The Practice and Theory of Bolshevism*
1921 *The Analysis of Mind*
1922 *The Problem of China*
1923 *Prospects of Industrial Civilisation* (with Dora Russell)
1923 *The ABC of Atoms* (out of print)
1924 *Icarus or the Future of Science* (USA only)
1925 *The ABC of Relativity*
1925 *What I Believe*
1926 *On Education*
1927 *An Outline of Philosophy*
1927 *The Analysis of Matter*
1928 *Sceptical Essays*
1929 *Marriage and Morals*
1930 *The Conquest of Happiness*
1931 *The Scientific Outlook*
1932 *Education and the Social Order*
1934 *Freedom and Organisation: 1814–1914*
1935 *In Praise of Idleness*
1935 *Religion and Science* (Oxford U.P.)
1936 *Which Way to Peace?* (out of print)
1937 *The Amberley Papers* (with Patricia Russell)
1938 *Power*
1940 *An Inquiry into Meaning and Truth*
1945 *History of Western Philosophy*
1948 *Human Knowledge: Its Scope and Limits*
1949 *Authority and the Individual*
1950 *Unpopular Essays*
1951 *New Hopes for a Changing World*
1952 *The Impact of Science on Society*
1953 *The Good Citizen's Alphabet* (Gaberbocchus)
1953 *Satan in the Suburbs* (out of print)
1954 *Nightmares of Eminent Persons* (out of print)
1954 *Human Society in Ethics and Politics*
1956 *Logic and Knowledge* (ed. by R. C. Marsh)
1956 *Portraits from Memory*
1957 *Why I am Not a Christian* (ed. by Paul Edwards)
1957 *Understanding History and other essays* (USA only)
1958 *Vital Letters of Russell, Khrushchev, Dulles* (Macgibbon and Kee) (out of print)
1958 *Bertrand Russell's Best* (ed. by Robert Egner)
1959 *Common Sense and Nuclear Warfare*
1959 *Wisdom of the West* (ed. by Paul Foulkes) (Macdonald)
1959 *My Philosophical Development*
1960 *Bertrand Russell Speaks his Mind* (USA only)
1961 *Fact and Fiction*
1961 *Has Man a Future?*
1961 *The Basic Writings of Bertrand Russell* (ed. by R. E. Egner and L. Denonn)
1963 *Unarmed Victory*
1967 *War Crimes in Vietnam*
1967 *The Archives of Bertrand Russell* (ed. by B. Feinberg, Continuum) (out of print)
1967 *Autobiography 1872–1914*
1968 *Autobiography 1914–1944*
1969 *Autobiography 1944–1967*
1969 *Dear Bertrand Russell . . .* (ed. by B. Feinberg and R. Kasrils)
1972 *The Collected Stories of Bertrand Russell* (ed. by B. Feinberg)

ESSAYS IN ANALYSIS

by

Bertrand Russell

edited by
Douglas Lackey

London · George Allen & Unwin Ltd
Ruskin House   Museum Street

First published in 1973

This book is copyright under the Berne Convention. All rights are reserved. Apart from any fair dealing for the purpose of private study, research, criticism or review, as permitted under the Copyright Act, 1956, no part of this publication may be reproduced, stored in a retrieval system, or transmitted, in any form or by any means, electronic, electrical, chemical, mechanical, optical, photocopying, recording or otherwise, without the prior permission of the copyright owner. Enquiries should be addressed to the publishers.

© George Allen & Unwin Ltd 1973

ISBN 0 04 108002 5

Printed in Great Britain
in 11 point Baskerville
by William Clowes & Sons, Limited
London, Beccles and Colchester

CONTENTS

Preface *page* 9

I. INTRODUCTION 11

II. RUSSELL'S CRITIQUE OF MEINONG 17
    1. Meinong's Theory of Complexes and Assumptions (1904) 21
    2. Review of: A. Meinong, *Untersuchungen zur Gegenstandstheorie und Psychologie* (1905) 77
    3. Review of: A. Meinong, *Uber die Stellung der Gegenstandstheorie im System der Wissenschaften* (1907) 89

III. DESCRIPTIONS AND EXISTENCE 95
    4. The Existential Import of Propositions (1905) 98
    5. On Denoting (1905) 103
    6. Mr Strawson on Referring (1957) 120

IV. CLASSES AND THE PARADOXES 127
    7. On Some Difficulties in the Theory of Transfinite Numbers and Order Types (1905) 135
    8. On the Substitutional Theory of Classes and Relations (1906) 165
    9. On 'Insolubilia' and their Solution by Symbolic Logic (1906) 190
    10. The Theory of Logical Types (1910) 215

V. PHILOSOPHY OF LOGIC AND MATHEMATICS 253
    11. The Axiom of Infinity (1904) 256
    12. On the Relation of Mathematics to Logic (1905) 260
    13. The Regressive Method of Discovering the Premises of Mathematics (1907) 272
    14. The Philosophical Implications of Mathematical Logic (1911) 284
    15. Is Mathematics Purely Linguistic? (1950–2) 295

VI. APPENDIX: FOUR PAPERS BY HUGH MACCOLL   307
Symbolic Reasoning (1905)   308
Three Notes from *Mind* (1905)   317

VII. BIBLIOGRAPHY   323
A. Historical background   325
B. Russell's Writings on Logic, published and unpublished   329
C. Secondary material   336

INDEX   343

PREFACE

In compiling this anthology I have been principally concerned with making clear the development of Russell's ideas in the crucial years from 1904 to 1913. Readers therefore may be surprised to see that the classic paper, 'Mathematical Logic as based on the Theory of Types' has been omitted. Since this paper is readily available in three recent anthologies (R. Marsh's *Logic and Knowledge*, J. van Heijenoort's *From Frege to Gödel*, and Copi and Gould's *Readings in Logical Theory*) I felt that it was better to devote the space to lesser known and less accessible works. The mature theory of types is represented by 'The Theory of Logical Types' from 1910. All unbracketed footnotes in the essays are by Russell, but the citations have been altered to conform to the bibliographies. The bibliographies run chronologically, then alphabetically. The reader may find this unusual at first, but by this means the bibliographies become readable surveys of the history of logic.

This book would not have been possible without the support and co-operation of the Bertrand Russell Archives of McMaster University. The Archives contributed three previously unpublished papers, and supplied the English manuscripts of two articles Russell published in French. The Archivist at McMaster, Mr Kenneth Blackwell, supplied a complete bibliography of Russell's works on Logic, published and unpublished. With the founding of the Russell Archives, the era of Russell scholarship can be considered inaugurated. Finally, this entire project rests on the consent and aid of the Bertrand Russell Estate, for which I am most grateful. All of the previously published essays in this volume are printed with their permission.

I am grateful to the Editors of *Mind* and of the *Proceedings of the London Mathematical Society* for use of papers from those publications. Professor Victor Lowe and Mrs T. North Whitehead gave kind permission to use quotations from Whitehead's letters to Russell, and Mr Frederick Bôcher granted the use of

PREFACE

letters from the mathematician Maxime Bôcher. Mr Harvey Goldman and Miss Laimdota Mazzarins worked out the translation of 'Sur la Relation de Mathématiques à la Logistique'. Throughout this project I have been most of all indebted to Miss Lyn Traverse for her help and patience.

Douglas P. Lackey
City University of
New York
Baruch College

I

INTRODUCTION

In 1956, Robert C. Marsh edited a collection of Russell's philosophical essays under the title *Logic and Knowledge*. That collection included 'On Denoting', 'Mathematical Logic as based on the Theory of Types', Russell's lectures on Logical Atomism, and other central works of Russell's philosophical career. But interests in philosophy have shifted since 1956, and so has interest in Russell's work. The rise of presupposition-free logics in the late 1950s sheds new light on Russell's debate with Hugh MacColl; the revival of philosophical Realism prompts re-reading of Russell's extensive essays on Alexius Meinong, and the same holds for a variety of current topics on which Russell had something original and important to say. The present volume is a response to these new concerns. It includes fifteen essays, three never before published, three published before only in French. All except one date from the years between the *Principles of Mathematics* and the publication of *Principia Mathematica* (1903–13), the decade in which, in common opinion, Russell did his finest work. All of the papers concern topics in logic, if one takes as 'logic' the full range of issues Russell considers under that heading in the *Principles of Mathematics*.

Russell's participation in the International Congress of Philosophy in July of 1900 marked the turning point for his early investigations in logic. It was there that he first met Giuseppe Peano, and obtained reprints of his work from him. In August of 1900, Russell mastered Peano's notation and methods, and in September he succeeded in extending them to the logic of relations. He wrote a paper describing these results, and containing a new definition of 'cardinal number' (discovered independently by Frege), and sent it in to Peano's

INTRODUCTION

journal.[1] In October of 1900, Russell commenced work on the *Principles of Mathematics*, and he finished the first draft, some 200,000 words, at the end of December.

The great successes of 1900 were followed by severe setbacks in 1901. In May of that year, Russell studied Cantor's proof that there is no greatest cardinal, and attempted to apply Cantor's argument to the class of all the things there are. The unintended result was Russell's discovery of a paradox in the notion of the class of all classes which are not members of themselves.[2] When the paradox resisted solution through 1901, Russell decided to complete the *Principles of Mathematics* without solving it. He revised the sections entitled 'The Indefinables of Mathematics' and 'Number', added a new chapter describing the contradiction, and included an appendix sketching a tentative solution, which he called 'The Doctrine of Types'.

The book was completed on 23 May 1902. On 16 June, Russell wrote to Frege describing his paradox, and six days later Frege replied that arithmetic had been shaken to its foundations.[3] Frege wrote an appendix to the forthcoming second volume of his *Grundgesetze der Arithmetik* in which he described the paradox and proposed a solution. Russell, for his part, wrote a second appendix to the *Principles*, giving the first systematic account in English of Frege's work.

Russell planned to write a second volume of the *Principles*, using Peano's notation throughout, but, since Whitehead was planning a second volume to his *Treatise of Universal Algebra* which covered similar ground, the two agreed to work together on what was to become the three volumes of *Principia Mathematica*. For the next eight years, Russell wrote drafts for the *Principia*, sent them to Whitehead for revision, and revised them again upon Whitehead's advice.[4] In lectures at Cambridge in

---

[1] See Russell *B* 1901*b*. This book contains three bibliographies, arranged chronologically, then alphabetically. This citation is to bibliography *B*, 1901, second entry. Bibliography *C* has five parts, necessitating *C*1, *C*2, etc.

[2] A fuller account is given of the paradoxes, Russell's and others, in the introduction to Part IV.

[3] Frege *A* 1902.

[4] See Russell *B* 1948*b*.

the fall of 1902, Russell sketched the plan for the forthcoming work.

Russell's own paradox, however, remained unresolved. In May of 1903, Russell thought that he could solve it by denying the existence of classes altogether, retaining in his logical system only the notation for propositional functions. Whitehead sent Russell a congratulatory telegram,[1] but these congratulations proved to be premature, as an exact analogue to the paradox was easily constructible in terms of propositional functions alone.

The rest of 1903 was given over to the study of Free Trade. In April 1904, Russell began working again at his paradox, continuing, with few intermissions, through January 1905.[2] The intellectual deadlock of this period is vividly described in Russell's *Autobiography*. Every day in the morning he would sit down before a blank piece of paper, and in the evening it would still be empty. Throughout this time he devoted much study to developing a theory of the meaning and denotation of phrases. The first positive result of these investigations was the discovery that a variable denoting function could be deduced from a variable propositional function. But progress, even on denoting, was blocked by the necessity of taking 'the' as indefinable, as is done in the *Principles of Mathematics*. During this period he retained a realistic ontology, as is evidenced by his sympathetic review of the realistic doctrines of Alexius Meinong (reprinted in Chapter 1 below).

In the spring of 1905, Russell and his first wife Alys moved to a house in Bagley Wood, near Oxford. There, in late spring, Russell discovered his Theory of Descriptions, an exposition of which appeared in *Mind* as 'On Denoting' (Chapter 5) in October of 1905. With the devices of the Theory of Descriptions at hand, it was no longer necessary to take 'the' as indefinable, and it was possible to diminish greatly the number of entities to which a logical system is ontologically committed. The new ontological stringency of this period is evident in the critical

[1] 21 May 1903. Now in the Bertrand Russell Archives.
[2] See Grattan-Guinness C1 1972.

reviews of Meinong and the Scotch logician Hugh MacColl that Russell wrote in this year (Chapters 2, 3, and 4).

Russell's next step was to apply the advances of the Theory of Descriptions to the logical paradoxes. For the first time, Russell began to consider the more mathematical paradoxes, such as Burali-Forti's, which he had hitherto thought to be solvable by some special rearrangement in the theory of transfinite ordinals. Various alternative solutions were proposed by Russell in a London Mathematical Society paper read in December 1905 (Chapter 7). Russell's favoured approach in this paper was the 'no classes' theory, which he developed further in a second London Mathematical Society paper in May 1906 (Chapter 8). In this second paper, Russell attempted a radical contextual definition of classes, even more reductionist than the definition of classes eventually adopted in *Principia*. At first Russell thought that this radical definition of classes could solve the paradoxes, but various technical difficulties obtruded, and Russell gradually returned to the type of approach suggested in the Appendix of the *Principles*.

Meanwhile, attacks on the *Principles of Mathematics* had been accumulating, and Russell began to answer them. In November 1905, he answered Pierre Boutroux (Chapter 12), and in November 1906, he answered repeated attacks directed by Henri Poincaré[1] against the logistic approach in mathematics (Chapter 9). The single point on which he was able to agree with Poincaré was that *all* the paradoxes then known seemed to involve some sort of vicious circle. The problem was to find a solution which would exclude these vicious circles without excluding patterns of reasoning common in established branches of mathematics. By the end of 1906, Russell felt that he had the solution, which involved the arrangement of individuals and functions into a hierarchy of types, and of functions into a further hierarchy of orders. Russell completed the development of this 'ramified' theory of types in 1907, and it was first published in the *American Journal of Mathematics* in 1908. Poincaré

---

[1] Poincaré *A* 1906.

promptly responded with a new attack in 1909,[1] and Russell's reply in 1910 (Chapter 10) finished off the Russell–Poincaré debate.

During these years the characteristic features of the *Principia* system were falling into place. The need for a separate 'multiplicative axiom' became apparent as early as the summer of 1904, the same year that Zermelo employed its equivalent, the 'axiom of choice', in his proof that every class can be well ordered. At first Russell and Whitehead thought that they had a proof of this principle, but it turned out that the proof of the previous proposition on which the proof was based implicitly assumed the axiom.[2] For a while they continued to attempt to prove the axiom, but soon they recognised that a proof was not forthcoming. Recognition of the need for an axiom of infinity, at first denied (Chapter 11), came sometime in 1906, and the choice of negation and disjunction as primitives came probably the same year. Finally, the axiom of reducibility was added as part of the ramified theory of types. By 1907, as Russell wryly put in his *Autobiography*, the only thing left to do was to write it out. This he did, working ten hours a day, eight months a year, for the next three years. When the manuscript neared completion in 1909, Whitehead wrote to Russell, 'Like the Greek ten thousand, we ejaculate Printing! Printing!'[3] The first volume appeared in 1910, the third and last in 1913.

Russell's interests after the writing of *Principia Mathematica* turned to more general philosophical topics and the history of his later opinions on logical subjects is difficult to trace. Wittgenstein's influence came in two waves: first from conversations in 1913 immediately before the war; second, from a reading of the manuscript of Wittgenstein's *Tractatus* in 1919. The impact of Wittgenstein's early work is registered in the Introduction and Appendices Russell wrote in about 1923 for the second edition of *Principia Mathematica*. In these Russell adopted the thesis of extensionality proposed by Wittgenstein in the

---

[1] Poincaré *A* 1909. [2] Grattan-Guinness *C*1 1972.
[3] Letter to Russell, 12 Oct. 1909, now in the possession of the Bertrand Russell Archives.

Tractatus, and succeeded in disposing with the axiom of reducibility in all cases where it was employed in mathematical induction. In 1925 and 1926, following in Wittgenstein's footsteps, F. P. Ramsey published two brilliant papers[1] criticising various doctrines of the *Principia*. Reviewing these in 1931,[2] Russell accepted Ramsey's division of the paradoxes into 'logical' and 'semantical' forms, and agreed with Ramsey that the hierarchy of types is sufficient in dealing with the former, while the hierarchy of orders is not practical in dealing with the latter. As late as 1959,[3] however, Russell maintained that *some* version of the theory of types is needed to solve the paradoxes.

Russell was personally dismayed by Wittgenstein's views on the nature of mathematics,[4] but having once accepted them, he never abandoned them in his later years. The realism that marked his comments on the philosophy of logic and mathematics while working on *Principia Mathematica* (Chapters 13 and 14), was supplanted by the belief that questions of logic concern the rules for manipulating expressions rather than the entities to which expressions referred. About 1951, he summarised his later view in his statement that 'The propositions of logic and mathematics are purely linguistic, and they are concerned with syntax'.[5] His arguments for this position are published here for the first time.

[1] Ramsey C5 1925, 1926.   [2] Russell B 1931.
[3] Russell B 1959a.   [4] Russell B 1944.
[5] 'Is Mathematics Purely Linguistic?' (Chapter 15).

II

RUSSELL'S CRITIQUE OF MEINONG

Readers familiar with Russell's discussions of Meinong in 'On Denoting' and *Introduction to Mathematical Philosophy* may receive the impression that Meinong was something of a madman whose main service to philosophy was to provide material for refutation by Russell. But a complete reading of Russell's articles on Meinong shows that Russell had the highest respect for Meinong and the Graz school of philosophers and psychologists. Between 1899 and 1907, Russell wrote seven reviews and articles on Meinong's work,[1] of which five are reprinted here (the remaining two deal mainly with matters of psychology). The famous debate on the status of such objects as the round square and the golden mountain occupies only a small part of the total discussion.

The first three articles, the three-part series 'Meinong's Theory of Complexes and Assumptions' (*Mind*, 1904) are an extended discussion of Meinong's article 'On Objects of Higher Order and their Relation to Inner Perception', and his book *On Assumptions*.[2] Russell in 1904 had not yet invented the theory of descriptions and held at this time to the liberal ontology defended in the *Principles of Mathematics*:

'Whatever may be an object of thought, or may occur in a true proposition, or can be counted as *one*, I call a *term*... Every term has being, i.e. *is* in some sense. A man, a moment, a number, a class, a relation, a chimera, or anything else that can be mentioned, is sure to be a term; and to deny that such a thing is a term must always be false.'[3]

Consequently these three articles contain none of the attacks on ontological liberalism that characterise Russell's later comments

[1] Russell B 1899b, 1904a, 1905d, 1906f, 1907d.
[2] Meinong A 1899, 1902.   [3] Russell B 1903a, section 47.

on Meinong. What the articles do contain is a careful discussion of topics typical of pure, descriptive psychology on the Continent at the turn of the century: the distinction between presentation, assumption, and judgment; the distinction between a mental act, its content, and its object, and so on.

Complexes are considered by Russell in the first article of the series, assumptions in the second. As regards complexes, or 'objects of higher order', Russell employs doctrines from the *Principles of Mathematics* to confute Meinong's view that a complex presupposes its constituents. Russell's own view is that a complex consists of a relation, itself unanalysable, and its terms, joined in a unity that also cannot be analysed – a position that he held right through the decade.[1] As regards assumptions, or propositions which are merely entertained and not asserted, Russell is in complete agreement with Meinong that they are essential in logical analysis. Propositions entertained are found in implications, such as 'p implies q'; propositions asserted are found in inferences, such as 'p, therefore q'; and the proper distinction of implication from inference was, in Russell's eyes, a major advance in logic.

In the third article, Russell considers what at the outset he calls 'the realistic thesis': that every perception and belief must have an object independent of itself. Meinong felt that in certain cases the object of a mental act was an 'immanent object' – a position that Russell strongly denies. Interestingly enough, Franz Brentano, who resurrected the scholastic notion of immanent objectivity in 1874 and made it a standard feature of early phenomenological investigation, himself came to deny that there are such immanent objects.[2] This leaves the alternative that the object is transcendent. Russell's candidates for these transcendent objects are propositions, which serve as the objects of mental states, including perceptions. This discussion is Russell's closest survey of key themes of twentieth-century phenomenology, and his reaction is generally positive.

Russell's 1905 review of *Investigations in the Theory of Objects and Psychology*, by Meinong and his associates, shows Russell in a

[1] See Russell *B* 1910*d*.   [2] See Brentano *A* 1911.

less liberal mood. By this time Russell had developed the theory of descriptions, and was prepared to deny that 'the round square' denoted any entity of any ontological grade. At the same time, Meinong had fully developed his theory of *Aussersein*, and was determined to maintain that even 'the round square' denoted an entity of some sort.

Russell's quarrel with the round square sprang from his belief that to maintain that the round square has being implies that something is both round and square, which violates the law of non-contradiction. Anticipating Meinong's reply that the round square, being non-existent, is not the kind of thing to which the law applies, Russell says, in a revival of the ontological argument, that on Meinong's principles, the existent round square exists, is round, and is square, and *this* surely is a violation of the principle of non-contradiction.

The source of Meinong's views on round squares was his thesis that '*So-Sein* is independent of *Sein*', i.e. that the properties possessed by an object are possessed by it independently of its ontological grade. Russell held to a related theory in 'On Denoting' (October 1905 and Chapter 5 in this volume) in which he maintained that 'Scott is the author of *Waverley*' consisted really of three assertions, (1) there is an author of *Waverley*, (2) there is at most one author of *Waverley*, and (3) he is identical with Scott. Meinong would say that the first assertion concerns the *Sein* of the author of *Waverley*, the third his *So-Sein*. But Russell and Meinong drew opposite conclusions from this separation of *So-Sein* from *Sein*, Russell maintaining that the truth of (1) is required if 'Scott is the author of *Waverley*' is to be true, Meinong maintaining that the truth of (1) is irrelevant.

In this controversy, Russell has usually appeared to be an apostle of common sense, while Meinong has appeared as a wild ontologiser hypostatising entities at will. But Meinong's theory says that 'Pegasus is a flying horse' is true, while Russell's says that this assertion is false. The average man, if he knows his mythology, would probably agree with Meinong.

Meinong responded to Russell's criticisms in *On the Place of the Theory of Objects in the System of Sciences,* and Russell in turn reviewed this book for *Mind* in 1907. In answer to Russell's charge that granting being to the round square violated the law of non-contradiction, Meinong argued that the law of non-contradiction did not apply to objects that neither exist nor subsist. As for Russell's existent round square, Meinong held that it is existent but it does not exist. Readers may find, as Russell did, an air of paradox in this assertion, but perhaps no more than in the argument that provoked it.

I

Meinong's Theory of Complexes and Assumptions[1]

First published in *Mind*, n.s. **13**, in three parts (April, July, October, 1904), pp. 204–19, 336–54, 509–24. Reprinted with the permission of the editor of *Mind*, and the Bertrand Russell Estate.

I

That every presentation and every belief must have an object other than itself and, except in certain cases where mental existents happen to be concerned, extra-mental; that what is commonly called perception has as its object an existential proposition, into which enters as a constituent that whose existence is concerned, and not the idea of this existent; that truth and falsehood apply not to beliefs, but to their objects; and that the object of a thought, even when this object does not exist, has a Being which is in no way dependent upon its being an object of thought: all these are theses which, though generally rejected, can nevertheless be supported by arguments which deserve at least a refutation.[2] Except Frege, I know of no writer on the theory of knowledge who comes as near to this position as Meinong. In what follows, I shall have the double purpose of expounding his opinions and of advocating my own; the points of agreement are so numerous and important that the two aims can be easily combined.

The theory of knowledge is often regarded as identical with logic. This view results from confounding psychical states with their objects; for, when it is admitted that the proposition

[1] The works concerned are: 'Uber Gegenstände hörerer Ordnung und deren Verhältnis zur ineren Wahrnehmung', *Zeitschrift für Psychologie und Physiologie der Sinnesorgane*, vol. xxi, pp 182–272 (1899) and *Uber Annahmen* (1902). There is an important article in the above periodical, 'Abstrahiren und Vergleichen', vol. xxiv, pp. 34–82 (1900), which, since its theme is not very closely connected with that of the above two works, I shall not deal with, although its contents appear to me almost wholly true, and deserving of careful attention.

[2] I have been led to accept these theses by Mr G. E. Moore, to whom, throughout the following pages, I am deeply indebted.

known is not identical with the knowledge of it, it becomes plain that the question as to the nature of propositions is distinct from all questions as to knowledge. And the refusal to recognise this distinction appears to have, apart from metaphysical consequences, two bad effects: it introduces irrelevant psychological considerations into logic, and at the same time excludes relevant psychological considerations from the theory of knowledge. It does the former, because knowledge cannot be other than psychical; and it does the latter because the distinction between logic and psychology is strongly felt, and is therefore constantly stated as a distinction between theory of knowledge and psychology. The theory of knowledge is in fact distinct from psychology, but is more complex: for it involves not only what psychology has to say about belief, but also the distinction of truth and falsehood, since knowledge is only belief in what is true. Thus the subject may be approached either through psychology or through logic, both of which are simpler than it is. Meinong has approached it through psychology, but with great logical acumen; it may be interesting, therefore, to confront his views with views which are suggested by the approach through logic.

Before entering upon details, I wish to emphasise the admirable method of Meinong's researches, which, in a brief epitome, it is quite impossible to preserve. Although empiricism as a philosophy does not appear to be tenable, there is an empirical manner of investigating, which should be applied in every subject-matter. This is possessed in a very perfect form by the works we are considering. A frank recognition of the data, as inspection reveals them, precedes all theorising; when a theory is propounded, the greatest skill is shown in the selection of facts favourable or unfavourable, and in eliciting all relevant consequences of the facts adduced. There is thus a rare combination of acute inference with capacity for observation. The method of philosophy is not fundamentally unlike that of other sciences: the differences seem to be only in degree. The data are fewer, but are harder to apprehend; and the inferences required are probably more difficult than in any other subject except mathematics. But the important point is that, in philosophy as elsewhere, there are self-evident truths from which we must start, and that these are discoverable by the process of inspection or observation, although the material to be observed is not, for the most part, composed of existent things. Whatever may ultimately prove to be the value of Meinong's particular contentions, the value of his method is undoubtedly very great; and on this account if on no other, he deserves careful study.

The following is a brief outline of Meinong's main theses. In all presentation and judgment, it is essential to distinguish the content from the object. The object, when it is what he calls an 'object of higher order', is complex. The article on this subject investigates the nature of complexity in objects, and contends that complex objects are perceptible. The book on assumptions (*Uber Annahmen*), which is at first sight on a different theme, is really closely connected with this article. It points out that judgment contains two elements, (1) conviction, (2) affirmation or denial, and that, in a large class of common facts, which are called *assumptions*, the second occurs without the first.[1] Both judgments and assumptions have reference to what Meinong calls Objectives, which are the propositions concerned: a judgment and an assumption differ, not in respect of the Objective, but in respect of the conviction which is present in the one but not in the other. It now appears that these Objectives always enter into the composition of complexes, even if they are not always identical with them.[2] But it is contended that complexes cannot be objects of presentation, since they require always an assumption, which is something radically different from presentation. Thus we have (1) simples, which can be presented; (2) complexes, which can be either assumed or judged, but not presented. The point of most importance for

---

[1] This had been already pointed out by Frege, but had by him only been applied over a very small part of the field covered by Meinong's investigations, and had, moreover, not been established with anything approaching the same wealth of argument and illustration. For references, see below.

[2] The identity of propositions and complexes was maintained in Moore *A* 1899, as was also the theory that truth and falsehood attach not to the judgment, but to the proposition, by which is meant the same as Meinong's Objective.

logic is, in my opinion, the connexion of complexes and propositions; for theory of knowlege, the objectivity of propositions, and the existence and functions of assumption as opposed to judgment.

The phrase 'objects of higher order' is used by Meinong to cover relations and what he calls *complexions*, or what, in English, it would probably be better to call *complexes*. To establish the perceptibility of such objects is the main purpose of the article which he devotes to them; but incidentally many other points of great importance receive an illuminating discussion.

In psychical matters, at any rate in the case of presentations and judgments, it is necessary, Meinong points out, to distinguish three elements, the act, the content, and the object. All presentations have in common the act of presentation, but the presentations of different objects differ in respect of their contents. It is necessary sharply to distinguish content and object: the content of a presentation exists when the presentation exists, but the object need not exist – it may be self-contradictory, it may be something which happens not to be a fact, such as a golden mountain, it may be essentially incapable of existence, as for instance equality, it may be physical, not psychical, or it may be something which did exist or will exist, but does not exist at present. What is called the existence of an object in presentation is really not existence at all: it may be called pseudo-existence. But though it is essential to distinguish content and object, the content tends to be ignored in favour of the object; there are no natural designations for contents, which have to be named and distinguished by their objects.

Among objects, there are some that have an intrinsic lack of independence; thus diversity, for example, can only be thought of in relation to differing terms. Such objects are based on others as indispensable presuppositions: Meinong calls them 'objects of higher order', and the presupposed objects he calls *inferiora*, in respect to which they (the objects of higher order) are *superiora*. An object which can have an *inferius* must have one; but an object which can have a *superius* need not have one (p. 190). Not all objects of higher order are relations: four nuts, e.g. are such, for they presuppose each of the nuts. A melody, again, is such; and so is a red square, being compounded of a shape and a colour (pp. 184–92).

The above instances make it fairly plain what class of objects Meinong has in view: they are relations, the complexes formed of terms related by a relation, and the kind of objects (which we may call plurals) of which numbers other than 0 and 1 can be asserted. But before proceeding to new points, we must examine the description which he gives of such objects. They have, he says (p. 189), an internal lack of independence in their nature; they are built on other objects as indispensable presuppositions (p. 190). Omitting plurals, for reasons which will be mentioned shortly, there are certain difficulties about this description.

In the first place, it is based upon logical priority: the *inferiora* are in some way prior to their *superius*. Now logical priority is a very obscure notion; and so far as can be seen at present, it is one which a careful discussion tends to destroy. For it depends upon the assumption that one true proposition may be implied by another true proposition, and not the other by the one; whereas, according to symbolic logic, there is a mutual implication of any two true propositions. The appearance of one-sided implication in such cases arises, it would seem, from an unconscious substitution of formal for material implication.[1] Thus it would result that the subsistence or being of a whole cannot presuppose that of its parts in any sense in which that of the parts does not presuppose that of the whole.[2]

---

[1] Russell *B* 1903, ch. iii.

[2] It must be admitted, however, that one-sided inferences can practically be made in many cases, and that consequently some relation or relations other than that considered by symbolic logic must be involved when we infer. One such relation is that with which Meinong is concerned, the relation of the simple to the complex: the simple is prior to the complex in the sense that *we* can infer it from the complex, whereas the converse inference, even when it is valid, can only be seen to be valid, as a rule, if the conclusion is already known to be true. In this sense, logical priority may be derived from relative simplicity; but when this is done, we cannot, of course, use logical priority in defining the relation of simple to complex. When logical priority is spoken of in what follows, it will be always in this derivative sense, in which the components of a complex are prior to the complex itself. But

Connected with this point is a second, namely, that it seems impossible to distinguish, among true propositions, some which are necessary from others which are mere facts. Thus the statement that a *superius must* have an *inferius*, while the converse is not necessary, must be questioned: any two terms have some relations, and the relations they do have are as necessary to them as they (the terms) are to the relations. Throughout Meinong's work, in many crucial points, use is made of the notion of necessity; and some of his most important arguments fail if necessity is not admitted. The difference of green and yellow, he says, is necessary; but not so the fact that the sun is shining now (*Uber Annahmen*, p. 188). But he adds in a footnote that this too, if considered in relation to its causes, may appear necessary, which seems to make the psychical process leading to a belief relevant in judging of necessity; and this, he admits, introduces a problem. Now when we consider what propositions we commonly call necessary, we find that they are: (1) all such as do not involve any particular parts of time – i.e. if they involve time at all, they involve all time; (2) all such as are seen to follow from true premisses, whether these are regarded as necessary or not. It is under the second head that an event becomes necessary when deduced from causes, for these, unless also so deduced, are not regarded as necessary. I cannot help suspecting that the whole feeling of necessity and contingency has been derived from the fact that a sentence containing a verb in the present tense – or indeed in the past or the future, unless with mention of a particular time – changes its meaning continually as the present changes, and thus stands for different propositions at different times, and as a rule sometimes for true ones, sometimes for false ones. And generally, when a proposition contains a term which we instinctively regard as variable, we feel that the proposition is contingent if some values of the variable make the proposition true, others false. For instance, when we say 'the number of this cab has four figures', we feel

this sense, though relevant in the theory of knowledge, appears to be inapplicable in logic: it would be better to call it epistemological priority, since it has an essential reference to our inferring.

that it might have had five, because we think of all the other cabs we might have taken. But when this often unconscious thought of the variable is excluded, I cannot see that temporal facts differ from others in any way that could be called contingency.[1]

A third objection is that relations, though not complexes, appear to be capable of being thought of apart from terms. If the impossibility is meant only in a psychological sense, it is probably true that most people find a difficulty in so thinking, though even then it is not any particular terms, but only the notion of some terms that is required. But it would seem that diversity, for example, or logical implication, is a simple notion, into whose composition the notion of terms does not enter; and that to learn to think of such a notion in itself is a feat which can be accomplished by practice. It may indeed be doubted whether relations can be adequately characterised by anything except the fact that they relate, or complexes by anything except the fact that they contain terms related. So far as any characterisation of complexes is possible, it is derived, in my opinion, from a certain kind of unity which Meinong himself has described later.

With regard to plurals, which are supposed by our author to have some unity making them more than a mere collection, it is impossible to speak without entering upon the whole question of classes and numbers, a question of the utmost difficulty, which I have discussed at length elsewhere.[2] Plurals, in any case, differ widely from relations and complexes, and involve a different kind of logical problems. It will be well, therefore, in what follows, to exclude them from our discussions.

Returning now to the exposition of Meinong's doctrine, we find a careful attempt to characterise the unity of a complex. A complex implies a relation, and *vice versa*; it is more than the collection of its constituents, in virtue of the combining relation. Although the relation is part of the complex, the complex is not composed of the terms and the relation, for the terms are related to the relation in consequence of being related by it – a fact

---

[1] See Moore *A*, 1900*b*.   [2] Russell *B*, 1903*a*, especially chs. vi, xv.

which leads to an endless regress, but of a harmless kind (pp. 193–4). A melody of four notes is not a fifth note, and generally a complex is not formed by adding an object to the constituents; nevertheless, something is added. What is added is the relation, but rightly related to the constituents: for red, green, and difference do not make 'red differs from green' (p. 236).

All these remarks appear to be perfectly just, as is the remark (p. 196) that a relation or complex may have more than two terms. But the unity of a complex raises a logical problem, of which Meinong seems to be not fully aware. What is added, we are told, is the relation, rightly related; but when we consider the relation as well as the terms, we do not obtain the complex. And if we add the relations of the relation to the terms, and all the relations generated in the resulting endless process, we still do not obtain again our original unity, but only an aggregate. Thus what distinguishes our complex is not any constituent at all, but simply and solely the fact of relatedness in a certain way. Out of given constituents, even when account is taken of all the infinitude of relating relations, different complexes can be constructed: thus, e.g. 'a is greater than b' and 'b is greater than a' differ in no respect which analysis can preserve. It is this special and apparently indefinable kind of unity which I should propose to employ in characterising the notion of a complex. The kind of unity in question belongs, as is evident, to all propositions; and the inadequacy of analysis appears, in this case, in the fact that propositions are true or false, while their constituents, in general, are neither.

Ideal objects, Meinong says, i.e. such as are incapable of existence, are always objects of higher order. Similarity, e.g. does not exist, but subsists (*besteht*); similarly quadruplicity does not exist where there are four nuts. But there are also real complexes and real relations: such are the occupation of time and place, the relation of desire to its object, and the relations of parts in the unity of consciousness (pp. 198–9). Real relations are not necessary, but ideal ones are: the latter he calls well-founded (*fundirt*), and objects of this sort he calls well-founded objects (p. 202).

To the last statement we may object, as before, our doubt as to the notion of necessity: and on the preceding contentions, while fully admitting the general distinction of existence and subsistence, some criticisms seem called for. If only what does exist, has existed, or will exist, is capable of existence, as we must hold if we reject the traditional distinctions of modality, then there certainly are ideal objects which are not of higher order. Such are the points of a non-Euclidean space, or the imaginary particles of rational dynamics. If, on the other hand, to be a possible existent is held to mean no more than to have such a resemblance to actual existents as belong to these points and particles, then there is danger of Meinong's contention becoming a mere tautology. Thus it may be questioned whether, in any significant sense, all ideal objects are objects of higher order. The converse, however, seems capable of being maintained in spite of the instances adduced. We tend to ascribe existence to whatever is intimately related to particular parts of space and time; but for my part, inspection would seem to lead to the conclusion that, except space and time themselves, only those objects exist which have to particular parts of space and time the special relation of *occupying* them. On a question of this kind argument seems scarcely possible; and I can only record the fact that my inspection does not yield the same results as Meinong's. It is possible to suspect, however, that he has been led to his opinion by the fact that some objects of higher order can be perceived, and that he holds as self-evident the doctrine that what does not exist is not perceptible (p. 200) – a doctrine to which I shall return presently.

We come now to a careful and interesting refutation of the opinion of Schumann, according to whom internal perception reveals no objects of higher order. With this opinion, Meinong admits, common sense is inclined at first sight to agree: when we see red and blue, we do not seem to see their difference also. Consider, he says, the presentation of a steeple: internal perception assures us only of the 'presented steeple', not of the real one. But internal perception yields not only the content, but also the (immanent) object – a fact which, since the latter has only pseudo-existence, involves a fundamental problem in the theory of knowledge (p. 207). Indeed the seeing is less perceptible to internal perception than what is seen: it would seem that, except physical objects, internal perception reveals nothing but feelings, if even these (pp. 208–9). This result is the outcome of Schumann's line of argument when pushed to its logical conclusion. But such a result cannot stand before a more careful examination of the observable facts. It is plain that we often know, without a process of inference, and therefore by perception, that such and such is our opinion; and in this case we perceive a judgment by internal perception. That we have perceptions, which is an undeniable fact, can only be discovered by internal perception. It is to be observed that all perception, including internal perception, is not merely presentation, but also judgment, namely of the existence of the object. Again we perceive that we desire, and what we desire, and the relation of desire to its object; and of feelings the same is true. And it is plain that presentations can be perceived, for many have non-existent objects, which, being non-existent, cannot be perceived, so that the knowledge of such presentations must be derived from perception of them, not of their objects (pp. 212–18).

In order to examine the last of these arguments, of which the validity seems as doubtful as the conclusion is irrefragable, it will be necessary to examine what Meinong says as to the nature of perception itself. It is generally assumed – and Meinong appears also to assume – that perception is a kind of knowledge, whereas it may, I think, be maintained that perception is merely knowledge of a kind of truths, i.e. that there is nothing distinctive, in perception, about the manner of knowing, but only about what is known. Before enlarging upon this thesis, however, I will set forth briefly what our author says upon this subject.

A thing is only perceived, we are told, when its existence is known immediately, i.e. without inference from premisses, and is (at least practically) simultaneous with the knowledge. This is not quite exact; for the fixed stars which we now perceive may have long ago ceased to exist; but this inexactness applies specially to external perception. A perception is characterised as internal (1) by its object being psychical, (2) by its pre-eminent certainty and evidence (p. 212). As regards the approximate simultaneity of the content and the object of perception, this can be proved to be *only* approximate by such cases as the perception of a melody or a motion or any single complex whose constituents are successive. The complex, in such a case, can only be perceived when all the parts have been perceived, and are still perceived: the temporally distinct *inferiora* of our complex must be given to presentation simultaneously, though not as simultaneous. When, after hearing the notes of a melody, I perceive the melody, the notes are not presented as still existing: their mutual time-relations and their relations to the time of presentation are all somehow involved, and the melody seems more or less past. It follows that a sequence in the object does not involve a corresponding sequence in the content, and that we can perceive what is past (pp. 244–55).

The above argument, which is set forth very fully, and appears quite unanswerable in regard to the perception of a temporal complex, leads to another, of rather more questionable validity, of which the conclusion is again that the past can be perceived. If we can only perceive what exists, not what did exist or will exist, it follows that we cannot perceive anything extended in time. But only what is real can be perceived, and an instant is only a limit, not anything real. Consequently it would follow that there is no perception. Not that we are to deny the existence of the point of time or space absolutely, but only of the point in isolation: the point does not exist, but subsist, yet where the point is, something may exist, only not confined to the point (pp. 259–60).

It is impossible, in this place, to argue the whole question of the nature of time; but as against Meinong, who appears to admit the existence of time, it may be enough to argue that instants are the ultimate constituents of time, and that a whole cannot exist if none of its parts exists. And if the existence of instants be admitted, the above argument fails: in order to retain anything of it, it will be necessary to assume (what is doubtless in some sense true), that we can only perceive existent things if they persist through a finite time.

Other less assailable arguments for the same conclusion follow. It is customary to speak of past and future as ideal in comparison with the actuality of the present; but we must admit the reality of past and future: the opposite course is unduly subjective, for the determination as past or future merely expresses a relation between the time of judgment and the time of the object, which is as irrelevant to the real as whether or when some one knows it. (This is a most lucid observation, by which a host of confusions are routed.) And there is no reason to limit perception to the present, for memory also is immediate, and grows more and more certain as the time elapsed grows shorter. Common sense supposes simultaneity of perception and its object, because it assumes a causal or conditional connexion between the two. But such a connexion, if causal, makes simultaneity impossible; if conditional, unnecessary. Thus we may conclude that we can perceive what is past, though not without limit: the perceptible part may be called the 'psychic present'. It is thus that we perceive change and motion. The distinction between memory and perception loses is sharpness by this theory, especially as, strictly speaking, we can *only* perceive what is past; but the sharpness of the distinction appears to be fictitious (pp. 260–6).

Omitting, in the above discussion of perception, the parts in regard to which no criticism seems called for, certain points remain to be examined. The non-simultaneity of perception and object, where internal perception is concerned, need cause no difficulty; but in regard to external perception, such simultaneity seems part of what is perceived, and yet, as in the case of the fixed stars, it is sometimes very far from true, and always, according to physical science, more or less erroneous. Yet physical science depends throughout upon the trustworthiness of perception: hence, it would seem, the assumption of such trustworthiness destroys itself. It may be a sufficient escape, however, merely to deny that *present* existence is what external perception affirms, although such a denial seems to contravene the results of inspection in the interests of theory. The next point concerns the Cartesian maxim of the greater evidence of internal perceptions. Hobbes objected that '*ambulo ergo sum*' was just as good an argument as '*cogito ergo sum*'; and this view seems to be that of common sense. Indeed, as Meinong himself says (p. 210), materialism is the natural view of the plain man. But, judging from the course and tenor of his argument, he would appear to hold that this belief in physical objects is derived from *internal* perception. A presentation, with the three elements of act, content and object, is taken to be wholly psychical, and the object, like the other two, is supposed to be part of the total mental state – so at least some passages suggest. Thus the object is spoken of as 'immanent', and in the case of the steeple, internal perception is said to assure us of the 'presented steeple', not of the real one. Consequently the materialism of the plain man, if such a derivation be correct, must be derived from perception of what belongs properly to psychology – a process whose complication seems very far from the facts. As against this view, I should prefer to advocate what is, presumably, the distinguishing feature of a common-sense philosophy, namely, that the object of a presentation is the actual external object itself, and not any part of the presentation at all. Thus to take the case of the steeple: we have (1) external perception, having as its object the actual steeple itself, or rather the existence of the steeple, the wholly extramental material thing; (2) purely internal perception, having as its object the existence of either the act or the content of the previous external perception; (3) the perception of the object of higher order, consisting of the perception and the existence of the steeple combined by the relation of cognition. (The objects of (1) and (2) are themselves of higher order, but that of (3) is a *superius* of which they are *inferiora*.) The reasons in favour of this common-sense view are briefly the following. As regards the external perception, if two people can perceive the same object, as the possibility of any common world requires, then the object of an external perception is not in the mind of the percipient. Consequently in this case, and therefore possibly in every case, the perception consists only of act and content, the object being an outside related entity, or rather proposition (namely the proposition that what is loosely called the object exists). As regards internal perception, it must be admitted that, in its pure form, it is exceedingly difficult: contents, as Meinong himself confesses, are *'wahrnehmungsflüchtig'*. Thus when we mean to think only of what is psychical, we are almost inevitably led to think instead of the cognitive complex, consisting of the knowledge together with what is known; hence what is known (the proposition) comes to be viewed as also psychical, in spite of the highly inconvenient consequence that two people, in that case, cannot know the same proposition.[1]

I have spoken hitherto, being concerned with what is commonly called perception, only of the awareness of *propositions*; for all the cases concerned are, as Meinong says (p. 216), cases where something is known to exist, and where, consequently, the object of perception is an existential proposition. But it seems undeniable that there is also a mere awareness, in which the object is not a proposition; for unless we were aware what redness is, we could not know that redness exists. Except, however, for this *a priori* argument, it would be more natural, as the result of inspection, to deny any such awareness; when we try to think of redness, we seem only to succeed in thinking of redness as existing, i.e. of what Meinong calls the *Annahme* 'redness exists'.[2] But however this may be, mere awareness, having as its object something neither true nor false, is widely different from cognition; and perception, in its usual significance, is a kind of cognition, namely cognition of existence.

Returning now to the question whether perception is to be defined by the way of knowing or by the kind of proposition known, we see that one mark at any rate is always associated with the word *perception*, and that is the absence of previous

---

[1] In his work *Uber Annahmen*, Meinong, as we shall see, approaches much nearer than in the earlier work to the position which I advocate.

[2] Meinong holds that a mere presentation does not have an object, but only acquires one through combination with an *Annahme*: *Uber Annahmen*, p. 101. See below.

inference. This certainly is not a property of what is known, for everything that is known might theoretically have been known by inference, except possibly a few of the fundamental principles of logic, which are presupposed in all inference. But it appears also to be not a property, in any strict sense, of the knowledge: for when the object of a judgment is given, it would seem that the judgment is also given – i.e. there is merely the knowledge of a given proposition, not different kinds of knowledge of it. Thus it follows that previous inference is a merely external relation of a cognition, which cannot affect its own nature. Yet, when we see Neptune and when we infer it, there is a wide difference of the two cases. This seems to be accounted for chiefly by two facts: (1) that a proposition perceived is not expressed in words, (2) that it always forms part of an infinitely complex spatio-temporal continuum, and is not, in perception, attended to in isolation. But in cases where the proposition concerned is abstract, say the principle 'when q follows from p and p is true, then q is true', the fact that no possible inference can warrant our belief in this proposition, since all inference employs it, does not alter the quality of our belief in any way. Analogous propositions which *are* inferred come to be assented to in a precisely similar manner, i.e. without any intrinsic difference in the feeling involved. Thus it is legitimate to suppose that, in the case of spatio-temporal propositions, the above two points may account for the felt difference.

But perception commonly implies also that what is perceived is an existential proposition concerning a time which is very nearly the present; and there is usually a more or less covert assumption that this mark is connected with that of not being inferred. That all premisses are obtained from perception in this sense, i.e. that whatever can be admitted without proof is an existential proposition concerning the present or the immediate past, is the creed of thorough-going empiricism – a creed, however, which cannot be held by any one who has ever considered that proof itself involves logical principles which cannot in turn be proved. This one instance (of logical principles) suffices to show that self-evident propositions need not be derived from perception in this narrow sense; and when the possibility is admitted, it becomes easy to see that immense numbers of non-existential unproved propositions are self-evident.

It follows, if what has been said is true, that there is no validity in Meinong's argument (p. 218) that presentations must be perceptible because we know of such as have non-existent objects, and the non-existent cannot be perceived. We must hold that the Being, or, as Meinong says, the subsistence, of the non-existent is often immediately known; and many other propositions are known concerning the non-existent otherwise than by inference. The process suggested by Meinong's argument is, in any case, exceedingly and curiously complicated. First we think of a golden mountain, then we perceive that we are thinking of it; thence, we infer that there is a presentation of a golden mountain, and thence finally that the golden mountain subsists or has Being. But when we originally thought of the golden mountain, we already perceived, or at least could perceive if we chose, that the golden mountain subsists; and the round-about road via our presentation seems quite superfluous. The doctrine that the object forms no part of the presentation must be extended to the case where the object is what we call imaginary, i.e. does not exist; and in the case of mathematical objects, such as numbers, this seems plain enough. And it is thus that the theory of knowledge becomes subsequent to logic and to the objects of knowledge in general: for, in Meinong's phrase, the objects of knowledge (propositions) are the *inferiora* for which and the cognition the cognitive relation is the *superius*. The theory of belief, in which no distinction is made between correct and erroneous belief, is a branch of psychology which is on a par with the study of the objects of belief; but belief is only knowledge where the cognitive relation subsists, i.e. where the object is true, and thus, if Meinong's doctrine of the local priority of *inferiora* to *superius* is to be maintained, the theory of knowledge must be subsequent both to logic and to psychology.

The relevant facts in regard to perception appear to me to be briefly these: Many propositions, of very various kinds, are self-evident, i.e. are accepted without being proved by means of other propositions. All self-evident propositions, or rather, such of them as are true, may, in the widest sense be said to be perceived. But there is a peculiar class of self-evident propositions concerned with particular parts of time, and only becoming self-evident at, or just after, the parts of time with which they are concerned. These, when they are true, may be said to be perceived in the second sense. But some of these, in my opinion, are not properly existential, being concerned with relations which *subsist*, but do not strictly exist, though Meinong maintains that they do exist. (These are what he calls *real* as opposed to *ideal* relations.) Thus we reach the third and narrowest meaning of perception by excluding from our second class all such propositions as are not existential.[1]

The very interesting theory of objects which are '*wahrnehmungsflüchtig*', or fugitive from perception, by which Meinong answers the doubt as to whether objects of higher order can be perceived at all, is almost purely psychological, and will therefore not be discussed here. I also pass by, as lying somewhat outside the main argument, an admirable analysis of the perception of continua considered as complexes. The chief criticisms of the article, from the standpoint which I have adopted, are (1) that the notion of perception, and its epistemological importance, are not made clear; (2) that the object of a presentation or perception is regarded as forming part of the presentation or perception, or at any rate as something necessarily psychical. In regard to this last point, it may be worth while to raise the following question for the consideration of the reader. Is it possible to have a presentation or belief to which no object corresponds? The converse possibility, except by those (of whom Meinong is not one) who hold that there can be nothing that is not known to some mind, will be at once admitted;

---

[1] The above method of defining perception, though it appears to give a first approximation, is liable to certain objections, which have led Mr G. E. Moore – with what justice, I do not attempt to decide – to introduce into the definition of perception a causal relation between that whose existence is known and the knowledge of its existence. See Moore *A* 1903*a*.

but the idea of a belief which is a belief in nothing seems at first sight quite inadmissible. Yet, by all analogy, it ought to be possible, if content and object are related as externally as I have contended, for either to subsist without the other. The chief importance of the question is in regard to error. What do we believe when we believe a false proposition? We believe in a relation (say) between two terms which, as a matter of fact, are not so related. Thus we seem to believe in nothing; for if there were such a relation as we believe in, the belief would not be erroneous. If a belief may be a content which has no object, then it may be true that, though we believe, there is nothing we believe in; and in this case correct beliefs would be distinguished from erroneous ones by the fact that they have an object, while the others have not. But this possibility seems too paradoxical to be maintained except in the last resort; and such cases as true hypotheticals of which the hypothesis is false seem to prove that false propositions must have some kind of extra-mental subsistence. This question is, however, a very large one, being indeed, no other than Pontius Pilate's 'What is truth?'. I shall return to it at the end of the present article.

II

Meinong's book, *Uber Annahmen*, is very important, for it introduces to notice a hitherto almost wholly neglected class of facts, and adduces such a wealth of evidence in their favour that their existence, henceforward, can hardly remain open to question.

The work is divided into nine chapters: On first principles, the characteristic functions of the sentence, the most obvious cases of assumptions, inferences with assumptions, the objectivity of the psychical, the apprehension of objects of higher order, the Objective (*das Objectiv*), the psychology of desire and value, elements of the psychology of assumptions. The last two of these chapters, however important in themselves, are devoted chiefly to themes lying outside epistemology, and will therefore be omitted in the following discussions; the other chapters all contain much that no theory of knowledge can safely neglect.

Chapter i defines the class of facts to be dealt with. Two

marks distinguish judgment from mere presentation: one is belief or conviction, the other is a certain attitude in regard to the opposition of affirmation and negation. Now although the first of these marks always implies the second, the second does not always imply the first: the main thesis to be established is, that affirmation and negation can occur without conviction, and so occur in what are to be called 'assumptions' (*Annahmen*) (pp. 2–3). An assumption or hypothesis might seem at first sight to be a mere presentation, but this view Meinong, erroneously in my opinion, believes to be capable of disproof. Direct perception alone, he remarks, now seems to him sufficient to establish the difference between a supposition and a presentation; but a formal proof can be obtained from the case of negative assumptions, as, for instance, 'Suppose the Boers had not been conquered'. Negation is never a matter of presentation: this may be taken as self-evident (p. 6). But how, in that case, are we to deal with such notions as 'not-red'? These are commonly regarded as presentations or concepts. But if so, is the negative element in the act, the content, or the object? Plainly not in the act or content, for we cannot have two kinds of presentation of one object. Thus we shall have to assume a negative object 'not-red', and this will have to be an object of higher order, for it cannot be thought of without at the same time thinking of red (pp. 6–8). If there are negative objects, they are plainly not objects of experience. To conceive not-A, we require not only A, but also another object M, of which it is judged that M is not A.[1] We might suppose that the negative, though a product of judgment, is itself an object of presentation, which can be apprehended without judgment, like 'different from A'. And this might tempt us to identify diversity and negation; but here inspection shows that we should be mistaken: 'there is no *perpetuum mobile*' does not mean 'whatever exists differs from the *perpetuum mobile*'; and 'x is not an a' cannot, by any analysis, be found to contain diversity. Consequently negation is a genuine element in a negative judgment

---

[1] Observe that the M here must be, in mathematical language, variable: i.e. no particular object will fulfil the purpose, but the notion '*any* object' is required.

(pp. 9–11). Returning now to our supposed object not-A, this, being an object of higher order, and not an object of experience, would have to be a well-founded object. But in that case, it would have to be connected necessarily with its fundament; yet many negations, e.g. 'stones do not rise', have no necessity. Consequently not-A is not a well-founded object, and is therefore not an object at all (pp. 12–13). It is true that 'something of which the judgment holds that it is not red' is a negative object, which we may call not-red; but it involves the negative judgment and its relation to that of which it holds, and such psychological and epistemological elements could hardly be involved in 'not-red' without being quite plainly visible, whereas, when we examine so-called negative presentations, we find (except perhaps in rare cases) no trace of any such roundabout process. Thus it is to be concluded that the opposition of yes and no makes no difference to the *act* of presentation, is only to be applied in an artificial manner to the object and therefore to the content of presentation, and never arises within mere presentation (pp. 13–14).

The above argument underlies much of what follows, and must therefore be examined with some minuteness. The contention derived from necessity is open to the same objection as was urged above in the same connexion; and if this objection is valid, the whole argument, as a piece of reasoning, collapses. But further points remain. In the first place, such an expression as 'not-red' is ambiguous, for it may apply to whatever is not red, or to whatever is not redness. In the latter sense, the thing which is red is included under 'not-red'. And in this sense, diversity does seem prior to, or at least co-ordinate with, negation. If A is an object, and not-A means 'whatever is not identical with A', then not-A means 'whatever is diverse from A'. Now diversity may, of course, be defined as the negation of identity; but this course, though suitable to formal logic, is perhaps hardly reconcilable with inspection, according to which diversity would by most people be judged fundamental. If, on the other hand, A is a predicate, not-A will usually mean whatever does not have the predicate A. It is quite necessary to keep these cases apart in considering not-A, for they give quite different kinds of objects. But the second, if not the first, involves the notion 'something of which the proposition so-and-so is false'. Meinong appears to reject such a meaning for not-A, on the ground that it involves psychological and epistemological elements. For my part, I cannot see that any such are involved: of any object x, if A is a predicate either 'x had the predicate A' or 'x does not have the predicate A' will be true quite objectively. But this raises the question whether propositions are psychological, to which I shall return later. Assuming, for the present, that they are not, it will follow that not-A, when A is a predicate, is also a predicate, and is just as much an object as A is, but an object which is a complex.

Admitting, as it seems we must, that negation can only be derived through propositions, there is an important distinction to be made, without which confusions will become almost unavoidable. To deny a proposition is not the same as to affirm its denial. The case of an assumption will itself make this clear. Given any proposition p, there is an associated proposition not-p. Either of these may, as Meinong points out, be merely supposed or assumed. But when we deny p, we are not concerned with a mere assumption, and there is nothing to be done with p that is logically equivalent to assuming not-p. And direct inspection, I think, will show that the state of mind in which we reject a proposition is not the same as that in which we accept its negation. Again, the law of excluded middle may be stated in the form: If p is denied, not-p must be asserted; this form, it is true, is too psychological to be ultimate, but the point is, that it is significant and not a mere tautology. Logically, the notion of denying a proposition p is irrelevant: it is only the truth of not-p that concerns logic. But psychologically, it would seem, there are two states of mind which both have p for their object, one affirming and the other denying; and two other states of mind, having not-p for their object, one affirming and the other denying. The assumption of p or not-p again has the same object as the affirmation or denial, but here the object is merely considered, not affirmed or denied.

The importance of the above distinction, in the present case, lies partly in the help which it affords in deciding a question as to which Meinong, though he nowhere discusses it, now appears to me to have decided rightly, whereas Frege, who approaches the subject through logic, has apparently come to the opposite conclusion.[1] The question is this: Does an assumption have a different object from the corresponding judgment, or does it merely have a different attitude to the same object (the proposition)? The case of belief and disbelief shows that it is possible to have different attitudes to the same object, and thus allows us to accept the view, which is *prima facie* the correct one, that there is no difference in the object. I have discussed elsewhere[2] the problems raised by this decision in the case of inference and hypothetical propositions.

One other preliminary point remains. Is there, in addition to the assumption and the assertion of a proposition, another attitude, in which the proposition is merely the object of a presentation? Meinong decides this question in the negative, for he holds that there is no presentation of a proposition or a complex (see above), and that 'the ill man' and 'the man is ill', of which the first is an assumption, the second a judgment, have the same object, though they do not express the same state of mind (pp. 24–5). In this point Frege, if I am not mistaken, again adopts the opposite opinion, for he regards 'the ill man' as referring to a different object from 'the man is ill' (*loc. cit.*). I agree with Meinong in identifying these two objects, but I differ from him in that I do not see in what sense an assumption is not a presentation of a proposition. But this point will occupy us again at a later stage.

Meinong's second chapter, after a brief discussion of signs, investigates the characteristics of the sentence. Not all sentences express judgments – e.g. questions and imperatives (p. 26). Dependent clauses also do not express judgments, for they are not asserted. 'I expect it will rain today' does not assert that it will rain; 'it is false that so-and-so' is not compatible with

---

[1] See Frege, *A* 1893, pp. x, 7–10.   [2] Russell *B* 1903*a*, pp. 503–4.

'so-and-so'. Clauses may be attached to a word in a way which leads to no judgment at all, as in 'the opinion that so-and-so'. Also, 'if p, then q', and 'p or q', do not assert either p or q. What is *expressed* by language is a thought, but what is *indicated is* an object: even when a man does not assert, we do not usually infer the speaker's state of mind – for example, when we hear a work of fiction read. In this case, as in the above cases of dependent clauses, it is necessary to replace judgments by assumptions.

The third chapter enumerates some of the more obvious instances of assumptions. The hypotheses of mathematical propositions, literary works of art, children's pretences, lies, and (instructive collocation) the theories of philosophers, can none of them be understood without assumptions. When a geometrical argument begins with 'let a right-angled triangle be given, having one of its sides double of the other', we have to do with a proposition which is not asserted: hence we have an assumption, not a judgment. Scientific hypotheses again, at least in their inception, are unasserted, and afford instances of assumptions. When children pretend, it is quite plain that they are not taken in by their own fancies: these fancies constitute assumptions; and the same applies to reading a novel. A liar wishes to produce, in another, belief in a proposition which he himself does not believe: if he is to be successful, he will have to entertain the assumption of the proposition in question. And this is why liars tend to believe their own lies – a mere presentation would not be so liable to turn into a judgment (p. 50). In understanding the theories of a philosopher whom we are reading, the same process is usually required: we *may* make the opinion in question the object of a presentation, and thence of a judgment based upon this presentation, or we may (and this is more usual) entertain the assumption which has the same object as the opinion to be examined (pp. 49–50). Meinong now returns to the subject of questions, which he had already discussed in the preceding chapter. A question expresses, if the answer to it is yes or no, the desire to have an assumption turned into the corresponding judgment or its opposite (p. 54).

And in all desire, since the opposition of yes or no occurs in the object of desire, we are necessarily concerned with an assumption: for mere presentation is inadequate, and the truth of what is desired is obviously no part of desire (p. 55).

Chapter iv, on assumptive inferences (*Annahmeschlüsse*), is very important for the analysis of reasoning. It begins by remarking (p. 61) that, though the *forms* of inference have been elaborately studied by formal logicians, the question, What facts were concerned in these inferences? has been left for the present time. If Meinong were himself a formal logician, he might have added that the forms of inference were studied in the past with the same blindness and inadequacy which the failure to analyse inference would lead one to expect. In our day, both defects have been largely remedied. Meinong does not know that Frege – a most unduly neglected author – had already, simply through analysis of inference, been led to distinguish assumptions from judgments.[1] It is in this connexion, more obviously perhaps than in any other, that assumptions can be seen to be absolutely indispensable.

There is very grave difficulty, in this subject, more, indeed, than in any other subject with which I am acquainted, in keeping perfectly clear the distinction of logic and theory of knowledge; this distinction, nevertheless, is hardly anywhere so indispensable, owing to the very startling lack of parallelism between the two standpoints in this matter. I have discussed elsewhere[2] the logical questions involved; in the present discussion I shall mention them only where confusions seem most likely to occur.

The fundamental logical fact, in this subject, is the relation of implications between propositions, expressed by 'p implies q', or 'q follows from p'. This relation, as is universally admitted, does not require either p or q to be true. But when p is true, we get the principle used in inference, namely, 'p, *therefore* q'. Here q is asserted with a reference to p; and it is a fact that, by this process, many propositions can be seen to be true, as to which

---

[1] The distinction is already to be found in Frege *A* 1891, p. 21.
[2] *Op. cit.* §§ 38, 52, 477 ff.

immediate inspection gives no decision. Meinong holds that a similar operation is possible with assumptions, i.e. an operation in which (in virtue of the fact that p implies q) we assume q with the same reference to the assumption of p as is involved in a true *therefore*-inference; and in this he sees the essence of the so-called hypothetical judgment, which, he declares, is really not a judgment at all (p. 89). There are thus three things to be distinguished, according to Meinong: (1) the relation of implication, (2) the *therefore*-inference, which operates with judgments, (3) the *if-then*-inference (as we may call it), which operates with assumptions.

The distinction of (1) and (2) is very important, and quite indubitable; but (3) appears open to doubt. Every *if-then* sentence, it seems plain, asserts something, and is either true or false; it is undeniable that the two propositions with which it is concerned are assumed, not asserted, but it seems also undeniable that a relation is asserted between them. Meinong affirms (p. 87) that such relations can only be affirmed, and that when we attempt to deny them we really deny something else. In testing this assertion, it is necessary to point out that almost all Meinong's instances contain variables, and therefore deal with what I call *formal* implication. 'If the sun shines, it need not therefore be hot', and 'if quadrilaterals are equilateral, they need not be squares' (p. 88), which he suggests and rejects as denials, both have this nature. In the first, a variable time is involved; in the second, a variable quadrilateral. He asserts (*ib.*) that *necessity* is denied in these propositions, whereas necessity is not a constituent in *if-then* statements. I have already remarked that necessity, in the old modal sense, appears to me inadmissible; there is, however, where propositions containing variables are concerned, a meaning for necessity, and that is, that the said propositions hold for all values of the variable. Now 'if the sun shines, it is hot' does assert something for all values of the variable; and this is what is denied in the suggested instance. Thus in the sense in which necessity occurs in the denial, it occurs in the affirmation also. Meinong discusses, as obviously of quite another kind, propositions where the connexion is temporal, as 'when a train leaves the station, a bell rings for the next station'. But these are precisely of the same kind as the other statements; the proposition is really the following: 'If x is a time at which a train leaves the station, x is a time at which a bell rings for the next station'. And it is to be observed that where variables occur, as in all these instances, neither hypothesis nor conclusion is a proposition at all, but only becomes one by giving a definite value to the variable. What is asserted is, that an implication holds *in all cases*; and it is, I think, from failure to perceive this, that the denial seems to Meinong so very different from the affirmation.

The notion of assumptive inferences seems, it must be confessed, to derive some support from observation of what actually occurs when we follow a chain of reasoning without assenting to the premises. There is, at every stage, first the recognition of the implication, then a new beginning with the conclusion, then a new recognition of an implication with the previous conclusion as premise. But what happens is, I think, as follows. First we assume a proposition p; then we judge that p implies q; then we assume q, and then we judge that q implies r. But what distinguishes this case from a *therefore*-inference is, that we might just as well assume q without perceiving that p implies it; whereas, in the other case, we actually *judge q*, which we do because of the implication. It is of course true that the *cause* of our assuming q may be, in part, our perception that p implies it; but this cannot be the *ground*, because assumptions do not require grounds and are incapable of having any.

With regard to what Meinong calls assumptive inferences, in which, by means of implications, we pass from one assumption to a second, which has what he calls relative evidence, there is a difficulty, which he himself recognises (pp. 261–5), in the fact that inconsistent assumptions can be combined, and that the rules of inference cannot bind our freedom of assuming. He seems to regard the making of self-contradictory assumptions as very rare; but, on his own theory of negation, it is implied in the statement of the law of contradiction itself. For this affirms that, if p be a proposition, p and not-p cannot both be true, i.e. it is false that p and not-p are both true. But this, being the negation of 'p and not-p are both true', can only be the outcome, on his view, of the assumption that p and not-p *are* both true (pp. 105–8). In view of the fact that assumptions are thus free, I cannot understand how the notion of assumptive inference, as distinct from judgments of implication, can be maintained.

The part of assumptions in inference, however, is very great even if this particular contention of Meinong's be false. For, whenever we judge that p implies q, we necessarily use the assumptions of p and q, since we are not judging either p or q; and this applies even if, in another judgment, we do actually assert p, and thence q. If there were no assumptions, inference would be inexplicable; and this is peculiarly evident where, as in the case of a *reductio ad absurdum*, premises and conclusion are actually disbelieved. The fifth, sixth and seventh chapters are closely interconnected, and must be considered jointly. The fifth, on the objectivity of the psychical, examines the relation of object and content in presentations, assumptions and judgments. No psychical occurrence, and in particular no presentation, is without an object; but in order to explain how a presentation comes to have an object, assumptions are indispensable (p. 93). It is well here to start from judgment. If I judge rightly that I feel pain, then the pain does as a matter of fact exist; and if I make a correct judgment which is not existential, but affirms that something subsists, then again the object must really subsist: in the first case the judgment has what may be called by the traditional name of transcendence, in the second case quasi-transcendence. In such cases the object of the judgment is that which is rightly affirmed to exist or subsist (pp. 94–5). But in the case of false affirmative or true negative judgments, this account of the object becomes inapplicable: for *ex hypothesi* these judgments cannot have the objects they would have if true and affirmative. The objectivity, in such a case, seems to belong only to the presentation involved; but the object of the presentation may not exist, and there seems to be only a capacity for an object. But capacities, though facts, are not perceivable, whereas the objectivity of presentations does seem perceivable (pp. 96–100). In this difficulty assumptions give the solution. The difficulty concerns only presentations and negative judgments; positive judgments, true or false, serve obviously for the apprehension of an object. But *pure* presentation is not directed to an object at all: it is only potentially objective.[1] When we seem to perceive direction to an object, this arises through the presence of an affirmative assumption: the object is presented 'as if it were real'. If not, the presentation has only *potential* objectivity. The introduction of assumptions in place of judgments enables us, in the above manner, to give objectivity even to such presentations as the round square, for assumptions are not bound by the law of contradiction. Thus the objectivity of a presentation is its capacity for being the basis of an affirmative assumption (pp. 101–3). And this applies also to negative judgments and assumptions; these are always based upon the corresponding positive assumption, and are only made when this has suggested itself (pp. 105–8).

In the above theory, there seem to me to be certain errors, which it will be well to examine at once. In the first place, not all propositions assert or deny being or existence. Meinong appears to hold that when a relation R is affirmed to hold between a and b, as in (say) 'a is the father of b', what is really affirmed is the being or subsistence of the relation.[2] But there are grave objections to this view. In the first place, it must be the relation particularised as relating a and b, not the abstract relation of paternity, whose being is supposed to be affirmed. But there are logical reasons for supposing that there are no such entities at all as particularised relations; most of these I have set forth elsewhere (*op. cit.*, § 55), but another is derived from false propositions. If what is actually meant by a relational proposition is the being of the particularised relation, then, when the proposition in question is not true, it must be meaningless: for it

[1] *Gegenständlich* is used by Meinong to mean *having* an object, not *being* one.
[2] In a later passage (pp. 143–6) Meinong says that he formerly held this view, but has now seen reason to abandon it. He holds, however, that no evil results can follow, as a rule, from assuming it when convenient. The above seems, nevertheless, to constitute a case where it does lead to errors, and where (as often happens) the influence of an opinion has persisted after the opinion has been renounced.

affirms the being of what, *ex hypothesi*, does not have being, and therefore there is nothing of which it affirms the being, and therefore it affirms nothing and is meaningless. In other words: every constituent of a proposition, whether this proposition be true or false, must have being; consequently, if the particularised relation is a constituent of the proposition in which it is supposed to occur, then, since such a proposition is significant when it is false, the particularised relation has being even when the terms are not related by the relation in question. Hence the being of the particularised relation is not what is asserted. It may be thought that this point has been unduly laboured; but it has a very important consequence. Since not all propositions assert or deny the existence or subsistence of an object, we cannot always take such object as the object of a judgment; and hence it is an easy step to the conclusion that we can never do so. What I wish to affirm is that the judgment or assumption 'A exists' has as its object, not A, but the existence of A, i.e. that which, in chapter vii, Meinong calls the *Objective* of the judgment or assumption. It would follow that there are not, as he appears to hold, two kinds of objects of a judgment, the one thing judged about, and the other the fact affirmed concerning it. In the above case, 'A is the father of B', we have already seen that the paternity is not the object, and it is obvious that neither A nor B is so: the conclusion remains that, if there is an object, it can only be the whole proposition. And this result, if valid, seems to throw doubt upon the view that presentations only acquire objects through assumptions, which, in any case, has a decided appearance of paradox. It is true, of course, that redness, e.g., is very difficult to think of without the assumption of its existence, which necessarily occurs in any visualising of a red colour. Yet if, as Meinong admits (p. 102), there are pure presentations, it is difficult not to suppose that the presentation of redness has redness for its object. And in the case of objects incapable of existence, a similar conclusion seems even more evident.

Chapter vi, which is very important, deals with the function of assumptions in the apprehension of objects of higher order;

it deals also (though the connexion is rather hard to see) with the nature of the difference between intuitive (*anschaulich*) and unintuitive presentation. The former problem is one in which, though I find few points to criticise in the discussion, a direct logical method seems to me to lead far more directly to the goal. Complexes, as soon as we examine them, are seen to be always products of propositions: one might be tempted to describe them, rather loosely, as propositions in which the truth or falsity has been left out. In any case, no analysis can be made of a complex except by reference to one or more propositions. This being so, it follows that the apprehension of a complex involves the apprehension of a proposition; and since the assertion of the proposition is not required, its assumption will be all that will be relevant. This is the direct logical road. The other way, which is pursued by Meinong, is to examine our apprehension of complexes, and to show that it contains or involves the apprehension of propositions. The supposed advantage of this method is, I imagine, that our apprehension exists, and is therefore supposed more amenable to inspection: but it is impossible to apprehend an object unless the object itself is amenable to inspection. The supposition is equivalent to assuming that we can find out about otherwise unknowable objects by examining our knowledge of them. Meinong, though he does not hold that only what exists is immediately knowable, seems still to feel that it is safer and more empirical to begin with what exists; and this recommends the psychological as opposed to the logical method. But except a certain cumbrousness in some problems, this method does not have any inevitable bad consequences.

The opposition of intuitive and unintuitive presentation, Meinong says, occurs only in the presentation of complexes: that of simple objects is of neither kind (pp. 114, 122). But the same object can be presented either intuitively or unintuitively; hence the distinction must not be sought in the object. And since it cannot lie in the act of presentation, it must lie in the content. It would seem that the same partial contents occur in both, but are combined into different complexes by a difference in the real relations existing between them (pp.

112–13). The intuitive combination seems natural, and offering itself without any act of ours; the other, more artificial, and produced, as a rule, by our intellectual activity. The first sort of combination he calls *Zusammensetzung*, the second *Zusammenstellung*. (I shall speak of the resulting complexes as *compounds* and *composites* respectively.) The first sort may be typified by 'the red cross', the second by 'the cross which is red' (pp. 116–17). But unintuitive presentation can also form 'the cross which is not red', which intuitive presentation cannot form. The presence of the negation indicates the need for an assumption; and the affirmative 'cross which is red' similarly requires an affirmative assumption. Thus all unintuitive presentations involve assumptions (pp. 118–19); and the same must be held concerning intuitive presentations, though where these are perceptions they involve judgments (pp. 120, 121, 137, 138). It is impossible to have a *presentation* of *a* and *b* standing in the relation R, for we must have R rightly related to *a* and *b*, and so on, whence an endless regress of a kind which, so long as judgments or assumptions are not introduced, is logically objectionable (pp. 122–3). This is reinforced by a long and difficult argument from the nature of knowledge, which, though I am not sure of understanding it, I shall do my best to reproduce. If truth requires the correspondence of ideas with facts, it must be the correspondence of the immanent objects of ideas with facts, not of the contents of ideas: for the content of the presentation of a square table is not square. When such correspondence subsists, there is a relation which we may call that of *adequacy*. A presentation is adequate when it is legitimated by a self-evident affirmation; but except where affirmative knowledge is concerned, there is a merely immanent object, and we say that the object is adequate to the presentation, not *vice versa*, for the presentation is here prior. Now the relation of content and object is ideal, not real, and ideal relations are never affected by real relations between their terms. Hence, taking as objects the contents of the presentations of *a* and *b* and R, no real relation between them can substitute for them, in presentation, the presentation of the one object '*a* and *b* in the relation R'; nothing we can do to them will give them the relation of adequacy to this object unless they have it already; consequently there is no *presentation* of this object at all (pp. 124–129).

This argument involves many points calling for criticism: in the first place, the idea of adequacy seems bound up with the notion that the object of a presentation is something which forms part of the presentation, and may be rightly called immanent. And as regards judgments, there seems no difference in the relation to their objects when they are correct and when they are incorrect; the difference is rather in the objects, which are true propositions in the one case, and false propositions in the other. Again the opposition of ideal and real relations seems to be bound up with the notion of necessity, and to be not capable of precision. But leaving all these points aside, there remains a simple fact, which forms probably the basis of the argument. The proposition '*a* has the relation R to *b*' is an object not to be obtained by juxtaposing *a* and R and *b*; it is a new object, having that special kind of unity that characterises propositions. And hence the presentations of *a* and R and *b* will not, of themselves, yield this object. But I do not see why the thought of this object should not be called a presentation; indeed, the question arises whether assumptions are anything more than presentations of propositions. It is the fact that propositions, and the complexes formed by means of them, have a kind of unity which, apart from truth and falsehood, distinguishes them among objects; but I do not see that the attitude towards a proposition, when it is assumed, differs in any way from the attitude towards objects which is called presentation. In short, the arguments adduced do not, to my mind, prove that the difference of an assumption and a presentation is not wholly derived from the difference between their objects.

By introducing judgments or assumptions, Meinong continues, it becomes possible, which so long as we confine ourselves to presentations it is not, subjectively to combine a *superius* with *inferiora* (p. 134). I should express what I believe to be the same fact as the one Meinong is analysing, by saying that the combination of *superius* and *inferiora* is what constitutes a proposition, and that therefore any state of mind, of which the object is or contains such a combination, has a proposition as the whole or part of its object. And a state of mind which has a proposition as the whole of its object is either a judgment[1] or an assumption, the latter being merely the presentation of a proposition, and differing from judgment both as regards the act and content and as regards the relation of content to object.

In the same chapter, Meinong raises a difficult point, which seems to involve the inner essence of relations. In the presentation of 'the cross which is red', the cross and the red are obvious, but there seems to be no presentation of their relation (p. 142). This fact leads Meinong to reject the view that a judgment of relation asserts the being of the relation (pp. 144–5) – a view which we have already seen reason to think erroneous. It leads also to the conclusion that the concomitance of complexes and relations cannot be maintained universally since a complex may be thought of without any presentation of the relation (p. 147). The fact itself, so far as I am able to judge from inspection, appears to me to be true. We can and do, apparently, think of objects in a certain relation, without thinking of the relation at all. And apart from inspection, the endless regress seems to prove that this is so; for if not, we should have to think also of the relation of the relation to the terms, and so on, which would make the apprehension of objects in relation impossible. This is, we may conjecture, the reason why common sense and many philosophers regard relations as less real, less substantial in some sense, than their terms. There is probably some logical fact corresponding to this, but I am at a loss to discover what it is. In some sense which it would be very desirable to define, a relational proposition seems to be *about* its terms, in a way in which it is not *about* the relation. And we distinguish between 'A is the father of B' and 'fatherhood holds between A and B': the latter, but not the former, is about fatherhood as well as A and B, and asserts, while the former does not, a relation of fatherhood to A and B. Hence, although, at first sight, the

[1] Including, for the moment, disbelief under *judgment*.

difference might seem to be a merely subjective difference of emphasis, it results that there is a real logical difference; and this difference may be relevant to the above question.

Chapter vii, on the Objective,[1] points out that judgment, in addition to what has hitherto been called its object, has reference also to something else which is like an object, namely to the something which is known, the something indicated by the whole sentence. If I say 'there was no disturbance', something positive is affirmed, which is plainly not the disturbance, since this is denied. We can say: 'It is a fact that there was no disturbance'; thus 'that there was no disturbance' is an object in a new sense: this Meinong calls the *Objective* of the judgment 'there was no disturbance' (pp. 150–3). When the judgment is false, the Objective is merely immanent, just as the object is in similar cases: the judgment always *has* its object and its Objective, but these do not necessarily have being – when the Objective is false, we can only say that the judgment is *directed towards* an Objective (pp. 154–5). This Objective of the judgment is what (following Mr G. E. Moore) I have called a proposition: it is to the Objective that such words as true and false, evident, probable, necessary, etc., apply (p. 174). That there are Objectives is made abundantly plain by instances. When we say, 'it is certain that the evidence is not concluded', it is not the judgment, but the Objective, that is certain. If A does not exist, we can say 'that A does not exist, is' – or, as would be more natural in English, 'there is the non-existence of A'. When we say, 'I believe that so-and-so', it is the Objective so-and-so, not the judgment, that we believe. (In all such cases, as is plain, we are really concerned with an appeal to inspection, which, to my mind, makes the Objective perfectly visible. If I say 'A is the father of B', I am not concerned with my own judgment, but with something quite outside it: in this sense, a judgment, like a presentation, has a reference to something other than itself, namely the fact asserted; and this is Meinong's Objective.)

[1] *Das Objectiv*. I shall use a capital O to distinguish this technical substantival sense from the usual adjectival one.

A curious difficulty arises for Meinong from the conclusion that there is no presentation of a proposition. The Objective, in his theory, cannot be the object of any presentation; and yet it can be the object of a judgment, as in 'p is certain', where p is an Objective. It would follow that we can think of something, namely an Objective, without having any presentation of it (p. 159). Some possible escapes are suggested from this paradox, but their acceptance is not urged upon the reader. Now I confess that, not being myself a psychologist, I have much difficulty in understanding what Meinong means by presentation; and the possibility here suggested adds to my difficulty. It is, therefore, with much diffidence that I venture upon criticism in this matter. But I fail to feel any force in the argument against the presentability of complexes. If *aRb* denotes '*a* has the relation R to *b*', Meinong proves, I admit, that no operation will produce the presentation of *aRb* out of those of *a* and R and *b*. But the further argument that there is no presentation of *aRb* seems to be made in forgetfulness of the Objective. For the presentation of a complex need not be a complex of presentations, when we remember that the complex is the Objective, and that therefore, if there is such a presentation, the complexity is primarily in the object of the presentation, i.e. in the Objective. It is, I admit, difficult to suppose that the content of the presentation of *aRb* does not contain those of *a* and R and *b*, for every property of the object seems to demand a strictly correlative property of the content, and the content, therefore, must have every complexity belonging to the object. Nevertheless it is not impossible to maintain that the content of the presentation of *aRb*, though it plainly involves those of *a* and *b*, does not involve that of R. No doubt difficulties might be found in this view, but I cannot think they would be greater than the difficulty of an unpresented object of thought. And, as Meinong's own arguments show, this view is one which, whether logically permissible or not, certainly commends itself to direct inspection. If we adopt this view, an assumption will be nothing other than the presentation of an Objective. Nevertheless, in his last chapter, Meinong asserts that the way in which, in chapters i and iii, assumptions first occurred, proves beyond all doubt that they are more than presentations (p. 276), and that, in fact, they are nearer to judgments than to presentations; they may, he says, be described as judgments without conviction, but it would be nonsense to describe them as presentations determined with respect to yes and no (p. 277). I should reply by distinguishing three kinds of opposition of yes and no, of which two are objective, and belong to the Objectives of assumptions, while one is subjective, and belongs to judgments but not to assumptions. Given a proposition p, there is first its truth or falsity: this belongs to the Objectives of assumptions. Next there is the opposition of p and not-p: this also belongs to the Objectives of assumptions, for either p or not-p may be assumed; and this is the opposition of yes and no which Meinong always employs in his arguments on this point. Thirdly, there is the subjective opposition of yes and no, which is that of belief or disbelief: either p or not-p may be believed or disbelieved, whether true or false; this is the opposition which specially characterises judgment, and is absent in assumption. Thus the opposition of yes and no, in the two senses in which it applies to assumptions, belongs to the object, and derivatively to the content, but not in any sense to the act; whereas in judgment, there is a yes or no in the act itself. Thus Meinong's argument is only valid if it is impossible to have a presentation of an object which contains a *not* as constituent – for the opposition of true and false is irrelevant in this matter, and only the opposition of p and not-p is in question. But we have already seen reason to doubt the conclusiveness of his reasoning on this point. The greater likeness of assumptions to judgments, we shall conclude, is derived from the identity of their objects and the close similarity of their contents; but in regard to the act, assumptions are to be classed with presentations, being merely the presentations of objects of a certain kind.

Meinong distinguishes 'objects of thought' from 'objects of presentation', the former being such as cannot be presented (p. 163), which are the same as those that involve Objectives. He points out that the division between objects and Objectives is not as sharp as might be supposed. 'Black' is an object of presentation, but 'the blackness of the board' is an object of thought, and so is 'the black', i.e. 'that which is black'. In fact, relations, attributes, and all complexes require Objectives, which occur everywhere except in the simple, or, speaking not quite precisely, in cases of complete intuitiveness with mere presentation (pp. 178-80). Again, it is always Objectives, i.e. that something should exist or not exist, that we desire, and to which we attach value (pp. 182-3).[1] Some general properties belong to all Objectives. They are all objects of higher order; they never have existence, but they have subsistence when true though not when false; and they are timeless (pp. 187-9). When Objectives occur as objects, it is usually the assumptions, not the judgments, of them that occur (p. 203). It is owing to their having been overlooked that no one has known hitherto what class of things were to be called true or false, or how to distinguish logic and epistemology from psychology; for without Objectives, only knowing (*Erkennen*), which is psychical, could be the object of epistemology, whereas this is really concerned *primarily*, not with knowing, but with knowledge (*Erkenntnis*). Meinong confesses that it is only since he has recognised Objectives that he has known *why* epistemology is not psychology; but he holds that both logic and epistemology must

---

[1] I do not intend to enter upon the non-epistemological parts of Meinong's work, but in this connexion one observation seems important. While agreeing entirely that desire is always directed to Objectives, I cannot think that these are always existential. Every mathematician, unless his patience is more than human, must often have wished, in regard to many general theorems, that there were fewer exceptional cases; yet here what is desired is not an existential proposition. And it would seem that value also may attach to non-existential propositions where these, as sometimes occurs, are felt to have beauty. Clifford felt, for example, that elliptic Geometry has more value than Euclidean; and it is difficult to suppose that the greater value attaches *only* to the knowledge, and in no respect to what is known. Another point, which, however, raises grave questions both of ethics and of logic, is, that value can only be held to attach to *true* propositions. The value attached to such as are false is only the value which they would have if they were true. This results very simply from the fact that otherwise a bad world would be as good as a good one, for the false existential propositions that were good would subsist just as much in the one as the true ones would in the other. This seems to show that judgment, not assumption, is relevant to questions of value; for the assumption 'A exists' only has a valuable Objective in case A really does exist and its existence is good.

concern themselves with knowing as well as with knowledge, and hence must be built upon a psychological basis, thus leaving psychology still the most central and fundamental part of philosophy (pp. 192–7).

These last remarks on the relations of logic, epistemology and psychology appear to me to contain remnants of the former theories through which Meinong has emerged, so far as he has emerged, from 'psychologism'; and doubtless they are much influenced by his belief in an 'immanent' object. For it is plain that logic must concern itself as much with false propositions as with true ones; but false propositions, according to Meinong, are the non-subsisting, merely pseudo-existing Objectives of erroneous judgments, and except through erroneous judgments they have no connexion either with existence or with subsistence. Hence, in order to survey the whole field of logic, it will be necessary to take account of judgment; and so psychology appears as fundamental. But if we deny the distinction between the immanent object and the (so to speak) external object, the positions become reversed. We shall now hold that a presentation or judgment is only capable of being directed to an object because such an object subsists, and that thus the subsistence of the object is prior to the presentation or judgment. We shall hold that, since psychological judgments, like all others, affirm propositions (i.e. Objectives), whatever can be said concerning propositions generally applies equally to those of psychology. We cannot say that logic is specially concerned with Objectives and psychology with the judgments that have those Objectives, for all knowledge is concerned with Objectives, psychological knowledge like the rest. But logic will certainly concern itself with the general nature of Objectives, with truth and falsehood, and whatever else may be discoverable of a like degree of generality. Psychology will concern itself (*inter alia*) with judgment; and the theory of knowledge will concern itself with the difference between correct and erroneous judgments, i.e. between such as affirm true and false propositions respectively. Since psychology consists of propositions, and wishes, at least, to consist of true ones, logic must be assumed in psychology; and not only the above very general kind of logic, but such matters also as the canons of inference; for these can only be inferred by assuming them, and are therefore necessarily presupposed in any argument from psychological data. For these reasons, it seems to result that logic, though not epistemology, is prior to psychology. And Meinong's own principle, that the *inferiora* are prior to the *superius*, makes the Objective necessarily prior to the relation involved in judgment.

III

It remains to establish, if this be possible, the principle that all presentations and all judgments have an object which is not merely immanent; and here, although the favourable arguments appear to me overwhelming, I must admit that the explanation of falsity presents grave difficulties. Let us, however, first consider the matter without regard to these difficulties.

Meinong holds – so it would seem – that the object of a presentation is sometimes immanent, but at other times not so; while the object of a judgment – which he calls an Objective, and I call a proposition – is always merely immanent (p. 257). Now for my part I do not see how an immanent object differs from no object at all. The immanent object does not exist, according to Meinong, and is therefore no part of the mental state whose object it is; for this mental state exists. Yet, although not part of any mental state, it is supposed to be in some sense psychical. But it cannot be in any way bound up with any particular mental state of which it is the object; for other states, at other times and in other people, may have precisely the same object, since an object or a proposition can be presented or believed more than once. I confess these facts seem to me to show, without more ado, that objects and propositions must always have being, and cannot be merely imaginary *relata* for what appears as a relation of presentation or judgment.

But let us examine directly the nature of the relation involved in judgment; and, in order to eliminate, to begin with, the problem of error, let us suppose the judgment to be correct. Suppose, for the sake of definiteness, that our judgment is 'A exists', where A is something that does as a matter of fact exist. Then A's existence, it seems plain, subsists independently of its being judged to subsist; for, if this were not so, the judgment would be erroneous. In this case, the Objective of the judgment – at least in the view of common sense – is as truly independent of the judgment as is A itself. But the peculiarity of the cognitive relation, which is what we wish to consider, lies in this: that one term of the relation *is* nothing but an awareness of the other term – an awareness which may be either that of presentation or that of judgment. This makes the relation more essential, more intimate, than any other; for the relatedness seems to form part of the very nature of one of the related terms, namely of the psychical term. This does not occur in any other relation that I know of; at first sight, it is as if, when A is greater than B, A were itself 'excess over B'. And yet it is different from this; for cognition is not awareness of a cognitive relation to an object, but only of an object. It seems, again, as though the psychical side were a complex, of which the other side formed a constituent; and this, I suppose, is what is meant by the immanent object: the object, in this view, enters always as an element into the cognition, even when there is, apart from the cognition, no object cognised, which is supposed to be the case with error. Here again, however, the very great difficulty of thinking of contents, as opposed to objects, has caused a confusion; there is no way of describing a particular judgment except as the judgment that so-and-so, i.e. by means of its object. But the judgment itself, in its purity, as something wholly psychical, is merely the content and the act: the object is not a part of the judgment. Thus the psychical side is not really a complex of content and object; and therefore the 'immanent' object may be discarded.

But now we are confronted with one or other of two alternatives. Either a presentation or judgment may be wholly destitute of an object, or else false propositions subsist just as much as true ones do. For false propositions may be assumed and even (unfortunately) believed. Let us endeavour to state the grounds for and against both views.

Direct inspection seems to leave no room whatever for doubt that, in all presentations and judgments, there is necessarily an object. If I believe that A is the father of B, I believe something; the subsistence of the something, if not directly obvious, seems to follow from the fact that, if it did not subsist, I should be believing nothing, and therefore not believing. And it is plain that others may believe the *same* thing; this, however, might be regarded as implying only sameness of content. Again, it is possible to count propositions, to make classes of them, and so on; but in doing so it is by no means necessary to confine ourselves to true propositions. It is a recognised principle that, if p implies q, then not-q implies not-p; but here, if p and q are true, not-p and not-q are false; thus, if, apart from judgment or assumption, there are only true propositions, there will be a gulf between 'p implies q' and 'not-p implies not-q', since the first will subsist, but not the second; but of such a gulf no trace is to be seen. Further, the proposition 'p implies q' may be true, though p be false: but in that case, since p is merely mental, the whole proposition will be merely mental, which we supposed true propositions not to be. And so throughout, the attempt to make a difference, as regards subsistence, between true and false propositions, leads to countless difficulties and to countless conflicts with what appear to be obvious facts.

It may be urged on the other side, first of all, that the argument that a content implies an object is one which makes the relation of content and object different from every other (except that of whole and part): in every other case, though a complex implies a relation, neither of the *inferiora* of the complex implies this relation. The supposed implication, it may be urged, arises solely from the fact that the content is elusive, and becomes confounded with the cognitive complex even where there is no such complex. And directly, if we consider a relation R between a and b, we should say, when it is false that this relation holds, that there is no such thing as the relation R between a and b. But this argument has been already disposed of, by the contention that the being of this relation is not what the proposition '*a* has the relation R to *b*' really affirms. Yet, when we consider such complexes as 'the difference between *a* and *b*', which must be admitted by some door, it seems plain that, when *a* and *b* are identical, there is no difference between *a* and *b*, which seems equivalent to 'the difference between *a* and *b* does not have being'. Consider, again, what it is we mean when we judge. At first sight, we seem to mean that a certain proposition is true; but '*p* is true' is not the same proposition as *p*, and therefore cannot be what we mean. And the complex '*p*'s truth' may be assumed just as *p* may: as assumed, it is not a judgment. Thus, when we affirm *p*, we are concerned only with *p*, and in no way with truth. This seems to show that truth and falsehood cannot lie in the Objective of the judgment; but that we affirm truly when the judgment has an Objective, and falsely when it has not.

The facts concerned may be summed up in the following survey.

(*a*) Among objects there are two kinds, the simple and the complex. The latter are characterised by a certain kind of unity, apparently not capable of definition, and not a constituent of the complexes in which it occurs. On one view, a complex is the same thing as a proposition, and is always either true or false, but has being equally in either case; on the other view, the only complexes are true propositions, and falsehood is a property of such judgments as have no Objectives.

(*b*) Two distinct attitudes occur towards objects, one that of presentation, the other that of judgment. The latter is only possible towards complex objects, but the former is possible towards all objects. We may say that the first gives acquaintance, while the second gives knowledge, or at least belief. These two attitudes towards the same object differ both as regards the act and as regards the content. Adopting Meinong's terminology, according to which words *express* a state of mind, but *indicate* (*bedeuten*) an object, 'the death of Cæsar' and 'Cæsar died' indicate the same object but express a different state of mind: the former merely apprehends the object in question, while the latter asserts it; the former is an *assumption*, the latter a *judgment*.

(*c*) On one view, knowledge is the affirmation of a true complex, error that of a false one. Affirmation must not be regarded as affirming that the complex in question is true, for this is a new affirmation, having a different complex as object; affirmation has as object merely the complex in question. On the other view, judgment has no object except when the object is a *true* proposition; an erroneous judgment is one which, though it seems to have an object, really has none. On this view, truth and falsehood apply most fitly to judgment; the object, when there is one, may be called a fact.

Between the two views here suggested, it is not easy to decide. For the purpose of reaching a decision, I shall enumerate five theories of knowledge, which appear to cover all, or nearly all, that have hitherto been suggested. I shall then resume the whole discussion from a general point of view.

The five theories of knowledge are as follows:

1. It may be urged that the knowledge does not differ from what is known, i.e. there is no *object* of knowledge.
2. We may admit the distinction of content and object, but hold that the latter is merely immanent.
3. We may hold that the object is immanent when false, transcendent when true.
4. We may hold that when a judgment is false there is no object; but when true, there is a transcendent object.
5. We may hold that the object is always transcendent.

These theories may be held both with regard to presentation and with regard to judgment; but in the case of presentation we shall have, in place of (3), that the object is transcendent when it exists, or when it has being (these are alternatives), and that otherwise it is immanent; with corresponding modifications in (4). Thus (3) requires that the theory of propositions should be developed before the theory of the transcendence of presentations. This seems to be Meinong's view, and to give the reason why he considers the transcendence of presentations to be derivative from that of judgments. Of the above views, Idealism oscillates between (1) and (2); Meinong holds to (3) in regard to presentations, and (2) in regard to judgments, common sense seems to prefer (4), Frege and Mr Moore advocate (5). Let us examine them in succession.

1. The theory that a presentation or judgment has no reference outside itself to an object seems sufficiently refuted by direct inspection; this argument has been adequately developed by Meinong. It is also incompatible, as regards presentations, with the obvious difference of content and object, as, e.g. that the presentation of redness is not red, that the presentation of extension is unextended, that the presentation of the past may be present, and that the presentation of the non-existent may exist. It leads also, in the case of presentations, to absolutely insoluble logical difficulties as regards identity. For, in this view, the whole realm of entities must be composed of particular psychical entities, and it becomes impossible to say in what respect two presentations agree which, in ordinary language, are said to be of the same object. If we say that they resemble one another, we can only mean that the judgment that they resemble one another exists, and this, in turn, can only mean that some one judges that this judgment exists, and so on. And if we say that strictly the *same* presentation may exist in different instances, this again can only mean that someone judges it to be so. In short, no logic is possible which does not admit identity to be independent of any judgment as to identity; and this decides that outside judgment there are objects and there is identity; and that there is identity outside judgment decides that some judgments at least have a transcendent object.

2. To admit the distinction of content and object, while holding that the latter is merely immanent, is a theory which is difficult to state precisely, owing to the doubt as to what is meant by an 'immanent' object. Internal perception, Meinong says, gives not only the content, but also the immanent object, of a presentation; and this fact constitutes, he admits, a fundamental problem in the theory of knowledge (*Gegenstände höherer Ordnung*, p. 207). Now it certainly would seem, so far as inspec-

tion can show, that any perception of a presentation involves also perception of an object. But here, I think, the greatest care and subtlety is required to avoid confusion. If all awareness be, as it seems to be, awareness of an object other than itself, then, when we are aware of an awareness, we are necessarily aware of an awareness of an object, and in this way the object seems to be also perceived. But I do not think this is really the case. The content being awareness of an object, the perception of the content involves the object as much as, but no more than, the content itself does. It is better and simpler, therefore, to study contents themselves, rather than the perception of them.

When we consider the presentation of something simple, say redness, it is evident that the presentation and the object are distinct. It is further evident that, if there be an immanent object at all, there is also an object which is not immanent. For, if this be denied, there can be no such thing as awareness of what is not part of the present psychical state: since awareness of an immanent object will not really be awareness of what is past in time or removed in space or otherwise distinct from my momentary thought. Thus the problem will arise as to the relation of the immanent object to the transcendent object; and identity is the only possible relation. And here it may be worth while to criticise the notion that truth consists in the correspondence of ideas with reality. This can only mean, as Meinong points out (*Annahmen*, p. 125), the correspondence of the immanent objects of ideas with reality, i.e. with the transcendent objects. But there is a difficulty in the mere supposition of non-correspondence: for an idea can only fail to correspond with an object by being the idea of something else; and in that case, the correspondence exists, but directed to a different object. People have in mind, apparently, such a case as failure to recognise a person: I see John coming along the road, and I think it is Peter. Here, it is supposed, the immanent object is Peter, and the transcendent object is John. But this is an error: for the immanent object is 'Peter is walking along the road'; and the fact that John is so walking is in no sense the transcendent object, but at most the *cause* of the erroneous judgment about Peter. Thus if there are immanent as distinct from transcendent objects, it would seem that erroneous judgments do not have transcendent objects at all.

But let us return to the analysis of awareness itself. In the case of presentation, to begin with, truth and falsehood do not occur; the presentation is of such and such an object, and a mistake as to what its object is would be a mistake in reflective analysis, not in the presentation itself. We have to consider the question: Is the presentation of a simple, such as redness, itself simple? If, as Meinong contends, it consists of content and object, then plainly it is not simple; it is a complex with a relation. But he admits, as indeed is evident, that the object, even the immanent object, does not exist in the presentation; consequently it seems to follow that the immanent object does not form part of the presentation; for any part of an existent exists. If, however, it is not part of the presentation, it seems not in any sense psychical, except when it happens to have formed part of some other psychical state. This argument seems to dispose of the immanent object.

Nevertheless, awareness is utterly unlike other relations, except that of whole and part, in that one of its terms presupposes the other. A presentation, we said, must have an object; and it seems plain that every awareness must be awareness *of* something: if there were no object, the awareness would be nothing, and this seems impossible. It is not maintained, of course, that the object must *exist*; that would be to maintain that a certain specific proposition must hold of the object, whereas all that seems essential is that there should *be* such an object; and the assertion of being, if not analytic, is yet more nearly so than any other assertion. Thus, although the object does not imply the content, the content does imply the object and the relation of content to object. In this, the relation in question distinguishes itself from all others except that of whole and part; and this fact probably accounts for the supposition that the object is part of the presentation. We have here a complex of an absolutely unique kind, where, though one term is prior to the complex, the other term is not, but is logically on a level with the complex and the relation. This makes the position of contents quite unlike that of other *inferiora* in complexes.

Thus the notion of a merely immanent object of presentations must be abandoned; but it remains to examine the case of judgments. Here the matter is complicated by error; for, though all presentations are alike in being awarenesses of objects, judgments differ by the fact that some are correct and others erroneous. In the case of such as are correct, the transcendence seems quite undeniable: there is a *fact*, of which we are aware, and the judgment is correct because of the fact. Things which exist, for example, really do exist, and are not merely judged to exist; for, if so, the judgment that they exist would only exist if some one judged that it existed, and so on through a vicious regress. Thus correct judgments have a transcendent object; but with regard to incorrect judgments, it remains to examine whether (1) the object is immanent, (2) there is no object, or (3) the object is transcendent. These possibilities constitute the third, fourth and fifth of the above theories.

3. We are now to suppose that true judgments have a transcendent object, while false ones have an immanent object. It must be objected *in limine* that the meaning of the phrase *immanent object* is obscure, and that our previous arguments in the case of presentations are still in large part applicable. But special objections apply to this theory. It will be necessary to suppose that correct judgments also have immanent objects; for, if not, it is hardly to be supposed that this difference of correct and erroneous judgments would be imperceptible, as it certainly is. But if so, we have the reduplication of immanent and transcendent objects which we found inadmissible in the case of presentations. Again, it is very hard to suppose that nothing is objectively false. Suppose, e.g. that A differs from B. This, being true, is objective and transcendent. But, in that case, 'A is identical with B' would seem to be objectively false. This, however, the theory will deny, though it must admit that 'A is not identical with B' is a judgment having a transcendent object. It seems quite impossible to maintain, as this view

requires, that a negation may be transcendent, when the corresponding affirmation is not so. To meet this, we might maintain that correct judgments do not always have transcendent objects, but only when they are affirmative. This modification will be considered under (5); for the present it seems plain that (3) is untenable.

4. All the arguments – and they are certainly not contemptible – which apply against transcendent objects in the case of erroneous judgments, apply, when the immanent object is discarded, in favour of the view that in such cases there is no object at all. When we examine the transcendent object of (say) a correct existential judgment, this object seems to be the actual existence of an object. It is easy enough to convince ourselves that this existence is a fact, and that we are aware of the fact when we judge. And the same holds of correct judgments even when they are not existential: they have as objects what, in a wide sense, may be called *facts*, and it is this (it would seem) that makes them correct. But when our judgment is erroneous, the error seems to consist precisely in the absence of such objects: if they have objects at all, these objects are at any rate not facts. If we judge that A is the father of B, we judge as to the subsistence of a relation, which, if we judge correctly, subsists independently of our judgment, and is thus a transcendent object. But if A is not the father of B, then the relation in question does not subsist, and there seems therefore to be no object for our judgment. Nevertheless, there seems to be involved *something* which is not a fact, and this something seems to be other than our judgment and independent of it. Moreover 'A is not the father of B' is, in this case, a fact, and seems equivalent to 'it is false that A is the father of B'. But if this last is transcendent, so is 'A is the father of B'; for the whole cannot be transcendent unless the parts are so.

In order to examine this question, several inquiries must be made. In the first place, How do we distinguish the judgment from the corresponding assumption? This we may answer, as before, by the theory that the assumption is the presentation of the same object as is asserted in the judgment. But if so, either

MEINONG'S THEORY OF COMPLEXES AND ASSUMPTIONS

all judgments have an object, or else all assumptions are of true propositions; for we agreed that a presentation always has an object. Now it is plain that we can assume the false as well as the true; hence, if only correct judgments have transcendent objects, we shall have to adopt Meinong's view, that assumption is something radically different from presentation.

Accepting, for the moment, the difference of assumption and presentation, we have next to inquire whether any relation of presentations can generate an assumption. For, if this were possible, an erroneous judgment aRb (i.e. 'a has the relation R to b') might be composed of the presentations of a and R and b suitably related, and might have no corresponding object. Meinong holds that this is impossible. Let us, however, examine the hypothesis afresh. The main point to be noted is, that the presentation of a relation is not itself a relation. Consequently, if the presentation of a is related to that of b, the presentation of R cannot be what relates them. It seems to follow that the presentation of aRb does not have a complexity exactly analogous to that of aRb itself; for the presentation of 'a and b related by R' is not the presentations of a and b related by the presentation of R. And it seems hardly possible that it should be constituted by the presentations of a and b related by some other relation R'. Nevertheless, if this were the case, the problem in question would be solved. In this view, a judgment would be constituted by a relation between presentations, and the object of the judgment (in the case of correctness) would be constituted by a different but correlative relation between the objects of the presentations. It might then very easily happen that the presentations would have a certain relation when their objects had not the correlative relation. And this would further account for the fact, if it be a fact, that in the assumption or judgment of aRb, the presentation of R appears to be absent.

Before examining this theory directly, we may observe that there must always be a relation between the presentations of a and b when we judge or assume aRb; for it seems, as a result of direct inspection, that the presentations of a and b are always present in such a case,[1] and therefore they must have some relation determined by the nature of the judgment or assumption made concerning *a* and *b*. Consequently, whether or not the judgment or assumption is constituted by a relation of presentations, such a relation is always present, and is determined by the proposition concerned. There is however, a fundamental and fatal objection to such a view, namely this: that if it were correct, we could never become aware of complexes. For, though we should, in the case supposed, have complexes of presentations, we should not have presentations of complexes, since presentations related cannot beget a new and different presentation. For this reason, if for no other, the theory in question must be dismissed.

We may now consider a different theory, namely this: that the presentation of a complex is not itself complex, but simple. We may, in fact, question what was above assumed as obvious, namely, that the presentations of *a* and *b* are always present in that of *aRb*. Take the complex '*a* existing'. It seems certain that, if *a* is redness, say, or anything else that we know as an existent, we do habitually, when we mean to think of *a*, think instead of *a* existing. And this is certainly a complex constituted by *a* and existence related in a definite way. But in the plain man's image of redness existing, it is very hard to discover any separate presentations of redness and existence: the two are amalgamated into one presentation, which, though its object is complex, has not itself the marks of a complex. And this theory would render more intelligible the curious fact that the apprehension of simples, so far from being easy, is possible only to minds with a high degree of philosophical capacity. Moreover, it accounts for the very great difference between the presentation of redness existing and the judgment that redness exists. For in the latter, it seems that the presentations of redness and existence do, in a way, separate themselves in our minds. The process of analysis – a process of which the difficulty is very surprising – would consist, on this view, in discovering the parts and constituents of an object of which the presentation is simple. If the

[1] We shall, however, shortly see reason to doubt this.

parts existed in the presentation, it is hard to believe that analysis would not be easier than it is.

But when the object is further removed from simplicity than 'redness existing', shall we still be able to maintain that the presentation is simple? In cases where a single word exists to express what is meant, this seems still possible. Monarchy, predestination, Parliament, empiricism, degeneracy, and many common words, express ideas of which the objects are quite bewilderingly complex; but it is by no means evident, even if it be true, that the ideas have complexity. On the other hand, where no single word exists, as in (say) 'the execution of Charles I', it seems quite evident, at first sight, that the presentation is complex: we think of executions, and we think of Charles I, and then we bring these two thoughts together. But whether it is the thoughts or their objects that we bring together, probably depends upon circumstances; certain it is that, so long as it is *only* the thoughts, we have not succeeded in thinking of Charles I's execution. At any rate, if any great theoretic advantage were obtainable from such a view, we might admit the theory that presentations are never complex even when their objects are so.[1] It is doubtful, however, whether the answer to this question in any way affects our main problem, which is as to the transcendence of erroneous judgments.

The questions involved are these: (*a*) When *a* and *b* do not have the relation R, can there be such an entity as 'Relation R between *a* and *b*'? To take a concrete instance, if I have a brown table, is there such a thing as the blackness of my table? (*b*) And, if there is such a thing, is it the object of the judgment 'my table is black'? (*c*) And if so, can this object be called false, and what is meant by calling it so?

(*a*) Taking the abstract proposition *aRb*, the first question must be: If the judgment '*aRb*' were *true*, would there be such a thing as 'Relation R between *a* and *b*'? This is open to grave doubt. There is a relation R, and there are terms *a* and *b*; but if R relates *a* and *b*, then 'Relation R between *a* and *b*' is

---

[1] It may be observed that presentations of complexes exist, and there is some sense in which whatever is a single existent must be simple.

simply the relation R, together with a reminder that *a* and *b* are related by it. If we try to mend matters by speaking of '*a* and *b* related by R', this again is merely '*a* and *b*, which, as a matter of fact, are related by R'. The point of these remarks is, that the whole proposition *aRb* seems essential, and that there is no relation particularised by its terms, as opposed to the abstract relation R; nor can we distinguish the terms as related from the terms simply, which as a matter of fact are related. Thus there seems no such entity as the blackness of the table: there is blackness, and the table, and the proposition 'the table is black'. When the table is black, 'the blackness of the table' is merely another expression for the proposition 'the table is black'; but it is an expression which is appropriate to the assumption rather than the judgment of the proposition.[1]

(*b*) It appears, therefore, that, if there is such a thing as the blackness of a table which is not black, then this is the object of the judgment 'the table is black'; but that, as a matter of fact, 'the blackness of the table' is a misleading expression.[2] This view, however, though it may be acceptable in the case of adjectives, such as blackness, seems in other cases less plausible. The view commended by inspection would rather be the following: There is, in any case, a proposition *aRb*, and in this proposition the abstract relation R occurs, not the relation particularised by its terms; but in the case where *aRb* is true, there is such an entity as the particularised relation, whereas, when *aRb* is false, there is no such entity. This entity, when it subsists, is distinct from the proposition. But the difficulty of this view is to see what it is that is denied when the particularised

---

[1] Against the exclusive applicability to the assumption, however, we may set certain cases such as 'the blackness of the table is delightful, or beautiful'. We cannot assert this if the table is not black; for the assumption can be made in any case, and therefore the world would be none the better for the existence of beautiful objects if only the assumption were relevant. If we admit that there are false propositions, we must admit that these are irrelevant in all ethical judgments: good and bad both apply only to propositions, and among propositions only to such as are true. We can say, however, of false propositions, that they *would* be good if they were true.

[2] Except, of course, where it refers to a particular kind of blackness – a meaning which is here irrelevant.

MEINONG'S THEORY OF COMPLEXES AND ASSUMPTIONS

relation is said not to subsist; and this difficulty seems fatal to the view in question.

(c) It is plain that, if *aRb*, when true, does involve a particularised relation, this is yet not what the proposition *aRb* asserts; and therefore it is not the particularised relation, nor yet 'the blackness of the table', that is true or false. The proposition, it would seem, must be somehow distinguishable from such complexes; but it is very difficult to see what the proposition is.

5. That even erroneous judgments have a transcendent object, and that this, in some cases at any rate, seems indistinguishable from a complex, appears readily from any concrete instance. Consider: (1) 'I went to town yesterday', (2) 'Your going to town was most adventurous'; (3) 'I did not go to town yesterday', (4) 'Your going to town would have been most unwise.' Here (1), (2), and (4) are concerned with a certain object, 'I (or you) went to town yesterday'. This object we will call p. (1) asserts p; (2), presupposing the assertion of p, ascribes an adjective to p; (4), presupposing the denial of p, again ascribes an adjective to p. As to (3), it may be held that this also is concerned with p, and denies it; or it may be held to assert not-p. If these two are distinct, the form of words is equally applicable to either; and we may assume that what is meant is the denial of p, so that here again we shall be concerned with p. Now it is perfectly obvious that the adventurousness and unwisdom do not apply to the judgment, which I make quietly at home; it is not the judgment that exposes me to the risks (whatever they are) that I incurred in London. It is the proposition p, expressed by the judgment, that was adventurous, or would have been unwise. But these adjectives attach to p equally whether it is true or false; and thus the false p must be just as transcendent as the true one. But the difference of *was* and *would have been* must be examined, if this conclusion is to be held indubitable. For *would have been* implies an unfulfilled condition, and this condition, obviously, is the truth of p. Thus (4) does not simply assign an adjective to p; the complete assertion is: 'If you had gone to town it would have been most unwise.' This, if we extract the implication of falsehood in the premise,

becomes 'p implies that p is unwise'. But this implication, as the previous statement shows, is not held to be true only when p is true: it is regarded as holding equally when p is false. Consequently there must be such an entity as p when p is false. And this applies to all such statements as 'p implies q'; if this only held when the hypothesis is true, we could not regard it as equivalent to 'not-q implies not-p', which as a matter of fact we do hold to be a self-evident equivalence. Thus we must allow false transcendent objects of judgment. And if not, we could not argue as to what would happen *if p* were true, except when p is true; for we here use the hypothesis 'p is true', which we suppose to be false. And all deliberation as to the future would be impossible if there were no false Objectives. We may imagine a rhetorically minded soldier in battle saying to himself: 'To advance is to die, to retreat is dishonour; better death than dishonour'. Here he is certainly not concerned with judgments; if he were, he might escape the painful alternative (as many naïve idealists seek to do), by retreating and at the same time judging that he advanced. And it cannot be said that, if he advances, it ceases to be true that to retreat is dishonour, although he does not retreat; the debate as to which he should do would have been impossible, unless it had been true that each decision entailed its own consequences, though only one decision could become fact. Thus the transcendence of false propositions must be admitted.

The position we have now arrived at is that there are, apart from and independently of judgment, true and false propositions, and that either kind may be assumed, believed or disbelieved.

Before examining the nature of false propositions, let us consider a preliminary question. Are there any propositions containing negations, or is negation merely an expression of disbelief? We have three oppositions to consider: (1) true and false, (2) affirmative and negative, (3) belief and disbelief; and we wish to examine whether it is necessary to distinguish (2) from (3). If, as inspection seems to show, we can discriminate between disbelief in p and belief in not-p, that of course proves that the distinction must be made. But the inspection involved is very difficult, and must not be trusted if it is quite unsupported. There is, however, another quite conclusive argument. Let p be a false affirmative proposition; then p may be either believed or disbelieved, but neither will give us knowledge of any truth. Yet it seems quite obvious that, if we believe not-p, we do know something true; consequently belief in not-p must be something which is not mere disbelief. This proves that there are negative propositions; but it leaves it doubtful whether disbelief is distinct from belief of the negation: it decides the logical point, whether not-p is anything other than 'p is false'; and this point is one which I know no way of deciding. It might also be doubted whether the simple assertion of p differs from 'p is true'; but here there is more ground for supposing a difference, since truth does not seem to be a constituent of most asserted propositions even when they are true.

It may be said – and this is, I believe, the correct view – that there is no problem at all in truth and falsehood; that some propositions are true and some false, just as some roses are red and some white; that belief is a certain attitude towards propositions, which is called knowledge when they are true, error when they are false. But this theory *seems* to leave our preference for truth a mere unaccountable prejudice, and in no way to answer to the feeling of truth and falsehood. The objection to such a view is not logical, but rather the kind of objection that we should feel to a person who told us that a horse is a pachydermous animal with tusks and a trunk – the description seems, at first sight, to apply to quite different objects from those concerned.

The fundamental objection may be simply expressed by saying that true propositions express *fact*, while false ones do not. This at once raises the problem: What is a fact? And the difficulty of this problem lies in this, that a fact appears to be merely a true proposition, so that what seemed a significant assertion becomes a tautology. It is very difficult to avoid recurring to the notion that a proposition is a judgment, and it might be thought that this is why the statement that true propositions express facts seems significant. But even when this error has been avoided, it *seems* to remain that, when a proposition is false, *something* does not subsist which would subsist if the proposition were true. In this respect, however, when we examine into it, we find that, on the theory in question, affirmative and negative propositions are not on a level. If 'A exists' is false, not only A does not exist, but also, we are to suppose, A's existence does not subsist; while if 'A does not exist' is false, A's existence does subsist. The point involved, therefore, comes to this: that it is hard to regard A's non-existence, when true, as a *fact* in quite the same sense in which A's existence would be a fact if it were true. It may be suspected, however, that this apparent difference is not logical, but derived from the nature of perception: all the propositions we perceive are affirmative, and the word *fact* applies most naturally to propositions which are either perceived or analogous to such as are perceived. It would seem that all the negative propositions which we believe are derived by inference from affirmative propositions, by means of implications of the form 'p implies not-q'; and this seems sufficient to account for the feeling that true affirmative propositions express fact in a sense in which no others do so.

Thus the analogy with red and white roses seems, in the end, to express the matter as nearly as possible. What is truth, and what falsehood, we must merely apprehend, for both seem incapable of analysis. And as for the preference which most people – so long as they are not annoyed by instances – feel in favour of true propositions, this must be based, apparently, upon an ultimate ethical proposition: 'It is good to believe true propositions, and bad to believe false ones'. This proposition, it is to be hoped, is true; but if not, there is no reason to think that we do ill in believing it.

2

Review of: A. Meinong, Untersuchungen zur Gegenstandstheorie und Psychologie[1]

A review, first published in *Mind*, n.s. 14 (October 1905), pp. 530–8. Reprinted with the permission of the editor of *Mind*, and the Bertrand Russell Estate.

This book consists of eleven essays, one by Meinong, the other ten by his pupils. Meinong's and the two which immediately follow it deal with what Meinong calls *Gegenstandstheorie*, and are largely concerned with matters of fundamental philosophical importance. The eighth, 'Uber Vorstellungsproduktion', deals with the relation of the apprehension of a complex to the apprehensions of its constituents, and is thus closely related to Meinong's non-psychological work. One deals with ethics; one with the principle of economy of thought; and the other five with special points of psychology. There is thus no very close unity, except what results from similarity of outlook and method. Especially the first three essays and the eighth belong together. The philosophy set forth in them is a development of that contained in Meinong's *Uber Annahmen*, and its value appears to me to be very great. Its originality consists mainly in the banishment of the psychologism which has been universal in English philosophy from the beginning and in German philosophy since Kant, and in the recognition that philosophy cannot concern itself exclusively with things that exist.

Presentations, judgments and assumptions, Meinong points out, always have *objects*; and these objects are independent of the states of mind in which they are apprehended. This independence has been obscured hitherto by the 'prejudice in favour of the existent' (*des Wirklichen*), which has led people to suppose that, when a thought has a non-existent object, there is really no object distinct from the thought. But this is an error: existents are only an infinitesimal part of the objects of

[1] Meinong *A* 1904.

knowledge. This is illustrated by mathematics, which never deals with anything to which existence is essential, and deals in the main with objects which *cannot* exist, such as numbers. Now we do not need first to study the knowledge of objects before we study the objects themselves; hence the study of objects is essentially independent of both psychology and theory of knowledge. It may be objected that the study of objects must be coextensive with *all* knowledge; but we may consider separately the more general properties and kinds of objects, and this is an essential part of philosophy. It is this that Meinong calls *Gegenstandstheorie*.

This subject is not identical with metaphysics, but is wider in its scope; for metaphysics deals only with the real, whereas the theory of objects has no such limitations. The theory of objects deals with whatever can be known *a priori* about objects, but knowledge of reality can only be obtained by experience. The theory of objects is not psychology, since objects are independent of our apprehension of them. It is also not theory of knowledge; for knowledge has two sides, the cognition, which belongs to psychology, and the object, which is independent. The theory of objects, Meinong contends, is also not to be identified with pure logic, since logic, in his opinion, is essentially practical in its aim, being concerned with right reasoning. (On this point, opinions will differ; but the question is in any case only one of nomenclature.) The conclusion is, that the theory of objects is an independent subject, and the most general of all philosophical subjects. Mathematics is essentially part of it, and thus at last finds a proper place; for the traditional division of sciences into natural and mental left no room for mathematics, because it took account only of the existent. Grammar may be a guide in the general theory of objects, as mathematics in more special parts of the theory.

The first great division of objects is into three classes, those which exist, those which subsist (*bestehen*), and those which neither exist nor subsist.[1] It is obvious that abstracts such as

---

[1] Meinong appears to use *Sein* and *bestehen* as synonyms, and I shall use *being* and *subsistence* as synonyms.

diversity or numbers do not exist; propositions, again, are non-existent; thus certainly there are objects which do not exist, and which yet in some sense subsist. But even when we include subsistence, we do not, it would seem, find a place for *all* objects; some, such as false propositions, the round square, etc., are objects and yet do not subsist.

There are two sorts of judgments, which may be called *thetic* and *synthetic*; the former assert the being of something, the latter assert its being so-and-so (*Sein* and *Sosein*). The latter sort may subsist when their subjects do not subsist; the round square is certainly both round and square, although the round square does not subsist. We may say, if we like, 'There are objects of which it is true to say that there are no such objects' (p. 9). Ameseder, the author of the second article ('Beiträge zur Grundlegung der Gegenstandstheorie'), discusses the three kinds of objects more in detail, and reduces existence to the being of a certain kind of objects. An object (*Gegenstand*) is either an *Objekt*[1] or an Objective – the latter being a proposition or something derivative from a proposition.[2] Objects may be divided into three classes, those whose being is respectively necessary, possible, and impossible. The being of what is possible, if the possible object is an *Objekt*, is defined as *existence*; but a possible Objective (e.g. the existence of a possible *Objekt*) has being, but not existence. Whatever is necessary is an Objective; but some Objectives are possible, and some are impossible (pp. 82–4). Still more definiteness is given to the subject of non-subsistent objects by Mally in the third article ('Zur Gegenstandstheorie des Messens'). A being-so (*Sosein*) whose subsistence excludes that of its *Objekt* (i.e. what would usually be called its subject) he defines as *contradictory*. An *Objekt* which has a non-contradictory being-so he defines as *possible*. 'The roundness of what is square' is an impossible being-so; but the roundness and squareness of the round square, so far from being impossible, are necessary, though contradictory. It is impossible

---

[1] As this word is used in a different sense from *Gegenstand* I shall leave it untranslated, using 'object' to translate *Gegenstand*.
[2] On the meaning of the word Objective see Russell *B* 1904*a*, pp. 349 ff.

a square should be round, but not that the round square should be round, which is necessary (p. 128). Again he says: 'Even if A . . . in fact is *not*, it is yet tautologically certain that the being of . . . "the subsistent A" subsists. By a judgment "the subsistent A subsists," no more is judged about the (factual) being or not-being of A . . . than by the hypothetical judgment: "If A is, it is". . . . The "being and not-being" of the "A which is and is not" subsists' (p. 133). Ameseder, in the preceding article, says, in the same spirit, that, if B is impossible, 'A differs from B' and 'A does not differ from B' may both be true (p. 88).

It is not customary for philosophers to face the round square with so much courage; and indeed few logicians can withstand its onset. But if we are to be clear about the supposed non-subsistent objects, it is quite essential that we should have a satisfactory theory about the round square. For my part, I am not convinced that there are any non-subsistent objects. But let us see what the arguments against them are.

Meinong's theory may be modified, (1) by denying his non-subsistent objects, (2) by denying that they do not subsist.[1] I should propose to apply the former process to the round square, the latter to false propositions. There is, Meinong admits (p. 12), one strong argument in favour of the subsistence of the objects which he regards as non-subsistent, and that is, that such objects can be subjects of true and therefore subsistent propositions. But this argument, he says, depends upon regarding a proposition as a complex, and its subject as a constituent of it; and such a view, he thinks, can only be taken figuratively. I should have thought the subject of a proposition was a constituent of a complex in the fundamental sense from which all others are derivative, and that therefore the argument would be sound. But the chief objection to Meinong's view seems to me to lie in the fact that it involves denying the law of contradiction when impossible objects are constituents. If 'A differs from B' and 'A does not differ from B' are to be both true, we cannot tell, for example, whether a class

---

[1] We might also invent a third kind of being, more tenuous even than subsistence. Meinong considers and rejects this plan (p. 11). His reasons seem to me not decisive; but I shall not further consider this plan.

composed of A and B has one member or two. Thus in all counting, if our results are to be definite, we must first exclude impossible objects. We cannot, if B is impossible, say 'A and B are two objects'; nor can we strictly say 'B is one object'. And the difficulty is that impossible objects often subsist, and even exist. For if the round square is round and square, the existent round square is existent and round and square. Thus something round and square exists, although everything round and square is impossible. This ontological argument cannot be avoided by Kant's device of saying that existence is not a predicate, for Ameseder admits (p. 79) that 'existing' applies when and only when 'being actual (*wirklich*)' applies, and that the latter is a *Sosein*. Thus we cannot escape the consequence that 'the existent God' both exists and is God; and it is hard to see how it can be maintained, as Mally implies (p. 133), that this has no bearing on the question whether God exists. Thus I should prefer to say that there is no such object as 'the round square'. The difficulties of excluding such objects can, I think, be avoided by the theory of denoting; in any case, it is plain that the admission of such objects is open to grave objections. But much credit is due to the authors of this book for the thoroughness with which their view is developed.

For those who agree with the general standpoint of the work, this question of impossible objects is the most important one of all that arise in considering it, and our view in regard to it will affect very many of our other views. There are certainly difficulties in either hypothesis; but I think the hypothesis adopted by Meinong, Ameseder and Mally involves the greater difficulties.

In place of the theory of denoting,[1] Mally, in the third essay, develops a theory of explicit and implicit *Objekte*, which serves a similar purpose. Mally's essay, before it reaches the subject of measurement, treats afresh all the fundamentals of the theory of objects; it does this in a series of definitions, often (I think) embodying important ideas, but so obscurely expressed that it

---

[1] i.e. Frege's distinction of *Sinn* and *Bedeutung*; cf. Frege *A* 1892*b*. See also Russell *B* 1905*c*.

is very hard to understand what they mean. I shall not attempt a summary, as no summary could be more condensed than the original, in which single pages contain more matter than one usually finds in twenty. But some attempt must be made to explain the nature of explicit and implicit objects, though I am not sure of having fully grasped the author's meaning.

An Objective of the form 'A is' or 'that A is' or 'A is b' or 'that A is b' is called an *explicit Objective*, and its subject[1] is an *explicit subject*, having the form 'A which is' or 'A which is b'. A determination which 'coincides essentially'[2] with an explicit Objective, without being one, is called an *implicit* determination; and a similar definition applies to an implicit subject. An explicit determination or subject with the determination of being implicit is called a *fictitious* determination or subject (pp. 137, 138). As an illustration, 'Number which is greater than 5' is an *explicit* object; this is not 6, or 7, or 8, or etc., nor yet the aggregate of all of these; but each of these 'coincides completely' (in Mally's sense) with this explicit object. Thus 6 e.g. is an *implicit* object having the kind of connexion in question with our explicit object. Now consider 'a *certain* number which is greater than 5'. This still has the same ambiguity as the *explicit* object, but it *says* it is a particular one of all the possible numbers 6, 7, 8. . . . Thus it is fictitious: it is a particular, but a *general* particular, if one may coin such a phrase. This distinction is an elusive one; at the same time, it is certainly genuine and important. For example, among the indemonstrable propositions which are the premises of mathematics there are two which may be roughly stated thus: (1) 'What holds of all, holds of any'; (2) 'What holds of all, holds of each'. The first, when we are given that all men are mortal, allows us to infer the proposition 'any man is mortal'; the second allows us to infer that Socrates is mortal, and also that Plato is mortal, and so on. In the second, we infer the mortality of a certain definite man; but when we state the principle generally, the definiteness is fictitious: we say it is

---

[1] I translate by 'subject' the word *Eigenschaftsgegenstand*, which is used very nearly in the usual sense of 'subject', though not quite.

[2] i.e. approximately, has the same predicates, or applies to the same subjects, as the case may be.

there, but in fact it is absent. This seems to be a case of a kind similar to that of Mally's fictitious objects. As to his explicit and implicit objects, their relation seems to be that of denoting concept to object denoted. The manner of statement, as opposed to that by means of *denoting*, seems to be determined by the admission of non-subsistent objects, which renders it unnecessary to make a sharp distinction of meaning and denotation such as we require for the denial of denotation in the case of impossible objects.

Mally passes next to the definition of *complexion* and *complex*, which is as follows: 'A quality with several objects of determination (*Bestimmungsgegenstände*) and *one* implicit subject (*Eigenschaftsgegenstand*) is to be called an implicit complexion. The implicit subject of a complexion is to be called an implicit complex. The objects of determination of an implicit complexion are called its *inferiora*. The objects of determination of an implicit complex are called its *constituents*, or also *inferiora* of the complex' (p. 147).[1]

I hope other readers do not find these definitions perfectly easy to follow. I believe the meaning is really quite definite, but the technical terms introduced are so numerous, and the fundamental ones so hard to apprehend, that the definitions become very puzzling. In the present case, an illustration is given which greatly eases matters. *Triplicity*, Mally says, is an implicit determination with several objects of determination, namely one, one, one. Its implicit subject is not many, but one, namely the implicit complex called *three*. This instance makes the meaning fairly clear; but I find it hard to believe that a definition of complexity can avoid circularity. In the above case, plurality is introduced, which is a particular 'complexion', and is definable when complexity is taken as indefinable.

Mally's theory of number is not very satisfactory. With every complex, he says, 'coincides' an aggregate-complex (*Mengenkomplex*) of its constituents. An aggregate-complex wholly determined by its complexion – i.e. composed of wholly indeterminate objects – is a *pure* aggregate-complex.

---

[1] The above definitions are restated in shorter form on p. 153.

Every aggregate-complex has a *degree*, which depends only on the complexion of the complex. An aggregate-complex of determinate degree is called a number-complex or number (pp. 163-165).

This theory, to begin with, will only apply to *finite* numbers; but this is not the only objection to it. There seems to me to be a confusion between a number and an aggregate to which it applies. Mally confesses (p. 166) that *couple, trio*, etc., seem more appropriate words than 2, 3, etc.; and in fact what he defines as the number 2 seems to be really an indeterminate couple. I should escape this indeterminateness by defining 2 as the class of couples; for one must, I think, as Mally does, reach the number 2 through couples. A similar remark applies to the above notion of a 'pure' aggregate. This is, it would seem, merely an indeterminate aggregate, that is to say, any aggregate. There cannot be an aggregate composed of indeterminate objects, except in a sense which makes the aggregate simply an indeterminate aggregate; but if this is so, there is not a variety of aggregates, called 'pure', and having the property that their constituents are indeterminate. Here and elsewhere, one feels the need of Frege's theory of the variable and of functions; but language is so ill-adapted to the fundamental notions of this subject and whoever is afraid of symbols can hardly hope to acquire exact ideas where it is necessary to distinguish (1) the variable in itself as opposed to its values, (2) any value of the variable, (3) all values, (4) some value. These ideas seem to occur in Mally's exposition, but their employment in complicated cases is very difficult for him.

Mally's theory of quantity closely follows Meinong's; it uses the same criterion of a series approaching zero; and it contains similar views as to differences and similarity considered as quantities. He holds, for reasons which seem not very convincing, that every quantity can be diminished, and that zero is therefore self-contradictory and non-subsistent. He has an interesting definition of a continuum (p. 169), which is reached as follows. A complex whose constituents are complexes of its own complexion is a *homoiomeric* complex; such is a couple of couples. If the constituents of the constituents, and the constituents of these again, and so on *ad infinitum*, are all of the same complexion as the original complex, then the original complex is said to be *throughout homoiomeric*. An implicit complex completely coincident with a throughout homoiomeric complex is a *continuum*. Though this definition is interesting, it is to be observed that it does not apply to mathematical space and time, and that it may well be doubted whether there can be any object to which it does apply. The latter question depends, however, upon whether we hold that every complex must be analysable into simple parts – a difficult question, which need not here be raised.

Mally's theory of the extension of number – negative, fractional, irrational and imaginary numbers – is not of a sort which will serve in mathematics. Since $-b$, in $a-b$, means the suppression, in an aggregate whose number is a, of a part whose number is b, it seems that $-b$ means the non-being of b. He says (p. 207): 'An (impossible) number, whose being is equal to the not-being of another number, is called *negative*'. (His theory of the other extensions of number is of the same kind.) But as a matter of fact, in $a-b$, it is not the number b itself that is suppressed, but an aggregate having b terms; here the earlier confusion of numbers with aggregate causes a fresh confusion as regards subtraction. Further, if a right theory of negative numbers is to be framed, we must distinguish the subtraction of b from the result of such subtraction performed on a number a. If we define $-b$ as $0-b$, we certainly get an impossible object, if 0 and b are the sort of numbers applicable to the counting of aggregates. In fact, $+b$ and $-b$ must both be defined as relations, and $+b$ must be distinguished from b just as much as $-b$ must. $+b$ and $-b$ are each other's converses; if two numbers (of the signless sort) a, c, are such that $a+b=c$, then a has to c the relation $+b$, and c has to a the relation $-b$[1]; in other words, what mathematicians would call the operation $+b$ turns a into c, and the operation $-b$ turns c into a. If negative numbers were in fact non-entities they would be useless, for a reason

---

[1] Or *vice versa*, according as we may choose to define.

which applies generally against the introduction of non-entities into special reasoning, namely this: Of every impossible object, two contradictory propositions hold. But if two contradictory propositions hold of an object, then *all* propositions concerning that object are true; for if p is any proposition, then every proposition is either implied by p or implied by not-p.[1] Hence if negative numbers are non-entities there is no more point in saying one thing about them than in saying another: a result which might be expected to follow from denying the law of contradiction.[2]

It is natural to consider, in connexion with the three fundamental essays on the theory of objects, the eighth essay, by Ameseder, 'Uber Vorstellungsproduktion'. He begins by setting forth briefly (pp. 481–3) the theory of sensation which is also explained elsewhere in the book.[3] According to this theory, sensations have objects and causes, but their objects are different from their causes. Thus the sensation of blue has *blue* for its object; but *blue*, though it subsists, does not exist. The *cause* of the sensation of blue is a thing-in-itself, and does exist. But *blue*, though it does not exist, is not dependent on sensation for its subsistence, and does not exist in the sensation of blue. Its subsistence does not, in fact, presuppose the subsistence of anything else. But this is not true of all objects. Founded (*fundierte*) objects[4] and the presentations which apprehend them have an inner dependence upon their *inferiora*; there can be no difference without objects which are different, and no presentation of a difference without presentations of objects which are different. The problem with which Ameseder is concerned is the problem as to the relation of the presentation of a founded object to the presentations of its *inferiora*. The presentation of a founded object is not itself founded, for nothing founded can exist. Nevertheless the presentation of a *superius* is built somehow on

---

[1] See Russell *B* 1903*a*, p. 18.
[2] This result might no doubt be avoided by modifying the theory of implication; but it seems probable that any modification adequate for this purpose would be inadmissible on other grounds.
[3] e.g. by himself, pp. 91–5.
[4] On the meaning of this term, cf. Russell *B* 1904*a*, pp. 210–11.

the presentations of the *inferiora*. This process is called *production*; it is involved in all perception which goes beyond sensation, for example in the perception of a melody. The conclusion reached is that the presentation of the founded object consists of the presentations of its *inferiora* standing in a *real* relation to each other (p. 496). This depends upon Meinong's distinction of real and ideal relations; the former are not necessary, and may exist, while the latter are necessary, and cannot exist. A real relation is such as that between the elements in a chemical compound; and the connexion of the produced presentation to the elementary presentations is thus conceived as being more or less like that of a chemical compound to its elements. This theory may or may not be satisfactory; in any case, the problem is very clearly stated, and its importance is quite undeniable.

The theory of production of presentations is used to account for the illusion in Müller-Lyer's figure, which is dealt with by Vittorio Benussi in a long and very interesting article (No. V.), 'Zur Psychologie des Gestalterfassens'. He distinguishes illusions of sensation, of judgment, and of production, and shows by a series of experiments that the illusion in question must be one of production. It appears that whatever, either in the figure or in the state of mind of the observer, increases the consciousness of the figure as a whole, increases the illusion as to the length of the central line of the figure. The illusion is not one of judgment, for it is unaffected by knowledge of the facts; it is not of sensation, for such illusions have the following marks, which it has not: (1) they depend on the stimulus, and cannot be modified by the subject; (2) they are uniquely determined by the stimulus; (3) their magnitude has in principle no limits; (4) they are not altered by practice. As regards (1) and (2), Benussi found that the illusion is diminished by telling the observer to concentrate attention on the central line, and increased by telling him to observe the whole figure. He concludes (p. 395) that contents in a real relation influence each other in the sense of their own natures; and that the presentation of shapes has this effect in a high degree because it involves a real relation of the presentations of the parts of the shapes.

The sixth essay, by Vittorio Benussi and Wilhelmine Liel, applies the same principles to the illusion of the shifted chessboard, and reaches a similar conclusion. The fourth essay, by Wilhelm Frankl, discusses the principles of Avenarius concerning economy of thought, and decides that, though certain principles of economy are valid, there are none so general or so fundamental as Avenarius contended. The seventh, by Vittorio Benussi, gives a new proof of the specific brightness of colours. The ninth, by Ameseder, 'Uber absolute Auffälligkeit der Farben', contends that this quality can be determined by experiments, some of which he has carried out and gives the results of. The tenth, by Wilhelmine Liel, 'Gegen eine voluntaristische Begründung der Werttheorie', is in the main a polemic against Schwarz, contending that value is derived from feeling, not from conation. The eleventh and last, by Robert Saxinger, 'Uber die Natur der Phantasiegefühle und Phantasiebegehrungen', contends that the feelings and desires of imagination are facts *sui generis*, differing from feelings and desires proper as assumptions differ from judgments. The argument is unconvincing to me, because I often dissent where he appeals to introspection. For example he says that all feelings proper weaken with the lapse of time, in the absence of fresh stimulus, whereas those of imagination are constant – a difference which to me is not apparent in experience.

The book as a whole does the highest credit to the Graz school of psychology and philosophy; and its main articles contain theories which demand and deserve careful study. The second and third articles, by Ameseder and Mally, contain so many important definitions in quick succession that it has been impossible to give an adequate idea of their contents in the space of a review. The first article gives what we may suspect is the final term of Meinong's development away from psychologism; his present position appears to me clear and consistent and fruitful of valuable results for philosophy.

3

Review of: A. Meinong, Uber die Stellung der Gegenstandstheorie im System der Wissenschaften[1]

A review, first published in *Mind*, n.s. 16 (October 1907), pp. 436–9. Reprinted with the permission of the editor of *Mind*, and the Bertrand Russell Estate.

This book is a defence of Meinong's views against various critics and a further explanation of the new science which he calls 'Gegenstandstheorie'. The necessity and importance of this science are vindicated, and reasons are given for not identifying it with logic or theory of knowledge or any other science which has hitherto received a name. The style is remarkably clear, and the polemical arguments appear to the present reviewer to be generally cogent, except (needless to add) when they are directed against himself.

After a brief introduction, Meinong proceeds to consider what he calls 'homeless objects', by which he means the non-existent objects of presentations which do or may exist. Such are for example, colours: these are not mental, for they are quite distinct from presentations of colours, and they are not physical, for they do not exist in the material world. (This might be questioned; but as Meinong has argued the question elsewhere, he is content to assume the result of his previous discussion.) Thus although presentations of colours exist, colours themselves do not exist. Yet there are many true propositions about colours, e.g. that black differs from white. To what science are such propositions to be assigned? Not to any of the sciences which deal essentially with what exists, but to a science which deals with objects as such, i.e. to *Gegenstandstheorie*.

The knowledge which composes this science is *a priori*, i.e. independent of experience in the narrow sense. Meinong explains that he does not require the *constituents* of a proposition to

[1] Meinong *A* 1907.

be known independently of experience; thus 'black differs from white' is for him *a priori*, in spite of the fact that black and white are given in experience. By *experience* he means apparently perception. Knowledge as to what exists always depends upon perception; but the knowledge which constitutes *Gegenstandstheorie* is independent of existence (*daseinsfrei*), and therefore independent of experience, i.e. *a priori*.

The question of the exact division of propositions into such as depend upon perception and such as do not appears to me to involve certain difficulties which Meinong (I think) overlooks, and which make them not identifiable with such as are existential.[1] For example, he considers the proposition 'ghosts do not exist' as existential; whatever affirms an existence or a non-existence, he says, is existential. Now it is plain that the knowledge derived immediately from perception is always affirmative, and that, therefore, any negative proposition can at most be *inferred* from propositions derived from perception, and that the implicational proposition by means of which the inference is made cannot be wholly derived from perception, but must either be or depend upon an *a priori* implicational proposition. Let us take an instance, say 'Jones is not in this room'. I do not perceive this; I merely perceive what *is* in this room; but I assume the proposition, 'If Jones were in this room, I should perceive him'. It would be difficult to disentangle the *a priori* element in this hypothetical, but it is plain that there *is* an *a priori* element, and that it is concerned with existence. It will be a proposition asserting that, under certain conditions, if a thing exists, it is perceived. Without some such premise, no perceptions can warrant negative conclusions. I think, therefore, that the proper distinction between the empirical and the *a priori* does not lie in the presence or absence of the assertion of existence, but in the presence or absence of a particular subject[2] given in perception. This, however, requires modification for

---

[1] Some difference is admitted by Meinong (e.g. p. 35), but of a different kind from that with which I am concerned.

[2] i.e. a subject actually perceived or defined by relation to what is or was actually perceived.

the case of general propositions arrived at by induction, such as the one instanced by Meinong, namely 'ghosts do not exist'. This proposition is of course empirical, and is derived by induction from the absence of ghosts on the occasions when they might reasonably be expected. But like all propositions obtained by induction, it is not certain, but only more or less probable. Thus we may say that propositions about existence which do not have a particular subject are either *a priori* or uncertain. To take a more important instance: 'every event has a cause' may, so far as its form shows, be either *a priori* and certain or empirical and only more or less probable. Thus it would seem that the form of a proposition alone does not decide as to whether it is empirical or *a priori*, provided we include propositions for which the evidence is inductive; while, if we exclude these as being not strictly *known* the empirical is whatever contains a constituent which is particular in the sense of being a *this*, while the *a priori* is what contains no such constituent.

A considerable amount of space is devoted to proving that geometry is *a priori* and independent of existence. Much of this discussion is excellent, particularly an utterly destructive criticism of Mach's 'Gedankenexperiment'. But unfortunately Meinong considers it necessary to his thesis to contend that the axiom of parallels is *a priori* certain. His argument on this subject rests, if I have not misunderstood him, on an elementary blunder, namely, on the supposition that in non-Euclidean spaces parallel lines intersect. He argues, quite rightly, that the intersection of parallels is impossible; but this is never denied. The question is whether, through a given point outside a given straight line, there is one parallel or two or none to the given straight line. He argues that it is not a mere tautology to say that parallel lines cannot meet; this seems to be because he thinks parallels can be defined as lines having the same direction. But 'direction', as a more intimate acquaintance with geometry would have taught him, is a notion which is only applicable when the axiom of parallels holds; and with any admissible definition of parallels it *is* a mere tautology to say that they cannot meet.

That pure geometry is *a priori*, is a thesis with which I am wholly in agreement; but in pure geometry the axioms are not assumed to be *true*, but are merely hypotheses in hypotheticals. Whether the space of the actual world is Euclidean or non-Euclidean, is not a question for pure geometry, but is an empirical question concerning what actually exists. Meinong argues at some length against the view that the space of the actual world might differ from a Euclidean space to an extent which would be beneath the threshold of observation. His reason is simply that 'parallel' and 'mutually inclined' are *precise* conceptions, concerning which *a priori* judgments are possible (p. 86). But this ground has no bearing on the question whether parallels are possible in the real world. This latter question is obscured for Meinong by the argument that straight lines, in any case, do not really exist, and that therefore no question concerning them can be one concerning what actually exists. This assumes that there is no such thing as absolute space, and further, that the world is not a plenum. But even with these two doubtful assumptions, it still remains possible to indicate respects in which what exists will differ according as actual space (however understood) is Euclidean or non-Euclidean, though the differences become more complicated than in the abstract geometrical statement.

There is an argument (pp. 14 ff.) in defence of impossible objects such as the round square, against criticisms passed in a previous review in *Mind*.[1] As the subject is important, I shall briefly state Meinong's contentions and indicate why they seem to me inconclusive. Impossible objects, it is admitted, do not obey the law of contradiction; but why should they? For after all, this law has never been explicitly asserted except of the actual and the possible, and there is no reason for assuming that it holds also of the impossible. This reply seems to overlook the fact that it is of *propositions* (i.e. of 'Objectives' in Meinong's terminology), not of subjects, that the law of contradiction is asserted. To suppose that two contradictory propositions can both be true seems equally inadmissible whatever their subjects

[1] Russell B 1905*d*, p. 532 ff.

may be. The next point urged by Meinong is that my objections apply equally to such objects as 'the golden mountain', which are not impossible, but merely non-existent. This I, of course, admit; indeed the object I specially attempted to demolish was 'the present King of France',[1] who is on a level with 'the golden mountain'. Meinong's next argument is an answer to my contention that, on his principles, 'the existent round square' exists. To this he replies that it is existent but does not exist. I must confess that I see no difference between existing and being existent; and beyond this I have no more to say on this head. Lastly, he argues that, although I affirm that there are no such things as impossible objects, yet I am compelled to make propositions about them, and thus implicitly to admit them. To this I reply that I was careful to provide an interpretation of propositions in which such objects seem to occur[2] and that therefore Meinong's argument was answered by anticipation. I see, therefore, no reason to admit that there are impossible objects; and the reasons against them still seem to me overwhelming.

In what precedes, I have dwelt chiefly on points in which Meinong seems open to criticism. But such points are few and slight compared to the points in which his views seem to me true and important. Moreover his contentions are in all cases clear, and whether right or not, they imperatively demand consideration.

[1] Russell *B* 1905*c*.   [2] *Ibid.*, p. 490.

III

DESCRIPTIONS AND EXISTENCE

In January of 1905, the Scottish logician Hugh MacColl published a paper in *Mind* (reprinted in the Appendix) in which he argued that the null class in logic should be taken as the class with all non-existents as its members. In the April issue Russell took MacColl to task in a short paper entitled 'The Existential Import of Propositions'. In this essay, Russell argued that the null class was the class with no members, and went on to expound for the first time the view of existence that became characteristic in his later philosophy. This view – that to assert existence properly is to assert that a propositional function is satisfied by at least one argument, or, correspondingly, that a certain class is non-empty – has come to be called the Frege–Russell analysis of existence. Russell, for one, certainly did not claim to originate it, since he describes it as 'the usual standpoint of Symbolic Logicians'. MacColl in turn replied to Russell, and the complete interchange can be read through by combining this section with the articles in the Appendix.

MacColl's stand on the null class, though not his symbolism, has been to a certain extent revived in recent years by logicians who have sought to free Russell's logic from its presupposition that *something* exists. If one takes the position, as Russell does here, that only existents are entities, and if one holds, as Russell and Whitehead do in *Principia Mathematica*, that '"$(x)Fx$"' implies "$(\exists x)Fx$"' is a logical truth (i.e. that what holds of all holds of some), then one presupposes that at least one entity exists, else there would be no 'some'. Thus the *Principia*, supposedly a system of *a priori* truths, presupposes the empirical truth that something exists, and Russell admitted in 1919 that this was a defect.[1] One of the ways of avoiding the presupposition is MacColl's view that there are entities which are not existents.

---

[1] Russell *B* 1919*a*, p. 203n.

'On Denoting' and its theory of descriptions need little introduction to readers; it is reprinted here because the development of Russell's thought in these years is incomprehensible without it. Its characteristic doctrine, that the grammatical form of a sentence need not be its logical form, was to guide Russell in much of his subsequent work. The device of contextual definition, in which any sentence containing a definite description can be replaced by an equivalent sentence which contains none at all, was almost immediately extended by Russell to the notation for class abstraction, and thus led to the view of classes that appears in *Principia*. Since definite descriptions were now defined out of the basic language, referents for definite descriptions were no longer required. Consequently, the rich ontology of the *Principles of Mathematics*, which postulated an entity for each definite description, was no longer needed. Russell never again returned to the extreme realism of his early work.

'On Denoting' contains the predictable criticisms of Meinong and MacColl, and also criticisms of Frege's theory of sense and reference.[1] The discussion of Frege is tortuous, and it is generally believed that Russell did not state Frege's theory correctly.[2] On the other hand, the arguments of 'On Denoting' are an excellent refutation of one earlier theory of denoting: Russell's own, stated first in the *Principles of Mathematics* and developed at length in papers probably written in late 1904.[3] In that theory Russell held that the meaning of 'the King of France' was a single definite entity called a denoting concept, or a denoting complex. In 'On Denoting' there is no single entity which is the meaning of 'the King of France', and Russell often said later that the phrase had no meaning, when considered apart from a sentence in which it occurs.

Criticisms of the theory of descriptions have come from two directions. First, there are philosophers who feel that the theory ignores certain features of the actual use of language and in general deviates too far from the forms of ordinary speech.

---

[1] See Frege *A* 1892*b*.   [2] See Searle *C*3 1958.
[3] Russell *B* 1904*d*, *e*, and *f*.

Russell's response to this group is found in 'Mr Strawson on Referring', written when Russell was 85. Next, there are logicians who charge that the theory of descriptions as it stands is formally inadequate because it lacks explicit conventions for the scope of quantifiers, and that when these conventions are added the theory becomes unduly complex.[1] To this criticism Russell did not reply; the issue arose long after he had ceased to do logic.

[1] This difficulty becomes acute in modal and other complex contexts. See Smullyan *C*3 1948, Montague and Kalish *C*3 1964, Linsky *C*3 1966.

4

The Existential Import of Propositions

First published in *Mind*, n.s. **14** (July 1905), pp. 398–401. Reprinted with the permission of the editor of *Mind*, and the Bertrand Russell Estate.

Mr MacColl's interesting paper in the January number of *Mind*, together with his note in the April number, raises certain points which call for an answer from those who (like myself) adhere to the usual standpoint of symbolic logicians on the subject of the existential import of propositions.

The first point in regard to which clearness is essential concerns the meaning of the word 'existence'. There are two meanings of this word, as distinct as stocks in a flower-garden and stocks on the Stock Exchange, which yet are continually being confused or at least supposed somehow connected. Of these meanings only one occurs in philosophy or in common parlance, and only the other occurs in mathematics or in symbolic logic. Until it is realised that they have absolutely nothing to do with each other it is quite impossible to have clear ideas on our present topic.

(*a*) The meaning of *existence* which occurs in philosophy and in daily life is the meaning which can be predicated of an individual: the meaning in which we inquire whether God exists, in which we affirm that Socrates existed, and deny that Hamlet existed. The entities dealt with in mathematics do not exist in this sense: the number 2, or the principle of the syllogism, or multiplication are objects which mathematics considers, but which certainly form no part of the world of existent things. This sense of existence lies wholly outside Symbolic Logic, which does not care a pin whether its entities exist in this sense or not.

(*b*) The sense in which existence is used in symbolic logic is a definable and purely technical sense, namely this: To say that

A exists means that A is a class which has at least one member. Thus whatever is not a class (e.g. Socrates) does not exist in this sense; and among classes there is just one which does not exist, namely, the class having no members, which is called the null-class. In this sense, the class of numbers (e.g.) exists, because 1, 2, 3, etc., are members of it; but in sense (a) the class and its members alike do not exist: they do not stand out in a part of space and time, nor do they have that kind of super-sensible existence which is attributed to the Deity.

It may be asked: How come two such diverse notions to be confounded? It is easy to see how the confusion arises, by considering classes which, if they have members at all, must have members that exist in sense (a). Suppose we say: 'No chimeras exist'. We may mean that the class of chimeras has no members, i.e. does not exist in sense (b), or that nothing that exists in sense (a) is a chimera. These two are equivalent in the present instance, because if there were chimeras, they would be entities of the kind that exist in sense (a). But if we say 'no numbers exist', our statement is true in sense (a) and false in sense (b). It is true that nothing that exists in sense (a) is a number; it is false that the class of numbers has no members. Thus the confusion arises from undue preoccupation with the things that exist in sense (a), which is a bad habit engendered by practical interests.

Mr MacColl assumes (p. 74) two universes, the one composed of existences, the other of non-existences. It will be seen that, if the above discrimination is accepted, these two universes are not to be distinguished in symbolic logic. All entities, whether they exist or whether they do not (in sense (a)), are alike real to symbolic logic and mathematics. In sense (b), which is alone relevant, there is among classes not a multitude of non-existences, but just one, namely, the null-class. All the members of every class are among realities,[1] in the only sense in which symbolic logic is concerned with realities.

---

[1] This holds even of the null-class. Of all the members of the null-class, *every* statement holds, since the null-class has no members of which it does not hold. See below, on the interpretation of the universal affirmative A.

But it is natural to inquire what we are going to say about Mr MacColl's classes of unrealities, centaurs, round squares, etc. Concerning all these we shall say simply that they are classes which have no members, so that each of them is identical with the null-class. There are no Centaurs; 'x is a Centaur' is false whatever value we give to x, even when we include values which do not exist in sense (a), such as numbers, propositions, etc. Similarly, there are no round squares. The case of nectar and ambrosia is more difficult, since these seem to be individuals, not classes. But here we must presuppose definitions of nectar and ambrosia: they are substances having such and such properties, which, as a matter of fact, no substances do have. We have thus merely a defining concept for each, without any entity to which the concept applies. In this case, the concept is an entity, but it does not denote anything. To take a simpler case: 'The present King of England' is a complex concept denoting an individual; 'the present King of France' is a similar complex concept denoting nothing. The phrase intends to point out an individual, but fails to do so: it does not point out an unreal individual, but no individual at all. The same explanation applies to mythical personages, Apollo, Priam, etc. These words have a *meaning*, which can be found by looking them up in a classical dictionary; but they have not a *denotation*: there is no entity, real or imaginary, which they point out.

It will now be plain, I hope, that the ordinary view of symbolic logicians as to existential import does not require Mr MacColl's modifications. This view is, that A and E do not imply the existence, in sense (b), of their subjects, but that I and O do imply the existence, in sense (b), of their subjects. No one of the four implies the existence, in sense (a), either of its subject or of any of the members of its subject. We have, adopting Peano's interpretation:

A. All S is P = For all values of x, 'x is an S' implies 'x is a P'.
E. No S is P = For all values of x, 'x is an S' implies 'x is not a P'.
I. Some S is P = For at least one value of x, 'x is an S' and 'x is a P' are both true.

O. Some S is not P = For at least one value of x, 'x is an S' and 'x is not a P' are both true.

Thus I and O require that there should be at least one value of x for which x is an S, i.e. that S should exist in sense (*b*). I also requires that P should exist, and O requires that not-P should exist. But A and E do not require the existence of either S or P; for a hypothetical is true whenever its hypothesis is false,[1] so that if 'x is an S' is always false, 'All S is P' and 'No S is P' will both be true whatever P may be.

The above remarks serve to answer the objection raised by Mr MacColl in the April number of *Mind* (p. 295) to the equation OA = O. To begin with, O does not represent the class of non-existences, but the non-existent class, i.e. the class which has no members. Thus, if 'XA = X' means 'every X is an A',[2] then 'OA = O' means 'every member of the class which has no members is an A', or 'for every value of x, "x is a member of the class which has no members" implies "x is an A"'. This hypothetical is true for all values of x, because its hypothesis is false for all values of x, and a hypothetical with a false hypothesis is true. Thus Mr MacColl's objection rests upon his taking O to be the class of non-existences, presumably in sense (*a*), since only so would O be a class with many members, all of them unreal, as he supposes it to be. The true interpretation of O, as the non-existent class, in sense (*b*), at once disposes of the difficulty.

The same principles solve Lewis Carroll's paradox, noticed by 'W' in the April number of *Mind* (p. 293). I cannot agree with 'W' in regarding the paradox as merely verbal; on the contrary, I consider it a good illustration of the principle that a false proposition implies every proposition. Putting p for 'Carr is out', q for 'Allen is out', and r for 'Brown is out', Lewis Carroll's two hypotheticals are:

(1) q implies r.
(2) p implies that q implies not-r.

---

[1] See Russell *B* 1903*a*, vol. i, p. 18.
[2] Not 'every X is A', as Mr MacColl says, and as most logicians say.

DESCRIPTIONS AND EXISTENCE

Lewis Carroll supposes that 'q implies r' and 'q implies not-r' are inconsistent, and hence infers that p must be false. But as a matter of fact, 'q implies r' and 'q implies not-r' must both be true if q is false, and are by no means inconsistent. The contradictory of 'q implies r' is 'q does not imply r', which is not a consequence of 'q implies not-r'. Thus the only inference from Lewis Carroll's premises (1) and (2) is that if p is true, q is false, i.e. if Carr is out, Allen is in. This is the complete solution of the paradox.

5

On Denoting

First published in *Mind*, n.s. 14 (October 1905), pp. 479-93. Reprinted with the permission of the editor of *Mind*, the Macmillan Co., and the Bertrand Russell Estate.

By a 'denoting phrase' I mean a phrase such as any one of the following: a man, some man, any man, every man, all men, the present King of England, the present King of France, the centre of mass of the Solar System at the first instant of the twentieth century, the revolution of the earth round the sun, the revolution of the sun round the earth. Thus a phrase is denoting solely in virtue of its *form*. We may distinguish three cases: (1) A phrase may be denoting, and yet not denote anything; e.g. 'the present King of France'. (2) A phrase may denote one definite object; e.g. 'the present King of England' denotes a certain man. (3) A phrase may denote ambiguously; e.g. 'a man' denotes not many men, but an ambiguous man. The interpretation of such phrases is a matter of considerable difficulty; indeed, it is very hard to frame any theory not susceptible of formal refutation. All the difficulties with which I am acquainted are met, so far as I can discover, by the theory which I am about to explain.

The subject of denoting is of very great importance not only in logic and mathematics, but also in theory of knowledge. For example, we know that the centre of mass of the Solar System at a definite instant is some definite point, and we can affirm a number of propositions about it; but we have no immediate *acquaintance* with this point, which is only known to us by description. The distinction between *acquaintance* and *knowledge about* is the distinction between the things we have presentations of, and the things we only reach by means of denoting phrases. It often happens that we know that a certain phrase denotes unambiguously, although we have no acquaintance with what it denotes; this occurs in the above case of the centre of mass. In perception we have acquaintance with the objects of perception, and in thought we have acquaintance with objects of a more abstract logical character; but we do not necessarily have acquaintance with the objects denoted by phrases composed of words with whose meanings we are acquainted. To take a very important instance: There seems no reason to believe that we are ever acquainted with other people's minds, seeing that these are not directly perceived; hence what we know about them is obtained through denoting. All thinking has to start from acquaintance: but it succeeds in thinking *about* many things with which we have no acquaintance.

The course of my argument will be as follows. I shall begin by stating the theory I intend to advocate[1]; I shall then discuss the theories of Frege and Meinong, showing why neither of them satisfies me; then I shall give the grounds in favour of my theory; and finally I shall briefly indicate the philosophical consequences of my theory.

My theory, briefly, is as follows. I take the notion of the *variable* as fundamental; I use '$C(x)$' to mean a proposition[2] in which x is a constituent, where x, the variable, is essentially and wholly undetermined. Then we can consider the two notions '$C(x)$ is always true' and '$C(x)$ is sometimes true'.[3] Then *everything* and *nothing* and *something* (which are the most primitive of denoting phrases) are to be interpreted as follows:

C(everything) means '$C(x)$ is always true';
C(nothing) means '"$C(x)$ is false" is always true';
C(something) means 'It is false that "$C(x)$ is false" is always true'.[4]

---

[1] I have discussed this subject in Russell *B* 1903*a*, ch. v, and para. 476. The theory there advocated is very nearly the same as Frege's, and is quite different from the theory to be advocated in what follows.

[2] More exactly, a propositional function.

[3] The second of these can be defined by means of the first, if we take it to mean, 'It is not true that "$C(x)$ is false" is always true'.

[4] I shall sometimes use, instead of this complicated phrase, the phrase '$C(x)$ is not always false', or '$C(x)$ is sometimes true', supposed *defined* to mean the same as the complicated phrase.

Here the notion 'C(x) is always true' is taken as ultimate and indefinable, and the others are defined by means of it. *Everything*, *nothing*, and *something* are not assumed to have any meaning in isolation, but a meaning is assigned to *every* proposition in which they occur. This is the principle of the theory of denoting I wish to advocate: that denoting phrases never have any meaning in themselves, but that every proposition in whose verbal expression they occur has a meaning. The difficulties concerning denoting are, I believe, all the result of a wrong analysis of propositions whose verbal expressions contain denoting phrases. The proper analysis, if I am not mistaken, may be further set forth as follows.

Suppose now we wish to interpret the proposition, 'I met a man'. If this is true, I met some definite man; but that is not what I affirm. What I affirm is, according to the theory I advocate:

'"I met x, and x is human" is not always false'.

Generally, defining the class of men as the class of objects having the predicate *human*, we say that:

'C (a man)' means '"C(x) and x is human" is not always false'.

This leaves 'a man', by itself, wholly destitute of meaning, but gives a meaning to every proposition in whose verbal expression 'a man' occurs.

Consider next the proposition 'all men are mortal'. This proposition[1] is really hypothetical and states that *if* anything is a man, it is mortal. That is, it states that if x is a man, x is mortal, whatever x may be. Hence, substituting 'x is human' for 'x is a man', we find:

'All men are mortal' means '"If x is human, x is mortal" is always true'.

This is what is expressed in symbolic logic by saying that 'all men are mortal' means '"x is human" implies "x is mortal" for all values of x'. More generally, we say:

[1] As has been ably argued in Bradley *A* 1883, Book I, ch. ii.

'C (all men)' means '"If x is human, then C(x) is true" is always true'.

Similarly

'C (no men)' means '"If x is human, then C(x) is false" is always true'.
'C (some men)' will mean the same as 'C (a man)',[1] and
'C (a man)' means 'It is false that "C(x) and x is human" is always false'.
'C (every man)' will mean the same as 'C (all men)'.

It remains to interpret phrases containing *the*. These are by far the most interesting and difficult of denoting phrases. Take as an instance 'the father of Charles II was executed'. This asserts that there was an x who was the father of Charles II and was executed. Now *the*, when it is strictly used, involves uniqueness; we do, it is true, speak of '*the* son of So-and-so' even when So-and-so has several sons, but it would be more correct to say '*a* son of So-and-so'. Thus for our purposes we take *the* as involving uniqueness. Thus when we say 'x was *the* father of Charles II' we not only assert that x had a certain relation to Charles II, but also that nothing else had this relation. The relation in question, without the assumption of uniqueness, and without any denoting phrases, is expressed by 'x begat Charles II'. To get an equivalent of 'x was the father of Charles II', we must add, 'If y is other than x, y did not beget Charles II', or, what is equivalent, 'If y begat Charles II, y is identical with x'. Hence 'x is the father of Charles II' becomes 'x begat Charles II; and "if y begat Charles II, y is identical with x" is always true of y'.

Thus 'the father of Charles II was executed' becomes:

'It is not always false of x that x begat Charles II and that x was executed and that "if y begat Charles II, y is identical with x" is always true of y'.

---

[1] Psychologically 'C (a man)' has a suggestion of *only one*, and 'C (some men)' has a suggestion of *more than one*; but we may neglect these suggestions in a preliminary sketch.

This may seem a somewhat incredible interpretation; but I am not at present giving reasons, I am merely *stating* the theory.

To interpret 'C (the father of Charles II)', where C stands for any statement about him, we have only to substitute $C(x)$ for 'x was executed' in the above. Observe that, according to the above interpretation, whatever statement C may be, 'C (the father of Charles II)' implies:

'It is not always false of x that "if y begat Charles II, y is identical with x" is always true of y',

which is what is expressed in common language by 'Charles II had one father and no more'. Consequently if this condition fails, *every* proposition of the form 'C (the father of Charles II)' is false. Thus, e.g. every proposition of the form 'C (the present King of France)' is false. This is a great advantage in the present theory. I shall show later that it is not contrary to the law of contradiction, as might be at first supposed.

The above gives a reduction of all propositions in which denoting phrases occur to forms in which no such phrases occur. Why it is imperative to effect such a reduction, the subsequent discussion will endeavour to show.

The evidence for the above theory is derived from the difficulties which seem unavoidable if we regard denoting phrases as standing for genuine constituents of the propositions in whose verbal expressions they occur. Of the possible theories which admit such constituents the simplest is that of Meinong.[1] This theory regards any grammatically correct denoting phrase as standing for an *object*. Thus 'the present King of France', 'the round square', etc., are supposed to be genuine objects. It is admitted that such objects do not *subsist*, but nevertheless they are supposed to be objects. This is in itself a difficult view; but the chief objection is that such objects, admittedly, are apt to infringe the law of contradiction. It is contended, for example, that the existent present King of France exists, and also does not exist; that the round square is round, and also not round; etc.

---

[1] See Meinong *A* 1904, the first three articles (by Meinong, Ameseder and Mally respectively).

But this is intolerable; and if any theory can be found to avoid this result, it is surely to be preferred.

The above breach of the law of contradiction is avoided by Frege's theory. He distinguishes, in a denoting phrase, two elements, which we may call the *meaning* and the *denotation*.[1] Thus 'the centre of mass of the Solar System at the beginning of the twentieth century' is highly complex in *meaning*, but its *denotation* is a certain point, which is simple. The Solar System, the twentieth century, etc., are constituents of the *meaning*; but the *denotation* has no constituents at all.[2] One advantage of this distinction is that it shows why it is often worth while to assert identity. If we say 'Scott is the author of *Waverley*', we assert an identity of denotation with a difference of meaning. I shall, however, not repeat the grounds in favour of this theory, as I have urged its claims elsewhere (*loc. cit.*), and am now concerned to dispute those claims.

One of the first difficulties that confront us, when we adopt the view that denoting phrases *express* a meaning and *denote* a denotation,[3] concerns the cases in which the denotation appears to be absent. If we say 'the King of England is bald', that is, it would seem, not a statement about the complex *meaning* 'the King of England', but about the actual man denoted by the meaning. But now consider 'the King of France is bald'. By parity of form, this also ought to be about the denotation of the phrase 'the King of France'. But this phrase, though it has a *meaning* provided 'the King of England' has a meaning, has certainly no denotation, at least in any obvious sense. Hence one would suppose that 'the King of France is bald' ought to be nonsense; but it is not nonsense, since it is plainly false. Or again

---

[1] See Frege *A* 1892*b*.

[2] Frege distinguishes the two elements of meaning and denotation everywhere, and not only in complex denoting phrases. Thus it is the *meanings* of the constituents of a denoting complex that enter into its *meaning*, not their *denotation*. In the proposition 'Mont Blanc is over 1,000 metres high', it is, according to him, the *meaning* of 'Mont Blanc', not the actual mountain, that is a constituent of the *meaning* of the proposition.

[3] In this theory, we shall say that the denoting phrase *expresses* a meaning; and we shall say both of the phrase and of the meaning that they *denote* a denotation. In the other theory, which I advocate, there is no *meaning*, and only sometimes a *denotation*.

consider such a proposition as the following: 'If *u* is a class which has only one member, then that one member is a member of *u*', or, as we may state it, 'If *u* is a unit class, *the u* is a *u*'. This proposition ought to be *always* true, since the conclusion is true whenever the hypothesis is true. But 'the *u*' is a denoting phrase, and it is the denotation, not the meaning, that is said to be a *u*. Now if *u* is *not* a unit class, 'the *u*' seems to denote nothing; hence our proposition would seem to become nonsense as soon as *u* is not a unit class.

Now it is plain that such propositions do *not* become nonsense merely because their hypotheses are false. The King in *The Tempest* might say, 'If Ferdinand is not drowned, Ferdinand is my only son'. Now 'my only son' is a denoting phrase, which, on the face of it, has a denotation when, and only when, I have exactly one son. But the above statement would nevertheless have remained true if Ferdinand had been in fact drowned. Thus we must either provide a denotation in cases in which it is at first sight absent, or we must abandon the view that the denotation is what is concerned in propositions which contain denoting phrases. The latter is the course that I advocate. The former course may be taken, as by Meinong, by admitting objects which do not subsist, and denying that they obey the law of contradiction; this, however, is to be avoided if possible. Another way of taking the same course (so far as our present alternative is concerned) is adopted by Frege, who provides by definition some purely conventional denotation for the cases in which otherwise there would be none. Thus 'the King of France', is to denote the null-class; 'the only son of Mr So-and-so' (who has a fine family of ten), is to denote the class of all his sons; and so on. But this procedure, though it may not lead to actual logical error, is plainly artificial, and does not give an exact analysis of the matter. Thus if we allow that denoting phrases, in general, have the two sides of meaning and denotation, the cases where there seems to be no denotation cause difficulties both on the assumption that there really is a denotation and on the assumption that there really is none.

A logical theory may be tested by its capacity for dealing with puzzles, and it is a wholesome plan, in thinking about logic, to stock the mind with as many puzzles as possible, since these serve much the same purpose as is served by experiments in physical science. I shall therefore state three puzzles which a theory as to denoting ought to be able to solve; and I shall show later that my theory solves them.

1. If a is identical with b, whatever is true of the one is true of the other, and either may be substituted for the other in any proposition without altering the truth or falsehood of that proposition. Now George IV wished to know whether Scott was the author of *Waverley*; and in fact Scott *was* the author of *Waverley*. Hence we may substitute *Scott* for *the author of Waverley*, and thereby prove that George IV wished to know whether Scott was Scott. Yet an interest in the law of identity can hardly be attributed to the first gentleman of Europe.

2. By the law of excluded middle, either 'A is B' or 'A is not B' must be true. Hence either 'the present King of France is bald' or 'the present King of France is not bald' must be true. Yet if we enumerated the things that are bald, and then the things that are not bald, we should not find the present King of France in either list. Hegelians, who love a synthesis, will probably conclude that he wears a wig.

3. Consider the proposition 'A differs from B'. If this is true, there is a difference between A and B, which fact may be expressed in the form 'the difference between A and B subsists'. But if it is false that A differs from B, then there is no difference between A and B, which fact may be expressed in the form 'the difference between A and B does not subsist'. But how can a non-entity be the subject of a proposition? 'I think, therefore I am' is no more evident than 'I am the subject of a proposition, therefore I am', provided 'I am' is taken to assert subsistence or being,[1] not existence. Hence, it would appear, it must always be self-contradictory to deny the being of anything; but we have seen, in connexion with Meinong, that to admit being also sometimes leads to contradictions. Thus if A and B do not differ,

---

[1] I use these as synonyms.

to suppose either that there is, or that there is not, such an object as 'the difference between A and B' seems equally impossible.

The relation of the meaning to the denotation involves certain rather curious difficulties, which seem in themselves sufficient to prove that the theory which leads to such difficulties must be wrong.

When we wish to speak about the *meaning* of a denoting phrase, as opposed to its *denotation*, the natural mode of doing so is by inverted commas. Thus we say:

> The centre of mass of the Solar System is a point, not a denoting complex;
> 'The centre of mass of the Solar System' is a denoting complex, not a point.

Or again,

> The first line of Gray's *Elegy* states a proposition.
> 'The first line of Gray's *Elegy*' does not state a proposition.

Thus taking any denoting phrase, say C, we wish to consider the relation between C and 'C', where the difference of the two is of the kind exemplified in the above two instances.

We say, to begin with, that when C occurs it is the *denotation* that we are speaking about; but when 'C' occurs, it is the *meaning*. Now the relation of meaning and denotation is not merely linguistic through the phrase: there must be a logical relation involved, which we express by saying that the meaning denotes the denotation. But the difficulty which confronts us is that we cannot succeed in *both* preserving the connexion of meaning and denotation *and* preventing them from being one and the same; also that the meaning cannot be got at except by means of denoting phrases. This happens as follows.

The one phrase C was to have both meaning and denotation. But if we speak of 'the meaning of C', that gives us the meaning (if any) of the denotation. 'The meaning of the first line of Gray's *Elegy*' is the same as 'The meaning of "The curfew tolls the knell of parting day"', and is not the same as 'The meaning of "the first line of Gray's *Elegy*"'. Thus in order to get the meaning we want, we must speak not of 'the meaning of C', but of 'the meaning of "C"', which is the same as 'C' by itself. Similarly 'the denotation of C' does not mean the denotation we want, but means something which, if it denotes at all, denotes what is denoted by the denotation we want. For example, let 'C' be 'the denoting complex occurring in the second of the above instances'. Then C = 'the first line of Gray's *Elegy*', and the denotation of C = The curfew tolls the knell of parting day. But what we *meant* to have as the denotation was 'the first line of Gray's *Elegy*'. Thus we have failed to get what we wanted.

The difficulty in speaking of the meaning of a denoting complex may be stated thus: The moment we put the complex in a proposition, the proposition is about the denotation; and if we make a proposition in which the subject is 'the meaning of C', then the subject is the meaning (if any) of the denotation, which was not intended. This leads us to say that, when we distinguish meaning and denotation, we must be dealing with the meaning: the meaning has denotation and is a complex, and there is not something other than the meaning, which can be called the complex, and be said to *have* both meaning and denotation. The right phrase, on the view in question, is that some meanings have denotations.

But this only makes our difficulty in speaking of meanings more evident. For suppose C is our complex; then we are to say that C *is* the meaning of the complex. Nevertheless, whenever C occurs without inverted commas, what is said is not true of the meaning, but only of the denotation, as when we say: The centre of mass of the Solar System is a point. Thus to speak of C itself, i.e. to make a proposition about the meaning, our subject must not be C, but something which denotes C. Thus 'C', which is what we use when we want to speak of the meaning, must be not the meaning, but something which denotes the meaning. And C must not be a constituent of this complex (as it is of 'the meaning of C'); for if C occurs in the complex, it will be its denotation, not its meaning, that will occur, and there is no backward road from denotations to meanings, because every object can be denoted by an infinite number of different denoting phrases.

Thus it would seem that 'C' and C are different entities, such that 'C' denotes C; but this cannot be an explanation, because the relation of 'C' to C remains wholly mysterious; and where are we to find the denoting complex 'C' which is to denote C? Moreover, when C occurs in a proposition, it is not *only* the denotation that occurs (as we shall see in the next paragraph); yet, on the view in question, C is only the denotation, the meaning being wholly relegated to 'C'. This is an inextricable tangle, and seems to prove that the whole distinction of meaning and denotation has been wrongly conceived.

That the meaning is relevant when a denoting phrase occurs in a proposition is formally proved by the puzzle about the author of *Waverley*. The proposition 'Scott was the author of *Waverley*' has a property not possessed by 'Scott was Scott', namely the property that George IV wished to know whether it was true. Thus the two are not identical propositions; hence the meaning of 'the author of *Waverley*' must be relevant as well as the denotation, if we adhere to the point of view to which this distinction belongs. Yet, as we have just seen, so long as we adhere to this point of view, we are compelled to hold that only the denotation can be relevant. Thus the point of view in question must be abandoned.

It remains to show how all the puzzles we have been considering are solved by the theory explained at the beginning of this article.

According to the view which I advocate, a denoting phrase is essentially *part* of a sentence, and does not, like most single words, have any significance on its own account. If I say 'Scott was a man', that is a statement of the form 'x was a man', and it has 'Scott' for its subject. But if I say 'the author of *Waverley* was a man', that is not a statement of the form 'x was a man', and does not have 'the author of *Waverley*' for its subject. Abbreviating the statement made at the beginning of this article, we may put, in place of 'the author of *Waverley* was a man', the following: 'One and only one entity wrote *Waverley*, and that one was a man'. (This is not so strictly what is meant as what was said earlier; but it is easier to follow.) And speaking generally, suppose we wish to say that the author of *Waverley* had the property ϕ, what we wish to say is equivalent to 'One and only one entity wrote *Waverley*, and that one had the property ϕ'.

The explanation of *denotation* is now as follows. Every proposition in which 'the author of *Waverley*' occurs being explained as above, the proposition 'Scott was the author of *Waverley*' (i.e. 'Scott was identical with the author of *Waverley*') becomes 'One and only one entity wrote *Waverley*, and Scott was identical with that one'; or, reverting to the wholly explicit form: 'It is not always false of x that x wrote *Waverley*, that it is always true of y that if y wrote *Waverley* y is identical with x, and that Scott is identical with x'. Thus if 'C' is a denoting phrase, it may happen that there is one entity x (there cannot be more than one) for which the proposition 'x is identical with C' is true, this proposition being interpreted as above. We may then say that the entity x is the denotation of the phrase 'C'. Thus Scott is the denotation of 'the author of *Waverley*'. The 'C' in inverted commas will be merely the *phrase*, not anything that can be called the *meaning*. The phrase *per se* has no meaning, because in any proposition in which it occurs the proposition, fully expressed, does not contain the phrase, which has been broken up.

The puzzle about George IV's curiosity is now seen to have a very simple solution. The proposition 'Scott was the author of *Waverley*', which was written out in its unabbreviated form in the preceding paragraph, does not contain any constituent 'the author of *Waverley*' for which we could substitute 'Scott'. This does not interfere with the truth of inferences resulting from making what is *verbally* the substitution of 'Scott' for 'the author of *Waverley*', so long as 'the author of *Waverley*' has what I call a *primary* occurrence in the proposition considered. The difference of primary and secondary occurrences of denoting phrases is as follows:

When we say: 'George IV wished to know whether so-and-so', or when we say 'So-and-so is surprising' or 'So-and-so is true', etc., the 'so-and-so' must be a proposition. Suppose now that 'so-and-so' contains a denoting phrase. We may either eliminate this denoting phrase from the subordinate proposition 'so-and-so', or from the whole proposition in which 'so-and-so' is a mere constituent. Different propositions result according to which we do. I have heard of a touchy owner of a yacht to whom a guest, on first seeing it remarked, 'I thought your yacht was larger than it is'; and the owner replied, 'No, my yacht is not larger than it is'. What the guest meant was, 'The size that I thought your yacht was is greater than the size your yacht is'; the meaning attributed to him is, 'I thought the size of your yacht was greater than the size of your yacht'. To return to George IV and *Waverley*, when we say, 'George IV wished to know whether Scott was the author of *Waverley*', we normally mean 'George IV wished to know whether one and only one man wrote *Waverley* and Scott was that man'; but we *may* also mean: 'One and only one man wrote *Waverley*, and George IV wished to know whether Scott was that man'. In the latter, 'the author of *Waverley*' has a *primary* occurrence; in the former, a *secondary*. The latter might be expressed by 'George IV wished to know, concerning the man who in fact wrote *Waverley*, whether he was Scott'. This would be true, for example, if George IV had seen Scott at a distance, and had asked 'Is that Scott?' A *secondary* occurrence of a denoting phrase may be defined as one in which the phrase occurs in a proposition p which is a mere constituent of the proposition we are considering, and the substitution for the denoting phrase is to be effected in p, not in the whole proposition concerned. The ambiguity as between primary and secondary occurrences is hard to avoid in language; but it does no harm if we are on our guard against it. In symbolic logic it is of course easily avoided.

The distinction of primary and secondary occurrences also enables us to deal with the question whether the present King of France is bald or not bald, and generally with the logical status of denoting phrases that denote nothing. If 'C' is a denoting phrase, say 'the term having the property F', then

'C has the property ϕ' means 'one and only one term has the property F, and that one has the property ϕ'.[1]

If now the property F belongs to no terms, or to several, it follows that 'C has the property ϕ' is false for *all* values of ϕ. Thus 'the present King of France is bald' is certainly false; and 'the present King of France is not bald' is false if it means

'There is an entity which is now King of France and is not bald',

but is true if it means

'It is false that there is an entity which is now King of France and is bald'.

That is, 'the King of France is not bald' is false if the occurrence of 'the King of France' is *primary*, and true if it is *secondary*. Thus all propositions in which 'the King of France' has a primary occurrence are false; the denials of such propositions are true, but in them 'the King of France' has a secondary occurrence. Thus we escape the conclusion that the King of France has a wig.

We can now see also how to deny that there is such an object as the difference between A and B in the case when A and B do not differ. If A and B do differ, there is one and only one entity x such that 'x is the difference between A and B' is a true proposition; if A and B do not differ, there is no such entity x. Thus according to the meaning of denotation lately explained, 'the difference between A and B' has a denotation when A and B differ, but not otherwise. This difference applies to true and false propositions generally. If 'aRb' stands for 'a has the relation R to b', then when aRb is true, there is such an entity as the relation R between a and b; when aRb is false, there is no such entity. Thus out of any proposition we can make a denoting phrase, which denotes an entity if the proposition is true, but does not denote an entity if the proposition is false. E.g. it is true (at least we will suppose so) that the earth revolves round

---

[1] This is the abbreviated, not the stricter, interpretation.

the sun, and false that the sun revolves round the earth; hence 'the revolution of the earth round the sun' denotes an entity, while 'the revolution of the sun round the earth' does not denote an entity.[1]

The whole realm of non-entities, such as 'the round square', 'the even prime other than 2', 'Apollo', 'Hamlet', etc., can now be satisfactorily dealt with. All these are denoting phrases which do not denote anything. A proposition about Apollo means what we get by substituting what the classical dictionary tells us is meant by Apollo, say 'the sun-god'. All propositions in which Apollo occurs are to be interpreted by the above rules for denoting phrases. If 'Apollo' has a primary occurrence, the proposition containing the occurrence is false; if the occurrence is secondary, the proposition may be true. So again 'the round square is round' means 'there is one and only one entity x which is round and square, and that entity is round', which is a false proposition, not, as Meinong maintains, a true one. 'The most perfect Being has all perfections; existence is a perfection; therefore the most perfect Being exists' becomes:

'There is one and only one entity x which is most perfect; that one has all perfections; existence is a perfection; therefore that one exists.' As a proof, this fails for want of a proof of the premise 'there is one and only one entity x which is most perfect'.[2]

Mr MacColl (*Mind*, n.s., Nos. 54, and again 55, p. 401) regards individuals as of two sorts, real and unreal; hence he defines the null-class as the class consisting of all unreal individuals. This assumes that such phrases as 'the present King of France', which do not denote a real individual, do, nevertheless, denote an individual, but an unreal one. This is essentially Meinong's

---

[1] The propositions from which such entities are derived are not identical either with these entities or with the propositions that these entities have being.

[2] The argument can be made to prove validly that all members of the class of most perfect Beings exist; it can also be proved formally that this class cannot have *more* than one member; but, taking the definition of perfection as possession of all positive predicates, it can be proved almost equally formally that the class does not have even one member.

theory, which we have seen reason to reject because it conflicts with the law of contradiction. With our theory of denoting we are able to hold that there are no unreal individuals; so that the null-class is the class containing no members, not the class containing as members all unreal individuals.

It is important to observe the effect of our theory on the interpretation of definitions which proceed by means of denoting phrases. Most mathematical definitions are of this sort: for example, '$m-n$ means the number which, added to n, gives m'. Thus $m-n$ is defined as meaning the same as a certain denoting phrase; but we agreed that denoting phrases have no meaning in isolation. Thus what the definition really ought to be is: 'Any proposition containing $m-n$ is to mean the proposition which results from substituting for "$m-n$" "the number which, added to n, gives m"'. The resulting proposition is interpreted according to the rules already given for interpreting propositions whose verbal expression contains a denoting phrase. In the case where m and n are such that there is one and only one number x which, added to n, gives m, there is a number x which can be substituted for $m-n$ in any proposition containing $m-n$ without altering the truth or falsehood of the proposition. But in other cases, all propositions in which '$m-n$' has a primary occurrence are false.

The usefulness of *identity* is explained by the above theory. No one outside a logic-book ever wishes to say 'x is x', and yet assertions of identity are often made in such forms as 'Scott was the author of *Waverley*' or 'thou art the man'. The meaning of such propositions cannot be stated without the notion of identity, although they are not simply statements that Scott is identical with another term, the author of *Waverley*, or that thou art identical with another term, the man. The shortest statement of 'Scott is the author of *Waverley*' seems to be: 'Scott wrote *Waverley*; and it is always true of y that if y wrote *Waverley*, y is identical with Scott'. It is in this way that identity enters into 'Scott is the author of *Waverley*'; and it is owing to such uses that identity is worth affirming.

One interesting result of the above theory of denoting is this:

when there is anything with which we do not have immediate acquaintance, but only definition by denoting phrases, then the propositions in which this thing is introduced by means of a denoting phrase do not really contain this thing as a constituent, but contain instead the constituents expressed by the several words of the denoting phrase. Thus in every proposition that we can apprehend (i.e. not only in those whose truth or falsehood we can judge of, but in all that we can think about), all the constituents are really entities with which we have immediate acquaintance. Now such things as matter (in the sense in which matter occurs in physics) and the minds of other people are known to us only by denoting phrases, i.e. we are not *acquainted* with them, but we know them as what has such and such properties. Hence, although we can form propositional functions $C(x)$, which must hold of such and such a material particle, or of So-and-so's mind, yet we are not acquainted with the propositions which affirm these things that we know must be true, because we cannot apprehend the actual entities concerned. What we know is 'So-and-so has a mind which has such and such properties' but we do not know 'A has such and such properties', where A *is* the mind in question. In such a case, we know the properties of a thing without having acquaintance with the thing itself, and without, consequently, knowing any single proposition of which the thing itself is a constituent.

Of the many other consequences of the view I have been advocating, I will say nothing. I will only beg the reader not to make up his mind against the view – as he might be tempted to do, on account of its apparently excessive complication – until he has attempted to construct a theory of his own on the subject of denotation. This attempt, I believe, will convince him that, whatever the true theory may be, it cannot have such a simplicity as one might have expected beforehand.

6

Mr Strawson on Referring

First published in *Mind*, n.s. **66** (July 1957), pp. 385–9. Reprinted with the permission of the editor of *Mind*, Simon and Schuster, Inc., and the Bertrand Russell Estate.

Mr P. F. Strawson published in *Mind* of 1950 an article called 'On Referring'. This article is reprinted in *Essays in Conceptual Analysis*, selected and edited by Professor Antony Flew. The references that follow are to this reprint. The main purpose of the article is to refute my theory of descriptions. As I find that some philosophers whom I respect consider that it has achieved its purpose successfully, I have come to the conclusion that a polemical reply is called for. I may say, to begin with, that I am totally unable to see any validity whatever in any of Mr Strawson's arguments. Whether this inability is due to senility on my part or to some other cause, I must leave readers to judge.

The gist of Mr Strawson's argument consists in identifying two problems which I have regarded as quite distinct – namely, the problem of descriptions and the problem of egocentricity. I have dealt with both these problems at considerable length, but as I have considered them to be different problems, I have not dealt with the one when I was considering the other. This enables Mr Strawson to pretend that I have overlooked the problem of egocentricity.

He is helped in this pretence by a careful selection of material. In the article in which I first set forth the theory of descriptions, I dealt specially with two examples: 'The present King of France is bald' and 'Scott is the author of *Waverley*'. The latter example does not suit Mr Strawson, and he therefore entirely ignores it except for one quite perfunctory reference. As regards 'the present King of France', he fastens upon the egocentric word 'present' and does not seem able to grasp that, if for the word 'present' I had substituted the words 'in 1905', the whole of his argument would have collapsed.

Or perhaps not quite the whole for reasons which I had set forth before Mr Strawson wrote. It is, however, not difficult to give other examples of the use of descriptive phrases from which egocentricity is wholly absent. I should like to see him apply his doctrine to such sentences as the following: 'the square-root of minus one is half the square-root of minus four', or 'the cube of three is the integer immediately preceding the second perfect number'. There are no egocentric words in either of these two sentences, but the problem of interpreting the descriptive phrases is exactly the same as if there were.

There is not a word in Mr Strawson's article to suggest that I ever considered egocentric words, still less, that the theory which he advocates in regard to them is the very one which I had set forth at great length and in considerable detail.[1] The gist of what he has to say about such words is the entirely correct statement that what they refer to depends upon when and where they are used. As to this, I need only quote one paragraph from *Human Knowledge* (p. 107):

'"This" denotes whatever, at the moment when the word is used, occupies the centre of attention. With words which are not egocentric what is constant is something about the object indicated, but "this" denotes a different object on each occasion of its use: what is constant is not the object denoted, but its relation to the particular use of the word. Whenever the word is used, the person using it is attending to something, and the word indicates this something. When a word is not egocentric, there is no need to distinguish between different occasions when it is used, but we must make this distinction with egocentric words, since what they indicate is something having a given relation to the particular use of the word.'

I must refer also to the case that I discuss (pp. 101 ff.) in which I am walking with a friend on a dark night. We lose touch with each other and he calls, 'Where are you?' and I reply 'Here I am!' It is of the essence of a scientific account of the world to reduce to a minimum the egocentric element in an

---

[1] Cf. Russell *B* 1940, ch. vii, and Russell *B* 1948a, Part II, ch. iv.

assertion, but success in this attempt is a matter of degree, and is never complete where empirical matter is concerned. This is due to the fact that the meanings of all empirical words depend ultimately upon ostensive definitions, that ostensive definitions depend upon experience, and that experience is egocentric. We can, however, by means of egocentric words, *describe* something which is not egocentric; it is this that enables us to use a common language.

All this may be right or wrong, but, whichever it is, Mr Strawson should not expound it as if it were a theory that he had invented, whereas, in fact, I had set it forth before he wrote, though perhaps he did not grasp the purport of what I said. I shall say no more about egocentricity since, for the reasons I have already given, I think Mr Strawson completely mistaken in connecting it with the problem of descriptions.

I am at a loss to understand Mr Strawson's position on the subject of names. When he is writing about me, he says: 'There are no logically proper names and there are no descriptions (in this sense)' (p. 109). But when he is writing about Quine, in *Mind*, October 1956, he takes a quite different line. Quine has a theory that names are unnecessary and can always be replaced by descriptions. This theory shocks Mr Strawson for reasons which to me, remain obscure. However, I will leave the defence of Quine to Quine, who is quite capable of looking after himself. What is important for my purpose is to elucidate the meaning of the words 'in this sense', which Mr Strawson puts in brackets. So far as I can discover from the context, what he objects to is the belief that there are words which are only significant because there is something that they mean, and if there were not this something, they would be empty noises, not words. For my part, I think that there must be such words if language is to have any relation to fact. The necessity for such words is made obvious by the process of ostensive definition. How do we know what is meant by such words as 'red' and 'blue'? We cannot know what these words mean unless we have seen red and seen blue. If there were no red and no blue in our experience, we might, perhaps, invent some elaborate description which we could substitute for the word 'red' or for the word 'blue'. For example, if you were dealing with a blind man, you could hold a red-hot poker near enough for him to feel the heat, and you could tell him that red is what he would see if he could see – but of course for the word 'see' you would have to substitute another elaborate description. Any description which the blind man could understand would have to be in terms of words expressing experiences which he had had. Unless fundamental words in the individual's vocabulary had this kind of direct relation to fact, language in general would have no such relation. I defy Mr Strawson to give the usual meaning to the word 'red' unless there is something which the word designates.

This brings me to a further point. 'Red' is usually regarded as a predicate and as designating a universal. I prefer for purposes of philosophical analysis a language in which 'red' is a subject, and, while I should not say that it is a positive error to call it a universal, I should say that calling it so invites confusion. This is connected with what Mr Strawson calls my 'logically disastrous theory of names' (p. 118). He does not deign to mention why he considers this theory 'logically disastrous'. I hope that on some future occasion he will enlighten me on this point.

This brings me to a fundamental divergence between myself and many philosophers with whom Mr Strawson appears to be in general agreement. They are persuaded that common speech is good enough not only for daily life, but also for philosophy. I, on the contrary, am persuaded that common speech is full of vagueness and inaccuracy, and that any attempt to be precise and accurate requires modification of common speech both as regards vocabulary and as regards syntax. Everybody admits that physics and chemistry and medicine each require a language which is not that of everyday life. I fail to see why philosophy, alone, should be forbidden to make a similar approach towards precision and accuracy. Let us take, in illustration, one of the commonest words of everyday speech: namely, the word 'day'. The most august use of this word is in the first chapter of Genesis and in the Ten Commandments.

DESCRIPTIONS AND EXISTENCE

The desire to keep holy the Sabbath 'day' has led orthodox Jews to give a precision to the word 'day' which it does not have in common speech: they have defined it as the period from one sunset to the next. Astronomers, with other reasons for seeking precision, have three sorts of day: the true solar day: the mean solar day; and the sidereal day. These have different uses: the true solar day is relevant if you are considering lighting-up time; the mean solar day is relevant if you are sentenced to fourteen days without the option; and the sidereal day is relevant if you are trying to estimate the influence of the tides in retarding the earth's rotation. All these four kinds of day – decalogical, true, mean, and sidereal – are more precise than the common use of the word 'day'. If astronomers were subject to the prohibition of precision which some recent philosophers apparently favour, the whole science of astronomy would be impossible.

For technical purposes, technical languages differing from those of daily life are indispensable. I feel that those who object to linguistic novelties, if they had lived a hundred and fifty years ago, would have stuck to feet and ounces, and would have maintained that centimetres and grams savour of the guillotine.

In philosophy, it is syntax, even more than vocabulary, that needs to be corrected. The subject-predicate logic to which we are accustomed depends for its convenience upon the fact that at the usual temperatures of the earth there are approximately permanent 'things'. This would not be true at the temperature of the sun, and is only roughly true at the temperatures to which we are accustomed.

My theory of descriptions was never intended as an analysis of the state of mind of those who utter sentences containing descriptions. Mr Strawson gives the name 'S' to the sentence 'The King of France is wise', and he says of me 'The way in which he arrived at the analysis was clearly by asking himself what would be the circumstances in which we would say that anyone who uttered the sentence S had made a true assertion'. This does not seem to me a correct account of what I was doing.

Suppose (which God forbid) Mr Strawson were so rash as to accuse his char-lady of thieving: she would reply indignantly, 'I ain't never done no harm to no one'. Assuming her a pattern of virtue, I should say that she was making a true assertion, although, according to the rules of syntax which Mr Strawson would adopt in his own speech, what she said should have meant: 'there was at least one moment when I was injuring the whole human race'. Mr Strawson would not have supposed that this was what she meant to assert, although he would not have used her words to express the same sentiment. Similarly, I was concerned to find a more accurate and analysed thought to replace the somewhat confused thoughts which most people at most times have in their heads.

Mr Strawson objects to my saying that 'the King of France is wise' is false if there is no King of France. He admits that the sentence is significant and not true, but not that it is false. This is a mere question of verbal convenience. He considers that the word 'false' has an unalterable meaning which it would be sinful to regard as adjustable, though he prudently avoids telling us what this meaning is. For my part, I find it more convenient to define the word 'false' so that every significant sentence is either true or false. This is a purely verbal question; and although I have no wish to claim the support of common usage, I do not think that he can claim it either. Suppose, for example, that in some country there was a law that no person could hold public office if he considered it false that the Ruler of the Universe is wise. I think an avowed atheist who took advantage of Mr Strawson's doctrine to say that he did not hold this proposition false, would be regarded as a somewhat shifty character.

It is not only as to names and as to falsehood that Mr Strawson shows his conviction that there is an unalterably right way of using words and that no change is to be tolerated however convenient it may be. He shows the same feeling as regards universal affirmatives – i.e. sentences of the form 'All A is B'. Traditionally, such sentences are supposed to imply that there are A's, but it is much more convenient in mathematical logic to drop this implication and to consider that 'All A is B' is true if there are no A's. This is wholly and solely a question of convenience. For some purposes the one convention is more convenient, and for others, the other. We shall prefer the one convention or the other according to the purpose we have in view. I agree, however, with Mr Strawson's statement (p. 127) that ordinary language has no exact logic.

Mr Strawson, in spite of his very real logical competence, has a curious prejudice against logic. On p. 121, he has a sudden dithyrambic outburst, to the effect that life is greater than logic, which he uses to give a quite false interpretation of my doctrines.

Leaving detail aside, I think we may sum up Mr Strawson's argument and my reply to it as follows:

There are two problems, that of descriptions and that of egocentricity. Mr Strawson thinks they are one and the same problem, but it is obvious from his discussion that he has not considered as many kinds of descriptive phrases as are relevant to the argument. Having confused the two problems, he asserts dogmatically that it is only the egocentric problem that needs to be solved, and he offers a solution of this problem which he seems to believe to be new, but which in fact was familiar before he wrote. He then thinks that he has offered an adequate theory of descriptions, and announces his supposed achievement with astonishing dogmatic certainty. Perhaps I am doing him an injustice, but I am unable to see in what respect this is the case.

IV

CLASSES AND THE PARADOXES

The discovery of the paradoxes discussed in the following four essays must rank as one of the most interesting chapters in the history of science. In the space of a few years, intuitions which had been the basis of a whole generation of development in logic and mathematics were called into question. Since all the essays presuppose familiarity with the paradoxes, a brief account of them will be given here.

The earliest of the modern paradoxes was discovered in Cantor's theory of transfinite ordinals by the Italian mathematician Cesare Burali-Forti in 1897,[1] and is fairly technical. It had by that time been demonstrated that (1) every well-ordered series has an ordinal number, (2) that a series of ordinals up to a given ordinal exceeds the given ordinal by 1, and (3) that the series of ordinals in order of magnitude is well ordered. Consider the series of all ordinals. From (1) and (3) it follows that this series has an ordinal number. Call it Ω. From (2) it follows that the series of all ordinals has the ordinal number $\Omega+1$. Hence Ω cannot be the ordinal number of the series of *all* ordinals.

A simpler paradox, now called Cantor's paradox, was known to Cantor in 1899.[2] Cantor had given proofs[3] that the number of sets in a given collection of terms is larger than the number of terms in the collection. This should hold for the collection of all sets as well. Thus the number of sets in the collection of all sets must be larger than the number of sets in the collection of all sets, a plain contradiction. Cantor did not publish this paradox, and Russell developed it independently in sections 344, 348, and 349 of the *Principles of Mathematics*, which are, I believe, the first published discussions of this difficulty. In the following

[1] Burali-Forti *A* 1897. [2] Cantor *A* 1899*b*. [3] Cantor *A* 1890.

essays it is referred to as 'the difficulty concerning the greatest cardinal'.

The simplest, and therefore the most fatal, of the modern paradoxes is Russell's own, discovered in May of 1901.[1] Some sets are members of themselves, and some are not. The set of all stones, for example, is not a member of itself, since it is not a stone, but the set of non-stones is a member of itself, since the set of non-stones is itself not a stone. Consider the set S of all sets that are not members of themselves. If we assume that S is a member of itself, by the definition of S it follows that it is not a member of itself. Since propositions which imply their opposites must be false, it follows that S is not a member of itself. But if S is not a member of itself, by the definition of S it follows that it is a member of itself. So S both is and is not a member of itself.

The next difficulty is referred to by Russell as that concerning 'the least indefinable ordinal'. The total number of possible definitions of transfinite ordinals is $\aleph_0$, but the total number of transfinite ordinals is greater than $\aleph_0$. Hence there are indefinable ordinals, and of these there must be a least. Consequently the least indefinable ordinal has a definition – it is the least indefinable ordinal.[2]

Richard's paradox,[3] about which Russell learned through Poincaré,[4] is similar to the preceding. Consider all the decimals definable in a finite number of words. If E is the class of such decimals, E has $\aleph_0$ terms; hence its members can be ordered as the 1st, 2nd, 3rd, etc. Let N be a number defined as follows. If the nth figure in the nth decimal is x, let the nth figure in N be $x+1$. Thus N cannot be a member of E, since the nth figure in N is always different from the nth figure in the nth decimal in E. Yet we have defined N in a finite number of words, so N must be in E.

G. G. Berry of the Bodleian Library at Oxford developed another paradox of definability which is confined wholly to finite numbers. Consider 'the least integer not nameable in

[1] The *Autobiography* (vol. 1, p. 236) says May 1901; the essay 'My Philosophical Development', Schilpp C1 1944, p. 13, says June.
[2] Konig *A* 1905*b*.   [3] Richard *A* 1905.   [4] Poincaré *A* 1906.

fewer than nineteen syllables'. The last sentence has given this integer a name which uses just eighteen syllables.

To all these must be added the Epimenides paradox, known in classical times. Its starkest form utilises the statement 'I am lying'. If the speaker is lying, he is telling the truth. But if his statement is the truth, he must be lying. Either way, we get a contradiction. The first two essays concern principally Russell's own paradox and Burali-Forti's. The second two concentrate on the paradoxes of definability and the Epimenides paradox.

Russell's first response to the paradoxes was the early theory of types developed in the Appendix to the *Principles of Mathematics*. In the theory, he distinguished between individuals, ranges of individuals (all the individuals satisfying a certain function), ranges of ranges of individuals, and so on. Each level in this hierarchy was called a type, and it was stipulated that if 'x is a u' is to be meaningful, u must be one type higher than x. Russell felt that this theory, as it stands, could not deal with Cantor's paradox, and hence was not ultimately satisfactory.

Russell's next move was to deny classes altogether in favour of propositional functions. In the *Principles* he had already said: 'In the case of classes, I have failed to perceive any concept fulfilling the conditions requisite for the notion of class. And the contradiction discussed in ch. x proves that something is amiss, but what this is I have hitherto failed to discover.'[1] In May of 1903, he set out to develop arithmetic without classes, using the functional symbol ϕ to do duty for class abstracts.

This approach, Russell wrote to Jourdain in 1906, 'went well until I came to consider the function $\overline{W}$, where $\overline{W}(\phi) . \equiv_\phi . \sim \phi(\phi)$. This brought back the contradiction, and showed that I had gained nothing by rejecting classes.'[2] After this failure, Russell returned to a realistic attitude towards classes,[3] which he maintained through 1904.

In late 1905, after the Theory of Descriptions had been developed, Russell started a fresh assault on the paradoxes, beginning with 'On Some Difficulties in the Theory of Transfinite

[1] Russell *B* 1903, Preface. [2] From Grattan-Guinness *C*1 1972.
[3] See 'On the Axiom of Infinity', chapter 11.

Numbers and Order Types', read in December before the London Mathematical Society. In this paper he developed three different approaches to the paradoxes, all of which became the basis for subsequent investigations. The first approach is the 'zig-zag' theory, which sets limits on the complexity of propositional functions considered as defining classes. This solution bears some similarity to that suggested by W. V. O. Quine in 'New Foundations for Mathematical Logic' in 1937.[1] The 'limitation of size' approach, discussed next, stipulates rules to prevent certain classes from becoming too large and spawning contradictions. Roughly speaking, this is the approach taken in the Zermelo–Frankel and Von Neumann–Bernays traditions in axiomatic set theory. The third approach is Russell's own 'no-classes' theory, a proposal once again to dispense with classes altogether.

The method by which classes are to be eliminated is left fairly unsettled in the 1905 paper. In a second paper, 'On the Substitutional Theory of Classes and Relations' read in May 1906 and published here for the first time, a definite plan for class elimination is outlined. The paper fared oddly. It was submitted to two referees: one gave an unfavourable report, the other took the paper off on vacation. When the Society finally voted to publish the paper in October of 1906, Russell was no longer satisfied with it and decided to withdraw it.

Perhaps remembering his previous failure to evade the paradoxes with propositional functions, Russell chose in this article to define away classes by a device employing propositions, constants, and the operation of substitution. With this 'substitutional' theory, it was possible to treat the notation for class abstraction as a mere 'symbolic convenience'. The new, nominalistic approach may have been partially due to the American mathematician Maxime Bôcher, with whom Russell had corresponded in April of 1905. Bôcher had written:

'The central point at issue is your "class as one". Your attitude towards this term is that of the realist, if I understand you

[1] Quine C4 1937.

correctly; mine is that of the nominalist. I cannot admit that a class is in itself an entity; it is for me *always* many entities (your "class as many"). When we speak of it as a single entity, we are considering a new object which we associate with the class, but not the class itself. That is, the "class as one" is merely a symbol or *name* which we may choose at pleasure.'[1]

Russell's original intention was to write the whole *Principia* using the new substitutional interpretation of classes. Had this plan been adopted, the *Principia* would have looked considerably different than it now looks. But Whitehead from the first steadfastly opposed the idea. On 21 February 1906, he wrote to Russell criticising the symbolism of the new theory, and said; 'I look upon these remarks as a protest against your excessive formalism. (There's a change of heart for you!)'[2] The next day he continued 'It founds the whole of mathematics on a typographical device and thus contradicts the main doctrines of Vol. I.'[3]

These comments indicate some of the intellectual tensions that arose between Whitehead and Russell during their collaboration on the *Principia*. Roughly speaking, Russell viewed the *Principia* as a *criticism* of mathematical reasoning; Whitehead viewed it as a *systematisation* of mathematical reasoning. Russell was more inclined to develop lines of attack based on philosophical conceptions, while Whitehead, on his side, was more inclined to relate lines of attack to actual mathematical practice. With regard to what was apparently an earlier attempt of Russell's to dispense with classes, Whitehead wrote to Russell:

'This extreme rigour must be tempered by practical considerations. *Classes* can be kept in use by the consideration that our object is to systematise the actual reasoning of mathematics, and this actual reasoning does in fact habitually employ classes when it need not do so. Thus our object is to

---

[1] Bôcher to Russell 25 April 1905. By permission of the Bertrand Russell Archives.
[2] Whitehead to Russell, 21 Feb. 1906.
[3] Whitehead to Russell, 22 Feb. 1906.

systematise the reasoning concerning classes, even when it is a primitive idea which might be avoided.'[1]

Russell experimented further with the substitutional method while developing a new theory of types designed to handle the Epimenides paradox and the paradoxes of definability. The technical complexity of combining the substitutional method with the new theory of types proved overwhelming; Whitehead got his way, and the *Principia* system in its present form was adopted.

In 1906, Henri Poincaré had launched an attack on Russell's 1905 London Mathematical Society paper and on the whole movement to formalise the foundations of mathematics,[2] the chief French defender of which was Louis Couturat. For a while the debate was confined to Poincaré and Couturat,[3] but in September 1906, Russell published his own reply, 'Les Paradoxes de la Logique' in the *Revue de Métaphysique et de Morale*. Oddly enough, Poincaré's side of the debate has been available in English, ever since an abbreviated version of his articles appeared in the English translation of *Science and Method* in 1914. Russell's side appears here in English for the first time.

The Couturat–Russell–Poincaré articles caused a sensation, and a fierce controversy ensued in which a number of distinguished logicians, mathematicians, and philosophers took part. A year later, in 1907, L. J. Brouwer[4] provided a more consistent and stringent exposition of Poincaré's viewpoint and the modern 'intuitionist' movement in mathematics was under way.

Russell developed his new theory of types in 'Mathematical Logic as based on the Theory of Types', written in 1907.[5] After a year's delay, the paper was published in the *American Journal of Mathematics*, and Poincaré replied with a further critique, 'La Logique de l'Infini',[6] in which he gave his own final suggestions on the paradoxes besetting logic:

[1] Whitehead to Russell, 30 April 1905.   [2] Poincaré *A* 1906.
[3] Couturat *A* 1904, 1906.   [4] Brouwer *A* 1907.   [5] Russell *B* 1908*a*.
[6] Poincaré *A* 1909.

1. Consider only objects that can be defined in a finite number of words;
2. Never forget that every proposition concerning infinity must be the translation, the abridged statement, of a proposition concerning the finite;
3. Avoid definitions and classifications that are not predicative.[1]

Russell responded to Poincaré's new criticisms in 1910 in 'La Théorie des Types Logiques', which partially overlaps the Introduction to *Principia Mathematica*. The article, here in English, presents Russell's mature theory, in which classes are defined in terms of propositional functions, and functions themselves are regimented by a ramified theory of types mitigated by the axiom of reducibility.

It would be out of place to attempt an evaluation of the mature theory here. But a few words should be said concerning Russell's 'reduction' of classes to propositional functions. The orthodox critical interpretation of Russell's reduction was given by Quine in 1941.[2] Quine says that Russell's definition does reduce classes to propositional functions, but the *Principia* system requires that propositional functions serve as variables of quantification. Consequently the *Principia* is committed to propositional functions *in re*, and the 'reduction' of classes turns out to be merely a reduction of classes to properties or attributes. Because Russell confused use and mention, he thought he had reduced classes to linguistic entities, while in fact he reduced them only to Platonic properties.

Russell's response to Quine's criticism would probably have been that properties are philosophically admissible, a position that he took in 1912 in *The Problems of Philosophy*. He certainly would have denied that he was unaware of his assumption of properties. It is hardly credible that Russell could have been unaware of the ontological commitments inherent in a system on which he had been working for ten years. And in a series of unpublished notes entitled 'The Paradox of the Liar', written in

---

[1] Poincaré *A* 1909, p. 482.   [2] Quine *C*4 1941.

1906, Russell wrote '... whatever can be an apparent variable must have some kind of being',[1] and specifically applies this rule to quantification over predicate variables. This passage anticipates Quine's own slogan 'to be is to be the value of a bound variable' by some forty years. Russell may have been wrong about properties, but he was certainly not confused.

[1] Russell *B* 1906*h*, p. 106. 'Apparent variable' was Peano's term for 'bound variable'.

7

On Some Difficulties in the Theory of Transfinite Numbers and Order Types

Received 24 November 1905 by the London Mathematical Society. Read on 14 December 1905 and published in the *Proceedings of the London Mathematical Society*, series 2, **4** (7 March 1906), pp. 29–53. Reprinted with permission of the editor of the *Proceedings*.

Dr Hobson's most interesting paper in the *Proceedings of the London Mathematical Society*[1] raises a number of questions which must be answered before the principles of mathematics can be considered to be at all adequately understood. I do not profess to know the complete answers to these questions, and most of the present paper will consist only of tentative suggestions, made as possibly a step towards the true solutions, not as themselves constituting solutions. With the greater part of Dr Hobson's paper I find myself in agreement; my purpose, therefore, will not be in the main polemical, but rather to carry the discussion a stage further by introducing certain distinctions which I believe to be relevant and important, and by generalising as far as possible the difficulties and contradictions hitherto discovered in the theory of the transfinite.

There are two wholly distinct difficulties to be considered in the theory of transfinite cardinal numbers, namely:

1. The difficulty as to *inconsistent* aggregates (as they are called by Jourdain);
2. The difficulty as to what we may call Zermelo's axiom.[2]

These two difficulties do not seem to be clearly distinguished by Dr Hobson; yet they are, so far as appears, largely independent and of very different degrees of importance. The first leads

---

[1] Hobson *A* 1905.
[2] See Zermelo *A* 1904. For statements of various forms of this axiom see the third part of this paper.

to definite contradictions, and renders all reasoning about classes and relations, *prima facie*, suspect; while the second merely raises a doubt as to whether a certain much used axiom is true, without showing that any *fundamental* difficulties arise either from supposing it true or from supposing it false. I shall consider these difficulties separately, beginning with the first, because it is more fundamental.

I

When Dr Hobson speaks of the necessity of a *norm* for constituting an aggregate, he appears sometimes to suppose that the *norm* is absent or ill-defined in the case of inconsistent aggregates, at other times to suppose it absent where Zermelo's axiom requires it. But the two cases are, in reality, quite distinct. The doubt as to the truth of Zermelo's axiom arises from the impossibility of discovering a *norm* by which to select one term out of each of a set of classes, while the difficulty of inconsistent aggregates arises from the presence of a perfectly definite *norm* combined with the demonstrable absence of a corresponding aggregate. This suggests that a *norm* is a necessary but not a sufficient condition for the existence of an aggregate; if so, the complete solution of our first set of difficulties would consist in the discovery of the precise conditions which a norm must fulfil in order to define an aggregate. Logical determinateness, it seems, is not sufficient, as Dr Hobson supposes (p. 173), and the meaning which he attaches to the term *aggregate* (p. 173) appears to be too wide. This is proved by a perfectly strict argument, which I shall try to state after explaining some ways of generating inconsistent aggregates.

In the first place, since the discussion belongs to symbolic logic, which already possesses technical names for the ideas we require, it is desirable to compare Dr Hobson's terms with those in current use. What he calls a *norm* is what I call a *propositional function*. A *propositional function* of x is any expression $\phi!x$ whose value, for every value of x, is a proposition; such is 'x is a man' or '$\sin x = 1$'. Similarly we write $\phi!(x, y)$ for a propositional function of two variables; and so on.

THEORY OF TRANSFINITE NUMBERS AND ORDER TYPES

In this paper I shall use the words *norm*, *property*, and *propositional function* as synonyms.

The word *aggregate* is used sometimes with an implication of order, sometimes without; I shall use *class* where there is no implication of order, and where there is order I shall consider the *relation* of *before* and *after* which generates the order. This last is necessary because every class which can be ordered at all can be ordered in many ways; so that only the ordering relation, not the class, determines what the order is to be. A *relation* will be used in an extensional sense, i.e. so that two relations are identical provided each holds whenever the other holds. We shall find that a propositional function $\phi!x$ may be perfectly definite, in the sense that, for every value of x, $\phi!x$ is determinably true or determinably false, while yet the values of x for which $\phi!x$ is true do not form a class. And, similarly, we shall find that a propositional function $\phi!(x, y)$ may be in the same sense definite, without there being any relation R which holds between x and y when and only when $\phi!(x, y)$ is true.

In order to eliminate at the outset a number of considerable but irrelevant difficulties, I may point out that the argument we are about to consider does not depend upon this or that view as to the nature of classes and relations. The refutable assumption as to the nature of classes and relations is only this: that a class is always uniquely determined by a *norm* or property containing one variable, and that two norms which are not *equivalent* (i.e. such that, for any value of the variable, both are true or both are false) do not determine the same class, with a similar assumption as regards relations. It is in no way essential to the argument to suppose that classes and relations are taken in *extension*, i.e. that two equivalent norms determine the same class or relation. Thus the argument proves that a norm itself is in general not an entity; that is, if we make statements of the form $\phi!x$ about a number of different values of x, we cannot pick out an entity ϕ which is the common *form* of all these statements, or is the property assigned to x when we state $\phi!x$. In other words, a statement about x cannot in general be analysed into two parts, x and what is said about x. There is no harm in talking of norms or properties so long as we remember this fact; but, if we forget it, we become involved in contradictions.

The two contradictions first discovered concerned respectively the greatest ordinal and the greatest cardinal.[1] Of these the cardinal contradiction is the simpler, and lends itself more readily to the removal from arithmetic to logic which I wish to effect for both. I shall therefore consider it first.

The cardinal contradiction is simply this: Cantor has a proof[2] that there is no greatest cardinal, and yet there are properties (such as '$x=x$') which belong to *all* entities. Hence the cardinal number of entities having such a property must be the greatest of cardinal numbers. Hence a contradiction.

If every logically determinate norm defines a class, there is no escape from the conclusion that there is a cardinal number of all entities. For, in that case, the norm '$x=x$' defines a class, which contains all entities: call this class V. Then the norm 'u is similar to V' defines a set of classes which may be taken as being the cardinal number of V, i.e. the greatest cardinal number.[3] Thus, if every logically determinate norm defines a class, it is impossible to escape the conclusion that there is a greatest cardinal.

The other horn of the dilemma yields more interesting results. Cantor's proof that there is no greatest cardinal may be simplified into the following: Let u be any class, and R a one–one correlation of all the members of u to some (or all) of the classes contained in u. There are such correlations, since one of them is obtained by correlating each member of u with the class whose only term is that member. Consider now the following norm: 'x is a member of u, but is not a member of the class with which R correlates it.' Suppose this norm defines a class w. Then w is omitted from the correlation: for, if w were correlated with x, then, if x is any member of w, it follows from

---

[1] The contradiction concerning the greatest ordinal was first set forth in Burali-Forti *A* 1897. The contradiction concerning the greatest cardinal is discussed in Russell, *B* 1903*a*, § 344ff.
[2] Cantor *A* 1890, p. 77.
[3] I shall consider later Dr Hobson's objection to this definition.

the definition of w that x is not a member of its correlate, i.e. is not a member of w; while, conversely, if x is not a member of w, it is a member of its correlate, i.e. of w. Hence the supposition that w is the correlate of x leads to a contradiction. Hence, in any one-time correlation of all the terms of u with classes contained in u, at least one class contained in u is omitted. Therefore, whatever class u may be, there are more classes contained in u than there are members of u.

We may test this conclusion, in the case of the class of all entities, by constructing, according to the method of the proof of the Schröder–Bernstein theorem, an actual one–one correlation of all terms with all classes, and then considering the class which Cantor shows to be omitted. This process leads us to the consideration of the norm: 'x is not a class which is a member of itself.' If this norm defines a class w, then the class w is omitted from our correlation. But it is easy to see that this norm does not define a class at all. For, if it defined a class w, we should find that, if w is a member of itself, then it is not a member of itself, and *vice versa*. Hence there is no such class as w. Essentially the same argument may be stated as follows: If u be any class, then, when $x = u$, the statement 'x is not an x' is equivalent to 'x is not a u'. Hence, whatever class u may be, there is one value of x – namely, u – for which 'x is not an x' is equivalent to 'x is not a u'; thus there is no class w such that 'x is not an x' is always equivalent to 'x is a w'. Hence, again, this norm does not define a class.

We thus find that, quite apart from any view as to the nature of cardinals, and without any considerations belonging to arithmetic, we can prove that at least one perfectly determinate norm does not define a class. By the same method, we can easily construct other such norms. Take any class u for which we can correlate all entities to some u's by a one–one correlation. By the method of the proof of the Schröder–Bernstein theorem, construct an actual one-one correlation of all the members of u to all classes contained in u, and then consider the norm: 'x is a member of u, which is not a member of its correlate according to the correlation in question'. This norm does not define a class. Thus from the class of all relations we obtain the norm: 'R is not a relation which is a member of its own domain.' From the class of all couples we obtain the norm: 'v is such that the couple whose members are (1) the class of all entities, (2) v, is not a member of v.' Thus it appears that the contradiction dealt with in chapter x of my *Principles of Mathematics* is a special case of a general type of contradictions which result from supposing that certain propositional functions determine classes, when, in fact, they do not do so. The above method of discovering such propositional functions is not required for proving, when they are discovered, that they are of the sort that do not define classes. In each case it is easy to discover a definite simple contradiction, analogous to that discussed in the above mentioned chapter, which results from supposing that the propositional functions in question do determine classes.

In like manner propositional functions of two variables do not always determine relations. For example, 'R does not have the relation R to S' does not determine a relation T between R and S, i.e. it is not equivalent, for all values of R and S, to 'R has the relation T to S'. For, if it were, substituting T for R and for S, we should have 'T does not have the relation T to T', equivalent to 'T has the relation T to T', which is a contradiction.

The following contradiction, of an analogous type to those discussed above, shows that a norm or property is not always an entity which can be detached from the argument of which it is asserted. Consider the norm: 'x does not have any property which it is.' If this assigns to x the property θ, then 'x has the property θ' is equivalent to 'x does not have any property which it is'. Hence, substituting θ for x, 'θ has the property θ' is equivalent to 'θ does not have any property which it is', which is equivalent to 'θ does not have the property θ'; whence a contradiction. The solution, in this case, is that properties are not always (if ever) separable entities which can be put as arguments either to other properties or to themselves. Thus, when we speak of properties we are sometimes (if not always) employing an abbreviated form of statement, which

THEORY OF TRANSFINITE NUMBERS AND ORDER TYPES

leads to errors if we suppose that the properties we are speaking of are genuine entities.

We have thus reached the conclusion that some norms (if not all) are not entities which can be considered independently of their arguments, and that some norms (if not all) do not define classes. Norms (containing one variable) which do not define classes I propose to call *non-predicative*; those which do define classes I shall call *predicative*. Similarly, by extension, a norm containing two variables will be called predicative if it defines a relation; in the contrary case it will be called non-predicative. Thus we need rules for deciding what norms are predicative and what are not, unless we adopt the view (which, as we shall see, has much to recommend it) that *no* norms are predicative.

I come now to Burali-Forti's contradiction concerning the greatest ordinal, and I shall show how this too reduces to a simple logical contradiction resulting from supposing that a certain non-predicative function is predicative.

Burali-Forti's contradiction may be stated, after some modification, as follows. If u is any segment of the series of ordinals in order of magnitude, the ordinal number of u is greater than any member of u, and is, in fact, the immediate successor of u (i.e. the limit of u has no last term, or the immediate successor of the last term if u has a last term). The ordinal number of u is always an ordinal number, and is never a member of u. But now consider the whole series of ordinal numbers. This is well ordered, and therefore should have an ordinal number. This must be an ordinal number, and yet must be greater than any ordinal number. Hence it both is, and is not, an ordinal number, which is a contradiction.

To generalise this contradiction, put $\phi!x$ in place of 'x is an ordinal', and $f`u$[1] in place of 'the ordinal number of $u$'. Then the case of the ordinals $\phi$ and $f$ are such that, if all the members of $u$ satisfy $\phi$, then $f`u$ satisfies ϕ and is not a member of u. Whenever these two conditions are satisfied for all values of u,

---

[1] The inverted comma may be read 'of'. The notation $f`u$ means the same as $f(u)$, but is for several reasons more convenient.

one or other of two conclusions follows: namely, either (1) $\phi!x$ is not a predicative property; or (2) if $\phi!x$ is predicative and defines the class w, then there must be no such entity as $f'w$. This is proved very simply as follows. If there is such a class as w, and such an entity as $f'w$, then, since every member of w satisfies ϕ, it follows that $f'w$ satisfies ϕ; but conversely, $f'w$ must be not a member of w, and must therefore not have the property ϕ, since w consists of all terms having the property ϕ. In the special case of the ordinals, our two alternatives are: (1) the ordinals do not form a class; (2) although they form a class, they have no ordinal number. The second alternative is equivalent to the assumption that either the whole series of ordinals is not well ordered, or, if it is well ordered, the dual property 'α and β are ordinal numbers, and α is less than β' is non-predicative; so that the series as a whole has no definite type, i.e. no ordinal number. The supposition that the whole series of ordinals is not well ordered can be disproved[1]; hence we are left with the alternatives that either (1) the property 'x is an ordinal number' is non-predicative, or (2), though 'x is an ordinal number' is predicative, 'x and y are ordinal numbers and x is less than y' is non-predicative.

We have seen that Burali-Forti's contradiction is a particular case of the following.

'Given a property ϕ and a function f, such that, if ϕ belongs to all the members of u, $f'u$ always exists, has the property ϕ, and is not a member of u; then the supposition that there is a class w of all terms having the property ϕ and that $f'w$ exists leads to the conclusion that $f'w$ both has and has not the property ϕ.'

This generalisation is important, because it covers all the contradictions that have hitherto emerged in this subject. In the case of the class of terms which are not members of themselves, we put 'x is not a member of x' for $\phi!x$, and u itself for

---

[1] This supposition can be disproved (by the generalised form of induction which applies throughout any well-ordered series) by means of the theorem that every segment of the series of ordinals is well ordered. It is not disproved by Jourdain's theorem, that every series which is not well ordered must contain a part of type $*\omega$; for this theorem depends upon Zermelo's axiom, of which the truth is doubtful.

$f`u$. In this case, owing to the fact that $f`u$ is u itself, we have only one possibility: namely, that 'x is not a member of x' is non-predicative. In other cases, we have two possibilities, and it may often be difficult to decide which of them to choose.

When we have a pair such as ϕ and f above, we can define, in terms of f alone, without introducing ϕ, a series ordinally similar to that of all ordinals, and obtain, as regards this series, a contradiction analogous to Burali-Forti's, provided f satisfies certain conditions. We do this as follows. Taking any class x, for which $f`x$ exists, take $f`x$ as the first term of our series, take the f of the class got by adding $f`x$ to x as the second term, and so on. Generally, the successor of any term is the f of the class consisting of that term together with all its predecessors and x, and the successor of a class u of terms having no maximum is the f of the class consisting of the whole segment defined by the class u. This gives Cantor's two principles of formation, and we can define the property of occurring in this series by the generalised form of induction.[1] We may then, subject to certain conditions as to f, substitute for ϕ the property of occurring in the f-series starting from x. If f has the property that, if u is composed of terms of the above series, then $f`u$ exists and is not a member of $u$, it will follow that the whole series does not form a class; for, if it did, its $f$ would both be and not be a member of the series. In the particular case of the ordinals, if $u$ is a class of ordinals, $f`u$ is their immediate successor; the whole series of ordinals can be generated by the above method, starting from o. In the case of 'x is not an x', $f`x$ is x itself: if we start from any class which is not a member of itself, and proceed by the above method, we obtain a series, like the series of all ordinals,[2] consisting entirely of classes which are not members of themselves, and the series as a whole does not form a class.

---

[1] This is done as follows: A property is *inductive* in the f-series if whenever it belongs to a class u it belongs to the class got by reading $f`u$ to u, and whenever it belongs to each of a set of classes it belongs to their logical sum, i.e. to the class of members of members of the set. A term belongs to the 'f-series starting from x' if it possesses every property which is possessed by x and is inductive in the f-series.

[2] I owe the proof that this series is well ordered and ordinally similar to the series of all ordinals to Mr G. G. Berry, of the Bodleian Library.

The above considerations point to the conclusion that the contradictions result from the fact that, according to current logical assumptions, there are what we may call *self-reproductive* processes and classes. That is, there are some properties such that, given any class of terms all having such a property, we can always define a new term also having the property in question. Hence we can never collect *all* the terms having the said property into a whole; because, whenever we hope we have them all, the collection which we have immediately proceeds to generate a new term also having the said property. It is probable, in view of the above general form for all known contradictions, that, if ϕ is any demonstrably non-predicative property, we can actually construct a series, ordinally similar to the series of all ordinals, composed entirely of terms having the property ϕ. Hence, if the terms satisfying ϕ can be arranged in a series ordinally similar to a segment of the series of ordinals, it follows that no contradiction results from assuming that ϕ is a predicative property. But this proposition is of very little use, until we know how far the series of ordinals goes; and at present it is not easy to see where this series begins to be non-existent, if such a bull may be permitted.

II

We have now seen the nature of the contradictions which beset the theory of the transfinite: we have seen that they are not an isolated few, but can be manufactured in any required number by a recipe; we have seen that all of them belong to a certain type, and we have seen that none of them are essentially arithmetical, but all belong to logic, and are to be solved, therefore, by some change in current logical assumptions. I propose, in this section, to consider three different directions in which such a change may be attempted. I shall endeavour to set forth the advantages and disadvantages of each of the three without *deciding* in favour of any one of them.

What is demonstrated by the contradictions we have considered is broadly this: 'A propositional function of one variable does not always determine a class.'[1]

In view of this fact, it is open to us, *prima facie*, to adopt one or other of two theories. We may decide that all ordinary straightforward propositional functions of one variable determine classes, and that what is needed is some principle by which we can exclude the complicated cases in which there is no class. In this view, the state of things is like that in the differential calculus, where every common place continuous function has a derivative, and only rather complicated and recondite functions have to be excluded. The other theory which suggests itself is that there are no such things as classes and relations and functions as entities, and that the habit of talking of them is merely a convenient abbreviation.

The first of these two theories itself divides into two, according as we hold that what classes have to avoid is excessive size, or a certain characteristic which we may call zigzagginess. Of these, the second is the more conservative, i.e. it preserves more of the theory of the transfinite than the first. Both preserve more of it than does the theory that there are no such things as classes. I shall consider these three theories in the following order, and by the following names:

(*a*) The zigzag theory.
(*b*) The theory of limitation of size.
(*c*) The no classes theory.

(*a*) *The Zigzag Theory*

Each of the three theories can be recommended as plausible by the help of certain *a priori* logical considerations. In the zigzag theory, we start from the suggestion that propositional functions determine classes when they are fairly simple, and only fail

---

[1] Here it is to be understood that the arguments which show that there is not always a class also show that there is not always a separable entity which is the propositional function (as opposed to its value); also that some propositional functions of two variables do not determine a relation either in intension or in extension, if we mean by a relation a separable entity which can be considered apart from related terms.

to do so when they are complicated and recondite. If this is the case, it cannot be bigness that makes a class go wrong; for such propositional functions as 'x is not a man' have an exemplary simplicity, and are yet satisfied by all but a finite number of entities. In this theory, as well as in the theory of limitation of size, we define a *predicative* propositional function as one which determines a class (or a relation, if it contains two variables); thus in the zigzag theory the negation of a predicative function is always predicative. In other words, given any class, u, all the terms which are not members of u form a class which may be called the class not-u.

If now $\phi!x$ is a non-predicative function, it follows that, given any class u, there must either be members of u for which $\phi!x$ is false, or members of not-u for which $\phi!x$ is true. (For, if not, $\phi!x$ would be true when, and only when, c is a member of u; so that $\phi!x$ would be predicative.) It thus appears that $\theta!x$ fails to be predicative just as much by the terms it does not include as by the terms it does. Again, given any class u, the property $\phi!x$ belongs either to some, but not all, of the members of u, or to some, but not all, of the members of not-u. This is the zigzag property which gives its name to the theory we are considering. This theory is specially suggested by the argument of Cantor's proof that there is no greatest cardinal. This proof, as we have already seen, constructs a would-be class w by the norm 'x is not a member of the class with which it is correlated by the relation R', where R is a relation which correlates individuals with classes. Such would-be classes, as we saw, are very apt to be not classes, and they all have a certain zigzag quality, in the fact that x is a w when x is not a member of its correlate, and is not a w when x is a member of its correlate.

The full development of this theory requires axioms as to the kinds of functions that are predicative. It has the great advantage that it admits as predicative all functions which can be stated simply, and only excludes such complicated cases as might well be supposed to have strange properties.[1]

---

[1] For suggestions of a solution more or less on the above lines, see Russell *B* 1903*a*, §§103, 104.

THEORY OF TRANSFINITE NUMBERS AND ORDER TYPES

The principal objection to this theory, so far as it is at present developed, is that the axioms as to what functions are predicative have to be exceedingly complicated, and cannot be recommended by any intrinsic plausibility. This is a defect which might be remedied by greater ingenuity, or by the help of some hitherto unnoticed distinction. But hitherto, in attempting to set up axioms for this theory, I have found no guiding principle except the avoidance of contradictions; and this, by itself, is a very insufficient principle, since it leaves us always exposed to the risk that further deductions will elicit contradictions. The general postulate, that predicative propositional functions must have a certain simplicity, does not lend itself readily to the decision whether this or that, propositional function has the requisite degree of simplicity. Nevertheless, since these difficulties are all such as further research might conceivably remove, the theory is not to be rejected wholly, but is rather to be retained as one of those that are possible. Speaking broadly, one may say that it applies better to cardinal than to ordinal contradictions: it deals more readily with such difficulties as that of the class of classes which are not members of themselves than with such difficulties as that of Burali-Forti.

The zigzag theory, in some form or other, is that assumed in the definitions of cardinal and ordinal numbers as classes of classes (if numbers are supposed to be entities). For all these classes of classes, if they are legitimate, must contain as many members as there are entities altogether; hence, if bigness makes classes go wrong, as we suppose in the 'limitation of size' theory, cardinals and ordinals so defined will be illegitimate classes. Dr Hobson has various criticisms on these definitions of cardinals and ordinals; but on the zigzag theory his criticisms can, I think, be all satisfactorily met.

Dr Hobson says[1]: 'It has been seen that the assumptions that an ordered aggregate possesses a definite order type and a definite cardinal number, which can be treated as objects, lead to the contradiction pointed out by Burali-Forti.' This statement seems

---

[1] P. 176, beginning of No. 5.

to me somewhat too sweeping. It is quite open to us to hold every ordered aggregate possesses a definite cardinal number, and that every ordered aggregate which is ordinally similar to a segment of the ordinals in order of magnitude possesses a definite ordinal number. All that Burali-Forti's contradiction forces us to admit is that there is no *maximum* ordinal, i.e. that the function 'α and β are ordinal numbers, and α is less than β' and all other functions ordinally similar to this one are non-predicative. In the same way the difficulty of the greatest cardinal is met by denying that the defining functions of Cantor's omitted classes are predicative in certain cases. Thus we conclude that in this theory there is a greatest cardinal, but there is no greatest ordinal: in each case contradictions are avoided by regarding certain functions as not predicative.

Dr Hobson distinguishes two methods of establishing the existence of a class of mathematical entities: the genetic method and the method by postulation. He rejects the former, as regards cardinals and ordinals; but he seems not to perceive that this can only be done by recognising that there may be no class even where there is a perfectly definite *norm*. From his No. 2 one would suppose that he regards the *norm* as a sufficient condition for the class; yet, later on, he refuses to admit classes which are defined by unimpeachable *norms*. It seems hardly correct to say, as he does: 'In the genetic method, as applied to the construction of the whole series of ordinal members, this notion of correspondence plays no part' (No. 6, p. 177). It is the notion of correspondence which defines the class of relations constituting an ordinal number; this class consists of all the relations which are *like*[1] a certain given relation. 'The existence of a number,' he truly says, 'is constantly inferred from that of a single unique ordered aggregate' (p. 177). But there can be no objection to this procedure, unless on the ground that, when P is given, 'Q is like P' is not predicative in respect of Q.

It is, of course, very easy to prove, when we have one series

[1] I use *like* to mean *ordinally similar to*. For the precise definition cf. Russell *B* 1903*a*, §253.

of a certain type, that there are an infinite number of series of the same type. To do this we need only substitute other terms for the terms of our series. Suppose, e.g. our series is composed of numbers. We may substitute Socrates for any terms of our series; this will give as many new series of the same type as there are terms in the given series. If our series is infinite, we can obtain $\aleph_0$ series of the same type by merely knocking off terms at the beginning; and so on. Thus, if multiplicity of series of a given type is desired, there is no difficulty in obtaining as many series of the given type as there are entities altogether, i.e. the maximum cardinal number of series of the given type. (For, instead of Socrates, we may substitute any other form not occurring in our series.) Thus it is not the case that the genetic method involves 'the setting up of a scale of standards, to which standards no aggregates not consisting of the preceding numbers conform' (No. 6, p. 179), though I do not see what harm there would be if this were the case.

The same remark applies to the criticism (No. 7, p. 179) of the definition of a cardinal as a class of similar classes.[1] It is very easy to show that the number of classes similar to the class of numbers from 0 to n is as great as the total number of entities; and, even if no other class were similar to this class, that would not, so far as I can see, constitute any objection. The number $n+1$ would, in that case, be the class whose only member is the class of numbers from 0 to n.

Dr Hobson explains that his opinion and mine are at variance as to the definition of cardinals because I, unlike him, 'regard the activities of the mind as irrelevant in questions of existence of entities' (No. 7, p. 180). This is a philosophical difference, and, like all philosophical differences, it ought not to be allowed to effect the detail of mathematics, but only the interpretation. Mathematics would be in a bad way if it could not proceed until the dispute between idealism and realism has been settled. When a new entity is introduced, Dr Hobson regards the entity as *created* by the activity of the mind, while I regard

[1] This definition is due to Frege. See Frege *A* 1884, pp. 79, 85.

it as merely *discerned*; but this difference of interpretation can hardly affect the question whether the introduction of the entity is legitimate or not, which is the only question with which mathematics, as opposed to philosophy, is concerned.

There is another passage in No. 7 (p. 179) which calls for explanations, namely the following:

'Russell objects to the conception of a number as the common characteristic of a family of equivalent aggregates on the ground that there is no reason to think that such a single entity exists with which the aggregates have a special relation, but that there may be many such entities. The mind does, however, in point of fact, in the case of finite aggregates at least, recognise the existence of such single entity, the number of the aggregates; and this is a valid result of our mental activity, subject to the law of contradiction.'

In the first place, it is not merely the case that 'there *may* be many such entities', but that there demonstrably are as many as there are entities altogether. Given any many–one relation having the property that when, and only when, u and v are similar classes, there is an entity α to which both u and v have the relation S, the converse domain of S (i.e. the terms to which classes have the relation S) will have all the formal properties of cardinal numbers.[1] Now, if there is one such relation as S, it is very easy to prove that there are as many as there are entities altogether; and, if there is no such relation as S, then there are no such entities as cardinal numbers. (There might be cardinal numbers for some classes and not for others, if there was a relation such as S which had some classes in its domain, but no relation such as S which had *all* classes in its domain.)

The supposition that there is no such relation as S is disproved by the fact that the relation of a class to the class of all classes similar to it has the properties we wish S to have. This

---

[1] For a development of this point of view see §2 of Russell *B* 1901*b*.

disproof is rejected by Dr Hobson, since he considers that it involves improper classes. His position seems to be that, at least in the case of finite aggregates, 'the mind' immediately recognises a certain relation of the sort required. The simplest formal statement of this point of view is, roughly, as follows:

In beginning cardinal arithmetic we introduce a new indefinable S, concerning which we lay down the indemonstrable properties[1]:

1. S is a many–one relation;
2. Every finite class (and, presumably, some infinite classes) have the relation S to some term;
3. When, and only when, two finite classes (and, presumably, some pairs of infinite classes) are similar they both have the relation S to the same term;
4. Things which are not classes do not have the relation S to anything.

The reason that S has to be indefinable and the above propositions indemonstrable is that, if we regard the above propositions as giving a definition of S 'by postulates', they do not determine S, since an infinite number of relations (if any) fulfil the above conditions, and every entity will, for a suitable S, be the cardinal number (in respect of that S) of some class which has a cardinal number. Moreover, the recognition by 'the mind', which Dr Hobson speaks of, is precisely the process of introducing an indefinable. It is a process of which, in certain cases, I fully recognise the validity and the necessity; but indefinables and indemonstrables are to be diminished in number as much as possible.[2] Moreover, in the case supposed, where Dr Hobson says that 'the mind' recognises such entities, I am unable to agree: if he said 'my mind', I should have taken his word for it; but personally, I do not perceive such entities as cardinal numbers, unless as classes of similar classes.

---

[1] It is probably possible to simplify the statement of these indemonstrables.
[2] This is merely the truism with which Dedekind begins 'Was sind und was sollen die Zahlen', namely: 'Was beweisbar ist, soll in der Wissenschaft nicht ohne Beweis geglaubt werden.'

(b) *The Theory of Limitation of Size*

This theory is naturally suggested by the consideration of Burali-Forti's contradiction, as well as by certain general arguments tending to show that there is not (as in the zigzag theory) such a thing as the class of all entities. This theory naturally becomes particularised into the theory that a proper class must always be capable of being arranged in a well-ordered series ordinally similar to a segment of the series of ordinals in order of magnitude; this particular limitation being chosen so as to avoid Burali-Forti's contradiction.[1] We still have the distinction of predicative and non-predicative functions; but the test of predicativeness is no longer simplicity of form, but is a certain limitation of size. In this theory, if u is a class, 'x is not a member of u' is always non-predicative; thus there is no such class as not u.

The reasons recommending this view are, roughly, the following: We saw, in the first part of this paper, that there are a number of processes, of which the generation of ordinals is one, which seem essentially incapable of terminating, although each process is such that the class of all terms generated by it (or a function of this class) ought to be the last term generated by that process. Thus it is natural to suppose that the terms generated by such a process do not form a class. And, if so, it seems also natural to suppose that any aggregate embracing all the terms generated by one of these processes cannot form a class. Consequently there will be (so to speak) a certain limit of size which no class can reach; and any supposed class which reaches or surpasses this limit is an improper class, i.e. is a non-entity. The existence of self-reproductive processes of this kind seems to make the notion of a totality of all entities an impossible one; and this tends to discredit the zigzag theory, which admits the class of all entities as a valid class.

This theory has, at first sight, a great plausibility and sim-

---

[1] This view has been advocated in Jourdain *A* 1904*a*; also Jourdain *A* 1905.

plicity, and I am not prepared to deny that it is the true solution. But the plausibility and simplicity tend rather to disappear on examination.

Let us first recall the generalisations of Burali-Forti's contradiction which we obtained in the first part of this paper. The fundamental proposition is: 'Given a property ϕ and a function f such that, if ϕ belongs to all the members of any class u, then $f'u$ always exists and has the property ϕ, but is not a member of u, it follows that either ϕ is non-predicative or, if ϕ is predicative and determines the class w, then $f'w$ does not exist.'

The theory of limitation of size neglects the second alternative (that $f'w$ may not exist), and decides for the first (that ϕ is not predicative). Thus, in the case of the series of ordinals, the second alternative is that the whole series of ordinals has no ordinal number, which is equivalent to denying the predicativeness of 'α and β are ordinal numbers, and α is less than β'. The adoption of this alternative would enable us to hold that all ordinals do form a class, and yet there is no greatest ordinal. But the theory in question rejects this alternative, and decides that the ordinals do not form a class. The only case in which this is the only alternative is when $f'u$ is u itself; otherwise we always have a choice.

A great difficulty of this theory is that it does not tell us how far up the series of ordinals it is legitimate to go. It might happen that ω was already illegitimate: in that case all proper classes would be finite. For, in that case, a series ordinally similar to a segment of the series of ordinals would necessarily be a finite series. Or it might happen that ω^2 was illegitimate, or ω^ω or ω_1 or any other ordinal having no immediate predecessor. We need further axioms before we can tell where the series begins to be illegitimate. For, in order that an ordinal α may be legitimate, it is necessary that the propositional function 'β and γ are ordinal numbers less than α, and β less than γ' should be predicative. (Here, of course, 'less than α' must be replaced by some property not involving α, but such that, if α is legitimate, the property is equivalent to being less than α.)

But our general principle does not tell us under what circumstances such a function is predicative.

It is no doubt intended by those who advocate this theory that all ordinals should be admitted which can be defined, so to speak, from below, i.e. without introducing the notion of the whole series of ordinals. Thus they would admit all Cantor's ordinals, and they would only avoid admitting the maximum ordinal. But it is not easy to see how to state such a limitation precisely: at least, I have not succeeded in doing so. The merits of this theory, therefore, would seem to be less than they at first appear to be.

(c) *The No Classes Theory*

In this theory classes and relations are banished altogether.[1] It is not necessary to the theory to assume that no functions determine classes and relations; all that is essential to the theory is to abstain from assuming the opposite. This is the strong point of the theory we are now to consider: the theory is constituted merely by abstinence from a doubtful assumption, and thus whatever of mathematics it permits us to obtain is indubitable in a way which anything involving classes or relations cannot be. The objections to the theory are (1) that it seems obvious to common sense that there are classes; (2) that a great part of Cantor's theory of the transfinite, including much that it is hard to doubt, is, so far as can be seen, invalid if there are no classes or relations; (3) that the working out of the theory is very complicated, and is on this account likely to contain errors, the removal of which would, for aught we know, render the theory inadequate to yield the results even of elementary arithmetic.

To explain fully how this theory is to be developed would take too much space. Some of its main points may, however, be briefly set forth.

[1] It must be understood that the postulate of the existence of classes and relations is exposed to the same arguments, *pro* and *con.*, as the existence of propositional functions as separable entities distinct from all their values. Thus, in the theory we are considering, anything said about a propositional function is to be regarded as a mere abbreviation for a statement about some or all of its values.

Instead of a function $\phi!x$, where the notation inevitably suggests the existence of something denoted by 'ϕ', we proceed as follows: Let p be any proposition, and a a constituent of p. (We may say broadly that a is a constituent of p if a is mentioned in stating p.) Then let '$p(x/a)$' denote what p becomes when x is substituted for a in the place or places where a occurs in p. For different values of x this will give us what we have been accustomed to call different values of a propositional function. In place of ϕ we have now two variables, p and a: in respect to the different values of $p(x/a)$, we may call p the prototype and a the *origin* or *initial subject*. (For a may be taken as being, in a generalised sense, the subject of p.) Consider now such a statement as '$p(x/a)$ is true for all values of x'. Let b be an entity which is not a constituent of p, and put $q = p(b/a)$; then '$q(x/b)$ is true for all values of x' is equivalent to '$p(x/a)$ is true for all values of x'. Thus, subject to a certain reservation, the statement '$p(x/a)$ is true for all values of x' is independent of the initial subject a, and thus may be said to depend only upon the *form of p*.[1] Statements of this sort replace what would otherwise be statements having propositional functions for their arguments. For example, instead of 'ϕ is a unit function' (i.e. 'There is one, and only one, x for which $\phi!x$ is true'), we shall have 'There is an entity b such that $p(x/a)$ is true when, and only when, x is identical with b'. There will not now be any such entity as the number 1 in isolation; but we shall be able to define what we mean by 'One, and only one, proposition of the type $p(x/a)$ (for a given p and a) is true'. Instead of saying 'The class u is a class which has only one member', we shall say (as above) 'There is an entity b such that $p(x/a)$ is true when, and only when, x is identical with b'. Here the values of x for which $p(x/a)$ is true replace the class u; but we do not assume that these values collectively form a single entity which is the class composed of them.

[1] The reservation is merely that the initial subject must not occur in the prototype except in the places which we wish to be variable. For example, if our prototype is '$3 > 2$', and our initial subject is 3, the substitution of x for 3 gives '$x > 2$'. But, if we now take 2 as our initial subject, so that our prototype is '$2 > 2$', the substitution of x gives '$x > x$', which is not the propositional function we want.

There is not much difficulty in re-wording most definitions so as to fit in with the new point of view. But now the existence theorems become hard to prove. We can manufacture enough different propositions to show what is now equivalent to the existence of ω and $\aleph_0$, though the process is cumbrous and artificial. We shall be able, by continuing a similar process, to prove the existence of various transfinite ordinal types. But we shall not be able to prove the existence of *all* the usual ordinal types. I do not know at what point the series begins to be non-existent; but I cannot at present, in this method, prove the existence of ω_1 or $\aleph_1$, which must therefore be considered for the moment as undemonstrated.

I hope in future to work out this theory to the point where it will appear exactly how much of mathematics it preserves, and how much it forces us to abandon. It seems fairly clear that ordinary arithmetic, analysis, and geometry, and indeed, whatever does not involve the later transfinite numbers, can be stated, though in a roundabout and difficult way, without the use of classes and relations as independent entities. A certain amount, also, of transfinite arithmetic can be preserved; but it is not easy to discover how much. The theory is safe, but drastic; and, if, in fact, there are classes and relations, it is unnecessarily difficult and complicated. For the present, therefor, it may be accepted as one way of avoiding contradictions, though not necessarily *the* way.

III

I come now to the second of our difficulties, namely, the doubt as to the truth of Zermelo's axiom. This is dealt with by Dr Hobson in his Nos. 10 and 11, with which I find myself in complete agreement.[1]

All that I wish to do is to state the question in various forms,

---

[1] Though I do not agree with his special criticism of Mr G. H. Hardy in No. 12, according to which the second figure in Mr Hardy's sequences 'would have indefinitely great values for all numbers β of the second class, and thus that for sufficiently great ordinal numbers of the second class the corresponding sequences can have no existence'.

and to point out some of its bearings. I shall assume the existence of classes and relations, for the sake of simplicity of statement. The difficulty is of a different kind, and is more easily apprehended by this form of statement.

Zermelo's axiom asserts the possibility of picking out one from each of the classes contained in a given class (excepting the null-class). It has hitherto been commonly assumed by mathematicians, and Zermelo has the merit of explicitly mentioning the assumption. The axiom may be stated as follows: 'Given any class w, there is a function $f'u$ such that, if u is an existent[1] class contained in w, then $f'u$ is a member of u.' That is, the axiom asserts that we can find some rule by which to pick out one term from each existent class contained in w. The axiom may also be stated: 'Given a set k of all existent classes contained in a certain class w, there is a many–one relation R, whose domain is k, which is such that, if u is a member of k, the term to which u has the relation R is a member of u.' The axiom can be stated in a form which does not involve classes, functions, or relations, but I shall not give this form of statement, as its complication makes it almost unintelligible.

A simple illustration may serve to show the nature of the difficulty as regards this axiom, and to introduce the analogous 'multiplicative axiom'. Given $\aleph_0$ pairs of boots, let it be required to prove that the number of boots is even. This will be the case if all the boots can be divided into two classes which are mutually similar. If now each pair has the right and left boots different, we need only put all the right boots in one class, and all the left boots in another: the class of right boots is similar to the class of left boots, and our problem is solved. But, if the right and left boots in each pair are indistinguishable, we cannot discover any property belonging to exactly half the boots. Hence we cannot divide the boots into two equal parts, and we cannot prove that the number of them is even. If the number of pairs were finite, we could simply choose one out of each pair; but we cannot choose one out of each of an

---

[1] An *existent* class is a class having at least one member.

CLASSES AND THE PARADOXES

infinite number of pairs unless we have a *rule* of choice, and in the present case no rule can be found.

The problem involved in the above illustration raises grave difficulties in regard to many elementary theorems about multiplication of cardinals. Multiplication has been defined as follows by Mr A. N. Whitehead[1]:

Let k be a set of classes no two of which have any common terms. Then we define the 'multiplicative class of k' (denoted by $\times\,'k$) as the class formed by picking one and only one term out of each class belonging to k, and doing this in all possible ways. That is, one member of $\times\,'k$ is a class consisting of one member of each class belonging to k. Then the number of terms in $\times\,'k$ is defined to be the product of the numbers of the various classes belonging to k. This definition is perfectly satisfactory when the number of classes which are members of k is finite, and also when each class which is a member of k has some peculiar term (for example, if each is given as a well-ordered series, and we can pick out the first term). But in other cases it is not obvious that there is any rule by which we can pick out just one term of each member of k, and therefore it is not obvious that $\times\,'k$ has any members at all. Hence, as far as the definition shows, the product of an infinite number of factors none of which is zero might be zero. Thus, in the case of the boots, we wished to pick out one boot from each pair, but we could find no rule by which this was to be done.

What is required is not that we should actually be able to pick out one term from each class which is a member of k, but that there should be (whether we can specify it or not) at least one class composed of one term from each member of k. If there is one, there must be many, unless all the members of k are unit classes; for, given one such class, if u is a member of k, and x is the member of u which is picked out, we can substitute for x any other member of u – say y – and we still have a member of $\times\,'k$. Thus the axiom we need may be stated: 'Given a mutually exclusive set of classes k, no one of which is

---

[1] Russell *B* 1902b.

null, there is at least one class composed of one term out of each member of k.'

This axiom is more special than Zermelo's axiom. It can be deduced from Zermelo's axiom; but the converse deduction, though it may turn out to be possible, has not yet, so far as I know, been effected. I shall call this the *multiplicative* axiom.

The multiplicative axiom has been employed constantly in proofs of theorems concerning transfinite numbers. It is open to everybody, as yet, to accept it as a self-evident truth, but it remains possible that it may turn out to be capable of disproof by *reductio ad absurdum*. It may also, of course, be capable of proof, but that is far less probable. A class of classes of which this axiom holds may conveniently be called a *multipliable* class of classes.

The above axiom is required for identifying the two definitions of the finite. We may define a finite cardinal number

(*a*) as a cardinal number which obeys mathematical induction starting from 0;

(*b*) as a cardinal number such that any class which has that number contains no part similar to itself.

We will for the present call any number of the kind (*a*) an *inductive* number, and any number of the kind (*b*) a *finite* number. Then it is easy to prove that all inductive numbers are finite; that every class whose number is infinite contains a part whose number is $\aleph_0$ (where $\aleph_0$ is defined as the number of inductive numbers), and *vice versa*; and that, if the number of classes contained in a finite class is always finite, then all finite numbers are inductive numbers. But, so far as I know, we cannot prove that the number of classes contained in a finite class is always finite, or that every finite number is an inductive number.[1]

---

[1] Burali-Forti has shown that the two definitions of the finite can be identified if we assume the following axiom: 'If u is any class of existent classes, the number of members of u is less than or equal to the number of members of members of u.' (Burali-Forti *A* 1896.) This axiom leads at once to the result that the number of classes contained in a finite class must be finite, whence the conclusion follows, as above indicated. The axiom as its stands is untrue: it is necessary to assume that the classes are mutually exclusive, or something analogous. Whether it will then give the desired result I do not know.

The multiplicative axiom is also required for proving that the number of terms in α sets of β terms is $\alpha \times \beta$, i.e. for connecting addition and multiplication. We cannot even prove, without this axiom, that the number of terms in α sets of β terms is always the same. Similarly, we cannot prove that the product of α factors each equal to β is βa (taking Cantor's definition of exponentiation),[1] or even that it is always the same number.

And in the case of the $\aleph_0$ pairs of boots we cannot prove that the number of boots is $\aleph_0$ (i.e. $\aleph_0 + \aleph_0$), except in the case where we can distinguish right and left boots.

The existence of $\times\,`k$ can be proved whenever any method exists of picking out one term from each member of $k$. If, for example, all terms which are members of members of $k$ belong to some one well-ordered series, we get a member of $\times\,`k$ by picking out the first terms of the various members of k (k being assumed to be a set of mutually exclusive existent classes). It does not follow that $\times\,`k$ exists when every member of k can be well ordered: for there will always be many ways of well ordering each member of k, and we need some rule for picking out one, in each case, of the various possible ways of well ordering each member. That is, we need a term of the multiplicative class of the class of which a single member is the class of relations by which a single member of k is well ordered.

If k is any set of mutually exclusive existent classes, and if we form another class k' by substituting for every member u of k the class (u') of all existent classes contained in u, then k' is a set of mutually exclusive existent classes, and $\times\,`k'$ exists, since $k$ is a member of $\times\,`k'$ (because each u is a member of its u').

Assuming that k is a set of mutually exclusive existent classes, there are certain cases in which the existence of $\times\,`k$ can be proved, because there is some structure which enables us to pick out particular terms from members of k. Such, for example, is the following case: Suppose there is some one–many relation P, such that each term of k consists of all the terms to which some term of the domain of P has the relation P, and suppose further that every term of the domain of P has the relation P to itself:

[1] Cantor *A* 1895, Section 4.

then the domain of P is a member of the multiplicative class of k.

If k is a set of mutually exclusive existent classes, $\times`k$ exists when, and only when, there is a one–one relation $S$ whose domain is $k$, and which relates each class $u$, belonging to $k$, to a member of $u$; for, when this condition is satisfied, the converse domain of $S$ is a member of $\times`k$; and given a term of $\times`k$, the relation of members of $k$ to the corresponding members of the given term of $\times`k$ is an S fulfilling the above conditions. Another way of stating the same thing is that $\times`k$ exists when, and only when, there is some function $f`u$ such that, if u is a member of k, $f`u$ is a member of $u$; for the $f$'s of the various members of $k$ make up a term of $k$. A *sufficient* condition for the existence of $\times`k$ whenever k is a set of mutually exclusive existent classes is that there should exist a function $f`u$ such that, if $u$ is any existent class, $f`u$ is a member of u. This is equivalent to Zermelo's axiom,[1] and it is not, so far as I know, a *necessary* condition for the existence of $\times`k$ in all such cases.

Zermelo's axiom is a generalised form of the multiplicative axiom, and is interesting because he has shown[2] that, if it is true, then every class can be well ordered. Since it is doubtful whether all classes obey Zermelo's axiom, we may define a Zermelo class as one which does obey the axiom; that is, w is a Zermelo class if there is at least one many–one relation R such that the domain of R consists of all existent classes contained in w, and if u has the relation R to x, then x is a member of u. That is, a class w is a Zermelo class if there is a method of correlating each existent class contained in w with one of its members. Zermelo proves that any class w for which this holds can be well ordered. The converse is obvious; for, if w is well ordered, we correlate each existent class u, contained in w, with the first term of u, which gives a relation R satisfying the above conditions. Hence Zermelo's axiom holds of those classes which can be well ordered, and of no others.

[1] Assuming that there is a class of all entities. But, if there is no such class, we only have to adopt the statement of Zermelo's axiom which does not assume that there are classes.
[2] Zermelo *A* 1904.

By applying his axiom to the class of all entities, we find that, if it holds universally, there must be a function $f'u$ such that, if u is any existent class, then $f'u$ is a member of u. Conversely, if there is such a function, Zermelo's axiom is obviously always satisfied. Hence, if there is a class of all entities, his axiom is equivalent to: 'There is a function $f'u$ such that, if u is any existent class, $f'u$ is a member of u.'

I think that Zermelo's axiom, applied in its functional form, and without the assumption that there are classes or relations, leads to the result that any propositional function only satisfied by terms of one type is such that all the terms satisfying it can be well ordered. If it should appear, on other grounds, that this is not always true, it would follow that Zermelo's axiom, in its functional form, is false. Whether or not it is true in the form in which it applies only to classes is a question which requires for its answer a previous decision as to what propositional functions are predicative: the more we restrict the notion of *class* the more likely this form of Zermelo's axiom is to be true, and the less information it gives us. To discover the conditions subject to which Zermelo's axiom and the multiplicative axiom hold would be a very important contribution to mathematics and logic, and ought not to be beyond the powers of mathematicians.

It is easy to see that, if w is any Zermelo class, and k is a set of mutually exclusive existent classes which between them contain all the terms w and no more, then k is a multipliable class of classes. For every member of k is an existent class contained in w; hence, if we pick out one term from each existent class contained in w, we incidentally pick out one term from each member of k. Thus the universal truth of Zermelo's axiom involves the universal truth of the multiplicative axiom. The converse, so far as I know, has not been proved, and may or may not be true.

It should be observed that, both in the case of Zermelo's axiom and in that of the multiplicative axiom, what we are primarily in doubt about is the existence of a norm or property such as will pick out one term from each of our aggregates; the doubt as to the existence of a *class* which will make this selection is derivative from the doubt as to the existence of a norm.

The problem concerned in such cases is like that of the 'lawless' decimal, which reduces to the problem of the 'lawless' class of finite integers. If we consider all the classes that can be formed of finite integers, it seems at first sight obvious that many will consist of a perfectly haphazard collection, not definable by any formula. But this is open to doubt. It would seem that, as Dr Hobson urges, an infinite aggregate requires a norm, and that such haphazard collections as seem conceivable are really non-entities. In the case of Cantor's 'proof' that there are more classes of finite numbers than there are finite numbers, it is shown that no one denumerable set of formulae will cover all classes of finite numbers; but the class shown to be left over in each case is defined by a formula in the process of showing that it is left over. Thus this process gives no ground for thinking that there are classes of finite numbers which are not definable by a formula.

To sum up: there are two analogous axioms – Zermelo's and the multiplicative axiom – which have been habitually employed by mathematicians in reasonings about the transfinite, but which, most likely, are not true without some restriction. Without them, we cannot, so far as at present appears, identify the two definitions of the finite, or establish the usual relations of addition, multiplication, and exponentiation. If Zermelo's axiom were true, every class would be well ordered, and also, I think, every aggregate of terms possessing some property. But in this respect the problem considered in our second part is dependent upon that considered in our first part.

The general position advocated in the foregoing paper may be briefly stated as follows.

When we say that a number of objects all have a certain property, we naturally suppose that the property is a definite object, which can be considered apart from any or all of the objects which have, or may be supposed to have, the property in question. We also naturally suppose that the objects which have the property form a *class*, and that the class is in some sense a new single entity, distinct, in general, from each member of the class. Both these natural suppositions can be proved, by arguments so short and simple that they scarcely admit a possibility of error, to be at any rate not *universally* true. We may, in view of this fact, adopt one of two courses: we may either decide that the assumptions in question are *always* false, or endeavour to find conditions subject to which they are true, these conditions being such as to exclude the cases where the falsehood of the assumptions can be proved. The latter course has the advantage of being more consistent with common sense, and of preserving more of Cantor's work; but it has, as yet, the disadvantage of great uncertainty and artificiality in detail, owing to the absence of any broad principle by which to decide as to which functions are predicative. The former course, in practice, merely involves abstaining from the doubtful assumptions, and does not commit us to the view that they are false; it is therefore, so long as any doubt subsists, the prudent plan to pursue the former course as far as possible. It appears on examination that, without supposing either of the suspected assumptions to be *ever* true, we can construct ordinary mathematics and most of the theory of the transfinite; and in this development we meet with no contradictions, so far as is known at present. Whether it is possible to rescue more of Cantor's work must probably remain doubtful until the fundamental logical notions employed are more thoroughly understood. And whether, in particular, Zermelo's axiom is true or false is a question which, while more fundamental matters are in doubt, is very likely to remain unanswered. The complete solution of our difficulties, we may surmise, is more likely to come from clearer notions in logic than from the technical advance of mathematics; but until the solution is found we cannot be sure how much of mathematics it will leave intact.

[*Note added 5th February 1906*. From further investigation I now feel hardly any doubt that the no-classes theory affords the complete solution of all the difficulties stated in the first section of this paper.]

8

On the Substitutional Theory of Classes and Relations

Received by the London Mathematical Society on 24 April 1906, and read before the Society on 10 May 1906. First publication by permission of the Bertrand Russell Archives, McMaster University.

The purpose of this paper is to explain what I believe to be the solution of the contradictions discovered by Burali-Forti and myself. I have discussed these contradictions, and given a brief sketch of the proposed solution, in a previous paper read before this society.[1] In the present paper, I shall endeavour to show more in detail how the contradictions are avoided, and how the elementary notions of mathematics are to be expressed according to the theory I wish to advocate.

The fundamental logical principle from which the theory starts is one which few people would deny. It is that, in any sentence, a single word, or a single component phrase, may often be quite devoid of meaning when separated from its context. In such a case, if the word or phrase is wrongly assumed to have an independent meaning, we get what may be called a 'false abstraction', and paradoxes and contradictions are apt to result. A simple case will illustrate what I mean.[2] If I say 'Socrates is bald', the word *Socrates* stands for a definite entity, to which I ascribe the property of baldness. But if I say 'the present King of France is bald', the phrase 'the present King of France' does not stand for anything and yet my statement has a perfectly definite meaning. Thus we cannot analyse the statement into 'the present King of France' (subject) and 'is bald' (predicate). What the statement really means seems to be 'one and only one man at present governs France, and that

---

[1] [The paper was 'On Some Difficulties in the Theory of Transfinite Numbers and Order Types', Russell *B* 1906*a*, reprinted in this volume, Chapter 7.]

[2] Cf. 'On Denoting', Russell *B* 1905*c*, and Chapter 5 in this volume.

one is bald'. This statement is false, but not meaningless. Now by parity of form, if I had said 'the present King of England is bald', the same analysis would have had to be made. Thus 'the present King of England', like 'the present King of France', has no meaning by itself, but only as part of a proposition.

The theory which I wish to advocate is that classes,[1] relations, numbers, and indeed almost all the things that mathematics deals with, are 'false abstractions', in the sense in which 'the present King of England', or 'the present King of France' is a false abstraction. Thus e.g. the question 'what is the number *one*?' will have no answer; the question which has an answer is 'what is the meaning of a statement in which the word *one* occurs?' And even this question only has an answer when the word occurs in a proper context. In this respect, 'the number one' is even more shadowy than 'the present King of England'; for every possible statement about a real entity remains significant if made about the present King of England, whereas only certain kinds of statements can be significantly made about the number one. 'The number one is bald' or 'the number one is fond of cream cheese' are, I maintain, not merely silly remarks, but totally devoid of meaning. In fact, all the statements about the number one that strike one as nonsensical are nonsensical in the strictest sense of the word, that is, they are phrases which do not express propositions at all. The same thing holds, on the theory in question, concerning all classes and relations. Thus such a statement as 'the class of human beings is a human being' will not be false, but meaningless, and it is equally meaningless to say 'the class of human beings is not a human being'. The reason is, that there are really no such things as classes, and statements apparently about a class will only be significant when they can be analysed into statements about all or some of the members of the class. Language which speaks about classes is, in fact, merely a form of short-hand, and becomes illegitimate as soon as it is incapable of translation into language which says nothing about classes.

---

[1] I use the word *class* as synonymous with *aggregate* or *manifold*.

SUBSTITUTIONAL THEORY OF CLASSES AND RELATIONS

In this general theory there is no novelty.[1] What, however, had always, until lately, kept me from adopting this view was that I saw no way, in detail, of stating the elementary propositions of arithmetic without the use of classes; and it seemed plain that a philosophy of mathematics must give some meaning to 'two and two are four'. Such a meaning *is* given by the substitutional theory of classes; and thus it now becomes possible to carry out in practice the policy of treating classes as mere linguistic fictions. But in order to explain this theory, it is necessary to go through a certain amount of preliminary logic.

The first point that has to be explained is the difference between *determination* and *substitution*. *Determination* consists in assigning a constant as the value of a variable; *substitution* consists in replacing one constant by another. *Determination* is required in answering such questions as 'What is the value of x^2+x+2 when $x=3$?' or 'what proposition results from "if x is a man, x is a mortal" by putting $x=$ Socrates?' *Substitution* is required if we say 'Plato was a philosopher whose sympathies were with the aristocratic party; and the same is true of Socrates', or '2 is an even prime, and this is not the case with any other number'. When we say 'the same' is true of Socrates, we mean that the proposition which results from substituting Socrates for Plato is true; when we say '*this* is not the case with any other number', we mean that if for 2 we substitute any other number in the proposition '2 is an even prime', the result is a false proposition. In both these cases, we might have started from a 'propositional function', and have compared two *determinations*: in the first case, 'x was a philosopher whose sympathies were with the aristocratic party' is true when $x=$ Plato and when $x=$ Socrates; in the second case, 'x is an even prime' is true when $x=2$ and not otherwise. Thus determination and substitution generally lead to the same result, and for this reason they are, as a rule, not clearly distinguished. But there

---

[1] It, or something very like it, has been advocated, for example, by Professor Maxime Bôcher. It is hinted at in 'The Fundamental Conceptions and Methods of Mathematics', Bôcher *A* 1904, and in private correspondence he has developed the view more fully.

are many cases in which they lead to different results, and it is then important not to confound them.

A simple instance of the difference between determination and substitution is afforded by the function '$x=a$', considered as a function of x. This is only true for the determination a; that is, if we give the value a to x, the resulting value of the function is true and not otherwise. But if we take this value ($a=a$) and substitute b for a, we get $b=b$, which is also true, but is not a value of $x=a$. Thus although $a=a$ is a determination (or value – the two words are synonyms) of $x=a$, yet none of the other determinations of $x=a$ can be got by substituting for a in $a=a$. From this case we may generalise: if ϕx is any propositional function, the result of substituting b for a in ϕa will usually be ϕb, but will not be ϕb if a occurs in ϕa otherwise than as each x occurs in its ϕx. For in that case, this other occurrence of a also will be replaced by b, whereas ϕb, as a rule, will still contain this occurrence of a. Thus from '$a=a$' by substitution we can obtain any value of the function '$x=x$', but we cannot obtain any value of the function '$x=a$' except '$a=a$' itself. Hence substitution is liable to limitation from which determination is exempt. There is, however, as we shall see later, a very important limitations to which determination is subject, but from which substitution is exempt.

We need some definitions before proceeding further. I use $p(x/a)!q$ or $p/a;x!q$ to mean 'q results from p by substituting x for a in all those places (if any) where a occurs in p'.[1] It is convenient to think of p (and therefore q) as a proposition, but this is not essential; all that is essential is that p should be the name of a genuine entity, and not a mere phrase like 'the King of France' or 'the King of England'. It results from the definition that if a does not occur in p at all, q will be the same as p. We may take this as the definition of 'not occurring in p', which we will write 'a ex p'. This is to hold, by definition, when, whatever x we take, the result of substituting x for a in p is p. If ϕx is any propositional function, we put

$(x).\phi x: = .\phi x$ is true for all values of x.

[1] The above two notations are both useful for different lines of development.

Thus '$(x).p(x/a)\,!p$' means 'for all values of x, the result of substituting x for a in p is p'. Hence our definition is

$$a \text{ ex } p. =: (x).p(x/a)\,!p \quad \text{Df}^1.$$

We then define 'a does occur in p', which we write 'a in p', as the negation of 'a ex p'. That is, 'a in p' holds if we can find an x such that the substitution of x for a alters p. We indicate the negation of a proposition q by the symbol $\sim q$; thus

$$\sim q. =. q \text{ is false.}$$

Thus we have

$$a \text{ in } p. =. \sim \{a \text{ ex } p\} \quad \text{Df.}$$

Another cognate notion which we need is that of *independence*: we say that p is independent of q when p and q have no common constituents, i.e. when there is no x which is in p and in q. This we write 'p ind q'; thus

$$p \text{ ind } q. =. (x). \sim (x \text{ in } p . x \text{ in } q) \quad \text{Df.}$$

that is 'p is independent of q' means 'for all values of x, it is false that x is both in p and in q'.

We can define identity by means of substitution: we shall say that x is identical with y if the result of substituting y for x in x is x. We may write this '$x=y$', thus

$$x=y. =. x(y/x)\,!x \quad \text{Df.}$$

It is obvious that the result of replacing x by y is y; thus it can only be x if x and y are identical; this justifies the definition. (We assume that the result of a substitution is always unique.) The q which satisfies $p(x/a)\,!q$ we write $p(x/a)$ or $p/a\text{;}x$. Thus

$$p(x/a) \text{ or } p/a\text{;}x. =. \text{ the result of substituting}$$
$$x \text{ for } a \text{ in } p \quad \text{Df}$$

In $p(x/a)$, we call (x/a) a *substitution*; in $p/a\text{;}x$, we call p/a a *matrix*. Both may be extended to any finite number of variables; we can substitute x and y for a and b, which gives us the

---

[1] The dots stand for brackets, as in Peano: a larger number of dots stands for an outside bracket.

CLASSES AND THE PARADOXES

substitution $(x,y)/(a, b)$ and the matrix $p/(a, b)$. These notions can be defined, though the definition is rather complicated; the definition of double substitution will be given presently. It is to be observed that a substitution or a matrix is not an entity, but a mere operation like d/dx; that is to say, the symbols x/a and p/a are wholly devoid of meaning by themselves and only become significant as parts of appropriate propositions.

The theory which I wish to advocate is that this shadowy symbol p/a represents a *class*. Similarly, $p/(a, b)$ will represent a dual (dyadic) relation, $p/(a, b, c)$ will represent a triple (triadic) relation, and so on. None of these are entities, and thus there are no such things as classes and relations.

Since absolutely everything there is is an entity, it may be asked what is the meaning of saying that a matrix is not an entity. When we say 'so-and-so is not an entity', the meaning is, properly speaking, 'The *phrase "so-and-so"* is not the name of an entity'. Thus when we say a matrix is not an entity, we mean that a matrix is a set of symbols, or a phrase, which by itself has no meaning at all, but by the addition of other symbols or words becomes part of a symbol or phrase which has meaning, i.e. is the name of something. Thus the matrix p/a is a symbol for the phrase 'the result of replacing a in p by', which is incomplete and meaningless; in order to acquire a meaning, we must add the name of the entity which is to replace a.[1] Similarly, $p/(a, b)$ stands for 'the result of simultaneously replacing a and b in p by'. Thus 'x is a member of the class p/a' is to be interpreted as 'the result of replacing a in p by x is true'. Here the phrase represented by p/a occurs as part of the whole sentence, but is obviously not a part which has an independent meaning of its own. Thus a matrix is part of a sentence, but is not a part which means anything in isolation. Thus it is not the name of an entity, but is a mere part of symbols which are the names of entities.

To show the grounds of the matrix theory, it will be necessary

---

[1] Strictly speaking, the phrase only becomes significant when we make a statement about the result of the substitution; but this point does not concern us at present.

SUBSTITUTIONAL THEORY OF CLASSES AND RELATIONS

first to explain briefly Frege's theory of classes,[1] which I formerly accepted, and then to give in outline the reasons for rejecting this theory.

The gist of Frege's theory is as follows. Whatever a class may be, it seems obvious that any propositional function ϕx determines a class, namely the class of objects satisfying ϕx. Thus 'x is human' defines the class of human beings, 'x is an even prime' defines the class whose only member is 2, and so on. We can then (so it would seem) define what we mean by 'x is a member of the class u', or 'x is a u' as we may say more shortly. This will mean: 'There is some function ϕ which defines the class u and is satisfied by x.' We then need an assumption to the effect that two functions define the same class when they are equivalent, i.e. such that for any value of x both are true or both false. Thus 'x is human' and 'x is featherless and two-legged' will define the same class. From this basis the whole theory of classes can be developed.

But if we assume, as Frege does, that the class is an entity, we cannot well escape the contradiction about the class of classes which are not members of themselves. For it is essential to an entity that it is a possible determination of x in any propositional function ϕx; that is, if ϕx is any propositional function, and a any entity, ϕa must be a significant proposition. Now if a class is an entity, 'x is a u' will be a propositional function of u; hence, 'x is an x' must be significant. But if 'x is an x' is significant, the best hope of avoiding the contradiction is extinguished.

The point where, as it seems to me, the above definition of 'x is a u' is faulty, is that it speaks of 'a function ϕ' without any argument. Now a function, as Frege himself has rightly urged, is nothing at all without some argument; hence, we can never say, of any formula containing a variable function, that it holds 'for some value of ϕ' or 'for all values of ϕ', because there is no such thing as ϕ and therefore there are no 'values of ϕ'. By the help of matrices, as I shall show, one can almost always express what is substantially the same thing as a formula asserted 'for all values of ϕ', but there are certain limiting cases where

[1] Frege *A* 1893.

CLASSES AND THE PARADOXES

matrices will not do this, and these cases are precisely those that lead to contradictions. We cannot, in the above, replace 'some value of ϕ' by 'some value of ϕz'; for here, if ϕ and z are both variable, 'some value of ϕz' is equivalent to 'some value of y', where y may be any *entity*; but if z is fixed, 'some value of ϕz' means 'something containing z'; and neither of these are the least what is required for the definition of 'x is a u'.

With the theory of matrices, on the contrary, all these difficulties are avoided. If p is ϕa, $p/a\mathbin{;}x$ is in general ϕx (i.e. if there is a value of x for which a is out of ϕx).[1] Thus $p/a\mathbin{;}x$ will, for most purposes, replace ϕx, and instead of 'all values of ϕ' we shall speak of 'all value of p and a'. Thus instead of one variable function ϕ, we shall have two variable entities, p and a. Any two entities p and a define a class, namely p/a, and x is a member of this class if $p/a\mathbin{;}x$ is true. (If p does not contain a, the class contains everything if p is true, and nothing if p is false.) To say that x is a member of the class α is now to say that for some values of p and a, α is the matrix p/a and $p/a\mathbin{;}x$ is true. Here, instead of the variable function ϕ, which could not be detached from its argument, we have the two variables p and a, which are entities, and may be varied. But now 'x is an x' becomes meaningless, because 'x is an α' requires that α should be of the form p/a, and thus not an entity at all. In this way membership of a class can be defined,[2] and at the same time the contradiction is avoided.

There is still an analogue to 'the class determined by ϕ', which is obtained as follows. If x is such as to be, for some value of y, out of ϕy, $(\phi x)/x\mathbin{;}z$ is ϕz, for any value of z. It follows that, for all x's satisfying this condition, $(\phi x)/x\mathbin{;}z$ has the same value, namely ϕz. Hence the class $(\phi x)/x$ has the same members as the class $(\phi x')/x'$, if x' is another term satisfying the above condition; the members in each case are the values of z for which ϕz is true. Thus we may define as 'the class determined by ϕ'

---

[1] [Russell introduces the phrase 'out of' without explanation. Apparently 'a ex p' is read 'a out of p'.]

[2] It should be observed that if 'x is a u' is taken as indefinable, as in Peano's system, the contradiction becomes still harder to avoid, since it becomes very difficult to set up any rule for excluding 'x is an x'.

SUBSTITUTIONAL THEORY OF CLASSES AND RELATIONS

the common value[1] of all the matrices $(\phi x)/x$ so long as x is, for some value of y, out of ϕy.

If we apply the above remarks to a concrete case, such as 'Plato is a man', or 'Plato is a member of the class of men', we must start from some proposition p not of the form 'x is a u'. Let us take 'Socrates is human' as p, and 'Socrates' as a. Then x belongs to the class p/a if, when x is substituted for Socrates in 'Socrates is human', the result is a true proposition. Thus if we define the class of men as the class p/a, we find that Plato is a man, because p/a؛Plato.=.Plato is human, which is a true proposition. If we start from the propositional function 'x is human', then the matrix $(x \text{ is human})/x$ will give the class of men, for any value of x which is independent of *humanity*, i.e. for any value of x except a concept containing a constituent also to be found in *humanity*. Thus, in particular, x may be any man or animal, or a particle of matter, or a point of space, or anything such that, when y is substituted for x in 'x is human', the result is 'y is human'.

In dealing with two variables, there is need of a rather complicated definition of 'simultaneous substitution', in order to effect the substitution of (say) x for a and y for b as if a and b were independent even in the cases when they are not so. For example, consider 'p/a؛x is true for all values of x', which is a function of p and a. We want to substitute p' and a' so that this becomes 'p'/a'؛x is true for all values of x'. But if p contains a, the substitution of a' for a will alter p, so that in general p will be not a constituent of the result. Hence there is no p left for which to substitute p'. This difficulty is avoided by the help of an auxiliary entity chosen so as to be independent of p and a. Thus the result of the 'simultaneous substitution' of x and y for a and b in p, which is denoted by $p(x,y)/(a,b)$ or $p/(a,b)$؛(x,y) is defined as follows: If b is in a, choose an entity u which is not in p, and is independent of b and y; substitute first u for a, then y for b, and last x for u; the result is $p(x,y)/(a,b)$. But if b is not

---

[1] Two matrices p/a and p'/a' are *defined* as having the same value when, for every x, p/a؛x and p'/a'؛x are both true or both false. In this case we write $p/a = p'/a'$. Equality in this sense is what occurs in mathematical equations, except in exceptional uses of the sign of equality.

in a, choose an entity u which is not in p, and is independent of a and x; substitute first u for b, then x for a, and last y for u; the result is $p(x, y)/(a, b)$. The object of this complicated definition is to secure that as often as possible the result of substituting x and y for a and b in $\phi(a, b)$ shall be $\phi(x, y)$.

A matrix of the form $p/(a, b)$ is a dual or dyadic relation. If we take any proposition containing two entities a and b, and imagine other entities x and y substituted for a and b, then if the result is true, x and y are said to have to each other the same relation as is asserted between a and b in asserting p. (It must be understood that this is a loose way of speaking, because in fact there are no such entities as relations.) Thus let a be Philip and b be Alexander, and let p be 'Philip is the father of Alexander'. Then $p/(a, b)\,;(x, y)$ is 'x is the father of y', which is true when and only when x has to y the relation of paternity, which is the relation that p affirms as subsisting between a and b. Thus the matrix $p/(a, b)$ may be taken as representing the relation of paternity. In this case also, exactly as in the case of one variable, we can define a matrix generated by any function $\phi(x, y)$, which will be the relation determined by the function $\phi(x, y)$, and will be the value of $\phi(x, y)/(x, y)$ except for exceptional values of x and y.

It should be observed that the relations identified with dual matrices are (approximately) relations in *extension*. If we say 'x begat y', the word *begat* expresses the same relation in *intension* as was expressed in extension by our matrix $p/(a, b)$. The drawback to relations in intension, from the standpoint of symbolic logic, is that not all propositional functions of two variables correspond to relations in intension, just as not all propositional functions of one variable correspond to predicates. Such a proposition as 'If Philip had not prepared the way, Alexander's conquests would have been impossible' cannot without distortion be put into a form which asserts a relation in intension between Philip and Alexander: but it gives rise to a matrix, which may be taken as the relation in extension. Relations in intension are of the utmost importance to philosophy and philosophical logic, since they are essential to complexity, and

SUBSTITUTIONAL THEORY OF CLASSES AND RELATIONS

thence to propositions, and thence to the possibility of truth or falsehood. But in symbolic logic, it is best to start with propositions as our data; what is prior to propositions is not yet, so far as I know, amenable to symbolic treatment, and it may even be doubted whether it will ever be amenable.

Although a matrix is more akin to a class or relation in *extension* than in *intension*, it is not quite extensional; for even if p/a and p'/a' define the same class, they can still be distinguished if p is different from p' or a from a'. Thus the theory here advocated is intermediate between that of intension and that of extension.

The next point to be considered is the definitions of classes of classes. This is particularly important because *cardinal numbers* are classes of classes. Before going into the general case, let us define the cardinals 0 and 1 by way of example.

Consider such a proposition as 'there are no snakes in Ireland'. This is equivalent to 'For all values of x, it is false that x is a snake in Ireland'. If we write p for 'Socrates is a snake in Ireland' and a for Socrates, the class p/a has no members, which is otherwise expressed by saying that the number of members of p/a is 0. Thus to say 'the number of members of the class p/a is 0' is equivalent to saying 'for all values of x, $p/a;x$ is false'. This statement contains p and a; let us call it q. Then 0 may be defined as the matrix $q/(p, a)$. For suppose p', a' have the relation $q/(p, a)$, i.e. suppose $q/(p, a);(p', a')$ is true. Effecting the substitution, we see that this states 'for all values of x, $p'/a';x$ is false', which states that p'/a' is a class which has no members, i.e. whose number is 0. Thus 0 is the value of the matrix $\{(x).\sim(p/a);x\}/(p, a)$ for all except certain exceptional values of p and a; it is, in fact, the matrix determined by the function $(x).\sim(p/a);x$. According to this definition, 0 is a relation between a proposition and an entity, namely the relation that, whatever we may substitute for the entity in the proposition, the result is always false.[1]

---

[1] It is not *necessary* that p should be a proposition: if p is any entity other than a proposition, and a is any entity other than p, $p/a;x$ will never be true, and thus p/a is null. But it is usually convenient to imagine p a proposition.

All the cardinal numbers are relations of the same sort. Consider the number 1. If p/a has just one member, then, if c is that member, $p/a\dot{}c$ is true, and $p/a\dot{}x$ is false if x is not identical with c. Thus 'p/a is a unit class' is equivalent to 'there is a c such that $p/a\dot{}x$ is true when and only when x is identical with c'; in other words, 'It is not false for all values of c that, for all values of x, $p/a\dot{}x$ is equivalent[1] to "x is identical with c".' This is a function of p and a; the value of the matrix determined by this function is the number 1.

It is obvious from the above two examples how any finite cardinal is to be defined. But we must now return to the general case of a class of classes. A class of classes, as appears from the above instances of 0 and 1, is a particular kind of dual relation, namely, the kind defined by a function of p and a, when p and a appear only in the form p/a. This, however, is not quite suitable for a formal definition. The formal definition is as follows: 'The matrix $q/(p, a)$ is called a *class of classes* if, for all values of r, c, r', c', provided $r/c = r'/c'$, then $q/(p, a)\dot{}(r, c)$ is equivalent to $q/(p, a)\dot{}(r', c')$.' For in this case the truth or falsehood of $q/(p, a)\dot{}(r, c)$ does not depend on r and c separately, but only upon the value of the matrix r/c. In such a case, we say that the class r/c is a member of the class of classes $q/(p, a)$ when $q/(p, a)\dot{}(r, c)$ is true. Thus in the above case of the definition of 0, we put $a =$ Socrates, $p = \sim$ Socrates is a snake in Ireland, $q. =: (x) . \sim (p/a)\dot{}x$. Then $q/(p, a)\dot{}(r, c) . =: (x) . \sim (r/c)\dot{}x$, i.e. '$r/c\dot{}x$ is false for all values of x'. If now $r'/c' = r/c$, i.e. if $r'/c'\dot{}x$ is always equivalent to $r/c\dot{}x$, it follows that if $r/c\dot{}x$ is always false, so is $r'/c'\dot{}x$; that is, if $q/(p, a)\dot{}(r, c)$ is true, so is $q/(p, a)\dot{}(r', c')$. Thus $q/(p, a)$ is a class of classes according to the definition, and thus 0 is a class of classes.

Exactly as classes of classes were defined, we can go on to define classes of classes of classes, which will be kind of triple (or triadic) relations. Similarly a dual relation between classes, such as similarity for example, will be a particular kind of quadruple (or tetradic) relation, and so on. A matrix of the form p/a is called of the first *type*; one of the form $p/(a, b)$ is

---

[1] Two propositions are called *equivalent* when they are both true or both false.

called of the second type, and so on. We shall be able to define substitution of a matrix for a matrix, so that we shall get such matrices as $q/(p/a)$, meaning 'the result of replacing p/a in q by'. Thus e.g. if q is 'x is a member of p/a', $q/(p/a) \cdot (p'/a')$ will be 'x is a member of p'/a''. This sort of matrix gives rise to classes of classes; it is merely a sub-division of matrices of the second type. It is sometimes not obvious at once what the type of a matrix is. Consider for example the ordinal number of a series of entities. This is a class of relations of entities, which will be defined by a matrix of the form $q/\{p/(a, b)\}$, which is a matrix of the third type. Suppose now we have a series of such ordinals; what will be the type of its ordinal number? This is a class of relations between such ordinals. Each ordinal is of the third type; hence a relation of two of them is of the sixth type, and a class of such relations is of the seventh type. Thus the ordinal number of a series of ordinals applicable to series of entities is a matrix of the seventh type.

Although it is easy to explain what we mean by a type, yet it is not strictly possible to define what we mean by a type, or to make any general statement about types, because statements which are significant for one type are in general not significant for another. Thus for example one might suppose that there would be $\aleph_0$ types, but this statement seems to be really devoid of meaning.

When a formula contains matrices, the test of whether it is significant or not is very simple: it is significant if it can be stated wholly in terms of entities. Matrices are nothing but verbal or symbolic abbreviations; hence any statement in which they occur must, if it is to be a significant statement and not a mere jumble, be capable of being stated without matrices. Thus for example '$p/a = q/b$' means: 'Whatever x may be, if x is substituted for a in p and for b in q, the results are equivalent.' Here nothing but entities occur. But if we try to interpret (say) '$p/a = q/(b, c)$', we find, on supplying x, that we have a proposition on the left and a matrix on the right.[1] Thus on the right

---

[1] In words, what we obtain by supplying x is 'the result of replacing a in p by x is identical with the result of replacing b in q by x and c in q by', which is nonsense.

another argument has to be supplied, but on the left there is no longer room for an argument. Hence the proposed formula is meaningless. (It is not *false*: its denial is just as meaningless as its affirmation.) Thus where matrices occur, significance demands homogeneity of type: this does not need to be stated as a principle, but results in each case from the necessity of getting rid of matrices in order to find out what the proposition really means.

By means of the ascending series of types and the requirement of homogeneity, the difficulties concerning the maximum cardinal and the maximum ordinal are both avoided. In each type, there is a maximum cardinal and a maximum ordinal; but both can always be surpassed in a higher type. And as there is no maximum type and no meaning in the totality of types, there is no absolute maximum either of cardinals or of ordinals. We have hitherto only defined the cardinal numbers of classes of entities; we must now define cardinals of higher types.

We say that the class p/a is a *member* of the matrix $q/(p_0, a_0)$ if not only $q/(p_0, a_0):(p, a)$ is true, but also, whenever $p'/a' = p/a$, then $q/(p_0, a_0):(p', a')$ is true. If $q/(p_0, a_0)$ has no members, in this sense, then, provided it is a class of classes, the number of its members is o_1, where o_1 means the class-zero, as distinguished from the entity-zero. Similarly, if there is a matrix p/a such that when and only when $p'/a' = p/a$, $q/(p_0, a_0):(p', a')$ is true, then the number of members of $q/(p_0, a_0)$ is 1_1, where 1_1 is the class-one, as opposed to the entity-one. Similarly we define o_2, 1_2, and so on. There is thus a whole hierarchy of o's or of 1's, applicable to matrices of different types. All the o's, or all the 1's, have definitions which are closely analogous in point of form, but they cannot be amalgamated, because each has its own conditions of significance.

We can, however, define what we mean by saying that two cardinals of different specified types are equal, or that one is greater than the other. For given a class of terms of a certain type, we can define a one–one relation of the terms of the said class to the terms of a class of the same or any other specified type, and thus we can define what we mean by saying that

SUBSTITUTIONAL THEORY OF CLASSES AND RELATIONS

classes of different types are similar. If we know the existence of a class of α terms of a certain type, we can prove the existence of a class of an equal number of terms of any higher type, but not, in general, of a class of an equal number of terms of a lower type. Consider now the theorem which gives rise to the difficulty concerning the greatest cardinal. This theorem asserts that, whatever cardinal α may be, 2^α is greater than α. It follows that there can be no greatest cardinal, although the cardinal number of *all* entities might seem, *prima facie*, to be as great as could reasonably be expected. We can see now, however, that in higher types we *shall* get greater cardinals than the cardinal number of all entities, and that $2^\alpha > \alpha$ is true without exception. The simplest definition of 2^α is as the cardinal number of classes contained in a class which has α members; Cantor has a definition according to which it is the number of many–one relations of a certain sort, which is equivalent but less simple. Whatever definition we adopt, the class whose number is defined as 2^α will always be of higher type than the class whose number is given as α. If we take the definition of 2^α as the number of classes contained in a class which has α members, then 2^α applies to a class of the next type above that to which α applies. Thus if α is the total number of entities, 2^α will be the total number of classes of entities: $2^\alpha > \alpha$ will be true, but there will be no class of *entities* having 2^α terms. Similarly 2^{2^α} will be the number of classes of classes of entities; and so on. We cannot take all these types together and ask 'what is the total number of objects, entities, matrices, and all?' For the comparison of a number in one type with a number in another is made according to a separate definition for each pair of types, and cannot be generalised. A series of numbers running through a *finite* number of types can be compared, because we can compare all the others with the highest of the types concerned; but if there is no highest type among those concerned, the comparison becomes impossible.

Thus the solution of the problem concerning the greatest cardinal lies simply in the fact that a class is not an entity, so that classes are not (as was supposed) a sub-class of entities.

Any two entities p, a define a class p/a; but a pair of entities is not one entity, and the number of pairs of entities may therefore, without the slightest contradiction, be greater than the number of entities.

The difficulties as regards ordinals are rather more complicated, and require a longer discussion; but the solution is closely analogous to the solution for cardinals.

The self-reproductive method of generating the series of ordinals assumes that, given any segment of this series, the ordinal number of the segment can be added at the end of the segment so as to give a new series whose ordinal number exceeds by 1 that of the given segment. This process, as is well-known, leads to Burali-Forti's contradiction to the effect that there is a maximum ordinal, which can nevertheless be increased by adding 1 to it. There is also another difficulty, not so serious, yet worth considering. The total number of objects definable in terms of a given finite set of fundamental terms is $\aleph_0$ [1]; hence if more than $\aleph_0$ ordinals can be defined we have a contradiction. But if not, there must be somewhere in the second class of ordinals a least indefinable ordinal; yet this ordinal might seem to be defined as the limit of the class of definable ordinals.

These two difficulties are, I think, satisfactorily met by the substitutional theory of classes and relations, as I shall try to show.

The method of generating ordinals by adding the ordinal number of a series to the series as an additional term at the end is vitiated by the fact that the ordinal number of a series is of a different logical *type* from the terms of the series. If the terms of the series are entities, the ordinal number of the series is a class of dual relations of entities. I shall call an ordinal of this sort an *entity*-ordinal, because it applies to series of entities. Similarly one which applies to series of classes will be called a *class*-ordinal, and so on. An ordinal number applicable to a series of entity-ordinals will very often have to be spoken of: I shall call

---

[1] This has been denied by Dr Hobson, but I shall try to show that there is reason to distrust his denial.

SUBSTITUTIONAL THEORY OF CLASSES AND RELATIONS

it an *ordinal*-ordinal. An ordinal number applicable to a series of ordinal-ordinals will be called an ordinal-ordinal-ordinal. If α is any logical type, an α-ordinal is never of type α, but is always a class of dual relations between terms of type α, and is thus of type $2\alpha + 1$. Hence, whatever type the terms of a series of ordinals may belong to, we can never form a new series by adding the ordinal number of the series at the end.

The question thus has to be asked afresh: What existence-theorems can be proved concerning ordinals? And first of all, what existence-theorems can we prove for *entity*-ordinals?

We can go a good way up the series of ordinals by a genetic method almost exactly like the method which has turned out fallacious. Let R be any dual entity-relation and a any entity; then we will call $R + a$ the relation which holds between x and y when either x and y have the relation R or x belongs to the field of R and y is a. That is, if R generates a series, $R + a$ generates the same series with a added at the end. To get a self-reproductive process, let a be taken to be the proposition bRc, where b and c are any constants. Put for R_1, a relation which only holds between b and c so that

$$xR_1 y \text{ is equivalent to } x = b . y = c.$$

Put $R_2 = R_1 + (bR_1 c)$ and generally $R_{n+1} = R_n + (bR_n c)$. It is easy to show that these relations are all different. R_n generates a series of entities which has the ordinal number n; hence all finite entity-ordinals exist.

We now define R_ω as a relation which holds between x and y whenever any one of the relations R_n holds. This is done by the use of induction as follows:

$xR_\omega y$ means: 'There is a relation Q between x and y such that, if s is any class of relations, then if R_1 is a member of s, and if, whenever R is a member of s, $R + (bRc)$ is also a member of s, then Q is a member of s.'

We then go on as before: $R_{\omega+1} = R_\omega + (aR_\omega b)$ and so on. $R_{\omega \cdot 2}$ is obtained from R_ω, $R_{\omega+1}$ etc., just as R_ω was obtained from R_1, R_2, etc. R_{ω^2} is similarly obtained from R, $R_{\cdot 2}$, $R_{\cdot 3}$, etc. In this way we can obtain every ordinal number of the second class that ever has been obtained. But we cannot in this way define the whole of the second class, nor, when it has been otherwise defined, can we show that every member of it can be obtained by such processes. On the contrary, we shall see reason to think that, though all ordinals of the second class exist as entity-ordinals, they cannot all be *defined* by means of the apparatus at our disposal.

The ordinal numbers of the second class may be defined as all those that are applicable to a denumerable set of terms. That is, given a class α of $\aleph_0$ terms, the ordinals of the second class are all ordinal numbers y such that there are series composed of the terms of α and having y as the ordinal number of their terms. The cardinal number of such ordinals is defined as $\aleph_1$. Observe that $\aleph_1$, as thus defined, is an ordinal-cardinal, i.e. the cardinal number of a class of ordinals. Its existence as an ordinal-cardinal results from the above definition, but its existence as an entity-cardinal remains in doubt, i.e. we have no reason to suppose that there is any class of $\aleph_1$ *entities*. It might be supposed that, given a class of matrices, we could always manufacture a class of propositions (which would be a class of entities) having the same cardinal number. But it is by no means always possible to do this. One might, for example, take the proposition $o = \alpha$ for all values of α in the given class. But there would be difficulties in proving that whenever $\alpha \neq \beta$, $o = \alpha$ is different from $o = \beta$. Hence we cannot be sure that there are as many different propositions of the form $o = \alpha$ as there are values of α. In this way inferences from a higher to a lower type are in general precarious, though inferences from a lower to a higher type are always possible.

Having now got a definition of all ordinals of the second class, the question arises whether they form a well-ordered series when arranged in order of magnitude. If so, their ordinal number when so arranged is ω_1, the first ordinal of the third class. I think it must be held demonstrable that they are a well-ordered series. The argument is Cantor's argument for proving, from the properties of segments, that of any two different

SUBSTITUTIONAL THEORY OF CLASSES AND RELATIONS

ordinal numbers, one must be the greater and the other the less.[1] This argument is long and intricate, but so far as I can discover, there is nothing in it that is affected by adopting the substitutional theory. Hence we are led to the existence of ω_1 as an ordinal-ordinal and of $\aleph_1$ as an ordinal-cardinal.

We can now proceed to prove the existence of ω_2 and $\aleph_2$ as an ordinal-ordinal-ordinal and an ordinal-ordinal-cardinal respectively. In this way we can obtain ω_n and $\aleph_n$ for any finite value of n. But we cannot, in this way, get beyond finite values of n, because the logical type is raised at each step, and there is no meaning in a type which is not of a finite degree.

We thus have the following results: There are series of entities having any ordinal of the second class; there are series of entity-ordinals having any ordinal of the third class; there are series of ordinal-ordinals having any ordinal of the fourth class; and so on; with corresponding propositions as regards the Aleph-cardinals. We have not found a proof or disproof of the existence of ω_1 or any subsequent ordinal as an *entity*-ordinal, nor of $\aleph_1$ and subsequent Alephs as entity-cardinals. But we have seen enough to know what must be the solution of Burali-Forti's contradiction.

This solution is as follows. If we arrange all the entity-ordinals in order of magnitude, they form a well-ordered series, which has an ordinal-ordinal. This ordinal-ordinal is greater than any entity-ordinal, and is the first that has this property. There is no contradiction in this, since it cannot be shown that there is any general method of manufacturing entity-series ordinally similar to given series of ordinals. If we again arrange all the ordinal-ordinals in order of magnitude, they form a well-ordered series having an ordinal-ordinal-ordinal, which is the first that is greater than any ordinal-ordinal; and so on. As far as appears from the above, it may be that ω_1 is the ordinal-ordinal of all entity-ordinals, ω_2 the ordinal-ordinal-ordinal of all ordinal-ordinals, and so on. But this is at present a mere possibility. The whole solution lies in

---
[1] Cf. Cantor *A* 1897 and also my article on well-ordered series, Russell *B* 1902*c*.

the fact that the ordinal number of a series is always of higher type than its members.

It remains to consider the question of the number of definables. The first proposition to be established here is that, given any finite set of fundamental terms, the number of definables cannot exceed $\aleph_0$. What is virtually this proposition has been maintained by Konig[1] and A. C. Dixon[2] and denied by Dr Hobson.[3] Dr Hobson's denial rests upon the fact that mathematics employs *variables* in addition to its fixed undefined notions. But this fact does not, to my mind, in any way affect the question. Whenever a variable occurs, we only have a definition if something is said about 'all values' or about 'some value or values'. The latter may be eliminated from our consideration, since the assertion that ϕx is true for some value or values of x is equivalent to the denial that ϕx is false for all values of x. Thus in any definable proposition of mathematics, if x occurs, the statement made is the assertion or denial of some proposition of the form 'ϕx is true for all values of x'. And no definable proposition contains more than a finite number of variables. So long as we do not take all values of x, or assign to x some value previously defined, our proposition is not definable. For example, we can define the proposition '$x = x$ for all values of x'. But the proposition 'Socrates = Socrates' cannot be defined in pure mathematics, since *Socrates* is not definable in terms of our apparatus of fundamental notions. The proposition '$1 = 1$' can be defined, because 1 is a constant which is mathematically definable. But if we assign to x any value except one of those that can be defined in mathematical terms, the proposition '$x = x$' is not definable in the sense concerned.

A definition, symbolically, consists of a certain finite number of marks. Such marks must be either the symbols of our undefined fundamental terms, or brackets, or letters standing for variables of which all values are to be taken.[4] In a definition containing n marks, there cannot certainly be more than n

---

[1] Konig *A* 1905*b*.   [2] Dixon *A* 1906.   [3] Hobson *A* 1906.
[4] I suppose each definition written out in full, i.e. without the use of any previous definition.

brackets, nor more than n variables. If the number of fundamental notions is c, the number of definitions containing n marks is therefore certainly not greater than the number of permutations of $2n+c$ things taken n at a time. This number is finite; the sum of all such numbers for different finite values of n is $\aleph_0$. Hence the total number of possible definitions, and therefore the total number of definable terms, cannot exceed $\aleph_0$.

Now the cardinal number of ordinals of the second class exceeds $\aleph_0$; hence some of these must be indefinable, and among those that are indefinable there must be a least. But this ordinal *seems* to be defined as 'the immediate successor of the ordinals that are definable'. At first sight this looks like a contradiction, but in fact it is not. For although every individual number less than this one is definable, the whole class of them is not definable. It *seems* to be defined as 'the class of definable ordinals'; but *definable* is relative to some given set of fundamental notions, and if we call this set of fundamental notions I, 'definable in terms of I' is never itself definable in terms of I. This may be regarded as proved by the above paradox; it is soon seen to be probable, apart from the paradox, when we try to find a definition. It is easy to define 'definable in terms of I' by means of a larger apparatus I'; but then 'definable in terms of I'' will require a still larger apparatus I'' for its definition, and so on. Or we may take 'definable in terms of I' as itself part of our apparatus, so that we shall now have an apparatus J consisting of I together with 'definable in terms of I'. In terms of this apparatus J, 'the least ordinal not definable in terms of I' is definable, but 'the least ordinal not definable in terms of J' is not definable. Thus the paradox of the least indefinable ordinal is only apparent.

I conclude, then, that, given any finite number of fundamental notions, only a selection of the ordinals of the second class consists of definable ordinals, while the others cannot be defined without enlarging our apparatus. This is just what appears when we set to work to define as many ordinals of the second class as possible. The only way of defining a particular entity-ordinal of the second class is to find a way of generating some series of entities having the given ordinal number of terms. Taking as an illustration the series of relations considered above, in which we put $R_{n+1} = R_n + (aR_n b)$, these relations, together with our former definition of the limit of a progression, take us up to a great many ordinals of the second class. But the limit of a progression of such relations must have a definition which gives the *law* of the progression. Now the law of the progression must enable us, for some finite value of m, to infer a term of the progression from its m predecessors. Thus in the case of the progression by which ω is defined, we have $R_{n+1} = R_n + (aR_n b)$, so that the immediate predecessor alone suffices for defining a term. This holds good of all limits of progression short of the number which Cantor calls ε_0, which is the smallest root of $\omega^x = x$. From ε_0 onwards, at least two predecessors are required for defining the next term in any progression whose limit is not of the form $x + \alpha$, where $\alpha < \varepsilon_0$. Then presently we shall reach a stage where three predecessors are required, and so on. If we take the first ordinal in each of these stages, we get a progression $0, \omega, \varepsilon_0, \ldots$ whose limit is, I think, the first indefinable ordinal of the second class. Here the defining progression has a law not expressible in terms of our data; at least it looks as if this law could not be so expressed. It is dangerous to be dogmatic as to what can *not* be done; but at any rate from the above it is clear how we can see that there are progressions of definable ordinals of the second class whose limits are not definable.

Finally, it should be observed that we may very well know what an ordinal is, without being able to define it in terms of the fundamental notions we are choosing to employ. There are many other notions which we apprehend, and an ordinal may be definable by their help when it is indefinable in terms of our apparatus. The point of the paradox about indefinability is that as we enlarge our apparatus we alter the notion 'definable in terms of our apparatus', and this notion, like the limit of a well-ordered series, always remains outside what can be defined in terms of our apparatus; so that, if I is any set of fundamental

SUBSTITUTIONAL THEORY OF CLASSES AND RELATIONS

notions, then, however I may be chosen, 'definability in terms of I' remains indefinable in terms of I.

To sum up: Every ordinal of the first or second class exists as an entity-ordinal, but not all of them are definable. The least indefinable ordinal of the second class is the ordinal number of those that are definable. All the ordinals of any given logical type form a well-ordered series in order of magnitude; the ordinal number of this series is greater and of a higher logical type than any member of the series. Every ordinal of the third class exists as an ordinal-ordinal, and $\aleph_1$ exists as an ordinal-cardinal. For a sufficiently high type, $\aleph_n$ and the ordinals of the $(n+2)$th class exist, so long as n is finite. We have not found means of deciding whether any entity-ordinals of the third class exist, nor whether there is any such cardinal (in any type) as α_ω, or any ordinal (in any type) not of the nth class for some finite value of n. I do not believe these questions are particularly difficult to decide, but I have not found the way to decide them.

As we go up the series of ordinals, the ordinals rise in type. Every segment of the series of ordinals is well-ordered, but there is no such thing as the whole series of ordinals, because there are only finite types, and any assigned type is surpassed by sufficiently great ordinals. Hence Burali-Forti's contradiction is at once explained and avoided.

The whole process of advancing from finite numbers to ω, or from any infinite series to its limit, is liable, in certain cases, to a curious limitation, of which, as appears from the above discussion, the series of types affords an illustration. It often happens that what is verbally and to all appearance a *general* theorem about *all* cases, is really only a theorem about each particular case. Such a theorem may be demonstrable in each particular case, and we may be able to see that it is demonstrable in each particular case, and yet there may be absolutely no way of stating the theorem generally. What, in such cases, looks like a general statement, may be called a *prescription*: it will work in each case, but there is, so to speak, no quintessence to be distilled from the various cases and stated as a general theorem. The most fundamental instance of this is presented by functions. As was explained earlier, we can state many propositions about ϕx, where ϕx may be any function of x we please; but it is meaningless to say that such propositions hold for all values of ϕ. For example, if x and y are identical, ϕx implies ϕy. This holds in each particular case, but we cannot say that it holds *always*, because the various particular cases have not enough in common. This distinction is difficult and subtle, and I do not know how to make it clear; but the neglect of it is the ultimate source of all the contradictions which have hitherto beset the theory of the transfinite.

A matrix is closely analogous, in use, to a propositional function; its great advantage is that it allows truly general statements, and not mere *prescriptions*. Thus in the above illustration, we cannot say 'x is identical with y when, and only when, ϕx implies ϕy for all values of ϕ', but we can say 'x is identical with y when, and only when, $p/a\!\cdot\! x$ implies $p/a\!\cdot\! y$ for all values of p and a'. It is for the sake of this generality that matrices have to be introduced in place of functions. The limitations which render contradictions avoidable are imposed entirely by the fact that matrices are not entities, with the resulting requirement of homogeneity.

The technical development of the principles of mathematics is, it must be confessed, rendered much more complicated by the substitutional theory. But as regards the fundamental assumptions, the primitive propositions upon which the deductive edifice is built, there is really a simplification: our assumptions are more modest than they were. All that is obtained by the substitutional method would still be true if there were after all such entities as classes and relations; we do not deny that there are such entities, we merely abstain from affirming that there are. The only serious danger, so far as appears, is lest some contradiction should be found to result from the assumption that *propositions* are entities; but I have not found any such contradiction, and it is very hard to believe that there are no such things as propositions, or to see how, if there were no propositions, any general reasoning would be possible. It would seem, therefore, that the chances of any important lurking fallacy in the method are not great. And this is confirmed by the delicate discrimination with which the substitutional method just avoids the results that lead to contradictions, while leaving almost everything else intact.

Of the philosophical consequences of the theory I will say nothing, beyond pointing out that it affords what at least seems to be a complete solution of all the hoary difficulties about the one and the many; for, while allowing that there are many entities, it adheres with drastic pedantry to the old maxim that, 'whatever is, is one'.

9

On 'Insolubilia' and their Solution by Symbolic Logic

First published as 'Les Paradoxes de la Logique' in the *Revue de Métaphysique et de Morale*, 14 (Sept. 1906), pp. 627–50. English version from the ms. 'On "Insolubilia" and their Solution by Symbolic Logic', now at the Bertrand Russell Archives. Published with the permission of the Bertrand Russell Archives. Quotations from Henri Poincaré in the English ms. are in French and have been translated by the editor.

M. Poincaré's article in this review, 'Les mathématiques et la logique'[1] illustrates what I believe to be a misapprehension as to the nature and purposes of logistic, which, since the article is largely concerned with my writings, it seems appropriate that I should endeavour to remove. At the same time, it suggests a solution of the paradoxes besetting the theory of the transfinite. M. Poincaré holds that these paradoxes all spring from some kind of vicious circle, and in this I agree with him. But he fails to realise the difficulty of avoiding a vicious circle of this sort. I shall try to show that, if it is to be avoided, something like my 'no-classes theory' seems necessary; indeed, it was for this purpose that I invented the theory. In the present article, I shall first deal with certain general preliminary questions; then I shall give a summary of the article[2] which M. Poincaré is criticising; then I shall consider certain extensions of the theory advocated in that article, which I now think necessary; and at the same time I shall try to reply to the more important of M. Poincaré's criticisms.

I

M. Poincaré begins his article by certain ironical concessions to M. Couturat, dismissing other points as of minor importance.

[1] Poincaré *A* May 1906.
[2] [The article was 'On Some Difficulties in the Theory of Transfinite Numbers and Order Types' reprinted in this section.]

On one question, however, he calmly reiterates his charge, without making any attempt whatever to reply to what purports to be a clear refutation of his previous observations. I refer to my supposed twofold enunciation of the principle of induction. M. Poincaré remarks: 'This confusion arises in a polemical article, but not in his principal work, and so I do not wish to hold it against him' (p. 301). I thank M. Poincaré for his generosity. It is like that of a man who, having brought an accusation of murder, and been met by an *alibi*, should reply: 'Well, I don't blame you much, for I dare say you were suffering from temporary insanity when you did the deed.'[1]

A point in which I must venture to differ respectfully from M. Poincaré is in his estimate of M. Peano; the more so as he supposes that my work, if sound, would be destructive of M. Peano's work, which is the opposite of my own opinion. M. Poincaré says:

'I have the highest respect for M. Peano, who has done some very nice things (for example his curve that fills a whole area) but, in the last analysis, he has gone no further, nor higher, nor faster, than the majority of wingless mathematicians, and he could have done all that he did by walking on the ground.' (p. 295.)

Now I would suggest to M. Poincaré that this is merely a way of stating that the bulk of what M. Peano has done does not interest him. M. Peano has forged an instrument of great potency for certain kinds of investigations. Some of us are interested in such investigations, and therefore do honour to M. Peano, who, as regards them, has gone, we think, so much farther and faster than the 'wingless' mathematicians that they have lost sight of him and do not know that he is in advance of them. Now there is no obligation upon a specialist to take an interest in the work of another specialist; but it is surely a part of courtesy to assume that the subjects one does not oneself study may also have their importance; indeed M. Poincaré recognises their importance by writing on them.

[1] See the lucid arguments of M. Couturat, Couturat *A* 1906, to which I have nothing to add on this point. [Note added in the French version.]

If M. Poincaré could divest himself of the belief that logistic is quite unlike any other part of mathematics, he would also realise that, in proposing not to regard classes as independent entities, I am not proposing a change which will make it necessary to 'remake all of logistic'; nor do I wish to forbid people to 'pronounce the word *class*' any more than Copernicus wished to forbid people speaking of the sunrise. 'What a change', he says, 'for the logisticians who speak only of classes and of classes of classes.' Perhaps an analogy will make it clear that the change is not so great after all. The infinitesimal calculus, as is now universally recognised, neither employs nor assumes infinitesimals. But how much has this altered 'the appearance of one page of' infinitesimal calculus? Hardly at all. Certain proofs are re-written, certain paradoxes which troubled the eighteenth century have been solved; otherwise, the formulae of the calculus have scarcely changed. But suppose the said paradoxes and their present solution had been discovered during the life-time of Leibniz's opponents, what would they have said?

'It is forbidden to pronounce the word "infinitesimal", and one has to substitute for it various circumlocutions. What a change for innovators who speak only of dx and d^2x! The whole calculus will have to be redone. Can one imagine what a page of calculus will look like after one has eliminated all the propositions which refer to the infinitesimal? There will be no more than a few scattered conclusions in the middle of a blank page. At any rate, the infinitesimal calculus will have to be rebuilt, and it's not too clear how much can be saved of the old one. It's unnecessary to add that Leibnizism alone is implicated, and that the true mathematics – algebra, geometry, and mechanics – will be able to continue to develop according to their own principles.'[1]

As little as the modern theory of the infinitesimal calculus is designed to undo the work of Leibniz and Newton, so little are

---

[1] Cf. pp. 306–7. [The preceeding beginning with 'One has to substitute . . .' was written by Russell in French.]

'INSOLUBILIA' AND SOLUTION BY SYMBOLIC LOGIC

the principles I propose intended to undo the work of M. Peano. I cannot recall any instance in which he has indulged in reasoning of the kind which leads to contradictions; all that is to be said is that his principles do not explicitly exclude such reasoning. Nor is my present view greatly different (as M. Poincaré supposes) from that of my *Principles of Mathematics*. In that work, I tentatively adopted the zigzag theory.[1] Also, I suggested the no-classes theory in the Preface (pp. v, vi): 'In the case of classes, I must confess, I have failed to perceive any concept fulfilling the conditions requisite for the notion of *class*. And the contradiction discussed in Chapter x proves that something is amiss, but what this is I have hitherto failed to discover.' *Technically*, the theory of types suggested in Appendix B differs little from the no-classes theory. The only thing that induced me at that time to retain classes was the technical difficulty of stating the propositions of elementary arithmetic without them – a difficulty which then seemed to me insuperable.

Before attempting to explain how I should propose to state the principles of logistic in a way which avoids contradictions, it is necessary to say something on the subject of 'intuition' and the nature of the evidence for the truth of propositions in logistic.

M. Poincaré says (p. 295):

'Must one follow your rules blindly? Yes – otherwise it would be intuition alone which would permit you to discriminate between them; but then they must be infallible. ... You have no right to say to us, "True, we make mistakes, but you make mistakes too." For us, making mistakes is a misfortune, a very great misfortune, but for you it is death.'

These remarks seem to me to embody a misconception of the claims of logistic, and of the nature of the evidence on which it relies. But the misconception is a very natural one, and may have been shared by some of its advocates as well as its enemies.[2]

---
[1] Cf. sections 103 and 484, end.
[2] Indeed, I shared it myself until I came upon the contradictions.

The subject is of considerable importance, not only to logistic, but to the general theory of the sciences; moreover it is necessary to explain it as a preliminary to dealing with the contradictions.

The method of logistic is fundamentally the same as that of every other science. There is the same fallibility, the same uncertainty, the same mixture of induction and deduction, and the same necessity of appealing, in confirmation of principles, to the diffused agreement of calculated results with observation. The object is not to banish 'intuition', but to test and systematise its employment, to eliminate the errors to which its ungoverned use gives rise, and to discover general laws from which, by deduction, we can obtain true results never contradicted, and in crucial instances confirmed, by intuition. In all this, logistic is exactly on a level with (say) astronomy, except that, in astronomy, verification is effected not by intuition but by the senses. The 'primitive propositions' with which the deductions of logistic begin should, if possible, be evident to intuition; but that is not indispensable, nor is it, in any case, the whole reason for their acceptance. This reason is inductive, namely that, among their known consequences (including themselves), many appear to intuition to be true, none appear to intuition to be false, and those that appear to intuition to be true are not, so far as can be seen, deducible from any system of indemonstrable propositions inconsistent with the system in question.

Among several systems fulfilling all these conditions, that one is to be preferred, aesthetically, in which the primitive propositions are fewest and most general; exactly as the law of gravitation is to be preferred to Kepler's three laws as the starting-point of mathematical deductions. If intuition were infallible, this complicated process of verification would be unnecessary. But, as is shown by the contradictions, intuition is not infallible. Hence an element of uncertainty must always remain, just as it remains in astronomy. It may, with time, be immensely diminished; but infallibility is not granted to mortals (except the Pope[1]), even when, as M. Poincaré advises, they carefully abstain from making their arguments cogent.

[1] [This phrase is omitted in the published French.]

'INSOLUBILIA' AND SOLUTION BY SYMBOLIC LOGIC

When M. Poincaré asks, 'Must one follow your rules blindly?', the answer is yes, in one sense, no, in another. While using a set of rules, it would be ridiculous to apply them with reservations, since thereby the inductive test of their validity would be rendered impossible. When a man of science wishes to establish a hypothesis, he does not, if he is wise, apply it only to the cases where it is most likely to succeed; he applies it also, and more particularly, to the cases where it might be expected to break down. If it does not break down, it is so far confirmed; if it does, it must be abandoned. One of the first services of logistic to philosophy has been to show that rules of logic hitherto universally accepted require emendation; its next service, one may hope, will be to provide the emendation required. If we had not applied our rules 'blindly', we should not have discovered that they were faulty.

But in another sense, the application of the rules ought to be by no means blind. That is to say, we ought to be constantly on the look-out for crucial cases where, if anywhere, they are likely to lead to error. For this purpose, we need a quick faculty of deducing consequences, and an imagination for the kind of consequences likely to be false. If, finally, we can arrive at a set of principles which recommend themselves to intuition, and which show exactly how we formerly fell into error, we may have a reasonable assurance that our new principles are at any rate nearer the truth than our old ones.

The question remains: How is logistic, pursued by such methods, related to ordinary mathematics? Logistic professes to be merely concerned with the principles employed in ordinary mathematics; its object is to discover these principles, to show deductively that ordinary mathematics follows from them, and to draw any other consequences from these principles that may seem interesting. It is in connection with the third point that logistic comes in contact with Cantor and with the contradictions. The principles employed in ordinary mathematics, when stated in their logical purity, still seem evident to intuition, because intuition (unless specially trained) pays no regard to queer cases, and in ordinary cases they hold. When M.

CLASSES AND THE PARADOXES

Poincaré clamours for the use of 'intuition' in reasoning, we may concede that positive errors are less likely to emerge if we only apply our rules where 'intuition' (i.e. common sense) suggests that we may safely do so. But there are some people who would prefer *true* rules of reasoning; and these people will be specially concerned with the queer cases from which common sense shrinks, in order to discover what, if any, are the limits to which the rules of ordinary mathematics are subject, and to discover rules in which all limitations (if any) are explicit. And until this labour has been performed, not only 'le cantorism', but also conventional mathematics, may be applying its rules to cases to which they do not apply. So long as we only know that a rule holds in 'ordinary' cases, without knowing what cases are ordinary, our mathematics is in a precarious condition.

I come now to the application of the above principles in the case of *insolubilia*. Such paradoxes have been known ever since the time of Epimenides the Cretan,[1] and the suggestion that they spring from a vicious circle appears to be due to William of Occam.[2] This suggestion, which is revived by M. Poincaré, is one with which I fully concur. But M. Poincaré, unlike William of Occam,[3] appears not to realise that, if vicious circles of this sort are to be avoided, some elaborate re-statement of logical principles, more or less resembling my no-classes theory, is absolutely indispensable. We may illustrate this by what M. Poincaré says concerning Richard's paradox. Having first put $E=$ 'all numbers definable in a finite number of words', we arrive at a paradox, due, says M. Poincaré, to our having included a number only definable in a finite number of words

---

[1] Assuming him to have really said that all Cretans are liars.

[2] See Baldwin's *Dictionary of Philosophy and Psychology*, art. 'Insolubilia'. The vicious circle is not mentioned explicitly, but it appears indubitable that the sense of the proposed solution is that which I attribute to it here. [The preceding sentence was added in the published French.]

[3] Baldwin, *Dictionary*: 'Occam ... admits the validity of the argumentation and its consequence, which is that there can be no such proposition, and attempts to show by other arguments that no proposition can assert anything of itself. Many logical writers follow Occam in the first part of his solution; but fail to see the need of the second part.'

'INSOLUBILIA' AND SOLUTION BY SYMBOLIC LOGIC

by means of E. This vicious circle he proposes to avoid by defining E as 'all numbers definable in a finite number of words without mentioning E.'[1] To the uninitiated, this definition looks more circular than ever. The same applies to what he says about induction. Induction is, apparently, that property of finite numbers in virtue of which they possess every property ϕ possessed by 0 and by the successor of every number possessing it, provided ϕ can be described without mentioning induction.[2] On the face of it, this does not seem a very promising plan for avoiding vicious circles.

Very similar remarks apply to what M. Poincaré says at the end of his article, on the subject of totality (pp. 316–17):

> '*There is no actual infinite*; the Cantorians have forgotten this, and they have fallen into contradiction ... The logisticians have forgotten this like the Cantorians, and they have encountered the same difficulties.'

On this we may remark in the first place that the contradictions have no essential reference to infinity. [Of] the *insolubilia* considered by the ancients, none of them introduce infinity; and of these, oddly enough, M. Poincaré mentions the Epimenides as being of the same nature as those that arise in the theory of the transfinite (p. 306). A simplification of this paradox is constituted by the man who says 'I am lying'; if he is lying, he is speaking the truth; but if he is speaking the truth, he is lying. Has this man forgotten that there is no actual infinite?

But further, in the paragraph headed 'The true solution', M. Poincaré has already given his adhesion to the vicious-circle theory, which makes no reference to infinity, and by no means

---

[1] Cf. p. 307: 'It seems to me that the solution can be found in a letter of M. Richard.... After exposing the antinomy that we have named the Richard antinomy, he gives an explanation of it.... E is the set of *all* the numbers which can be defined using a finite number of words, *without introducing the notion of the set E itself*. Otherwise, the definition of E would involve a vicious circle; one cannot define E by means of the set E itself.'

[2] P. 309: 'An inductive number is one which belongs to all recurrent classes; if we wish to avoid a vicious circle we must understand by this: all recurrent classes in the definition of which the notion of an inductive number is not already included.'

excludes infinite collections; that is to say, it admits infinite collections in exactly the same sense in which it admits finite collections. I shall try to show that the only sense in which Cantor and the logisticians need admit the actual infinite is the sense that we can make statements about any or some of the terms having a certain property, even when the number of such terms is not finite. And in this sense M. Poincaré himself must admit the actual infinite, for in the paragraph immediately preceding the one in which the above italicised denial of the actual infinite occurs, he says, 'The word "all" is quite appropriate when it applies to a finite number of objects'. In other words, the word *all* can be legitimately applied to *any* finite class of objects. But the number of finite classes is not finite; hence, in the sense which is required in logistic (according to the no-classes theory), M. Poincaré himself concedes what is required. In the other sense, in which the no-classes theory does not assume infinite collections, it does not assume finite collections either; that is, it does not assume that a class is ever a single individual.

I recognise, however, that the clue to the paradoxes is to be found in the vicious-circle suggestion; I recognise further this element of truth in M. Poincaré's objection to totality, that whatever in any way concerns *all* of *any* or *some* (undetermined) of the members of a class must not be itself one of the members of a class. In M. Peano's language, the principle I wish to advocate may be stated: 'Whatever involves an apparent variable must not be among the possible values of that variable'. But before explaining how this is to be secured, I will give a résumé of the article[1] which M. Poincaré has criticised.

II

The article in question deals only with the paradoxes that arise in the theory of classes and relations. In order to deal with the *Epimenides* and its kindred, which concern propositions, we need an extension of the doctrines contained in that article, which I will explain later. It is very probable that the views which at

[1] Russell *B* 1906a.

'INSOLUBILIA' AND SOLUTION BY SYMBOLIC LOGIC

present seem to me the best require considerable modification. But imperfect theories may often be useful as stepping-stones, and it seems therefore desirable to set them forth even if there cannot yet be any great certainty that they are quite right.

The first point is to distinguish two separate and almost unconnected questions, namely (1) the question of the paradoxes, (2) the question of Zermelo's axiom. In the article in question, both were discussed, but for the present we may confine ourselves to the first. In discussing the paradoxes, I sought first to show that all of them are rather logical than arithmetical, i.e. that if they are to be solved, it must be by a modification of current logical assumptions. By 'current logical assumptions' I do not mean such (if any) as are peculiar to logisticians, but such as are universally admitted, at least tacitly, except when people are reminded of the awkward results to which they lead. I showed that Burali-Forti's contradiction, and the contradiction about the class of classes which are not members of themselves, and all analogous contradictions (of which any number can be manufactured on a system) are particular cases of the following:

'Given a property ϕ and a function f, such that, if ϕ belongs to all the members of u, fu always exists, has the property ϕ, and is not a member of u; then the supposition that there is a class ω of all terms having the property ϕ and that $f\omega$ exists leads to the conclusion that $f\omega$ both has and has not the property ϕ.'

Thus in those cases in which it seems, at first sight, as if ω and $f\omega$ existed, we must find a way of admitting that they do not both exist. It appeared on examination that this required us to admit that some, at least, among propositional functions (i.e. among properties ϕ such as the above) do not determine classes, it being supposed that classes are entities, which can be significantly put as arguments to any function which requires one entity as its argument. The question then arises: what precisely are the limitations to which a property ϕ must be subject if it is to define a class?

Three theories were considered, which I called respectively

the zigzag theory, the theory of limitation of size, and the no-classes theory. Of these, the first two, in any form in which I have hitherto been able to give them, proved quite unservicable. My reason for mentioning them was partly historical, partly that it seemed possible they might hereafter be better stated. But the third theory was found to be more satisfactory, and to be capable of solving the paradoxes for the sake of which it was invented.

The contention of the 'no-classes' theory is that all significant propositions concerning classes can be regarded as propositions about all or some of their members, i.e. about all or some of the terms satisfying some propositional function ϕx. It appears that the only propositions about classes which cannot be so regarded are propositions of the type which gives rise to contradictions. Hence it is natural to suppose that classes are merely linguistic or symbolic abbreviations. Thus, e.g. when we say 'men are contained among mortals', we may seem to be making a statement about the class of men collectively; but when we say 'all men are mortal' we do not necessarily assume that there is a new entity, the class of men, in addition to all men individually. To carry out this mode of interpretation thoroughly is a rather complicated matter; but it can be done, and when it is done it is found to exclude only such propositions as lead to paradoxes.

The method of substitution, by which I have proposed to effect this interpretation, is more or less in the nature of a technical device, to be replaced by a more convenient device if one should be discovered. The important point is merely to provide a mode of interpreting the ordinary statements about classes without assuming that classes are entities. In the substitutional theory, this is effected as follows.

Let p be a proposition, and a a constituent of p. Then '$p\frac{b}{a}!q$' is to mean 'q results from p by substituing b for a whenever a occurs in p'. We then define $p\frac{b}{a}$ or $p/a;b$ as 'the q which satisfies $p\frac{b}{a}!q$'. Strictly speaking, as in all cases of phrases beginning with *the*, we do not define $p/a;b$ itself, but we define any statement in which it occurs. Thus '$p/a;b$ has the property ϕ' is to mean: 'There is a q such that $p\frac{b}{a}!r$ is true when and only when r is identical with q, and q has the property ϕ'.[1] We call p/a the *matrix* of the substitution; it has no meaning by itself, since it stands for 'the result of replacing a in p by ...'. A *matrix* has all the formal properties of a *class*; thus the members of p/a are the values of x for which $p/a;x$ is true, and so on. In order to insure that a statement about p/a holds of 'all classes', we have to state that it holds for 'all values of p and a', so that instead of one variable we have two. The notion of a class being a member of itself becomes meaningless; though it is easy to construct a definition of what we mean when we say that a class is a member of a class of classes. Similarly we obtain *relations* by substituting for two of the constituents of a proposition, and so on. In this way, we obtain a series of types, such that, in all cases where formerly a paradox might have emerged, we now have a difference of type rendering the paradoxical statement meaningless.

The various types that emerge in this process: classes, classes of classes, classes of classes of classes, dual relations, classes of dual relations, dual relations of classes to entities, triple relations, and so on; all these are merely incomplete phrases like 'the result of replacing a in p by ...'. Thus a certain supplement is always required to produce anything significant. What the supplement is, is always evident at once. Take, e.g. 'the relations $p/(a, b)$ and $q(c, d)$ have the same extension'. This will mean: 'For any values of x and y, the propositions $p/(a, b);(x, y)$[2] and $q/(c, d);(x, y)$ are equivalent', i.e. both true or both false. We define this as the *equality* of two dual relations; i.e. when the above holds, we write: $p/(a, b) = q/(c, d)$. In counting a class of relations, equal relations are regarded as identical; and the same applies to all matrices. But if we try to give a meaning to (say) $p/(a, b) = q$, or $p/(a, b) = q/c$, we cannot

---

[1] Cf. 'On Denoting', Russell *B* 1905*c*.
[2] Here $p/(a, b);(x, y)$ means 'the result of replacing a and b in p by x and y'.

do so. The test of significance for a formula containing matrices is that, when fully written out, it should be found to contain only entities; and by this test, the equality of a relation and an entity, or a relation and a class, or a class and an entity, is meaningless. In this way, Burali-Forti's paradox and the rest are avoided.

We may illustrate the theory of substitution by considering, e.g. the definition of the cardinal number 1. This will still be a class of classes, but, like all matrices, it will have no meaning in isolation. Instead of 'u is a unit class', we shall have 'p/a is a unit class', which we define as meaning: 'There is a c such that $p\dfrac{x}{a}$ is true when, and only when, x is identical with c'. If we call this proposition q, then the matrix $q/(p, a)$ has the same value however p and a may be chosen (provided p and a are not identical); that is to say, if q' is the proposition; 'There is a c such that $p'\dfrac{x}{a'}$ is true when and only when x is identical with c', then $q'/(p', a') = q(p, a)$. The common value of all such matrices is defined as the number 1.

In the above-mentioned article, the no-classes theory was merely sketched in the briefest outline, nor did I then know how much of the theory of the transfinite it was possible to express in this language. I have since come to the conclusion that, so far at least as I can yet discover, hardly anything is ruled out except the paradoxes. It may be worth while briefly to explain the method by which former results are re-stated.

Some of the main existence-theorems are obtained as follows. We assume as a primitive proposition that, given any proposition p, there is at least one entity u which is not explicitly mentioned in stating p. We also assume that what is true for all values of x is true for some value of x (or some equivalent of this assumption). This is equivalent to the assumption that there is at least one entity.[1]

---

[1] Some assumption of this kind is necessary; for if there were none, there would be no propositions, and therefore there would be no possibility of inconsistencies. If the statement 'there are no propositions' itself enunciated a proposition, it would of

'INSOLUBILIA' AND SOLUTION BY SYMBOLIC LOGIC

Given one entity a, we have the proposition $a=a$; and by the axiom at the beginning of the last paragraph, there is an entity u such that u is not mentioned in '$a=a$'. This entity is not a, since a is mentioned in '$a=a$'. Hence there are at least two entities. There will be similarly an entity not mentioned in '$a=u$', which must be neither a nor u. We can in this way show that, if n is any finite number, there are more than n entities, and by taking propositions into account, we can manufacture $\aleph_0$ entities. E.g. put

$$p_0 . = . a = u, \qquad p_{n+1} . = . p_n = u;$$

it is not hard to prove that the successive p's are all different, and that there are therefore at least $\aleph_0$ entities. Hence the cardinals up to and including $\aleph_0$ exist, and the ordinals finite and of the second class exist. These are *entity*-ordinals, i.e. they are the ordinals of series of entities. If we arrange these ordinals in order of magnitude, we get a new ordinal, ω_1, the first of the third class. But this is an *ordinal*-ordinal,[1] not an *entity*-ordinal; it is thus of higher logical type than an entity-ordinal, and is neither equal to, greater than, nor less than any entity-ordinal, except in virtue of a new definition introduced *ad hoc*. In this way we find that, although the existence-theorem can be proved for $\omega, \omega_1, \omega_2, \ldots \omega_n, \ldots$, it is proved at each stage for a higher type. Consequently, there is no proof (at least so far as appears by this method) of the existence of ω_ω, and there is a proof that there is no such thing, in any sense, as the whole series of ordinals of all types. For such a series would have to transcend, sooner or later, any given type; hence it would not fulfil the conditions of significance for expressions containing matrices. Thus Burali-Forti's paradox receives the following

---

course refute itself; but according to the theory to be explained later, such a statement is either meaningless or does not apply to itself, and the contention that it refutes itself embodies the fallacy of the vicious circle. Thus we need an axiom of some sort to state that there is at least one entity. No such axiom is given in the article concerned, because in that article it is assumed that general propositions (i.e. such as contain apparent variables) are entities whereas in the present article I propose to dispense with this assumption, treating only particular propositions as entities. Cf. below.

[1] I.e. the ordinal number of a series of entity-ordinals.

solution: There is such a matrix as the ordinal number of all the ordinals of a given type; this is not of the given type, and is (with a suitable definition of *greater* and *less*) the first ordinal greater than any of the given type. In the type to which it belongs, it is not the greatest. Thus every segment of the series of ordinals is well-ordered, there is no greatest ordinal, and the whole series of ordinals of all types is a fiction.

III

The above doctrine solves, so far as I can discover, all paradoxes concerning classes and relations; but in order to solve the *Epimenides* we seem to need a similar doctrine as regards propositions. For the avoidance of the vicious-circle fallacy, we require, as we saw at the end of section I, the principle: 'Whatever involves an apparent variable must not be among the possible values of that variable'. Let us call this the 'vicious-circle principle'. The important case of this principle may be less exactly stated as follows: 'Whatever involves *all* must not be one of the *all* which it involves'. Thus a statement about *all* propositions must either be meaningless, or a statement of something which is not a proposition in the sense concerned. Any statement about *all* propositions involves a proposition as apparent variable; hence to avoid vicious circles, we need a meaning of *proposition* according to which no proposition can contain an apparent variable. This result can, so it seems to me, be secured by deciding that a statement about *all* (or about *any*, which comes to the same thing) is really an affirmation of an ambiguous one of the several propositions got from particular cases. E.g. if we state: 'Whatever x may be, $x=x$', we are stating an ambiguous one of the propositions of the form '$x=x$'; thus though we have a new *statement*, we do not have a new proposition. Our statement can only be true if the proposition is true however the ambiguity may be decided; but since the truth of a statement is different from the truth of a proposition, we do not get an opportunity for the sort of inference which would expose us to the vicious-circle fallacy.

'INSOLUBILIA' AND SOLUTION BY SYMBOLIC LOGIC

It is important to observe that the vicious-circle principle is not itself the solution of vicious-circle paradoxes, but merely the result which a theory must yield if it is to afford a solution of them. It is necessary, that is to say, to construct a theory of expressions containing apparent variables which will yield the vicious-circle principle as an outcome. It is for this reason that we need a reconstruction of logical first principles, and cannot rest content with the mere fact that the paradoxes are due to vicious circles.

The difficulty of applying the vicious-circle principle arises from the argument by which, as it seems, we can prove that our variables must be capable of *all* values. The older symbolic logicians had a doctrine of the *universe of discourse*, setting, as it were, bounds of decency, outside which no well-conducted variable would wander. Thus when they asserted that (say) ϕx was always true, they only meant that it was always true so long as x was within the universe. Let us call the universe i. Then they really meant: '"x is an i" implies ϕx'. But was this to hold only when x is an i? If so, we should have to say '"x is an i" implies that "x is an i" implies ϕx'. And so on *ad infinitum*. Thus a statement, such as ϕx, which is true under an hypothesis, can only be stated to be true under that hypothesis if the statement that the hypothesis implies ϕx can be made without any limitation on x. Any limitation on x is part of the whole which is really asserted; and as soon as the limitation is explicitly stated, the resulting implicational proposition remains true when the limitation is false. Thus a variable must be capable of *all* values. This argument may be fallacious, but I have never seen any attempt to refute it.

There is one way in which we might seek to evade this conclusion. We may say that 'ϕx is always true' means 'ϕx is true whenever it is significant' or 'ϕx is never false'. We might then say that a given function ϕx will always have a certain *range of significance* which will be either *individuals*, or *classes*, or *classes of classes*, or *dual relations of individuals*, or etc. The difficulty of this view lies in the proposition (say) 'ϕx is only significant when x is a class'. This proposition must not be restricted, as to its range, to the case when x *is* a class; for we want it to imply 'ϕx is not significant when x is not a class'. We thus find that we are brought back after all to variables with an unrestricted range. If this is to be avoided, the range of significance must be somehow given with the variable; this can only be done by employing variables having some internal *structure* for such as are to be of some definite logical type other than individuals. For example, M. Peano's symbol 'xɜ(ϕx)' can only stand for a class, and no explicit statement to this effect is needed in particular cases. But then we have to assume that a single letter, such as x, can only stand for an individual; and that can only be the case if individuals are really all entities, and classes, etc., are merely a *façon de parler*. Thus our variable x now again has an unrestricted range, since it may be any individual, and there is really nothing that is not an individual. Hence to reconcile the unrestricted range of the variable with the vicious-circle principle, which might seem impossible at first sight, we have to construct a theory in which every expression which contains an apparent variable (i.e. which contains such words as *all*, *any*, *some*, *the*) is shown to be a mere *façon de parler*, a thing with no more independent reality than belongs to (say) $\frac{d}{dx}$ or $\int_a^b$. For in that case, if (say) ϕx is true for *every* value of x, it will be not true, but meaningless, if we substitute for x an expression containing an apparent variable. And such expressions include all descriptive phrases (the so-and-so), all classes, all relations in extension, and all *general* propositions, i.e. all propositions of the form 'ϕx is true for all (or some) values of x'.

To show in detail how this is to be done would require much mathematics, and is impossible in the present article. I shall content myself, in this article, with showing how the above principle solves the contradictions, and how the no-classes theory embodies the application of the principle to classes.

Let us begin with the man who says 'I am lying'. We need, in the first place, different words for the case in which a man's assertion contains an apparent variable, and the case in which it does not. In the latter case, we assume that there is a genuine

'INSOLUBILIA' AND SOLUTION BY SYMBOLIC LOGIC

entity, the proposition, which is what the man asserts. If I say, 'Socrates is mortal', there is a fact corresponding to my assertion, and this fact is what I will call the proposition. I assume that there is such a thing as the proposition even in cases where it is false,[1] but not in cases where it is *general*. Such a statement as 'Whatever x may be, $x=x$', or 'For all values of x, $x=x$', I take to be an ambiguous statement of any one of the various propositions of the form '$x=x$'. There is thus not a new proposition, but merely an unlimited undetermined choice among a number of propositions. Similarly if I assert 'I met a man', I assert *some one* of the propositions of the form 'I met x, and x is human', without in any way deciding as to which one I assert. Thus the word *proposition* will, in what follows, be confined to what is affirmed by a statement containing no apparent variable.[2]

We can now solve the paradox as to the man who says 'I am lying'. This statement is capable of various interpretations; the simplest is: 'There is a proposition p which I am affirming and which is false'. This statement contains an *apparent* variable p; hence it does not state a definite proposition, in the sense which we have given to *proposition*.[3] This statement may be false if I affirm a proposition p which is true, or if I do not affirm any proposition. The first hypothesis involves a contradiction. The second is impossible unless a general statement does not affirm a definite proposition. It is this latter hypothesis which we are adopting. Hence the man's statement is false, not because he is stating a *true* proposition, but because, though he is making a statement, he is not stating a *proposition*. Thus when he says he is lying, he is lying, and the inference that he must therefore be stating what is true fails. He cannot mean: 'I am now making a statement which is false', because there is no way of speaking of statements *in general*: we can speak of statements of propositions, or statements containing one, two, three . . . apparent variables, but not of statements in general. If we want to

[1] Russell *B* 1904*a*, p. 521.
[2] This use of the word *proposition* is proposed solely for the purposes of the present discussion. Elsewhere it would probably prove inconvenient.
[3] [The following four sentences do not appear in the English ms.]

say what is equivalent to 'I am making a false statement containing n apparent variables', we must say something like: 'There is a propositional function $\phi(x_1, x_2, \ldots x_n)$ such that I assert that $\phi(x_1, x_2, \ldots x_n)$ is true for any values of $x_1, x_2 \ldots x_n$, and this is in fact false'. This statement contains $n+1$ apparent variables, namely $x_1, x_2, \ldots x_n$ and ϕ. Hence it does not apply to itself. In this way we avoid all paradoxes of the type of the *Epimenides*, since, with any proposed statement, we can show that it does not apply to itself. This result cannot be obtained by the usual theory of statements; yet unless we can obtain it, our theory will not avoid vicious-circle fallacies.

The point may be illustrated further by considering (say) the law of excluded middle, in the form 'every proposition is either true or false'. If this is true, most people would regard it as legitimate to infer that the law of excluded middle itself is either true or false; yet that is an inference precisely of the kind which led to the paradox of the liar. In the restricted sense which we have given to *proposition*, the law of excluded middle is not a proposition, since it contains an apparent variable. It is a true *statement*; but *true* here has a different meaning, namely that all the propositions which the statement ambiguously denotes are true (in the previous sense). As applied to *statements* the meaning of the word *true* varies as the number of apparent variables in the statements varies.

The broad result for the sake of which the above theory is adopted is this: If ϕx is true for all values of x, it does not follow that ϕx is true of the statement that ϕx is true for all values of x.[1] Thus the vicious-circle paradoxes which would result if this did follow are avoided.

M. Poincaré's method of avoiding the vicious circle would be to say that when we affirm 'all propositions are either true or false', which is the law of excluded middle, we mean tacitly to exclude the law of excluded middle itself. The difficulty is to legitimate this tacit exclusion without reviving the vicious

---

[1] That is, writing '$(x).\phi x$' for 'ϕx is true for all values of x', we do not have $(x).\phi x . \supset . \phi\{(x).\phi x\}$.

circle. If we say 'all propositions are true or false, except the proposition that all propositions are true or false', we have not avoided the vicious circle. For this is a statement about *all* propositions, namely 'all propositions are either true or false or identical with the proposition that all propositions are true or false'. And it assumes that we know the meaning of '*all* propositions are true or false' where the *all* has no exception. Its purport may be stated by defining the law of excluded middle as 'all propositions except the law of excluded middle are true or false', in which the circle is glaring. Hence we must find some way of stating the law of excluded middle so that it shall not apply to itself, although in stating it we have not said that it is not to apply to itself. This we do by confining its scope to propositions containing no apparent variable, provided we can do this without saying that they are to contain no apparent variable. We can then infer a new law of excluded middle applying to statements with one apparent variable; this law will contain more than one apparent variable, and will thus be again outside its own scope. We can then go on to three, four, ... apparent variables, but we never reach a law applying to *all* statements.

I come now to other paradoxes, and shall try to show briefly how they are solved by the principles advocated above.

As regards Richard's puzzle about the number not definable in a finite number of words, the answer here must be one from which it results that the class which M. Poincaré calls E shall not contain any member defined in terms of E. But in this case the result is reached by showing that E is an ill-defined notion. The reason of this is that, in defining E, we use the notion of *definition*, and this, oddly enough, is not definable, and is indeed not a definite notion at all. For any number of apparent variables may occur in a definition; thus if we take any finite number n, there are definitions containing more than n apparent variables. But when this happens, there is no possible way of making a statement about *all* or *any* or *some* (undefined) of the members of our collection. Hence there is no such collection as E – not only in the sense in which all classes are to be nonentities, but in the sense that there is no property common and peculiar to the members of E.

The same remarks apply to 'the least indefinable ordinal', which might seem to be defined by the very phrase which announces its indefinability; and to 'the least integer not nameable in fewer than nineteen syllables', which might seem to be thus named in eighteen syllables.[1]

In paradoxes concerning classes, we escape the vicious circle by the fact that classes are now not single entities, but matrices, which are composed of two entities, p and a, and are only parts of significant phrases, without being themselves significant in isolation. In this we have an illustration of the vicious-circle principle; for we may regard a class as 'all the x's such that ϕx is true' or 'all the x's such that $p\dfrac{x}{a}$ is true', but however we regard it, it will always involve an apparent variable in all its possible significant occurrences. Thus we require, if the vicious-circle principle is to be verified, that classes should not be among the possible values of a wholly unrestricted variable, which is another way of saying that we require that there should be no classes. We cannot then give any meaning to the supposition of a class being a member of itself, and thus we escape the paradox which concerns this supposition.[2]

A few words seem called for as regards mathematical induction. M. Poincaré quotes me as saying: 'But, so far as I know, we cannot prove that the number of classes contained in a finite class is always finite, or *that every finite number is an inductive number*'. I thought the context had made it plain that what I meant was that we cannot prove this without the multiplicative axiom; for the paragraph in question begins 'The above axiom is required for identifying the two definitions of the finite'. It is on account of doubt as to the multiplicative axiom that I am now not contented with the proof of this identification

[1] This paradox was suggested to me by Mr G. G. Berry of the Bodleian Library, Oxford. It has the merit of not going outside finite numbers.

[2] We can give a definition, easily enough, of what is meant by saying that a class is a member of a class of classes; but a class of classes is a matrix of the form $q/(p, a)$, and is thus never possibly equal to a class.

referred to by M. Poincaré.[1] His further criticism, that this proof involves the vicious-circle fallacy, is formally true according to the view advocated above; but the fallacy can be avoided if we admit a certain assumption which is required for other reasons, and to which, so far as I know, there is no serious objection.

Leaving the question whether the principle of induction is a definition or an axiom, let us consider how to state the principle. I presume M. Poincaré would assent to the statement: 'Any property which belongs to 0, and belongs to the successor of any number having the property, belongs to all finite[2] numbers'. Now in this statement, 'any property' must, if the vicious-circle fallacy is to be avoided, be restricted to properties ϕx which can be stated without introducing any apparent variables. A statement of the form '$\phi(x, y)$ is true for all values of y' (or any complication of this form) must not be regarded as a statement of the form ϕx. This is suggested by a variant of the 'Epimenides'. Suppose Epimenides asserts 'All propositions of the form ϕx affirmed by Epimenides are false'. If this is of the form ψ(Epimenides), we get a contradiction. Hence a statement involving an apparent function-variable must not be of the form ϕx even when it contains x; and it is natural to extend this to statements containing apparent entity-variables. Thus the properties concerned in the enunciation of induction must be only such as can be stated without the use of such words as *any, all, some, the*.

But unless this restriction is mitigated by an axiom, it will render most of the usual uses of induction fallacious; and in other ways it will destroy many pieces of ordinary mathematical reasoning. Take such a proposition as: 'If m and n are finite numbers, either $m < n$ or $m = n$ or $m > n$'. If we consider this as a property of m, n is an apparent variable; thus induction does not warrant the conclusion that this holds for all finite numbers from the facts that it holds for 0, and that if it holds for m it

[1] Russell B 1902b.
[2] *Finite* here means what I have proposed to call *inductive*; but I use the word *finite* to avoid involving questions in dispute with which I am not at present concerned.

holds for $m+1$. The objection to such an inference is precisely the same as M. Poincaré's objection to the use of induction which he criticises (No. XI).

But the above modification of the *Epimenides* only proves that a statement containing a real variable x and an apparent variable is not *identical* with any statement of the form ϕx. It by no means proves that it is not *equivalent* to any such statement. Indeed, in the instance of Epimenides's assertion, this assertion *is* equivalent to one of the form ϕ(Epimenides). For, however loquacious he may have been, he can only have affirmed a finite number of propositions containing no apparent variables. If we deny these one by one, we get a statement containing no apparent variable and equivalent to the statement that all his assertions of this form are lies. Thus there is no objection, on the score of the *Epimenides*, to the assumption that every statement containing x and an apparent variable is *equivalent*, for all values of x, to some statement ϕx containing no apparent variable. With this assumption, the usual uses of induction become justified, and with them the use criticised by M. Poincaré also becomes justified.

The above discussion illustrates an important peculiarity of the *Epimenides*. In most of the sort of statements we wish to make in mathematics, if a proposition p occurs otherwise than in a matrix, it may be replaced by any other equivalent proposition[1] without altering the truth or falsehood of our statement. And if a function ϕx occurs, where the argument x is an apparent variable, ϕ may usually be replaced by any other function ψ having the same extension, i.e. true for the same values of x. And the same holds of a matrix p/a. But in the case of the *Epimenides*, this does not hold. The actual statements made by him are relevant and it will not do to substitute equivalent statements not containing the same number of apparent variables. Thus our assumption that a statement containing x and an apparent variable always has the same extension as some statement containing x and no apparent variable does not enable us to substitute the one for the other

[1] A proposition is equivalent to p if both are true or both false.

in the *Epimenides*, but does enable us to make this substitution in all ordinary cases.

We may now briefly recapitulate the theory outlined above. The paradoxes besetting logistic are attributed by M. Poincaré to two sources: vicious circles, and the belief in the actual infinite. In the former suggestion we agreed with him, but not in the latter. The vicious circles involved, however, were found to be peculiar by the fact that we could not avoid them by merely observing that they occurred; for the statement that they were to be avoided would, if it was not accompanied by a re-statement of logical first principles, itself embodies one of the very circles whose avoidance it prescribes. The vicious circles arise where a phrase containing such words as *all* or *some* (i.e. containing an apparent variable) appears itself to stand for one of the objects to which the words *all* or *some* are applied. This appearance must, therefore, be deceptive. The difficulty is, that there is reason to hold that *all* must be capable of meaning *absolutely all*; thus the phrases in question must not stand for entities at all. This result we secured, in the case of statements, by saying that a statement about all things states an ambiguous proposition about any one among things, and in the case of classes and relations, by saying that these are to be regarded as merely verbally or symbolically parts of statements, not as parts of the facts expressed by the statements in question.[1] A brief sketch was given of a way in which the principles of mathematics may be stated in conformity with the theory, and it was shown that the theory, whether true or not, at any rate avoids all known contradictions, while at the same time preserving nearly the whole of Cantor's work on the transfinite.

To set forth precisely and in detail the theory outlined in the present article is only possible by means of a lengthy symbolic development. If the theory is right, the beginnings of logistic are much more difficult than has been hitherto supposed, but this is only what the contradictions would have led us to expect. M. Poincaré informs us that 'clearer notions in logic' are not

---

[1] This principle is an extension of the method applied to denoting phrases in my article 'On Denoting', Russell *B* 1905*c*.

what is wanted; but he does not reveal the process by which he has made this important discovery. For my part, I cannot but think that his attempts to avoid the vicious circle illustrate the fate of those who despise logic. There seems reason to hope that the method proposed in this article avoids all the contradictions, and at the same time preserves Cantor's results; but a long and patient labour of analysis and reconstruction will probably be necessary before the principles of mathematics can be stated in the absolutely best form. Success in this task is sure to throw great light on philosophy and logic; and the measure of success already obtained has conquered for mathematics many provinces previously abandoned to the vague conjectures called 'philosophy'. I do not believe that the subject is best advanced either by dogmatic acceptance of solutions which perhaps do not go to the root of the difficulties, or by refusing to make suggestions which may be found to stand in need of more or less correction, as will no doubt be the case with the suggestions in the present article.

10

The Theory of Logical Types

First published as 'La Théorie des Types Logiques' in the *Revue de Métaphysique et de Morale*, **18** (May 1910), pp. 263–301. English version from the ms. 'The Theory of Logical Types', now in the Bertrand Russell Archives, McMaster University. Published with the permission of the Russell Archives.

M. Poincaré, in his interesting article in a recent number of this Review[1] has explained, with his usual lucidity, what are his reasons for not wholly accepting any of the theories recently put forward to explain the paradoxes of logic. As one of the authors concerned, I gratefully recognise that his article is not polemical in tone, and I freely admit that, on the points as to which he complains of my having given insufficient explanations, the article to which he was referring is no doubt too concise.[2] As this article appeared in a mathematical journal, I was unwilling to devote more space to philosophical interpretations than appeared absolutely indispensable. From M. Poincaré's criticisms, however, I see that certain obscurities resulted from the endeavour to be brief. These obscurities I shall try to remove in the following pages, of which the purpose is explanatory rather than controversial.

I THE NATURE OF PROPOSITIONAL FUNCTIONS

It is agreed that the paradoxes to be avoided all result from a certain kind of vicious circle. The vicious circles in question all arise from supposing that a collection of objects may contain members which can only be defined by means of the collection as a whole. Thus, for example, the collection of *propositions* will

[1] 'La Logique de l'Infini', Poincaré *A* 1909.
[2] [The article was 'Mathematical Logic as based on the Theory of Types', Russell *B* 1908*d*.]

be supposed to contain a proposition stating that 'all propositions are either true or false'. It would seem, however, that such a statement could not be legitimate unless 'all propositions' referred to some already definite collection, which it cannot do if new propositions are created by statements about 'all propositions'. We shall, therefore, have to say that statements about 'all propositions' are meaningless. More generally, given any set of objects such that, if we suppose the set to have a total, it will contain members which presuppose this total, then such a set cannot have a total. By saying that a set has 'no total', we mean, primarily, that no significant statement can be made about 'all its members'. Propositions, as the above illustration shows, must be a set having no total. The same is true, as we shall shortly see, of propositional functions, even when these are restricted to such as can significantly have as argument a given object a. In such cases, it is necessary to break up our set into smaller sets, each of which is capable of a total. This is what the theory of types aims at effecting.

The paradoxes of symbolic logic concern various sorts of objects: propositions, classes, cardinal and ordinal numbers, etc. By means of the theory (to be explained below) which reduces statements that are verbally concerned with classes and relations to statements that are concerned with propositional functions, the paradoxes are reduced to such as concern propositions and propositional functions. The paradoxes that concern propositions are such as the *Epimenides*, and are only indirectly relevant to mathematics. The paradoxes that more nearly concern the mathematician are all concerned with *propositional functions*. By a 'propositional function' I mean something which contains a variable x, and expresses a *proposition* as soon as a value is assigned to x. That is to say, it differs from a proposition solely by the fact that it is ambiguous: it contains a variable of which the value is unassigned. It agrees with the ordinary functions of mathematics in the fact of containing an unassigned variable: where it differs is in the fact that the values of the function are propositions. Thus e.g. 'x is a man' or 'sin $x = 1$' is a propositional function. We shall find that it is possible

THEORY OF LOGICAL TYPES

to incur a vicious-circle fallacy right at the very outset by admitting as possible arguments to a propositional function terms which presuppose the function. This form of the fallacy is very instructive, and its avoidance leads, as we shall see, to the hierarchy of types.

The question as to the nature of a function[1] is by no means an easy one. It would seem, however, that the essential characteristic of a function is *ambiguity*. Take, for example, the law of identity in the form 'A is A', which is the form in which it is usually enunciated. It is plain that, regarded psychologically, we have here a single judgment. But what are we to say of the object of the judgment? We are not judging that Socrates is Socrates, nor that Plato is Plato, nor any other of the definite judgments that are instances of the law of identity. Yet each of these judgments is, in a sense, within the scope of our judgment. We are in fact judging an ambiguous instance of the propositional function 'A is A'. We appear to have a single thought which does not have a definite object, but has as its object an undetermined one of the values of the function 'A is A'. It is this kind of ambiguity that constitutes the essence of a function. When we speak of 'ϕx', where x is not specified, we mean one value of the function, but not a definite one. We may express this by saying that 'ϕx' *ambiguously denotes* ϕa, ϕb, ϕc, etc., where ϕa, ϕb, ϕc, etc., are the various values of 'ϕx'.

When we say that 'ϕx' ambiguously denotes ϕa, ϕb, ϕc, etc., we mean that 'ϕx' means one of the objects ϕa, ϕb, ϕc, etc., though not a definite one, but an undetermined one. It follows that 'ϕx' only has a well-defined meaning (well-defined, that is to say, except in so far as it is of its essence to be ambiguous) if the objects ϕa, ϕb, ϕc, etc., are well-defined. That is to say, a function is not a well-defined function unless all its values are already well-defined. It follows from this that no function can have among its values anything which presupposes the function, for if it had, we could not regard the objects ambiguously denoted by the function as definite until the function was definite

---

[1] When the word 'function' is used in the sequel, 'propositional function' is always meant. Other functions will not be in question.

while conversely, as we have just seen, the function cannot be definite until its values are definite. This is a particular case, but perhaps the most fundamental case, of the vicious-circle principle. A function is what ambiguously denotes some one of a certain totality, namely the values of the function; hence this totality cannot contain any members which involve the function, since, if it did, it would contain members involving the totality, which, by the vicious-circle principle, no totality can do.

It will be seen that, according to the above account, the values of a function are presupposed by the function, not vice versa. It is sufficiently obvious, in any particular case, that a value of a function does not presuppose the function. Thus for example the proposition 'Socrates is human' can be perfectly apprehended without regarding it as a value of the function 'x is human'. It is true that, conversely, a function can be apprehended without its being necessary to apprehend its values severally and individually. If this were not the case, no function could be apprehended at all, since the number of values (true and false) of a function is necessarily infinite and there are necessarily possible arguments with which we are unacquainted. What is necessary is not that the values should be given individually and extensionally, but that the totality of the values should be given intensionally, so that, concerning any assigned object, it is at least theoretically determinate whether or not the said object is a value of the function.

It is necessary practically to distinguish the function itself from an undetermined value of the function. We may regard the function itself as that which ambiguously denotes, while an undetermined value of the function is that which is ambiguously denoted. If the undetermined value is written 'ϕx', we will write the function itself '$\phi \hat{x}$'. (Any other letter may be used in place of x.) Thus we should say 'ϕx is a proposition', but '$\phi \hat{x}$ is a propositional function'. When we say 'ϕx is a proposition', we mean to state something which is true for every possible value of x, though we do not decide what value x is to have. We are making an ambiguous statement about any value of the function. But when we say '$\phi \hat{x}$ is a function', we are not making an ambiguous statement. It would be more correct to say that we are making a statement about an ambiguity, taking the view that a function is an ambiguity. The function itself, $\phi\hat{x}$, is the single thing which ambiguously denotes its many values; while ϕx, where x is not specified, is one of the denoted objects, with the ambiguity belonging to the manner of denoting.

We have seen that, in accordance with the vicious-circle principle, the values of a function cannot contain terms only definable in terms of the function. Now given a function $\phi\hat{x}$, the values for the function[1] are all propositions of the form ϕx. It follows that there must be no propositions, of the form ϕx, in which x has a value which involves $\phi\hat{x}$. (If this were the case, the values of the function would not all be determinate until the function was determinate, whereas we found that the function is not determinate unless its values are previously determinate.) Hence there must be no such thing as the value for $\phi\hat{x}$ with the argument $\phi\hat{x}$, or with any argument which involves $\phi\hat{x}$. That is to say, the symbol '$\phi(\phi\hat{x})$' must not express a proposition, as 'ϕa' does if ϕa is a value for $\phi\hat{x}$. In fact '$\phi(\phi\hat{x})$' must be a symbol which does not express anything: we may therefore say that it is not significant. Thus given any function $\phi\hat{x}$, there are arguments with which the function has no value, as well as arguments with which it has a value. We will call the arguments with which $\phi\hat{x}$ has a value 'possible values of x'. We will say that $\phi\hat{x}$ is 'significant with the argument x' when $\phi\hat{x}$ has a value with the argument x.

The above limitation upon the possible arguments for $\phi\hat{z}$ solves many paradoxes. Take for example the following. Let '$f(\phi\hat{z})$' mean '$\phi\hat{z}$ is not satisfied by itself as argument', i.e. '$\phi(\phi\hat{z})$ is false'. (If this were significant, it would be true in all ordinary cases. For example, it cannot be true that the function '$\hat{x}$ is a man' is a man; if therefore it is either true or false that it is a man, it must be false.) Let us now denote by $f(\hat{\phi})$ the

---

[1] We shall speak of 'values for $\phi\hat{x}$' and of 'values of ϕx', meaning in each case the same thing, namely ϕa, ϕb, ϕc, etc. The distinction of phraseology serves to avoid ambiguity where several variables are concerned.

function for which $f(\phi\hat{z})$ is the value for the argument $\phi\hat{z}$, and let us inquire whether $f(f\hat{\phi})$ is true or false. If $f(f\hat{\phi})$ is true that means, by the definition of f, '$f(f\hat{\phi})$ is false'. If $f(f\hat{\phi})$ is false, that means, by the definition of f, 'it is false that $f(f\hat{\phi})$ is false', whence it follows that $f(f\hat{\phi})$ is true. Thus whether we suppose $f(f\hat{\phi})$ true, or whether we suppose it false, we are led into a contradiction. This contradiction disappears if '$\phi(\phi\hat{z})$' is meaningless.

The paradox about the class of classes which are not members of themselves is also solved by the above considerations, if it is admitted that a class must always be defined by a propositional function. For then the class to be considered is the class of those classes which do not satisfy their defining functions. But as the class is derived from the function, it cannot, according to our principle, be an argument to its defining function, and therefore it neither satisfies nor does not satisfy its defining function.

When it is said that e.g. '$\phi(\phi\hat{z})$' is meaningless, and therefore neither true nor false, it is necessary to avoid a misunderstanding. If '$\phi(\phi\hat{z})$' were interpreted as meaning 'the value for $\phi\hat{z}$ with the argument $\phi\hat{z}$ is true', that would be not meaningless, but false. It is false for the same reason for which 'the King of France is bald' is false, namely because there is no such thing as 'the value for $\phi\hat{z}$ with the argument $\phi\hat{z}$'. But when, with some argument a, we assert ϕa, we are not meaning to assert 'the value for $\phi\hat{x}$ with the argument a is true'; we are meaning to assert the actual proposition which *is* the value for $\phi\hat{x}$ with the argument a. Thus for example if $\phi\hat{x}$ is '$\hat{x}$ is a man', ϕ (Socrates) will be 'Socrates is a man', *not* 'the value for the function "$\hat{x}$ is a man", with the argument Socrates, is true'. Thus in accordance with our principle that '$\phi(\phi\hat{z})$' is meaningless, we cannot legitimately deny 'the function "$\hat{x}$ is a man" is a man', because this is nonsense, but we can legitimately deny 'the value for the function "$\hat{x}$ is a man" with the argument "$\hat{x}$ is a man" is true', not on the ground that the value in question is false, but on the ground that there is no such value for the function.

We will denote by the symbol '$(x).\phi x$' the proposition 'ϕx

THEORY OF LOGICAL TYPES

always[1]', i.e. the proposition which asserts *all* the values for $\phi\hat{x}$. This proposition involves the function $\phi\hat{x}$, not merely an ambiguous value of the function. The assertion of ϕx, where x is unspecified, is a different assertion from the one which asserts all values for $\phi\hat{x}$, for the former is an ambiguous assertion, whereas the latter is in no sense ambiguous. It will be observed that '$(x).\phi x$' does not assert 'ϕx with all values of x', because, as we have seen, there must be values of x with which 'ϕx' is meaningless. What is asserted by '$(x).\phi x$' is all propositions which are values for $\phi\hat{x}$; hence it is only with such values of x as make 'ϕx' significant, i.e. with all *possible* arguments, that ϕx is asserted when we assert '$(x).\phi x$'. Thus a convenient way to read '$(x).\phi x$' is 'ϕx is true with all possible values of x'. This is, however, a less accurate reading than 'ϕx always', because the notion of *truth* is not part of the content of what is judged. When we judge 'all men are mortal', we judge truly, but the notion of truth is not necessarily in our minds, any more than it need be when we judge 'Socrates is mortal'.

II DEFINITION AND SYSTEMATIC AMBIGUITY OF TRUTH AND FALSEHOOD

Since '$(x).\phi x$' involves the function $\phi\hat{x}$, it must, according to our principle, be impossible as an argument to ϕ. That is to say, the symbol '$\phi\{(x).\phi x\}$' must be meaningless. This principle would seem, at first sight, to have certain exceptions. Take, for example, the function 'p is false', and consider the proposition '$(p).p$ is false'. This should be a proposition asserting all propositions of the form 'p is false'. Such a proposition, we should be inclined to say, must be false, because 'p is false' is not always true. Hence we should be led to the proposition

'$\{(p).p$ is false$\}$ is false',

i.e. we should be led to a proposition in which '$(p).p$ is false' is

---

[1] I use 'always' as meaning 'in all cases', not 'at all times'. Similarly 'sometimes' will mean 'in some cases'.

the argument to the function '$\hat{p}$ is false', which we had declared to be impossible. Now it will be seen that '$(p).p$ is false', in the above, purports to be a proposition about all propositions, and that, by the general form of the vicious-circle principle, there must be no propositions about *all* propositions. Nevertheless, it seems plain that, given any function, there is a proposition (true or false) asserting all its values. Hence we are led to the conclusion that 'p is false' and 'q is false' must not always be the values, with the arguments p and q, for a single function '$\hat{p}$ is false'. This, however, is only possible if the word 'false' really has many different meanings, appropriate to propositions of different kinds.

That the words 'true' and 'false' have many different meanings, according to the kind of proposition to which they are applied, is not difficult to see. Let us take any function $\phi\hat{x}$, and let ϕa be one of its values. Let us call the sort of truth which is applicable to ϕa 'first truth'. (This is not to assume that this would be first truth in another context: it is merely to indicate that it is the first sort of truth in our context.) Consider now the proposition $(x).\phi x$. If this has truth of the sort appropriate to it, that will mean that every value ϕx has 'first truth'. Thus, if we call the sort of truth that is appropriate to $(x).\phi x$ '*second* truth', we may define '$\{(x).\phi x\}$ has second truth' as meaning 'every value for $\phi\hat{x}$ has first truth', i.e. '$(x).(\phi x$ has first truth)'. Similarly, if we denote by '$(\exists x).\phi x$' the proposition 'ϕx sometimes', i.e. as we may less accurately express it, 'ϕx with some value of x', we find that $(\exists x).\phi x$ has second truth if there is an x with which ϕx has first truth; thus we may define '$\{(\exists x).\phi x\}$ has second truth' as meaning 'some value for $\phi\hat{x}$ has first truth', i.e. '$(\exists x).(\phi x$ has first truth)'. Similar remarks apply to falsehood. Thus '$\{(x).\phi x\}$ has second falsehood' will mean 'some value for $\phi\hat{x}$ has first falsehood'; i.e. '$(\exists x).(\phi x$ has first falsehood)', while '$\{(\exists x).\phi x\}$ has second falsehood' will mean 'all values, for $\phi\hat{x}$ have first falsehood', i.e. '$(x).(\phi x$ has first falsehood)'. Thus the sort of falsehood that can belong to a general proposition is different from the sort that can belong to a particular proposition.

Applying these considerations to the proposition '$(p).p$ is false', we see that the kind of falsehood in question must be specified. If, for example, first falsehood is meant, the function 'p has first falsehood' is only significant when p is the sort of proposition which has first falsehood or first truth. Hence '$(p).p$ is false' will be replaced by a statement which is equivalent to 'all propositions having either first truth or first falsehood have first falsehood'. This proposition has *second* falsehood, and is not a possible argument to the function 'p has *first* falsehood'. Thus the apparent exception to the principle that '$\phi\{(x).\phi x\}$' must be meaningless disappears.

Similar considerations will enable us to deal with 'not-p' and with 'p or q'. It might seem as if these were functions in which *any* proposition might appear as argument. But this is due to a systematic ambiguity in the meanings of 'not' and 'or', by which they adapt themselves to propositions of any order. To explain fully how this occurs, it will be well to begin with a definition of the simplest kind of *truth* and *falsehood*.

The universe consists of objects having various qualities and standing in various relations. Some of the objects which occur in the universe are complex. When an object is complex, it consists of interrelated parts. Let us consider a complex object composed of two parts a and b standing to each other in the relation R. The complex object 'a-in-the-relation-R-to-b' may be capable of being *perceived*; when perceived, it is perceived as one object. Attention may show that it is complex; we then *judge* that a and b stand in the relation R. Such a judgment, being derived from perception by mere attention, may be called a 'judgment of perception'. This judgment of perception, considered as an actual occurrence, is a relation of four terms, namely a and b and R and the percipient. The perception, on the contrary, is a relation of two terms, namely 'a-in-the-relation-R-to-b', and the percipient. Since an object of perception cannot be nothing, we cannot perceive 'a-in-the-relation-R-to-b' unless a is in the relation R to b. Hence a judgment of perception, according to the above definition, must be true. This does not mean that, in a judgment which *appears* to us to be one of perception, we are sure of not being in error, since we may err in thinking that our judgment has really been derived merely by analysis of what was perceived. But if our judgment has been so derived, it must be true. In fact, we may define *truth*, where such judgments are concerned, as consisting in the fact that there is a complex *corresponding* to the discursive thought which is the judgment. That is, when we judge 'a has the relation R to b', our judgment is said to be *true* when there is a complex 'a-in-the-relation-R-to-b', and is said to be *false* when this is not the case. This is a definition of truth and falsehood in relation to judgments of this kind.

It will be seen that, according to the above account, a judgment does not have a single object, namely the proposition, but has several interrelated objects. That is to say, the relation which constitutes judgment is not a relation of two terms, namely the judging mind and the proposition, but is a relation of several terms, namely the mind and what are called the constituents of the proposition. That is, when we judge (say) 'this is red', what occurs is a relation of three terms, the mind, and 'this', and red. On the other hand, when we *perceive* 'the redness of this', there is a relation of two terms, namely the mind and the complex object 'the redness of this'. When a judgment occurs, there is a certain complex entity, composed of the mind and the various objects of the judgment. When the judgment is *true*, in the case of the kind of judgments we have been considering, there is a corresponding complex of the *objects* of the judgment alone. Falsehood, in regard to our present class of judgments, consists in the absence of a corresponding complex composed of the objects alone. It follows from the above theory that a 'proposition', in the sense in which a proposition is supposed to be *the* object of a judgment, is a false abstraction, because a judgment has several objects, not one. It is the severalness of the objects in judgment (as opposed to perception) which has led people to speak of thought as 'discursive', though they do not appear to have realised clearly what was meant by this epithet.

Owing to the plurality of the objects of a single judgment, it follows that what we call a 'proposition' (in the sense in which this is distinguished from the phrase expressing it) is not a single entity at all. That is to say, the phrase which expresses a proposition is what we call an 'incomplete' symbol; it does not have meaning in itself, but requires some supplementation in order to acquire a complete meaning. This fact is somewhat concealed by the circumstance that judgment in itself supplies a sufficient supplement, and that judgment in itself makes no *verbal* addition to the proposition. Thus 'the proposition "Socrates is human"' uses 'Socrates is human' in a way which requires a supplement of some kind before it acquires a complete meaning; but when I judge 'Socrates is human', the meaning is completed by the act of judging, and we no longer have an incomplete symbol. The fact that propositions are 'incomplete symbols' is important philosophically, and is relevant at certain points in symbolic logic.

The judgments we have been dealing with hitherto are such as are of the same form as judgments of perception, i.e. their subjects are always particular and definite. But there are many judgments which are not of this form. Such are 'all men are mortal', 'I met a man', 'some men are Greeks'. Before dealing with such judgments, we will introduce some technical terms.

We will give the name of 'a *complex*' to any such object as 'a in the relation R to b' or 'a having the quality q', or 'a and b and c standing in the relation S'. Broadly speaking, a *complex* is anything which occurs in the universe and is not simple. We will call a judgment *elementary* when it merely asserts such things as 'a has the relation R to b', 'a has the quality q' or 'a and b and c stand in the relation S'. Then an *elementary* judgment is true when there is a corresponding complex, and false when there is no corresponding complex.

But take now such a proposition as 'all men are mortal'. Here the judgment does not correspond to *one* complex, but to many, namely 'Socrates is mortal', 'Plato is mortal', 'Aristotle is mortal', etc. (For the moment, it is unnecessary to inquire whether each of these does not require further treatment before we reach the ultimate complexes involved. For purposes of illustration, 'Socrates is mortal' is here treated as an elementary judgment, though it is in fact not one, as will be explained later. Truly elementary judgments are not very easily found.) We do not mean to deny that there may be some relation of the concept *man* to the concept *mortal* which may be *equivalent* to 'all men are mortal', but in any case this relation is not the same thing as what we affirm when we say that all men are mortal. Our judgment that all men are mortal collects together a number of elementary judgments. It is not, however, composed of these, since (e.g.) the fact that Socrates is mortal is no part of what we assert, as may be seen by considering the fact that our assertion can be understood by a person who has never heard of Socrates. In order to understand the judgment 'all men are mortal', it is not necessary to know what men there are. We must admit, therefore, as a radically new kind of judgment, such general assertions as 'all men are mortal'. We assert that, given that x is human, x is always mortal. That is, we assert 'x is mortal' of *every* x which is human. Thus we are able to judge (whether truly or falsely) that *all* the objects which have some assigned property also have some other assigned property. That is, given any propositional functions $\phi\hat{x}$ and $\psi\hat{x}$, there is a judgment asserting ψx with every x for which we have ϕx. Such judgments we will call *general judgments*.

It is evident (as explained above) that the definition of *truth* is different in the case of general judgments from what it was in the case of elementary judgments. Let us call the meaning of *truth* which we gave for elementary judgments 'elementary truth'. Then when we assert that it is true that all men are mortal, we shall mean that all judgments of the form 'x is mortal', where x is a man, have elementary truth. We may define this as 'truth of the second order' or 'second-order truth'. Then if we express the proposition 'all men are mortal' in the form

'$(x).x$ is mortal, where x is a man',

and call this judgment p, then 'p is true' must be taken to mean 'p has second-order truth', which in turn means

'$(x).$"x is mortal" has elementary truth, where x is a man'.

In order to avoid the necessity for stating explicitly the limitation to which our variable is subject, it is convenient to replace the above interpretation of 'all men are mortal' by a slightly different interpretation. The proposition 'all men are mortal' is equivalent to '"x is a man" implies "x is mortal", with all possible values of x'. Here x is not restricted to such values as are men, but may have any value with which '"x is a man" implies "x is mortal"' is *significant*, i.e. either true or false. Such a proposition is called a 'formal implication'. The advantage of this form is that the values which the variable may take are given by the function to which it is the argument: the values which the variable may take are all those with which the function is significant.

We use the symbol '$(x).\phi x$' to express the general judgment which asserts all judgments of the form 'ϕx'. Then the judgment 'all men are mortal' is equivalent to

'(x). "x is a man" implies "x is a mortal"',

i.e. to

'$(x).x$ is not a man or x is mortal'.

The meaning of *truth* which is applicable to this proposition is not the same as the meaning of *truth* which is applicable to 'x is a man' or to 'x is mortal'. And generally, in any judgment $(x).\phi x$, the sense in which this judgment is or may be true is not the same as that in which ϕx is or may be true. If ϕx is an elementary judgment, it is true when it *points to* a corresponding complex. But $(x).\phi x$ does not point to a single corresponding complex: the corresponding complexes are as numerous as the possible values of x.

It follows from the above that such a proposition as 'all the judgments made by Epimenides are true' will only be *prima facie* capable of truth if all his judgments are of the same order. If they are of varying orders, of which the nth is the highest, we may make n assertions of the form 'all the judgments of order m made by Epimenides are true', where m has all values up to n. But no such judgment can include itself in its own scope, since

CLASSES AND THE PARADOXES

such a judgment is always of higher order than the judgments to which it refers.

Let us consider next what is meant by the negation of a proposition of the form '$(x).\phi x$'. We observe, to begin with, that 'ϕx in some cases', or 'ϕx sometimes', is a judgment which is on a par with 'ϕx in all cases', or 'ϕx always'. The judgment 'ϕx sometimes' is true if one or more values of x exist for which ϕx is true. We will express the proposition 'ϕx sometimes' by the notation '$(\exists x).\phi x$', where '$\exists$' stands for 'there exists', and the whole symbol may be read 'there exists an x such that ϕx'. We take the two kinds of judgment expressed by '$(x).\phi x$' and '$(\exists x).\phi x$' as primitive ideas. We also take as a primitive idea the negation of an *elementary* proposition. We can then define the negations of $(x).\phi x$ and $(\exists x).\phi x$. The negation of any proposition p will be denoted by the symbol '$\sim p$'. Then the negation of $(x).\phi x$ will be *defined* as meaning

$$'(\exists x).\sim \phi x',$$

and the negation of $(\exists x).\phi x$ will be *defined* as meaning '$(x).\sim \phi x$'. Thus, in the traditional language of formal logic, the negation of a universal affirmative is to be defined as the particular negative, and the negation of the particular affirmative is to be defined as the universal negative. Hence the meaning of negation for such propositions is different from the meaning of negation for elementary propositions.

An analogous explanation will apply to disjunction. Consider the statement 'either p, or ϕx always'. We will denote the disjunction of two propositions p, q by '$p \vee q$'. Then our statement is '$p . \vee .(x).\phi x$'. We will suppose that p is an elementary proposition, and that ϕx is always an elementary proposition. We take the disjunction of two elementary propositions as a primitive idea, and we wish to *define* the disjunction

$$'p . \vee .(x).\phi x'.$$

This may be defined as '$(x).p \vee \phi x$', i.e. 'either p is true, or ϕx is always true' is to mean '"p or ϕx" is always true'. Similarly we will define

$$'p . \vee .(\exists x).\phi x'$$

THEORY OF LOGICAL TYPES

as meaning '$(\exists x) . p \vee \phi x$', i.e. we define 'either p is true or there is an x for which ϕx is true' as meaning 'there is an x for which either p or ϕx is true'. Similarly we can define a disjunction of two universal propositions: '$(x) . \phi x . \vee . (y) . \psi y$' will be defined as meaning '$(x, y) . \phi x \vee \psi y$', i.e. 'either ϕx is always true or ψy is always true' is to mean '"ϕx or ψy" is always true'. By this method we obtain definitions of disjunctions containing propositions of the form $(x) . \phi x$ or $(\exists x) . \phi x$ in terms of disjunctions of elementary propositions; but the meaning of 'disjunction' is not the same for propositions of the forms $(x) . \phi x$, $(\exists x) . \phi x$, as it was for elementary propositions.

Similar propositions could be given for implication and conjunction, but this is unnecessary, since these can be defined in terms of negation and disjunction.

III WHY A GIVEN FUNCTION REQUIRES ARGUMENTS OF A CERTAIN TYPE

The considerations so far adduced in favour of the view that a function cannot significantly have as argument anything defined in terms of the function itself have been more or less indirect. But a direct consideration of the kinds of functions which have functions as arguments and the kinds of functions which have arguments other than functions will show, if we are not mistaken, that not only is it impossible for a function $\phi\hat{z}$ to have itself or anything derived from it as argument, but that, if $\psi\hat{z}$ is another function such that there are arguments a with which both 'ϕa' and 'ψa' are significant, then $\psi\hat{z}$ and anything derived from it cannot significantly be argument to $\phi\hat{z}$. This arises from the fact that a function is essentially an ambiguity, and that, if it is to occur in a definite proposition, it must occur in such a way that the ambiguity has disappeared, and a wholly unambiguous statement has resulted. A few illustrations will make this clear. Thus '$(x) . \phi x$', which we have already considered, is a function of $\phi\hat{x}$; as soon as $\phi\hat{x}$ is assigned, we have a definite proposition, wholly free from ambiguity. But it is obvious that we cannot substitute for the function something which is not a function: '$(x).\phi x$' means 'ϕx in all cases', and depends for its significance upon the fact that there are 'cases' of ϕx, i.e. upon the ambiguity which is characteristic of a function. This instance illustrates the fact that, when a function can occur significantly as argument, something which is not a function cannot occur significantly as argument. But conversely, when something which is not a function can occur significantly as argument, a function cannot occur significantly. Take, e.g. 'x is a man', and consider '$\phi \hat{x}$ is a man'. Here there is nothing to eliminate the ambiguity which constitutes $\phi \hat{x}$; there is thus nothing definite which is said to be a man. A function, in fact, is not a definite object, which could be or not be a man; it is a mere ambiguity awaiting determination, and in order that it may occur significantly it must receive the necessary determination, which it obviously does not receive if it is merely substituted for something determinate in a proposition. This argument does not, however, apply directly as against such a statement as '$\{(x).\phi x\}$ is a man'. Common sense would pronounce such a statement to be meaningless, but it cannot be condemned on the ground of ambiguity in its subject. We need here a new objection, namely the following: A proposition is not a single entity, but a relation of several; hence a statement in which a proposition appears as subject will only be significant if it can be reduced to a statement about the terms which appear in the proposition. A proposition, like such phrases as 'the so-and-so', where grammatically it appears as subject, must be broken up into its constituents if we are to find the true subject or subjects. But in such a statement as 'p is a man', where p is a proposition, this is not possible. Hence '$\{(x).\phi x\}$ is a man' is meaningless.

IV THE HIERARCHY OF FUNCTIONS AND PROPOSITIONS

We are thus led to the conclusion, both from the vicious-circle principle and from direct inspection, that the functions to which a given object a can be an argument are incapable of being arguments to each other, and that they have no term in common with the functions to which they can be arguments. We are thus led to construct a hierarchy. Beginning with a and the other terms can be arguments to the same functions to which a can be argument, we come next to functions to which a is a possible argument, and then to functions to which such functions are possible arguments, and so on. But the hierarchy which has to be constructed is not so simple as might at first appear. The functions which can take a as argument form an illegitimate totality, and themselves require division into a hierarchy of functions. This is easily seen as follows. Let $f(\phi\hat{z}, x)$ be a function of the two variables $\phi\hat{z}$ and x. Then if, keeping x fixed for the moment, we assert this with all possible values of ϕ, we obtain a proposition:

$$(\phi).f(\phi\hat{z}, x).$$

Here, if x is variable, we have a function of x; but as this function involves a totality of values of $\phi\hat{z}$ [1] it cannot itself be one of the values included in the totality, by the vicious-circle principle. It follows that the totality of values of $\phi\hat{z}$ concerned in $(\phi).f(\phi\hat{z}, x)$ is not the totality of all functions in which x can occur as argument, and that there is no such totality as that of all functions in which x can occur as argument.

It follows from the above that a function in which $\phi\hat{z}$ appears as argument requires that '$\phi\hat{z}$' should not stand for *any* function which is capable of a given argument, but must be restricted in such a way that none of the functions which are possible values of '$\phi\hat{z}$' should involve any reference to the totality of such functions. Let us take as an illustration the definition of identity. We might attempt to define 'x is identical with y' as meaning 'whatever is true of x is true of y', i.e. 'ϕx always implies ϕy'. But here, since we are concerned to assert all values of 'ϕx implies ϕy' regarded as a function of ϕ, we shall be compelled to impose upon ϕ some limitation which will prevent us from including among values of ϕ values in which 'all possible values of ϕ' are referred to. Thus for example 'x is identical with a' is a function of x; hence, if it is a legitimate value of ϕ in 'ϕx always implies

---

[1] When we speak of 'values of $\phi\hat{z}$' it is ϕ, not $\hat{z}$, that is to be assigned.

ϕy', we shall be able to infer, by means of the above definition, that if x is identical with a, and x is identical with y, then y is identical with a. Although the conclusion is sound, the reasoning embodies a vicious-circle fallacy, since we have taken '$(\phi).\phi x$ implies ϕa' as a possible value of ϕx, which it cannot be. If, however, we impose any limitation upon ϕ, it may happen, so far as appears at present, that with other values of ϕ we might have ϕx true and ϕy false, so that our proposed definition of identity would plainly be wrong. This difficulty is avoided by the 'axiom of reducibility', to be explained later. For the present it is only mentioned in order to illustrate the necessity and the relevance of the hierarchy of functions of a given argument.

Let us give the name 'a-functions' to functions that are significant for a given argument a. Then suppose we take any selection of a-functions, and consider the proposition 'a satisfies all the functions belonging to the selection in question'. If we here replace a by a variable, we obtain an a-function; but by the vicious-circle principle this a-function cannot be a member of our selection, since it refers to the whole of the selection. Let the selection consist of all those functions which satisfy $f(\phi \hat{z})$. Then our new function is

$$(\phi).\{f(\phi \hat{z}) \text{ implies } \phi x\},$$

where x is the argument. It thus appears that, whatever selection of a-functions we may make, there will be other a-functions that lie outside our selection. Such a-functions, as the above instance illustrates, will always arise through taking a function of two arguments, $\phi \hat{z}$ and x, and asserting all or some of the values resulting from varying ϕ. What is necessary, therefore, in order to avoid vicious-circle fallacies, is to divide our a-functions into 'types', each of which contains no functions which refer to the whole of that type.

When something is asserted or denied about all possible values or about some (undetermined) possible values of a variable, that variable is called *apparent*, after Peano. The presence of the words *all* or *some* in a proposition indicates the presence of an apparent variable; but often an apparent variable is really present where language does not at once indicate its presence. Thus for example 'A is mortal' means 'there is a time at which A will die'. Thus a variable time occurs as apparent variable.

The clearest instances of propositions not containing apparent variables are such as express immediate judgments of perception, such as 'this is red' or 'this is painful', where 'this' is something immediately given. In other judgments, even where at first sight no variable appears to be present, it often happens that there really is one. Take (say) 'Socrates is human'. To Socrates himself, the word 'Socrates' no doubt stood for an object of which he was immediately aware, and the judgment 'Socrates is human' contained no apparent variable. But to us, who only know Socrates by description, the word 'Socrates' cannot mean what it meant to him; it means rather 'the person having such-and-such properties', (say) 'the Athenian philosopher who drank the hemlock'. Now in all propositions about 'the so-and-so' there is an apparent variable, as I have shown elsewhere.[1] Thus in what *we* have in mind when we say 'Socrates is human' there is an apparent variable, though there was no apparent variable in the corresponding judgment as made by Socrates, provided we assume that there is such a thing as immediate awareness of oneself.

Whatever may be the instances of propositions not containing apparent variables, it is obvious that propositional functions whose values do not contain apparent variables are the source of propositions containing apparent variables, in the sense in which the function $\phi\hat{x}$ is the source of the proposition $(x).\phi x$. For the values for $\phi\hat{x}$ do not contain the apparent variable x, which appears in $(x).\phi x$; if they contain an apparent variable y, this can be similarly eliminated, and so on. This process must come to an end, since no proposition which we can apprehend can contain more than a finite number of apparent variables on the ground that whatever we can apprehend must be of finite complexity. Thus we must arrive at last at a function of as many variables as there have been stages in reaching it from

[1] Cf. 'On Denoting', Russell *B* 1905*c*, and this volume, ch. 5.

our original proposition, and this function will be such that its values contain no apparent variables. We may call this function the *matrix* of our original proposition and of any other propositions and functions to be obtained by turning some of the arguments to the function into apparent variables. Thus for example, if we have a matrix-function whose values are $\phi(x, y)$, we shall derive from it

$(y) . \phi(x, y)$, which is a function of x,
$(x) . \phi(x, y)$, which is a function of y,

$(x, y) . \phi(x, y)$, meaning '$\phi(x, y)$ is true with all possible values of x and y'.

This last is a proposition containing no *real* variable, i.e. no variable except apparent variables.

It is thus plain that all possible propositions and functions are obtainable from matrices by the process of turning the arguments to the matrices into apparent variables. In order to divide our propositions and functions into types, we shall, therefore, start from matrices, and consider how they are to be divided with a view to the avoidance of vicious-circle fallacies in the definitions of the functions concerned. For this purpose, we will use such letters as a, b, c, x, y, z, w, to denote objects which are neither propositions nor functions. Such objects we shall call *individuals*. Such objects will be constituents of propositions or functions, and will be *genuine* constituents, in the sense that they do not disappear on analysis, as (for example) classes do, or phrases of the form 'the so-and-so'.

The first matrices that occur are those whose values are of the forms

$$\phi x, \psi(x, y), \chi(x, y, z \ldots),$$

i.e. where the arguments, however many there may be, are all individuals. The functions $\phi, \psi, \chi \ldots$, since (by definition) they contain no apparent variables, and have no arguments except individuals, do not presuppose any totality of functions. From the functions $\psi, \chi \ldots$ we may proceed to form other functions of x, such as $(y) . \psi(x, y)$, $(\exists y) . \psi(x, y)$, $(y, z) . \chi(x, y, z)$, $(y) : (\exists z) . \chi(x, y, z)$, and so on. All these presuppose no totality except that of individuals. We thus arrive at a certain collection of functions of x, characterised by the fact that they involve no variables except individuals. Such functions we will call '*first-order* functions'.

We may now introduce a notation to express 'any first-order function'. We will denote any first-order function by '$\phi!\hat{x}$' and any value for such a function by '$\phi!x$'. Thus '$\phi!x$' stands for any value for any function which involves no variables except individuals. It will be seen that '$\phi!x$' is itself a function of *two* variables, namely $\phi!\hat{z}$ and x. Thus $\phi!x$ involves a variable which is not an individual, namely $\phi!\hat{z}$. Similarly '$(x).\phi!x$' is a function of the variable $\phi!\hat{z}$, and thus involves a variable other than an individual. Again, if a is a given individual,

'$\phi!x$ implies $\phi!a$ with all possible values of ϕ'

is a function of x, but it is not a function of the form $\phi!x$, because it involves an (apparent) variable ϕ which is not an individual. Let us give the name 'predicate' to any first-order function $\phi!\hat{x}$. (This use of the word 'predicate' is only proposed for the purposes of the present discussion.) Then the statement '$\phi!x$ implies $\phi!a$ with all possible values of ϕ' may be read 'all the predicates of x are predicates of a'. This makes a statement about x, but does not attribute to x a *predicate* in the special sense just defined.

Owing to the introduction of the variable first-order function $\phi!\hat{z}$, we now have a new set of matrices. Thus '$\phi!x$' is a function which contains no apparent variables, but contains the two real variables $\phi!\hat{z}$ and x. (It should be observed that when ϕ is assigned, we may obtain a function whose values do involve individuals as apparent variables, for example if $\phi!x$ is $(y).\psi(x,y)$. But so long as ϕ is variable, $\phi!x$ contains no apparent variables.) Again, if a is a definite individual, $\phi!a$ is a function of the one variable $\phi!\hat{z}$. If a and b are definite individuals, '$\phi!a$ implies $\psi!b$' is a function of the two variables $\phi!\hat{z}, \psi!\hat{z}$, and so on. We are thus led to a whole set of new matrices,

$$f(\phi!\hat{z}), g(\phi!\hat{z}, \psi!\hat{z}), F(\phi!\hat{z}, x), \text{ and so on.}$$

CLASSES AND THE PARADOXES

These matrices contain individuals and first-order functions as arguments, but (like all matrices) they contain no apparent variables. Any such matrix, if it contains more than one variable, gives rise to new functions of one variable by turning all its arguments except one into apparent variables. Thus we obtain the functions

$(\phi).g(\phi!\hat{z}, \psi!\hat{z})$, which is a function of $\psi!\hat{z}$.
$(x).F(\phi!\hat{z}, x)$, which is a function of $\phi!\hat{z}$.
$(\phi).F(\phi!\hat{z}, x)$, which is a function of x.

We will give the name of *second-order matrices* to such matrices as have first-order functions among their arguments, and have no arguments except first-order functions and individuals. (It is not *necessary* that they should have individuals among their arguments.) We will give the name of *second-order functions* to such as either are second-order matrices or are derived from such matrices by turning some of the arguments into apparent variables. It will be seen that either an individual or a first-order function may appear as argument to a second-order function. Second-order functions are such as contain variables which are first-order functions, but contain no other variables except (possibly) individuals.

We now have various new classes of functions at our command. In the first place, we have second-order functions which have one argument which is a first-order function. We will denote a variable function of this kind by the notation $f!(\hat{\phi}!\hat{z})$, and any value of such a function by $f!(\phi!\hat{z})$. Like $\phi!x$, $f!(\phi!\hat{z})$ is a function of two variables, namely $f!(\hat{\phi}!\hat{z})$ and $\phi!\hat{z}$. Among possible values of $f!(\phi!\hat{z})$ will be $\phi!a$ (where a is constant), $(x).\phi!x$, $(\exists x).\phi!x$, and so on. (These result from assigning a value to f, leaving ϕ to be assigned.) We will call such functions 'predicative functions of first-order functions'.

In the second place, we have second-order functions of two arguments, one of which is a first-order function while the other is an individual. Let us denote undetermined values of such functions by the notation

$$f!(\phi!\hat{z}, x).$$

As soon as x is assigned, we shall have a predicative function of $\phi!\hat{z}$. If our function contains no first-order function as apparent variable, we shall obtain a predicative function of x if we assign a value to $\phi!\hat{z}$. Thus, to take the simplest possible case, if $f!(\phi!\hat{z}, x)$ is $\phi!x$, the assignment of a value to ϕ gives us a predicative function of x, in virtue of the definition of '$\phi!x$'. But if $f!(\phi!\hat{z}, x)$ contains a first-order function as apparent variable, the assignment of a value to $\phi!\hat{z}$ gives us a second-order function of x.

In the third place, we have second-order functions of individuals. These will all be derived from functions of the form $f!(\phi!\hat{z}, x)$ by turning ϕ into an apparent variable. We do not, therefore, need a new notation for them.

We have also second-order functions of two first-order functions, or of two such functions and an individual, and so on.

We may now proceed in exactly the same way to third-order matrices, which will be functions containing second-order functions as arguments, and containing no apparent variables, and no arguments except individuals and first-order functions and second-order functions. Thence we shall proceed, as before, to third-order functions; and so we can proceed indefinitely. If the highest order of variable occurring in a function, whether as argument or as apparent variable, is a function of the nth order, then the function in which it occurs is of the $n+1$th order. We do not arrive at functions of an infinite order, because the number of arguments and of apparent variables in a function must be finite, and therefore every function must be of a finite order. Since the orders of functions are only defined step by step, there can be no process of 'proceeding to the limit', and functions of an infinite order cannot occur.

We will define a function of one variable as *predicative* when it is of the next order above that of its argument, i.e. of the lowest order compatible with its having that argument. If a function has several arguments, and the highest order of function occurring among the arguments is the nth, we call the function predicative if it is of the $n+1$th order, i.e. again, if it is of the lowest order compatible with its having the arguments it has.

A function of several arguments is predicative if there is one of its arguments such that, when the other arguments have values assigned to them, we obtain a predicative function of the one undetermined argument.

It is important to observe that all possible functions in the above hierarchy can be obtained by means of predicative functions and apparent variables. Thus, as we saw, second-order functions of an individual x are of the form

$$(\phi).f!(\phi!\hat{z}, x) \quad \text{or} \quad (\exists\phi).f!(\phi!\hat{z}, x)$$
$$\text{or} \quad (\phi, \psi).f!(\phi!\hat{z}, \psi!\hat{z}, x) \quad \text{or etc.,}$$

where f is a second-order predicative function. And speaking generally, a non-predicative function of the nth order is obtained from a predicative function of the nth order by turning all the arguments of the $n-1$th order into apparent variables. (Other arguments also may be turned into apparent variables.) Thus we need not introduce as variables any functions except predicative functions. Moreover, to obtain any function of one variable x, we need not go beyond predicative functions of *two* variables. For the function $(\psi).f!(\phi!\hat{z}, \psi!\hat{z}, x)$, where f is given, is a function of $\phi!\hat{z}$ and x, and is predicative. Thus it is of the form $F!(\phi!\hat{z}, x)$, and therefore $(\phi, \psi).f!(\phi!\hat{z}, \psi!\hat{z}, x)$ is of the form $(\phi).F!(\phi!\hat{z}, x)$. Thus speaking generally, by a succession of steps we find that, if $\phi!\hat{u}$ is a predicative function of a sufficiently high order, any assigned non-predicative function of x will be of one of the two forms

$$(\phi).F!(\phi!\hat{u}, x), \ (\exists\phi).F!(\phi!\hat{u}, x),$$

where F is a predicative function of $\phi!\hat{u}$ and x.

The nature of the above hierarchy of functions may be restated as follows. A function, as we saw at an earlier stage, presupposes as part of its meaning the totality of its values, or, what comes to the same thing, the totality of its possible arguments. The arguments to a function may be functions or propositions or individuals. (It will be remembered that individuals were defined as whatever is neither a proposition nor a function.) For the present we neglect the case in which the

THEORY OF LOGICAL TYPES

argument to a function is a proposition. Consider a function whose argument is an individual. This function presupposes the totality of individuals: but unless it contains functions as apparent variables, it does not presuppose any totality of functions. If, however, it does contain a function as apparent variable, then it cannot be defined until some totality of functions has been defined. It follows that we must first define the totality of those functions that have individuals as arguments and contain no functions as apparent variables. These are the *predicative* functions of individuals. Generally, a predicative function of a variable argument is one which involves no totality except that of the possible values of the argument, and those that are presupposed by any one of the possible arguments. Thus a predicative function of a variable argument is any function which can be specified without introducing new kinds of variables not necessarily presupposed by the variable which is the argument.

A closely analogous treatment can be developed for propositions. Propositions which contain no functions and no apparent variables may be called *elementary propositions*. Propositions which are not elementary, which contain no functions, and no apparent variables except individuals, may be called *first-order propositions*. (It should be observed that no variables except *apparent* variables can occur in a proposition, since whatever contains a *real* variable is a function, not a proposition.) Thus elementary and first-order propositions will be values of first-order functions. (It should be remembered that a function is not a constituent in one of its values: thus for example the function '$\hat{x}$ is human' is not a constituent of the proposition 'Socrates is human'.) Elementary and first-order propositions presuppose no totality except (at most) the totality of individuals. They are of one or other of the three forms

$$\phi!x; \quad (x).\phi!x; \quad (\exists x).\phi!x,$$

where $\phi!x$ is a predicative function of an individual. It follows that, if p represents a variable elementary proposition or a variable first-order proposition, a function fp is either $f(\phi!x)$ or

$f\{(x).\phi!x\}$ or $f\{(\exists x).\phi!x\}$. Thus a function of an elementary or a first-order proposition may always be reduced to a function of a first-order function. It follows that a proposition involving the totality of first-order propositions may be reduced to one involving the totality of first-order functions; and this obviously applies equally to higher orders. The propositional hierarchy can, therefore, be derived from the functional hierarchy, and we may define a proposition of the nth order as one which involves an apparent variable of the $n-1$th order in the functional hierarchy. The propositional hierarchy is never required in practice, and is only relevant for the solution of paradoxes; hence it is unnecessary to go into further detail as to the types of propositions.

V THE AXIOM OF REDUCIBILITY

It remains to consider the 'axiom of reducibility'. It will be seen that, according to the above hierarchy, no statement can be made significantly about 'all a-functions', where a is some given object. Thus such a notion as 'all properties of a', meaning 'all functions which are true with the argument a', will be illegitimate. We shall have to distinguish the order of function concerned. We can speak of 'all predicative properties of a', 'all second-order properties of a', and so on. (If a is not an individual, but an object of order n, 'second-order properties of a' will mean 'functions of order $n+2$ satisfied by a'.) But we cannot speak of 'all properties of a'. In some cases, we can see that some statement will hold of 'all nth-order properties of a', whatever value n may have. In such cases, no practical harm results from regarding the statement as being about 'all properties of a', provided we remember that it is really a number of statements, and not a single statement which could be regarded as assigning another property to a, over and above all properties. Such cases will always involve some systematic ambiguity, such as that involved in the meaning of the word 'truth', as explained above. Owing to this systematic ambiguity, it will be possible, sometimes, to combine into a single verbal statement what are really a number of different statements, corresponding to different orders in the hierarchy. This is illustrated in the case of the liar, where the statement 'all A's statements are false' should be broken up into different statements referring to his statements of various orders, and attributing to each the appropriate kind of falsehood.

The axiom of reducibility is introduced in order to legitimate a great mass of reasoning, in which, *prima facie*, we are concerned with such notions as 'all properties of a' or 'all a-functions', and in which, nevertheless, it seems scarcely possible to suspect any substantial error. M. Poincaré surmises that the axiom of reducibility may be really another form of the axiom of complete induction. This, however, is by no means the case. The axiom of reducibility is very much more general in its scope, and serves many purely logical purposes with which mathematical induction has nothing to do.[1] These purposes must now be explained.

If we call a *predicate* of an object a predicative function which is true of that object, then the predicates of an object are only some among its properties. Take for example such a proposition as 'Napoleon had all the qualities that make a great general'. We may interpret this as meaning 'Napoleon had all the predicates that make a great general'. Here there is a predicate which is an apparent variable. If we put '$f(\phi!\hat{z})$' for '$\phi!\hat{z}$ is a predicate required in a great general', our proposition is

$$(\phi):f(\phi!\hat{z}) \text{ implies } \phi!(\text{Napoleon}).$$

Since this refers to a totality of predicates, it is not itself a predicate of Napoleon. It by no means follows, however, that there is not some one predicate common and peculiar to great

---

[1] M. Poincaré's statement of the axiom of mathematical induction, Poincaré *A* 1906, p. 867, may be summarised as follows: A *recurrent* class is one to which o belongs, and to which $n+1$ belongs if n belongs. An inductive number is one belonging to every recurrent class. A *finite* number is one such that $n < n+1$. Then the axiom of induction states that every finite number is inductive. To my mind, this axiom, so far from being evident, is extremely doubtful: I have myself the gravest doubts of its truth. Moreover there is very little in mathematics that is invalidated by supposing it false. And it is by no means impossible that it may be found hereafter to be capable either of proof or of disproof. Under these circumstances, I cannot see any good reason for assuming it as an axiom.

generals.[1] In fact, it is certain that there is such a predicate. For the number of great generals is finite, and each of them certainly possessed some predicate not possessed by any other human being – for example, the exact instant of his birth. The disjunction of such predicates will constitute a predicate common and peculiar to great generals. If we call this predicate $\psi!\hat{z}$, the statement we made about Napoleon was equivalent to $\psi!$(Napoleon). And this equivalence holds equally if we substitute any other individual for Napoleon. Thus we have arrived at a predicate which is always equivalent to the property we ascribed to Napoleon, i.e. it belongs to those objects which have this property, and to no others. The axiom of reducibility states that such a predicate always exists, i.e. that every property of an object belongs to the same collection of objects as those that possess some predicate.

We may next illustrate our principle by its application to *identity*. In this connexion, it has a certain affinity with Leibniz's identity of indiscernibles. It is plain that, if x and y are identical, and ϕx is true, then ϕy is true. Here it cannot matter what sort of function $\phi\hat{x}$ may be: the statement must hold for *any* function. But we cannot say, conversely: 'If, for all values of ϕ, ϕx implies ϕy, then x and y are identical', because 'all values of ϕ' is inadmissible. If we wish to speak of 'all values of ϕ', we must confine ourselves to functions of one order. We may confine ϕ to predicates, or to second-order functions, or to functions of any order we please. But we must necessarily leave out functions of all but one order. Thus we shall obtain, so to speak, a hierarchy of different degrees of identity. We may say 'all the predicates of x belong to y', 'all second-order properties of x belong to y', and so on. Each of these statements implies all its predecessors: for example, if all second-order properties of x belong to y, then all predicates of x belong to y, for to have all the predicates of x is a second-order property, and this property belongs to x. But we cannot, without the help of an axiom, argue

---

[1] Where a (finite) group of predicates is given by an effective enumeration, their disjunction is a predicate, because no predicate occurs in the disjunction as an apparent variable. [Note added in the French version.]

conversely that if all the predicates of x belong to y, all the second-order properties of x must also belong to y. Thus we cannot, without the help of an axiom, be sure that x and y are identical if they have the same predicates. Leibniz's identity of indiscernibles supplied this axiom. It should be observed that by 'indiscernibles' he cannot have meant two objects which agree as to *all* their properties, for one of the properties of x is to be identical with x, and therefore this property would necessarily belong to y if x and y agreed in *all* their properties. Some limitation on the common properties necessary to make things indiscernible is therefore implied by the necessity of an axiom. For purposes of illustration (not of interpreting Leibniz) we may suppose the common properties required for indiscernibility to be limited to predicates. Then the identity of indiscernibles will state that if x and y agree as to all their predicates, they are identical. This can be proved if we assume the axiom of reducibility. For in that case, every property belongs to the same collection of objects as is defined by some predicate. Hence there is some predicate common and peculiar to the objects which are identical with x. This predicate belongs to x, since x is identical with itself; hence it belongs to y, since y has all the predicates of x; hence y is identical with x. It follows that we may *define* x and y as identical when all the predicates of x belong to y, i.e. when $(\phi):\phi!x$ implies $\phi!y$. But apart from the axiom of reducibility, or some axiom equivalent in this connection, we should be compelled to regard identity as indefinable, and to admit (what seems impossible) that two objects may agree in all their predicates without being identical.

The axiom of reducibility is even more essential in the theory of classes. It should be observed, in the first place, that, if we assume the existence of classes, the axiom of reducibility can be proved. For in that case, given any function $\phi\hat{z}$ of whatever order, there is a class α consisting of just those objects which satisfy $\phi\hat{z}$. Hence 'ϕx' is equivalent to 'x belongs to α'. But 'x belongs to α' is a statement containing no apparent variable, and is therefore a predicative function of x. Hence if we assume the existence of classes, the axiom of reducibility becomes

CLASSES AND THE PARADOXES

unnecessary. The assumption of the axiom of reducibility is therefore a smaller assumption than the assumption that there are classes.

This latter assumption has hitherto been made unhesitatingly. I prefer, however, both on the ground of the contradictions, which require a more complicated treatment if classes are assumed, and on the ground that it is always well to make the smallest assumption required for proving our theorems – I prefer, on these grounds, to assume the axiom of reducibility rather than the existence of classes. But in order to explain the use of the axiom in dealing with classes, it is necessary first to explain the theory of classes.

VI THE THEORY OF CLASSES

To explain the theory of classes, it is necessary first to explain the distinction between *extensional* and *intensional* functions of functions. This is effected by the following definitions:

The *truth-value* of a proposition is its truth if it is true, and its falsehood if it is false. (This expression is due to Frege.)

Two propositions are said to be *equivalent* when they have the same truth-value, i.e. when they are both true or both false.

Two propositional functions are said to be *formally equivalent* when they are equivalent for every possible argument, i.e. when any argument which satisfies the one satisfies the other, and vice versa. Thus '$\hat{x}$ is a man' is formally equivalent to '$\hat{x}$ is a featherless biped'; '$\hat{x}$ is an even prime' is formally equivalent to '$\hat{x}$ is identical with 2'.

A function of a function is called *extensional* when its truth-value for any argument is the same as for any formally equivalent argument. That is to say, $f(\phi\hat{z})$ is an extensional function of $\phi\hat{z}$ if, provided $\psi\hat{z}$ is formally equivalent to $\phi\hat{z}$, $f(\phi\hat{z})$ is equivalent to $f(\psi\hat{z})$. But since ϕ and ψ are apparent variables in this definition, it is necessary to limit them to one type; we will limit them to *predicative* functions. Thus $f(\phi!\hat{z})$ is an extensional function if, for every ϕ and ψ, provided $\phi!\hat{z}$ is formally equivalent to $\psi!\hat{z}$, then $f(\phi!\hat{z})$ is equivalent to $f(\psi!\hat{z})$.

A function of a function is called *intensional* when it is not extensional.

The nature and importance of the distinction between intensional and extensional functions will be made clearer by some illustrations. The proposition '"x is a man" always implies "x is a mortal"' is an extensional function of the function '$\hat{x}$ is a man', because we may substitute, for 'x is a man', 'x is a featherless biped', or any other statement which applies to the same objects to which 'x is a man' applies, and to no others. But the proposition 'A believes that "x is a man" implies always "x is a mortal"' is an intensional function of "$\hat{x}$ is a man", because A may never have considered the question whether featherless bipeds are mortal, or may believe wrongly that there are featherless bipeds which are not mortal. Thus even if 'x is a featherless biped' is formally equivalent to 'x is a man', it by no means follows that a person who believes that all men are mortal must believe that all featherless bipeds are mortal, since he may have never thought about featherless bipeds, or have supposed that featherless bipeds were not always men. Again the proposition 'the number of arguments that satisfy the function $\phi!\hat{z}$ is n' is an extensional function of $\phi!\hat{z}$, because its truth or falsehood is unchanged if we substitute for $\phi!\hat{z}$ any other function which is true whenever $\phi!\hat{z}$ is true, and false whenever $\phi!\hat{z}$ is false. But the proposition 'A asserts that the number of arguments satisfying $\phi!\hat{z}$ is n' is an intensional function of $\phi!\hat{z}$, because, if A asserts this concerning $\phi!\hat{z}$, he certainly cannot assert it concerning all predicative functions that are equivalent to $\phi!\hat{z}$, because life is too short. Again, consider the proposition 'two white men have reached the North Pole'. This proposition states 'two arguments satisfy the function "$\hat{x}$ is a white man who has reached the North Pole".' The truth or falsehood of this proposition is unaffected if we substitute for '$\hat{x}$ is a white man who has reached the North Pole' any other statement which holds of the same argument or arguments, and of no others. Hence it is an extensional function. But the proposition 'It is a strange coincidence that two white men should have reached the North Pole', which states 'it is a strange coincidence that two arguments should satsify the function "$\hat{x}$ is a white man who has reached the North Pole"', is not equivalent to 'It is a strange coincidence that two arguments should satisfy the function "$\hat{x}$ is Dr Cook or Commander Peary".' Thus 'it is a strange coincidence that $\phi!\hat{x}$ should be satisfied by two arguments' is an intensional function of $\phi!\hat{x}$.

The above instances illustrate the fact that the functions of functions with which mathematics is specially concerned are extensional, and that intensional functions of functions only occur where non-mathematical ideas are introduced, such as what somebody believes or affirms, or the emotions aroused by some fact. Hence it is natural, in a mathematical logic, to lay special stress on *extensional* functions of functions.

When two functions are formally equivalent, we may say that they *have the same extension*. In this definition, we are in close agreement with usage. We do not assume that there is such a thing as an extension: we merely define the whole phrase 'having the same extension'. We may now say that an extensional function of a function is one whose truth or falsehood depends only upon the extension of its argument. In such a case, it is convenient to regard the statement concerned as being about the extension. Since extensional functions are many and important, it is natural to regard the extension as an object, called a *class*, which is supposed to be the subject of all the equivalent statements about various formally equivalent functions. Thus, e.g. if we say 'there were twelve Apostles', it is natural to regard this statement as attributing the property of being twelve to a certain collection of men, namely those who were Apostles, rather than as attributing the property of being satisfied by twelve arguments to the function '$\hat{x}$ was an Apostle'. This view is encouraged by the feeling that there is something which is identical in the case of two functions which 'have the same extension'. And if we take such simple problems as 'how many combinations can be made of n things?' it seems at first sight necessary that each 'combination' should be a simple object which can be counted as one. This, however, is certainly not necessary technically, and I see no reason to suppose that it is true philosophically. The technical procedure by which the apparent difficulty is overcome is as follows.

We have seen that an extensional function of a function may be regarded as a function of the class determined by the argument-function, but that an intensional function cannot be so regarded. In order to obviate the necessity of giving different treatment to intensional and extensional functions of functions, we construct an extensional function derived from any function of a function, and having the property of being equivalent to the function from which it is derived provided this function is extensional.

The derived function is defined as follows: Given a function $f(\phi\hat{z})$, our derived function is to be 'There is a predicative function which is formally equivalent to $\phi\hat{z}$ and satisfies f.' If $\phi\hat{z}$ is a predicative function, our derived function will be true whenever $f(\phi\hat{z})$ is true. If $f(\phi\hat{z})$ is an extensional function, and $\phi\hat{z}$ is a predicative function, our derived function will not be true unless $f(\phi\hat{z})$ is true; thus, in this case, our derived function is equivalent to $f(\phi\hat{z})$. If $f(\phi\hat{z})$ is not an extensional function, and if $\phi\hat{z}$ is a predicative function, our derived function may sometimes be true when the original function is false. But in any case the derived function is always extensional. The reason for confining ourselves to a *predicative* function formally equivalent to $\phi\hat{z}$ is that the function formally equivalent to $\phi\hat{z}$ has to be an apparent variable, and therefore must be of some one specified type, and it is natural to take the type of predicative functions as the simplest. It will be found that in all the cases of extensional functions that occur in practice, two formally equivalent functions, when taken as arguments,[1] give the same truth-value, even when either or both are not predicative; but this cannot be stated in the definition of extensional functions, because it would require a functional apparent variable not restricted to any one type. Whenever two formally equivalent functions give the same truth-value to $f(\phi\hat{z})$ even when they are

[1] Here the conjunction or disjunction is supposed to be given qualitatively (intensionally). If it is given in extension (that is to say by enumeration) no assumption is required; but in this case the number of predicates referred to must be finite. [Note added in the French version.]

not both predicative, then the function 'there is a predicative function formally equivalent to $\phi\hat{z}$ and satisfying f' will be equivalent to $f(\phi\hat{z})$, provided there is any predicative function formally equivalent to $\phi\hat{z}$. But if there is no such function, the derived function is necessarily false, even if the original function was true and f is extensional. At this point, we make use of the axiom of reducibility, according to which there always is a predicative function $\psi!\hat{z}$ formally equivalent to $\phi\hat{z}$.

In order that the derived function should be significant for any function $\phi\hat{z}$, of whatever order, provided it takes arguments of the right type, it is necessary and sufficient that $f(\psi!\hat{z})$ should be significant, where $\psi!\hat{z}$ is any *predicative* function. The reason of this is that we only require, concerning an argument $\phi\hat{z}$, the hypothesis that it is formally equivalent to some predicative function $\psi!\hat{z}$, and formal equivalence has the same kind of systematic ambiguity as to type that belongs to truth and falsehood, and can therefore hold between functions of any two different orders, provided the functions take arguments of the same type. Thus by means of our derived function we have not merely provided extensional functions everywhere in place of intensional functions, but we have *practically* removed the necessity for considering differences of type among functions whose arguments are of the same type. This effects the same kind of simplification in our hierarchy as would result from never considering any but predicative functions.

As was explained above, it is convenient to regard an extensional function of a function as having for its argument not the function, but the class determined by the function. Now we have seen that our derived function is always extensional. Hence, if our original function was $f(\psi!\hat{z})$, we write the derived function $f\{\hat{z}(\phi z)\}$, where '$\hat{z}(\phi z)$' may be read 'the class of arguments which satisfy $\phi\hat{z}$', or more simply 'the class determined by $\phi\hat{z}$'. Thus '$f\{\hat{z}(\phi z)\}$' will mean: 'There is a predicative function $\psi!\hat{z}$ which is formally equivalent to $\phi\hat{z}$ and is such that $f(\psi!\hat{z})$ is true.' This is in reality a function of $\phi\hat{z}$, but we treat it symbolically as if it had an argument $\hat{z}(\phi z)$. By the help of the axiom of reducibility, we find that the usual properties of

THEORY OF LOGICAL TYPES

classes result. For example, two formally equivalent functions determine the same class, and conversely, two functions which determine the same class are formally equivalent. Also to say that x is a member of $\hat{z}(\phi z)$, i.e. of the class determined by $\phi\hat{z}$, is true when ϕx is true, and false when ϕx is false. Thus all the mathematical purposes for which classes might seem to be required are fulfilled by the purely symbolic objects $\hat{z}(\phi z)$, provided we assume the axiom of reducibility.

In virtue of the axiom of reducibility, if $\phi\hat{z}$ is any function, there is a formally equivalent predicative function $\psi!\hat{z}$. Hence the class $\hat{z}(\phi z)$ is identical with the class $\hat{z}(\psi!z)$. Hence every class can be defined by a predicative function. Hence the totality of the *classes* to which a given term can be significantly said to belong or not to belong is a legitimate totality, although the totality of *functions* which a given term can be significantly said to satisfy or not to satisfy is not a legitimate totality. The classes to which a given term a belongs or does not belong are the classes defined by a-functions; they are also the classes defined by *predicative* a-functions. Let us call them a-classes. Then 'a-classes' form a legitimate totality, derived from that of predicative a-functions. Hence many kinds of general statements become possible which would otherwise involve vicious-circle paradoxes. These general statements are none of them such as to lead to contradictions, and many of them such as it is very hard to suppose illegitimate. The fact that they are rendered possible by the axiom of reducibility, and that they would otherwise be excluded by the vicious-circle principle, is to be regarded as an argument in favour of the axiom of reducibility.

It is worth while to note that all the purposes served by the axiom of reducibility are equally well served if we assume that there is always a function of the nth order (where n is fixed) which is formally equivalent to $\phi\hat{x}$, whatever may be the order of $\phi\hat{x}$. Here we shall mean by 'a function of the nth order' a function of the nth order relative to the arguments to $\phi\hat{x}$; thus if these arguments are absolutely of the nth order, we assume the existence of a function formally equivalent to $\phi\hat{x}$ whose absolute order is the $m+n$th. The axiom of reducibility in the form

CLASSES AND THE PARADOXES

assumed above takes $n = 1$, but this is not necessary to the use of the axiom. It is also unnecessary that n should be the same for different values of m; what is necessary is that n should be constant so long as m is constant. What is needed is that, where extensional functions of functions are concerned, we should be able to deal with any a-function by means of some formally equivalent function of a given type, so as to be able to obtain results which would otherwise require the illegitimate notion of 'all a-functions'; but it does not matter what the given type is. It does not appear, however, that the axiom of reducibility is rendered appreciably more plausible by being put in the above more general but more complicated form.

The axiom of reducibility is equivalent to the assumption that 'any combination or disjunction of predicates is equivalent to a single predicate', i.e. to the assumption that, if we assert that x has all the predicates that satisfy a function $f(\phi!\hat{z})$, there is some one predicate which x will have whenever our assertion is true, and will not have when it is false, and similarly if we assert that x has some one of the predicates that satisfy a function $f(\phi!\hat{z})$. For by means of this assumption, the order of a non-predicative function can be lowered by one; hence after some finite number of steps, we shall be able to get from any non-predicative function to a formally equivalent predicative function. It does not seem probable that the above assumption could be substituted for the axiom of reducibility in symbolic deductions, since its use would require the explicit introduction of the further assumption that by a finite number of downward steps we can pass from any function to a predicative function, and this assumption could not well be made without developments that are scarcely possible at an early stage. But on the above grounds it seems plain that in fact, if the above alternative axiom is true, so is the axiom of reducibility. The converse which completes the proof of equivalence is of course evident.

VII REASONS FOR ACCEPTING THE AXIOM OF REDUCIBILITY

That the axiom of reducibility is self-evident is a proposition which can hardly be maintained. But in fact self-evidence is never more than a part of the reason for accepting an axiom, and is never indispensable. The reason for accepting an axiom, as for accepting any other proposition, is always largely inductive, namely that many propositions which are nearly indubitable can be deduced from it, and that no equally plausible way is known by which these propositions could be true if the axiom were false, and nothing which is probably false can be deduced from it. If the axiom is apparently self-evident, that only means, practically, that it is nearly indubitable; for things have been thought to be self-evident and have yet turned out to be false. And if the axiom itself is nearly indubitable, that merely adds to the inductive evidence derived from the fact that its consequences are nearly indubitable: it does not provide new evidence of a radically different kind. Infallibility is never attainable, and therefore some element of doubt should always attach to every axiom and to all its consequences. In formal logic, the element of doubt is less than in most sciences, but it is not absent, as appears from the fact that the paradoxes followed from premises which were not previously known to require limitations. In the case of the axiom of reducibility, the inductive evidence in its favour is very strong, since the reasonings which it permits and the results to which it leads are all such as appear valid. But although it seems very improbable that the axiom should turn out to be false, it is by no means improbable that it should be found to be deducible from some other more fundamental and more evident axiom. It is possible that the use of the vicious-circle principle, as embodied in the above hierarchy of types, is more drastic than it need be, and that by a less drastic use the necessity for the axiom might be avoided. Such changes, however, would not render anything false which had been asserted on the basis of the principles explained above: they would merely provide easier proofs of the same theorems. There would seem, therefore, to be but the slenderest ground for fearing that the use of the axiom of reducibility may lead us into error.

One point in M. Poincaré's article on 'La logique de l'infini' calls for a word of explanation. He asserts (p. 469): 'The theory of types remains incomprehensible, unless one supposes the theory of ordinals already established.' This assertion appears to me to rest upon a confusion. That the types *have* an order is admitted; but it is not admitted that it is necessary to study this order as an order. The steps of a deduction have an order, but it is not necessary to the deduction to study the order of the steps, although, when we turn our attention to the order, we see that it is essential to the deduction. So with types: they have an order, and when we study it, we see that it is important. But we can make all the uses of them that are required without studying the order, just as we can distinguish a function $\phi\hat{x}$ from a function $\phi(\hat{x}, y)$ without knowing that the first has one argument while the second has two, though it would be idle pedantry to avoid all phrases which involve this knowledge, as soon as we have seen that we could avoid such phrases if we chose. So, with types, we may speak of their order in words which, strictly speaking, involve a knowledge of the ordinals, because it is obvious that we could make all the necessary uses of types without such words. Instead of speaking of functions of the first order, we should speak of 'functions $\phi!\hat{x}$'; instead of functions of the second order, 'functions $f!(\hat{\phi}!\hat{x})$', and so on. Thus although types have an order, the ordinals are not presupposed in the theory of types, and there is no logical circle in subsequently basing the theory of ordinals upon a basis which assumes the theory of types.

V

PHILOSOPHY OF LOGIC AND MATHEMATICS

Although Russell was usually a tireless explainer of his opinions on philosophical subjects, he spent little time explaining precisely what was involved in his claim that all of mathematics is reducible to logic. He considered *Principia Mathematica* explanation enough. But the *Principia* lacks any explicit formal semantics, nor does it contain any metalinguistic investigations of the system's scope and limits. The *Introduction to Mathematical Philosophy*, written in 1918, gives no help: it is an admirable exposition of the *Principia*, but not an explanation, at a higher level, of what it is all about. The following five essays show Russell in a more reflective mood, either considering his own work, or criticising the views of others on logical subjects.

The first essay. 'On the Axiom of Infinity' dates from 1904. In 1903, the Columbia mathematician C. J. Keyser had argued that the current theory of transfinite numbers required the assumption, in an axiom, of the existence of a denumerably infinite number of entities.[1] In his reply, Russell agreed that the existence of an infinite number of entities was required for the theory, but denied that a separate assumption to this effect was needed, because the existence of an infinite number of entities could be proved from prior principles. The proof he provided, in which the infinite 'entities' all turn out to be classes, was criticised by Whitehead,[2] but Russell eventually decided that Keyser was right. It is difficult to establish just when the decision was made to incorporate an 'axiom of infinity'[3] into the

[1] Keyser *A* 1903. See also Keyser *A* 1904. Keyser's axiom was not stated as such, but in a form logically equivalent to this.

[2] 'Does not the theory require the explicit recognition of at least an indefinite plurality, if not of the definite cardinal numbers?' Whitehead to Russell, 23 April 1905, Bertrand Russell Archives.

[3] *Principia* ∗120.04, labelled the 'axiom of infinity' is equivalent to Keyser's assumption.

Principia system, but in May 1906, Whitehead wrote to Russell, 'I don't like to have to assume as a Pp $\aleph_0$ entities, nor blocks of $\aleph_0$ Pp's.'[1] which shows that Russell, at least, had considered it by that time. Of this axiom Russell wrote in 1911:

> 'The axiom of infinity is purely empirical. Whatever v is, provided that it is a finite or transfinite cardinal number, it is possible *a priori* that v be the number of individuals in the universe. But, according to empirical evidence, and the divisibility of finite objects, it seems artificial to suppose that there are a finite number of objects in the universe. It doesn't seem to me that empirical data are enough to demonstrate that the number of individuals is not finite, but it is sufficient to demonstrate that the finitist hypothesis is much more difficult and less simple than the other, and the logic of infinity demonstrates that the finitist hypothesis is no way preferable *a priori*. I conclude, for reasons which usually decide scientific hypotheses, that it is better to presume that the number of individuals is infinite.'[2]

'On the Relation of Mathematics to Logic' (1905) is a reply to the French philosopher P. Boutroux, and shows Russell's patient attempts to disentangle logical from psychological and epistemological considerations. The general campaign against psychologism was already won in Germany through the efforts of Frege and Husserl, and, in England, by the work of Russell himself, but in France the question was still alive. Russell's essay appears here in English for the first time.

In 'The Regressive Method of Discovering the Premises of Mathematics' (1907), Russell argues that mathematics is a nonempirical but *inductive* science, a thesis that has been revived in recent years now that the rigid division of propositions into 'analytic' and 'synthetic' has been generally abandoned. Russell's views on the nature of systems, as indicated in this essay, are remarkable and have been little noted. It is generally

---

[1] Whitehead to Russell, 9 May 1906. 'Pp' is the *Principia* abbreviation for 'primitive proposition'.

[2] Russell *B* 1911*c*, p. 32. Translated by L. Mazzarins.

assumed that the attempt to 'reduce mathematics to logic' is motivated by the belief that logic is in some sense more secure than mathematics, and justifies its validity. But Russell believed that the theorems in logical systems justified the axioms more than the axioms justified the theorems. Consequently, in works like the *Principia*, it is mathematics that justifies logic[1] rather than the other way around. 'The Philosophical Importance of Mathematical Logic' was a lecture delivered in Paris at the Ecole des Hautes Etudes Sociales in 1911. General in scope, it indicates Russell's belief at the time that what the *Principia* system describes is the non-linguistic structure of implication between propositions. The late essay, 'Is Mathematics Purely Linguistic?' reverses ground on just this issue, and argues that the propositions of mathematics are all assertions concerning logical syntax. The date of this essay is not known, but to judge from the references to Truman's presidency and Rudolf Carnap's *Logical Foundations of Probability*, published in 1950, it must have been written between 1950 and 1952.

[1] 'Logic' for Russell, includes property theory, i.e. set theory.

11

The Axiom of Infinity

First published in the *Hibbert Journal*, **2** (July 1904), pp. 809–12.
Reprinted with the permission of the Bertrand Russell Estate.

Professor Keyser's very interesting article 'On the Axiom of Infinity'[1] contains a contention of capital importance for the theory of infinity. The view advocated by those who, like myself, believe all pure mathematics to be a mere prolongation of symbolic logic, is, that there are no new axioms at all in the later parts of mathematics, including among these both ordinary arithmetic and the arithmetic of infinite numbers. Professor Keyser maintains, on the contrary, that a special axiom is covertly invoked in all attempted demonstrations of the existence of the infinite. I believe that, in so thinking, he has been misled by the brevity, and perhaps obscurity, with which writers on this subject have usually stated their arguments. I am myself, as yet, obnoxious to the same charge; for the strict and detailed proof, with all the apparatus of logical rigour, is too long to be given incidentally, and was therefore reserved by me for Vol. ii of my *Principles of Mathematics*. It is possible, however, with a little care, so to set forth the outline of the proof as to make it appear that, whether 'exquisite' or not, it is certainly not 'round'.[2]

I presuppose, in setting forth the argument, the definition of number, and the proof that, with the suggested definition, every class has some perfectly well-defined number of terms. These matters I have discussed at length in Part II of the above mentioned work; and so far as appears, Professor Keyser has no fault in regard to them.

The first step is to demonstrate that there is such a number as 0. The number of things fulfilling any condition which nothing fulfils is defined to be 0; and it may be shown that there are

[1] Keyser *A* 1904.   [2] *Ibid*. pp. 549–50.

such conditions. For example, nothing is a proposition which is both true and false. Consequently, the number of things which are propositions which are both true and false is 0. Thus there is such a number as 0.

We next define the number 1 as follows. The number of terms in a class is 1 if there is a term in the class such that, when that term is taken away, the number of terms remaining is 0. That classes having one member exist is not hard to prove; for example, the class of things identical with the number 0 consists of the number 0 alone, and has only one member.

We proceed in like manner to the number 2, and we prove that the class consisting of the number 0 and 1 has two members, from which it follows that the number 2 exists.

It is in the next stage of the argument that, if I am not mistaken, Professor Keyser has been misled by undue brevity. He appears to think that, at this point, the advocates of infinity are content with a vague 'and so on' – a sort of *etcetera* which is intended to cover a multitude of sins. But *etceteras*, common as they are in ordinary mathematics, where they are represented by rows of little dots, are not tolerated by the stricter symbolic logicians. I shall try to show how it is that the argument proceeds without them.

We first prove the principle of mathematical induction[1] – a principle which, in this domain, does work for us such as hardly could be expected but from an *etcetera*. This principle states that any property possessed by the number 0, and possessed by $n+1$ when it is possessed by n, is possessed by all finite numbers. By means of this principle, we prove that, if n be any finite number, the number of numbers from 0 to n, both inclusive, is $n+1$. Consequently, if n exists, so does $n+1$. Hence, since 0 exists, it follows by mathematical induction that all finite numbers exist. We prove also that, if m and n be two finite numbers other than 0, $m+n$ is not identical with either m or n. It follows that, if n be any finite number, n is not the number of finite numbers, for the number of numbers from 0 to n is $n+1$, and $n+1$ is different

[1] I omit the proofs of propositions here assumed. Some of these proofs will be found in section 4 of Russell *B* 1901*b*; others in Whitehead *A* 1902.

from n. Thus no finite number is the number of finite numbers; and therefore, since the definition of the cardinal numbers[1] allows no doubt as to the existence of a number which is the number of the finite numbers, it follows that this number is infinite. Hence, from the abstract principles of logic alone, the existence of infinite numbers is rigidly demonstrated.

The above is a strict proof appropriate to pure mathematics, since the entities with which it deals are exclusively those belonging to the domain of pure mathematics. Other proofs, such as the one from the fact that the idea of a thing is different from the thing, are not appropriate to pure mathematics, since they do, as Professor Keyser points out, assume premises not mathematically demonstrable. But such proofs are not on that account circular or otherwise fallacious. Accepting the five postulates enumerated by Professor Keyser as assumed by Dedekind, I deny wholly that any one of the five *presupposes* the actual infinite. It is true that they together *imply* the actual infinite; it is indeed their purpose to do so. But it is too common, in philosophising, to confound implications with presuppositions. At this rate, all deduction would be circular. The contention advanced by Professor Keyser is essentially the following: If the conclusion (the existence of the infinite) were untrue, one of the premises would be untrue; consequently the premises beg the conclusion, and the argument is circular. But in all correct deductions, if the conclusion is false, so is at least one of the premises. The falsehood of the premises presupposes the falsehood of the conclusion, but it by no means follows that the truth of the premises presupposes the truth of the conclusion. The root of the error seems to be that, where a deduction is very easily drawn, it comes to be viewed as actually part of the premises; and thus very elementary arguments acquire the appearance, quite falsely, of *petitiones principii*.

Another point that calls for criticism is the psychological form of Professor Keyser's statement of the axiom of infinity. He states this axiom (p. 551) as follows: 'Conception and logical inference alike presuppose absolute certainty that an act

[1] See Russell *B* 1903, ch. xi.

AXIOM OF INFINITY

which the mind finds itself capable of performing is intrinsically performable endlessly.' This statement is rendered vague by the word *intrinsically*; but I sincerely hope there is no such presupposition in inference, since it is a most certain empirical fact that the mind is not capable of endlessly repeating the same act. Even apart from the fact that man is mortal, he is doomed to intervals of sleep; when he is drunk, he cannot perform mental acts which he can perform when he is sober, and so on. I am aware, of course, that such accidents are intended to be eliminated by the word *intrinsically*; but when they are, as they must be, explicitly and in terms eliminated, we get an axiom so complicated, and so plainly full of empirical elements, that it would require extraordinary boldness to present it as underlying all logic. The only escape would be to say that 'the mind' is to be taken to mean God's mind. But few will maintain nowadays that the existence of God is a necessary premise for all logic.[1]

The truth is that, throughout logic and mathematics, the existence of the human or any other mind is totally irrelevant; mental processes are studied by means of logic, but the subject-matter of logic does not presuppose mental processes and would be equally true if there were no mental processes. It is true that, in that case, we should not know logic; but our knowledge must not be confounded with the truths we know, and in the case of logic, although our knowledge of course involves mental processes, that which we know does not involve them. Logic will never acquire its proper place among the sciences until it is recognised that a truth and the knowledge of it are as distinct as an apple and the eating of it.

[1] See Russell *B* 1900*a*, ch. xv, especially section 111.

12

On the Relation of Mathematics to Logic

First published as 'Sur la Relation des Mathématiques à la Logistique' in the *Revue de Métaphysique et de Morale*, **13** (Nov. 1905), 906–17. English translation by H. S. Goldman and L. Mazzarins. Reprinted with the permission of the Bertrand Russell Estate.

The primary intention of this article is to respond to certain points in the discussion of Mr P. Boutroux: 'Mathematical Correspondence and Logical Relation'.[1] But as certain of the criticisms in that discussion derive from a rather serious misapprehension of my opinions, and as that misapprehension is probably owing to obscurities in the manner in which I set them forth, I will have to explain again very briefly, at this time, a few points.

Mr Boutroux asserts that *correspondence* and *order* are, according to me, indefinable (pp. 620, 626). Concerning *order*, I cannot understand how he was able to arrive at such an interpretation, considering the lengthy considerations by which I sought to establish the definition of that notion.[2] With regard to *correspondence*, he must have supposed that I regard it as undefinable, either because I regard *function* as undefinable, or because I regard *relation* as undefinable. But neither of these two notions is identical with that of *correspondence*. A correspondence is created by an equation of the form: $y = f(x)$, and in mathematics we are accustomed to speak of a relation when one has such an equation, and to imagine that this is the general type of all relations. But in reality such an equation defines only a uniform relation of x to y, which is a special and particular case. For example, 'x is a cousin of y', or 'sin x = sin y', cannot be reduced to the form $y = f(x)$. The idea of relation which is fundamental in logic is not the idea of a uniform relation, but the more general idea of which this is a particular case.

[1] Boutroux *A* 1905.
[2] Russell *B* 1903a, chs. xxiv, xxv. Cf. especially section 207.

RELATION OF MATHEMATICS TO LOGIC

Furthermore, the sort of function which is fundamental in logic is not the sort to which f belongs in the equation $y = f(x)$. Much confusion is caused by the diverse senses that one can attach to the word 'function'. The sort of function which is fundamental in logic is the *propositional* function; and the functions customary in mathematics are defined by means of this. To avoid misunderstandings, I am going to enumerate briefly the principal points of this development.

The undefinable of which I speak is the notion[1] of an expression which contains one or more variables, such as 'x is a man', 'x is a cousin of y', 'x is greater than 2', 'x implies y', and so on. I represent by $\phi!x$ every expression which contains x; likewise by $\phi!(x, y)$ every expression which contains x and y; etc. Such expressions are *propositional functions*; they are called *simple*, *double*, *triple*, etc. according to the number of variables which they contain.[2]

The ordinary functions of mathematics, such as $2x$, x^2, $\sin x$, $\log x$, etc., are not propositional, but what I call *denoting* functions. One can define not only particular denoting functions, but one can define also the general concept of denoting functions. Here is how. Let $\phi!(x, y)$ be a propositional function. It can happen that, for certain values of x, there is one value, and one only, of y for which $\phi!(x, y)$ is true. Now, for such values, 'The y for which $\phi!(x, y)$ is true' is a function of x, of the kind that I call *denoting* function. For any other value of x, that is, for a value for which $\phi!(x, y)$ is satisfied by no value of y or is satisfied by many, the expression 'The y for which $\phi!(x, y)$ is true' is meaningless, and denotes nothing.[3] Thus, 'The y for which $\phi!(x, y)$ is true' is a function of x defined for certain values

---

[1] I think that this notion could be replaced as well by the more primitive notion of the *substitution* of a variable for a constant, and that by this means one can avoid the contradictions in the matter of certain paradoxical classes, for example the contradiction discovered by Mr Burali-Forti. Mr Boutroux does not approach the difficulties which raise these contradictions, and consequently I do not discuss them here.

[2] These names are necessary only in order to speak of the functions in question. Their treatment in symbols does not require in any way that one be able to *count* the number of variables.

[3] On the interpretation of propositions where such expressions occur, see my article, 'On Denoting', Russell *B* 1905c, and ch. 5 in this volume.

of x, and meaningless for all other values. Every denoting function can be obtained in this manner. I employ for such a function the notation $f`x$, where the apostrophe can be read 'of'. The denoting function of $x$ derived from $\phi!(x,y)$ by the above procedure can be represented by $\phi\text{ı}`x$ [1] (the sign ı being introduced by analogy with the sign ı of Peano). Thus, for example, $2x$ is 'the y such that every class whose cardinal number is y can be divided into two exclusive parts whose cardinal number is x'. Likewise, denoting functions of two variables are derived from propositional functions of three variables; and so on.

With respect to relations, a relation in *intension* is simply a double propositional function $\phi!(x,y)$. Relations in *extension* are perhaps required for certain problems, for example, for counting the number of permutations of elements of a class. They can, like classes, be introduced by a new undefinable, or can be defined, by a rather complicated procedure by means of classes of propositional functions. It is only in the particular case where, for a given x, there is one value, and one only, of y for which $\phi!(x,y)$ is true, that $\phi!(x,y)$ is equivalent to an equation of the form $y=f`x$; thus, such equations do not express the general type of relations, but only those which are uniform. Every equation $y=f`x$ gives a correspondence of y to x; that correspondence is *reciprocal*, if two different values of x never give the same value of y. The notion of correspondence is thus not indefinable; it can be defined very simply in logical terms.[2]

The special arguments cited by Mr Boutroux (1905, pp. 630–

[1] Speaking rigorously, we do not define (in accordance with the theory of denotation developed in the article previously cited) the denoting function $\phi\text{ı}`x$ itself, but we define every proposition where that function occurs. Here is how: Let $\psi!y$ be a propositional function containing $y$. Then for each value of $x$, $\psi!\phi\text{ı}`x$ signifies by definition: 'There is one value, and one only, of y for which $\phi!(x,y)$ is true and this value satisfies $\psi!y$'. And here the phrase 'There is one value, and one only, of y for which $\phi!(x,y)$ is true' is itself defined as: 'There is a y such that, for every value of z, $\phi!(x,z)$ is equivalent to 'z is identical to y'. Thus $\phi\text{ı}`x$ by itself makes no sense, but every assertion with this subject has a well-defined sense.

[2] I do not intend to affirm that this is the only manner of treating denoting relations and functions, but only that, among many possible methods, this one appears to me the most convenient. I do not recognise at all a necessary divergence of principles between myself and authors who, like Mr Peano, prefer a different method.

632) to show that the notion of *function* is obscure and ambiguous, are ruled out, I hope, by the above demonstration. Nevertheless, these arguments contain certain points which demand explanation. In the first place, there is no ambiguity in having two different and clearly distinguished notions, as are the two types of functions of Mr Peano. These two types are in reality the function in *intension* and the function in *extension*: the u in ux can be regarded as an *operation*, which is understood in intension; whereas the 'defined function' F is in reality a correlation between x and ux for a given class of values of x; this function is extensive, and can be identified with my 'relation in extension'. It is not correct to say that 'an infinity of conditions' (Boutroux, 1905, p. 632) enters into the definition of a correlation: the only condition expressed by the propositional function $\phi!(x,y)$, which x and y must satisfy, is sufficient, since that function determines a corresponding extension.[1] To object to a correlation for being 'an impoverishment of the general idea of function' (p. 633), is as if one objected to the idea of *man* for being an impoverishment of the general idea of animal. The two notions have their use; and although the conception which Mr Peano develops of the function in intension could, in my opinion, be perfected, nevertheless it in no way lays itself open to the criticisms of Mr Boutroux.

There is thus no reason whatever to consider 'the mathematical correspondence as an intuitive fact analogous to physical law, as an object which it is the mission of science to analyse and whose content will be drawn out little by little through ongoing work' (pp. 620, 621). In order to justify such an opinion, it would be necessary to find a definite gap in the preceding deductions; but I do not see that Mr Boutroux has done so. He shows that the word *function* is, grammatically, capable of many meanings; this is a fact to interest the lexicographer. He shows, moreover, that the definition of this or that particular function is sometimes difficult. But this does not

---

[1] That the *practical determination* of the extension can be 'one of the objects which we are pursuing' (pp. 632-3), is perfectly true; but the extension is logically determined, otherwise we could not set ourselves to discover it. Mr Boutroux confuses here what is logically determined with what is known.

obscure the meaning of the word *function*, any more than a doubt about the identity of the Iron Mask obscures the meaning of the word *man*. It seems to me that Mr Boutroux attaches too much importance to *names*. He seems to believe that, if the *word* 'function' is employed first in one sense, then in another, the *object* designated first by this name has become the *object* designated afterward by this word. But objects, clearly, are in no way affected by the names which it pleases us to give them, and remain unchanged whatever the variations of our nomenclature and of our knowledge might be.

This particular case illustrates, if I am not mistaken, a confusion which vitiates many of the lines of argument of Mr Boutroux, to wit, the confusion between the act of discovery and the proposition discovered. He seems to believe that, because our knowledge of mathematics changes, mathematics itself changes. Thus he says (p. 629): 'If we adopt the views of Mr Hilbert, we will thus have to consider mathematics as a science which evolves, which grows, and which is enriched. What now becomes of the eight logical constants of Mr Russell?' In the first place, it is perfectly possible that the development of mathematics consists in defining and studying new complex notions formed by means of logical constants. An argument analogous to that of Mr Boutroux would be this: 'If we adopt the opinions of the historians, the Carolingians were a family which evolved, grew and spread. What now becomes of Charlemagne?' But this is not the main point. The main point is that what evolves is our *knowledge* of mathematics, and not the body of truths which we gradually discover. That evolution makes it very likely that a list of eight constants drawn up in the present situation of our knowledge will need correction; but it does not in the least degree make it likely that there cannot be found any list of constants at all. Because I think of one thing, then of another, it does not follow that the *things* have changed. The variability of things, according to Mr Boutroux, seems to consist in our applying the same name to different things at different times. But if there were no constancy whatever in the objects of thought, it is difficult to see how we could become aware of changes in thinking. For it is necessary to be able to compare the objects of two different thoughts, and to see that they are different, in order to recognise some change. Whereas, in order for the theory of Mr Boutroux to be legitimate, it would be necessary that the old object entirely disappeared, having become itself, by evolution, the new object.

Mr Boutroux remarks (p. 622) that we can consider a mathematical concept from the point of view of what it tends to become, or from the point of view of what it is in its present state. Here again there is some confusion. In what sense does a concept retain its identity while undergoing its alleged development? Does not Mr Boutroux rather have in mind the following process: Certain theorems are known to be valid for a concept that we will call N; then one finds that these theorems hold for a different and more general concept, to which we then transfer the name N. Thus, in practice, a mathematical concept is constituted by a considerable collection of theorems which hold for it: its present sense will be the most general sense for which the theorems in question are *known* at present to be true, whereas the sense towards which the concept is supposed to tend (admitting an optimistic opinion concerning the intellectual future of mankind) is the most general sense for which the theorems in question are really true. But the present concept is just as legitimate as the future one, in as much as we lack the temerity to affirm that it is incapable of a further useful generalisation.

In any case, it is difficult to see how one can take the point of view of what a concept ought to be, without possessing the gift of prophecy. When we think of what will be thought later on, we ordinarily want to speak of what we ourselves already think, though the bulk of our contemporaries do not accept it. But this involves the undemonstrable premise that we are wiser than our contemporaries. Consequently, it is impossible to take the point of view of what a science will be, and one can only really speak of the present state of a science.

The theory of intuition of Mr Boutroux is not easy to understand, for me at least. He says (p. 624): 'We will say that a piece of knowledge is intuitive if, on the one hand, it is not the result of sense experience, and if, on the other hand, it is not deduced from previous knowledge by analysis or synthetic combination.' But this is less clear than what he says previously (p. 623): 'It is possible that the notion of correspondence is undefinable and yet we cannot dispense with definition. This is what will happen if, on the one hand, the content of this notion is infinite and undetermined (cannot be expressed by a finite number of words), and if it nevertheless is impossible to argue about the mathematical correspondence short of defining it.'

That hypothesis raises many difficulties which suffice, in my opinion, to show that it is untenable. In the first place, one supposes necessarily that we have an idea of correspondence, by comparison with which we examine successive definitions and establish that they are more or less inadequate. The idea that we have of correspondence must not change as our definitions change; it must remain constant; for, if the idea changed, the successive definitions would not be inadequate, but would be the adequate definitions of varying ideas. We have thus an idea of correspondence, and nevertheless that idea has an infinite complexity. But is it not evident that none of our ideas has an infinite complexity? Our ideas of infinite classes, for example, are always obtained by means of concepts which have only a finite complexity. Surely, the opinion that we are able to imagine ideas of an infinite complexity is new, and as for me, I see no reason to believe it true.

But the principal criticism of the theory of Mr Boutroux results from the supposition that, although all the definitions proposed for correspondence are false, some definition is nevertheless necessary in order to reason about it. Because it follows that all the deductions founded on the proposed definitions could be false, since the definition, which by hypothesis is false, could be false in a manner which renders our deductions false. Thus, if Mr Boutroux were correct, we would be able to know absolutely nothing concerning correspondence, although we would know enough of it to check the various successive definitions of it. But this state of affairs is contradictory.

In my opinion, the only way to maintain without contradiction something analogous to the theory in question, would be to admit openly the idea of correspondence as one of our undefinable terms, and to regard the alleged definitions as primitive propositions concerning correspondence. In this case, all the successive stages would be correct, although unequally complete. Our primitive propositions would be true, although there might exist other true primitive propositions which would be necessary in order to deduce other properties of the correspondence. This theory is not contradictory; but it is not the theory of Mr Boutroux, and, in fact, there is every reason to believe that correspondence is not undefinable.

I conclude, thus, that the proposed theory of intuition becomes, when one purges it of all contradiction, the theory of undefinables and undemonstrables, and that there is no reason to place correspondence among our undefinables.

I come now to some questions of a less general character raised by Mr P. Boutroux's article. He doubts that Analysis can be entirely explained by means of the undefinables enumerated in my *Principles of Mathematics*. Apparently he does not dispute that the concepts that I have explicitly treated can be explained thus. He cites (p. 626, note 2) a passage where I enumerated 'number, infinity, continuity, the various spaces of geometry, and movement', and he supposes that I have intended to make there a *complete* enumeration of mathematical concepts. I did not have, in fact, any such intention, since evidently the number of mathematical concepts is infinite. For example the cardinal number 3,210 is certainly one of the concepts of mathematics, and yet I have given no definition of it. Having defined 0, 1, and 2, I thought that it was sufficiently evident that the process could be continued. In the same way, with regard to Analysis, I defined complex numbers (section 360),[1] the continuity of a function, its derivative and its integral (sections 304, 305, 307). But these are expressly the notions from which Analysis proceeds: the rest of the construction is in the textbooks.

There seem to be two reasons on account of which Mr

[1] P. 379, line 27, 'real' is a printing error, which should be replaced by 'complex'.

Boutroux believes that the theory of functions goes beyond logic, to wit: (1) the multiplicity of functions that the theory deals with, and (2) the motives that cause mathematicians to study certain functions rather than others. On the first point, he says (p. 630): 'The theory of functions is the representation, by means of quantified relations, of the correspondences capable of existing between variables. The work of the mathematician consists here in determining, particularising, and representing concretely the correspondences that he perceives by intuition.' He continues[1] (and here is the important point): 'We thus fall back on the conclusions mentioned above. The notions of mathematical Analysis are undefined (their definition is never completed).' In this passage, as in others, it seems that Mr Boutroux confuses the definition of a class with the enumeration of its elements; otherwise, there would not be the appearance of a connection between his premises and his conclusion. The argument seems to be this: 'Mathematicians find, without end, new functions, and this progress can have no termination. Thus, the *notion* of function is infinitely complex, and can never be completely defined.' If it is this that is meant, it involves a confusion, pure and simple, between intension and extension. In virtue of the same argument, the sense of 'finite cardinal number' would be infinitely complex; since the whole human race could devote itself from now until the death of the last man, to the enumeration of new finite cardinal numbers without coming any closer to the end of this process. Mr Boutroux would reply, perhaps, that he is thinking not only of different individual functions, but of different *types* of functions. But each new cardinal number belongs also to an infinite number of classes to which none of its predecessors belongs, and is consequently, not only of a new type, but of an infinity of new types. Thus, following the argument in question, the concept 'finite cardinal number' has an infinite complexity, 'which evolves, which grows, and becomes richer' just as millionaires are led by the needs of their accounts to consider greater and greater numbers. Likewise, as long as infants continue being brought

[1] After an interval, it is true; but the reasoning seems to be continued.

RELATION OF MATHEMATICS TO LOGIC

into the world, the meaning of 'human being' is uncertain. And thus for all: if we are not able to provide a list of all the examples of a concept, one claims that the *meaning* of this concept is uncertain. To this one must respond that we are, by hypothesis, capable of deciding, of each object given, whether it is or is not an example of the concept in question; but this would be impossible if the concept were not fixed independently of the question of knowing whether it does or does not include the object under consideration. Speaking logically, the extension of a concept is determined as soon as the concept is determined; speaking psychologically, it is perfectly possible to know the concept perfectly, without thereby knowing all of its extension. What I am maintaining is that logic suffices to define the *intension* of 'correspondence', and consequently also, speaking logically, its *extension*. But, regarding our knowledge, logic permits us only to decide if this or that object is or is not a correspondence, without furnishing us the means of giving a complete enumeration of all of the infinitely numerous correspondences which exist.

One can express the opinion of Mr Boutroux in another form: 'To have a thorough knowledge of a class-concept, it is not sufficient to know *a single* attribute common and particular to the elements of the class, it is necessary to know *all* of the analogous attributes. It is the sum total of these attributes which one can call *the* intension of the class. But, in a case like that of correspondences, we always find that the attributes which we supposed necessarily united are in reality separable. Consequently, we do not know completely the intension in question.'

To this thesis, we would respond that the intension, in this sense, is simply an extension of class-concept, to wit, the extension of 'all the class-concepts which have the given extension'. That is not a fundamental logical entity, and it is *never* necessary or possible to know *all* the class-concepts having a given extension, since their number is always equal to the number of all entities. And it is not the possibility of knowing that extension that one means when one says that a class is definable. What one means is that a class-concept, whose extension is the given class, can be constructed by means of concepts already known. In this sense, nothing that Mr Boutroux has said tends to show that the class of correspondences is undefinable.

The confusion which I believe I have discovered between the motives of study and the objects studied appears in many of the arguments directed against the reduction of mathematics to logic. Take for example the following passage (p. 627):

'It is in the choice of the class of functions studied, in the choice of the propositions taken for definitions, that the discovery and proper work of the mathematician principally will reside. Essentially undetermined with regard to their form, the problems of mathematical Analysis could not be confined within any definition.'

What is curious is that immediately after, the author avows that the problem of continuity presents itself in a determined form. This is curious, because the problem has only this peculiarity, that it is resolved, and that the solution was obtained by the same methods that Mr Boutroux does not like. But this is not the point. The point is that no one pretended that logic alone could tell us what problems we should study, and that the choice of problems to study is, everyone will agree, a matter of individual judgment. But this has nothing to do with the question of knowing if the solution of mathematical problems can be obtained in terms of logic. It would be just as logical to say: 'It is not by means of railroads that people travel; for the railroads alone cannot decide where I should take my vacation, which is the important point after all.' What Mr Boutroux says is true, applied to the psychology of the mathematician; but the psychology of the mathematician is not mathematics.

In sum, the principal points with respect to which, if the previous arguments are correct, the discussion of Mr Boutroux opens itself to criticism, are the following:

1. He believes that a class-concept can only be known if its extension is known.

2. He confuses the act of discovery with the proposition discovered.

3. He reasons as if, when one transfers a name from one concept to another, the first concept is itself changed into the other.

4. His theory of intuition leads to this result, that we can know much about an object which is described as necessarily unknowable.

5. He confuses logical constancy, which consists simply in being a definite entity, with historical constancy, which does not concern things, but our manner of knowing them.

If one admits that these are errors, the thesis that correspondence cannot be defined and that Analysis contains extra-logical concepts no longer seems tenable.

13

The Regressive Method of Discovering the Premises of Mathematics

Read before the Cambridge Mathematical Club, 9 March 1907. Reprinted with the permission of the Bertrand Russell Archives, McMaster University.

My object in this paper is to explain in what sense a comparatively obscure and difficult proposition may be said to be a premise for a comparatively obvious proposition, to consider how premises in this sense may be discovered, and to emphasise the close analogy between the methods of pure mathematics and the methods of the sciences of observation.

There is an apparent absurdity in proceeding, as one does in the logical theory of arithmetic, through many rather recondite propositions of symbolic logic, to the 'proof' of such truisms as $2+2=4$: for it is plain that the conclusion is more certain than the premises, and the supposed proof therefore seems futile. But of course what we are really proving is not the truth of $2+2=4$, but the fact that from our premises this truth can be deduced. The proposition $2+2=4$ itself strikes us now as obvious; and if we were asked to prove that 2 sheep + 2 sheep = 4 sheep, we should be inclined to deduce it from $2+2=4$. But the proposition '2 sheep + 2 sheep = 4 sheep' was probably known to shepherds thousands of years before the proposition $2+2=4$ was discovered; and when $2+2=4$ was first discovered, it was probably inferred from the case of sheep and other concrete cases. Thus we see that the word 'premise' has two quite different senses: there is what we may call the 'empirical premise', which is the proposition or propositions from which we actually are led to believe the proposition in question; and there is what we will call the 'logical premise', which is some logically simpler proposition or propositions from which, by a valid deduction, the proposition in question can be obtained. Thus the empirical premises for $2+2=4$ will be '2 sheep $+2$ sheep $=4$ sheep', and other like facts; whereas the logical premises will be certain principles of symbolic logic.

We may distinguish the proximate from the ultimate logical premise of a given proposition. The proximate logical premise will be whatever proposition comes just before the given proposition in the proof. Thus in Euclid, the proximate premise consists of the propositions referred to in the proof, while the relatively ultimate premise consists of the axioms and postulates. And premises which are ultimate in one investigation may cease to be so in another; that is, we may find logically simpler propositions from which they can be deduced.

The 'logical simplicity' of a proposition is measured, roughly speaking, by the number of its constituents. Thus $2+2=4$ is simpler than 2 sheep $+2$ sheep $=4$ sheep, because the latter contains all the constituents of the former with one addition, namely 'sheep'. It is a mistake to suppose that a simpler idea or proposition is always easier to apprehend than a more complicated one; and this mistake has been the source of many of the errors of *a priori* philosophers. The propositions that are easiest to apprehend are somewhere in the middle, neither very simple nor very complex. Generally speaking, they become simpler as civilisation advances. Thus *we* probably find it easier to think of fishing than of trout-fishing or salmon-fishing; but I am told that savages are apt to have a verb for trout-fishing and another for salmon-fishing, but no verb for fishing. When we get beyond the degree of complexity which makes propositions easiest, the empirical premise and the proximate logical premise will generally coincide. Thus in mathematics, except in the earliest parts, the propositions from which a given proposition is deduced generally give the reason why we believe the given proposition. But in dealing with the principles of mathematics, this relation is reversed. Our propositions are too simple to be easy, and thus their consequences are generally easier than they are. Hence we tend to believe the premises because we can see that their consequences are true, instead of believing the consequences because we know the premises to be true. But the inferring of premises from consequences is the essence of induction; thus the method in investigating the principles of mathematics is really an inductive method, and is substantially the same as the method of discovering general laws in any other science.

In every science, we start with a body of propositions of which we feel fairly sure. These are our empirical premises, commonly called the facts, which are generally got by observation. We may then ask either: What follows from these facts? or, what do these facts follow from? The general laws of a science are propositions logically simpler than the empirical premises of the science, but such that the empirical premises, or some of them, can be deduced from these laws. The laws only become as certain as the empirical premises if we can show that no other hypotheses would lead to the empirical premises, or if (what may happen in mathematics) the laws, once obtained, are found to be themselves obvious, and thus to be capable of themselves becoming empirical premises. The law of contradiction, for example, must have been originally discovered by generalising from instances, though, once discovered, it was found to be quite as indubitable as the instances. Thus it is both an empirical and a logical premise. But when the general laws are neither themselves obvious, nor demonstrably the only hypotheses to account for the empirical premises, then the general laws remain merely probable; though the degree of probability may be indefinitely heightened as observation and experiment increase the number of empirical premises which they account for.

In induction, if p is our logical premise and q our empirical premise, we know that p implies q, and in a text-book we are apt to begin with p and deduce q. But p is only believed on account of q. Thus we require a greater or less probability that q implies p, or, what comes to the same thing, that not-p implies not-q. If we can *prove* that not-p implies not-q, i.e. that p is the only hypothesis consistent with the facts, that settles the question. But usually what we do is to test as many alternative hypotheses as we can think of. If they all fail, that makes it probable, more or less, that any hypothesis other than p will fail. But in this we are simply betting on our inventiveness: we think it unlikely that we should not have thought of a better hypothesis if there were one. Perhaps, however, we may reinforce this rather slender ground of belief by the observation that, when inductive hypotheses require correction, the new hypothesis is generally not much changed from the old one, so that we are very likely to have something like the right hypothesis. And this is rendered probable by the fact that the consequences of a false hypothesis are true and false in equal numbers; if, therefore, the whole of a haphazard collection of consequences of a given hypothesis are found to be true, that gives a high degree of probability that the hypothesis is true, or that, if not wholly true, it can be split into a true part and a false part, of which only the true part is really relevant in obtaining the collection of true consequences.

The advantage of obtaining simple logical premises in place of empirical premises is partly that it gives a greater chance of isolating a possible pervading element of falsehood, partly that it organises our knowledge, and partly that the logical premises have, as a rule, many more consequences than the empirical premises, and thus lead to the discovery of many things which could not otherwise be known. The law of gravitation, for example, leads to many consequences which could not be discovered merely from the apparent motions of the heavenly bodies, which are our empirical premises. And so in arithmetic, taking the ordinary propositions of arithmetic as our empirical premises, we are led to a set of logical premises from which we can deduce Cantor's theory of the transfinite.

It may be worth while to specify the process in arithmetic more in detail. The usual elementary propositions, such as $2+2=4$, were once, as we saw, comparatively general laws collected from empirical premises; but by now they have become sufficiently obvious to be themselves taken as empirical premises. Assuming, then, that elementary arithmetic is true, we may ask for the fewest and simplest logical premises from which it can be deduced. Peano reduced the special premises required for arithmetic to five, using three primitive ideas. The primitive ideas are o, *natural number*, and *successor of*. The five primitive propositions are:

1. o is a natural number.
2. If a is a natural number, so is the successor of a.
3. If a, b are natural numbers having the same successor, then $a = b$.
4. o is not the successor of any natural number.
5. If s is a class of which o is a member, and if, whenever x is a member of s, the successor of x is a member of s, then every natural number is a member of s. (This is the principle of mathematical induction.)

Peano shows that these five primitive propositions suffice to found arithmetic. It is to be observed that they go beyond the empirical premises out of which they are distilled. For the particular facts known in arithmetic all deal with numbers not exceeding some finite though indefinitely extensible size. But Peano's premises are recommended not only by the fact that arithmetic follows from them, but also by their inherent obviousness. These two grounds together make their probability so great as to be almost certainty.

Peano's premises are not the ultimate logical premises of arithmetic. Simpler premises and simpler primitive ideas are to be had by carrying our analysis on into symbolic logic. Peano's axioms may be stated as an existence-theorem, namely 'there is a class called the *natural numbers*, containing a relation called *succession*, and a certain member, called o, and having the following properties' – and then we repeat the five axioms. Thus if we can prove this existence-theorem by means of logically simpler premises, the regress towards ultimate logical premises will have been carried a stage farther. It is known that all ordinary pure mathematics, including the existence-theorems for the various geometries, follows from arithmetic, and therefore from Peano's five premises: this represents a previous stage in the regress. Thus for the present we may take

DISCOVERING THE PREMISES OF MATHEMATICS

Peano's five premises as our empirical premises, regarding them, so to speak, as hostages for the whole of ordinary pure mathematics.

Peano prefaces his arithmetic by an exposition of symbolic logic; and symbolic logic is used by him in deducing arithmetic from his five premises. Thus the premises of symbolic logic are in any case *necessary* to arithmetic; if they can be shown to be also *sufficient*, the five premises will cease to be logical premises, and will take their place as theorems. The first serious attempt in this direction is that of Frege, who showed that a cardinal number may be defined as a class of similar classes. Then 0 is the class of all classes which have no members, i.e. it is the class whose only member is the null-class; and the natural numbers may be *defined* as those that obey mathematical induction starting from 0. In this way the existence-theorem which we saw to be equivalent to Peano's five axioms is deduced from purely logical propositions which Peano requires just as much as Frege does. These logical propositions are therefore more ultimate logical premises than Peano's five premises.

It is not worth while to remember Frege's premises in detail, but it is worth while to know what sort of propositions they are. I shall therefore enumerate them without comment.

Frege divides his premises into *principles* and *rules*. The principles, translated as nearly as possible into ordinary language, are the following:

I. If a and b are both true, then a is true. If a is true, then a is true.

II. If $f(a)$ is true for all values of a, it is true for any value. (This principle is separately stated for the cases where a is an object and where a is a function.)

III. Any statement about the proposition 'a is identical with b' implies the corresponding statement about the proposition: 'every property of b is also a property of a'.

IV. 'a is true' is equivalent either to 'b is true', or to 'b is not true'.

V. Two propositional functions fx and gx determine the same class when, and only when, fx is equivalent to gx for all values of x.

VI. a is the only object which is identical with a.

The rules, again translated as nearly as possible into ordinary language, are as follows:

1. The proposition 'it is true that p is true' may be replaced by 'p is true'.
2. If p implies that q implies r, then q implies that p implies r.
3. If p implies q, then not-q implies not-p.
4. If p occurs more than once in the hypothesis of a hypothetical, we may omit all but one of its occurrences (e.g. if p and q and p together imply r, then p and q together imply r).
5. If, whatever x may be, the proposition $f(x)$ is true, then $f(x)$ is true for all values of x.
6. A true premise in an implication may be dropped.
7. If p implies q, and q implies r, then p implies r.
8. If q follows both from p and from not-p, then q must be true.
9. When a proposition containing two or more variables is true whatever values we give to the variables, we may identify the variables. [At least I think this is his meaning.]

10 & 11 only concern notation.

12. A definition may always be treated as a true proposition.

These principles and rules are sufficient for the proof of the whole of pure mathematics.

With this result, the regressive investigation would be completed, but for the well-known contradictions, of which Burali-Forti's was the first to be discovered. I do not propose to discuss possible solutions of these contradictions now – I merely propose to point out their connection with general questions of method and the nature of proof.

Of the logical premises enumerated by Frege, some are far more intrinsically obvious than others. Since the contradictions show that the premises need correction, we shall naturally begin with those that are least obvious. To deny the universal validity of the law of contradiction, say, would be a very desperate remedy, not to be adopted save in the last resort. (I once attempted a partial denial of the law of excluded middle as an escape from the contradictions; but plainly it is better to attempt other denials first.) Some of the logical premises are not very obvious – for example, that whatever can be said significantly of an individual can be said significantly (not necessarily truly) of a class. (This premise is not explicit in the list, but is embodied in explanations.) Such principles are premises in the sense of being logically simple propositions from which the desired consequences follow, but they are not empirical premises, in the sense of being intrinsically obvious. If, therefore, we can substitute other premises, from which we get the desired consequences without the admixture of demonstrable falsehood, our problem is solved.

The function of intrinsic obviousness in any body of knowledge demands some consideration. It is to be observed that it gives necessarily the basis of all other knowledge: our empirical premises must be obvious. In the natural sciences, the obviousness is that of the senses, while in pure mathematics it is an *a priori* obviousness, such as that of the law of contradiction. But there are three important points to be observed as regards obviousness. (1) It is a matter of degree, and, in a case of conflict, the more obvious is to be preferred, *caeteris paribus*, to the less obvious. (2) Even where there is the highest degree of obviousness, we cannot assume that we are infallible – a sufficient conflict with other obvious propositions may lead us to abandon our belief, as in the case of a hallucination afterwards recognised as such. (3) Assuming the usual laws of deduction, two obvious propositions of which one can be deduced from the other both become more nearly certain than either would be in isolation; and thus in a complicated deductive system, many parts of which are obvious, the total probability may become all but absolute certainty. Thus although intrinsic obviousness is the basis of every science, it is never, in a fairly advanced science, the whole of our reason for believing any one proposition of the science.

When, therefore, we are faced with a problem such as that of the contradictions in symbolic logic, the method to be pursued must be, first, to make a kind of hierarchy of obviousness among the results to which our premises ought to lead, then to isolate, if possible, the premises from which contradictions flow, and the kind of reasoning which gives rise to the contradictions, and then to invent various modifications of the guilty premises, applying to such modifications the two tests (1) that they must yield the more obvious of the results to be obtained, (2) that they must not yield any demonstrably false results. The second of these conditions cannot be secured with certainty. The most that can be done is to try the kind of deductions from which contradictions are most likely to spring. Thus we cannot hope to be sure that our new premises are free from error. But if we seem to have discovered precisely *why* our previous premises led to contradictions, so that what (apart from consequences) seemed obviously true, now seems obviously false, and if the whole kind of reasoning from which the contradictions sprang is ruled out by our new premises, we may have a reasonable confidence that we have at least made the right kind of modification, and that if more modification is required, it will be more of the same sort. The chief difficulty throughout consists in reconciling the two aims of avoiding the false and keeping what we cannot but think true: a modification of our premises which is inconsistent with $2+2=4$ is almost as bad as a modification which does not avoid contradictions. All this is very like the procedure of other sciences. Boyle's law, e.g. is only approximately true; therefore our premises must both prove it approximately true, and not prove it quite true. Thus Frege's premises undoubtedly give a first approximation, and the exact truth must be very like them.[1]

Taking account of the contradictions, Frege's premises may, I think, be replaced by some such list as the following. In the following list, 'ϕx is always true' is to mean 'every proposition of the form ϕx is true', *not* 'ϕx is true for all values of x', for there will usually be values of x for which ϕx is nonsense. Our

[1] Similar remarks are made by Bôcher *A* 1904, pp. 111–120, who speaks of 'successive approximations'.

DISCOVERING THE PREMISES OF MATHEMATICS

premises may then be divided into three sets. There are first six principles of deduction, concerning which it is almost impossible to entertain any reasonable doubt. These principles are:

1. Whatever is implied by a true proposition is true.
2. If either p is true or p is true, then p is true.
3. If q is true, then either p is true or q is true.
4. If p or q is true, then q or p is true.
5. If either p is true or q or r is true, then either q is true or p or r is true.
6. If q implies r, then p or q implies p or r.

The next four principles, which are nearly as indubitable as the previous six, concern the notion 'ϕx is always true', where ϕx is a function whose values are propositions.

7. If all values of ϕx are true, then any value of ϕx is true.
8. If ϕx is true whatever possible argument x may be, then all values of ϕx are true.
9. If all values of ϕx are true, then this or that value is true.
10. If 'p implies ϕx' is always true as x varies, then p implies that ϕx is always true.

There remain two principles, less evident, but indispensable if we are both to avoid contradictions and to preserve ordinary mathematics. The first of these concerns the distinction between a general propositional function of x and a function assigning a property to x. We assume that:

11. Any propositional function of x is equivalent to one assigning a property to x.

The second principle similarly distinguishes between a general propositional function of x and y and one which asserts a relation between x and y, and assumes:

12. Any propositional function of x and y is equivalent to one asserting a relation between x and y.

These twelve principles, with possible modifications or additions as regards the last two, seem to embody what mathematics requires, and at the same time to avoid contradictions. Their full scope can only be made clear by lengthy explanations; I have only mentioned them to show the *kind* of residuum to which our regress leads us.

It should be mentioned that, unless much of arithmetic is to be wholly trivial, we require the further assumption that no finite number is the total number of things in the universe.

The above premises are obtained by analysing the procedure and the propositions of mathematics: they are the hitherto irreducible minimum of assumptions from which ordinary mathematics can be deduced.

If the contentions of this paper have been sound, it follows that the usual mathematical method of laying down certain premises and proceeding to deduce their consequences, though it is the right method of exposition, does not, except in the more advanced portions, give the order of knowledge. This has been concealed by the fact that the propositions traditionally taken as premises are for the most part very obvious, with the fortunate exception of the axiom of parallels. But when we push analysis farther, and get to more ultimate premises, the obviousness becomes less, and the analogy with the procedure of other sciences becomes more visible. The various sciences are distinguished by their subject-matter, but as regards method, they seem to differ only in the proportions between the three parts of which every science consists, namely (1) the registration of 'facts', which are what I have called empirical premises; (2) the inductive discovery of hypotheses, or logical premises, to fit the facts; (3) the deduction of new propositions from the facts and hypotheses.

If we are asked as to the use of such investigations, several important uses may be mentioned. In the first place, when a number of facts are shown to follow from a few premises, this is not only a new truth in itself, but also an organisation of our knowledge, making it more manageable and more interesting. In the second place, the premises, when discovered, are pretty certain to lead to a number of new results which could not otherwise have been known: in the sciences, this is so obvious that it needs no illustration, and in mathematics it is no less true. In the third place, in the particular case of the principles of mathematics, the philosophical consequences are far-reaching and of vast importance. Mathematics being admittedly more certain than any other knowledge, most philosophers have based their theory of knowledge to a large extent upon mathematics; and any new discovery as to mathematical method and principles is likely to upset a great deal of otherwise plausible philosophising, as well as to suggest a new philosophy which will be solid in proportion as its foundations in mathematics are securely laid.

14

The Philosophical Implications of Mathematical Logic

Lecture delivered in French at the Ecole des Hautes Etudes Sociales, 22 March 1911. First publication in the *Revue de Métaphysique et de Morale*, **19** (Sept. 1911), pp. 281–91. English translation by P. E. B. Jourdain with revisions by Russell in *The Monist*, **22** (Oct. 1913), pp. 481–93. Reprinted with the permission of the Bertrand Russell Estate.

In speaking of 'mathematical logic', I use this word in a very broad sense. By it I understand the works of Cantor on transfinite numbers as well as the logical work of Frege and Peano. Weierstrass and his successors have 'arithmetised' mathematics; that is to say, they have reduced the whole of analysis to the study of integer numbers. The accomplishment of this reduction indicated the completion of a very important stage, at the end of which the spirit of dissection might well be allowed a short rest. However, the theory of integer numbers cannot be constituted in an autonomous manner, especially when we take into account the likeness in properties of the finite and infinite numbers. It was, then, necessary to go farther and reduce arithmetic, and above all the definition of numbers, to logic. By the name 'mathematical logic', then, I will denote any logical theory whose object is the analysis and deduction of arithmetic and geometry by means of concepts which belong evidently to logic. It is this modern tendency that I intend to discuss here.

In an examination of the work done by mathematical logic, we may consider either the mathematical results, the method of mathematical reasoning as revealed by modern work, or the intrinsic nature of mathematical propositions according to the analysis which mathematical logic makes of them. It is impossible to distinguish exactly these three aspects of the subject, but there is enough of a distinction to serve the purpose of a framework for discussion. It might be thought that the inverse

IMPLICATIONS OF MATHEMATICAL LOGIC

order would be the best; that we ought first to consider what a mathematical proposition is, then the method by which such propositions are demonstrated, and finally the results to which this method leads us. But the problem which we have to resolve, like every truly philosophical problem, is a problem of analysis; and in problems of analysis the best method is that which sets out from results and arrives at the premises. In mathematical logic it is the conclusions which have the greatest degree of certainty: the nearer we get to the ultimate premises the more uncertainty and difficulty do we find.

From the philosophical point of view, the most brilliant results of the new method are the exact theories which we have been able to form about infinity and continuity. We know that when we have to do with infinite collections, for example the collection of finite integer numbers, it is possible to establish a one-to-one correspondence between the whole collection and a part of itself. For example, there is such a correspondence between the finite integers and the even numbers, since the relation of a finite number to its double is one-to-one. Thus it is evident that the number of an infinite collection is equal to the number of a part of this collection. It was formerly believed that this was a contradiction; even Leibniz, although he was a partisan of the actual infinite, denied infinite *number* because of this supposed contradiction. But to demonstrate that there is a contradiction we must suppose that all numbers obey mathematical induction. To explain mathematical induction, let us call by the name 'hereditary property' of a number a property which belongs to $n+1$ whenever it belongs to n. Such is, for example, the property of being greater than 100. If a number is greater than 100, the next number after it is greater than 100. Let us call by the name 'inductive property' of a number a hereditary property which is possessed by the number zero. Such a property must belong to 1, since it is hereditary and belongs to 0; in the same way, it must belong to 2, since it belongs to 1; and so on. Consequently the numbers of daily life possess every inductive property. Now, amongst the inductive properties of numbers is found the following. If any collection has the number n, no part of this collection can have the same number n. Consequently, if all numbers possess all inductive properties, there is a contradiction with the result that there are collections which have the same number as a part of themselves. This contradiction, however, ceases to subsist as soon as we admit that there are numbers which do not possess all inductive properties. And then it appears that there is no contradiction in infinite number. Cantor has even created a whole arithmetic of infinite numbers, and by means of this arithmetic he has completely resolved the former problems on the nature of the infinite which have disturbed philosophy since ancient times.

The problems of the *continuum* are closely connected with the problems of the infinite and their solution is effected by the same means. The paradoxes of Zeno the Eleatic and the difficulties in the analysis of space, of time, and of motion, are all completely explained by means of the modern theory of continuity. This is because a non-contradictory theory has been found, according to which the continuum is composed of an infinity of distinct elements; and this formerly appeared impossible. The elements cannot all be reached by continual dichotomy; but it does not follow that these elements do not exist.

From this follows a complete revolution in the philosophy of space and time. The realist theories which were believed to be contradictory are so no longer, and the idealist theories have lost any excuse there might have been for their existence. The flux, which was believed to be incapable of analysis into indivisible elements, shows itself to be capable of mathematical analysis, and our reason shows itself to be capable of giving an explanation of the physical world and of the sensible world without supposing jumps where there is continuity, and also without giving up the analysis into separate and indivisible elements.

The mathematical theory of motion and other continuous changes uses, besides the theories of infinite number and of the nature of the continuum, two correlative notions, that of a *function* and that of a *variable*. The importance of these ideas may be shown by an example. We still find in books of philosophy a statement of the law of causality in the form: 'When the same cause happens again, the same effect will also happen.' But it might be very justly remarked that the same cause never happens again. What actually takes place is that there is a constant relation between causes of a certain kind and the effects which result from them. Wherever there is such a constant relation, the effect is a function of the cause. By means of the constant relation we sum up in a single formula an infinity of causes and effects, and we avoid the worn-out hypothesis of the *repetition* of the same cause. It is the idea of functionality, that is to say the idea of constant relation, which gives the secret of the power of mathematics to deal simultaneously with an infinity of data.

To understand the part played by the idea of a function in mathematics, we must first of all understand the method of mathematical deduction. It will be admitted that mathematical demonstrations, even those which are performed by what is called mathematical induction, are always deductive. Now, in a deduction it almost always happens that the validity of the deduction does not depend on the subject spoken about, but only on the form of what is said about it. Take for example the classical argument: All men are mortal, Socrates is a man, therefore Socrates is mortal. Here it is evident that what is said remains true if Plato or Aristotle or anybody else is substituted for Socrates. We can, then, say: If all men are mortal, and if x is a man, then x is mortal. This is a first generalisation of the proposition from which we set out. But it is easy to go farther. In the deduction which has been stated, nothing depends on the fact that it is men and mortals which occupy our attention. If all the members of any class α are members of a class β, and if x is a member of the class α, then x is a member of the class β. In this statement, we have the pure logical form which underlies all the deductions of the same form as that which proves that Socrates is mortal. To obtain a proposition of pure mathematics (or of mathematical logic, which is the same thing), we must submit a deduction of any kind to a process analogous to that which we have just performed, that is to say, when an argument remains valid if one of its terms is changed, this term must be replaced by a variable, i.e., by an indeterminate object. In this way we finally reach a proposition of pure logic, that is to say a proposition which does not contain any other constant than logical constants. The definition of the *logical constants* is not easy, but this much may be said: A *constant* is *logical* if the propositions in which it is found still contain it when we try to replace it by a variable. More exactly, we may perhaps characterise the logical constants in the following manner: If we take any deduction and replace its terms by variables, it will happen, after a certain number of stages, that the constants which still remain in the deduction belong to a certain group, and, if we try to push generalisation still farther, there will always remain constants which belong to this same group. This group is the group of logical constants. The logical constants are those which constitute pure form; a formal proposition is a proposition which does not contain any other constants than logical constants. We have just reduced the deduction which proves that Socrates is mortal to the following form: 'If x is an α, then, if all the members of α are members of β, it follows that x is a β.' The constants here are: *is-α*, *all*, and *if-then*. These are logical constants and evidently they are purely formal concepts.

Now, the validity of any valid deduction depends on its form, and its form is obtained by replacing the terms of the deduction by variables, until there do not remain any other constants than those of logic. And conversely: every valid deduction can be obtained by starting from a deduction which operates on variables by means of logical constants, by attributing to variables definite values with which the hypothesis becomes true.

By means of this operation of generalisation, we separate the strictly deductive element in an argument from the element which depends on the particularity of what is spoken about. Pure mathematics concerns itself exclusively with the deductive element. We obtain propositions of pure mathematics by a

IMPLICATIONS OF MATHEMATICAL LOGIC

process of *purification*. If I say: 'Here are two things, and here are two other things, therefore here are four things in all', I do not state a proposition of pure mathematics because here particular data come into question. The proposition that I have stated is an *application* of the general proposition: 'Given any two things and also any two other things, there are four things in all.' The latter proposition is a proposition of pure mathematics, while the former is a proposition of applied mathematics.

It is obvious that what depends on the particularity of the subject is the verification of the hypothesis, and this permits us to assert, not merely that the hypothesis implies the thesis, but that, since the hypothesis is true, the thesis is true also. This assertion is not made in pure mathematics. Here we content ourselves with the hypothetical form: *If* any subject satisfies such and such a hypothesis, it will also satisfy such and such a thesis. It is thus that pure mathematics becomes entirely hypothetical, and concerns itself exclusively with any indeterminate subject, that is to say with a *variable*. Any valid deduction finds its form in a hypothetical proposition belonging to pure mathematics; but in pure mathematics itself we affirm neither the hypothesis nor the thesis, unless both can be expressed in terms of logical constants.

If it is asked why it is worth while to reduce deductions to such a form, I reply that there are two associated reasons for this. In the first place, it is a good thing to generalise any truth as much as possible; and, in the second place, an economy of work is brought about by making the deduction with an indeterminate x. When we reason about Socrates, we obtain results which apply only to Socrates, so that, if we wish to know something about Plato, we have to perform the reasoning all over again. But when we operate on x, we obtain results which we know to be valid for every x which satisfies the hypothesis. The usual scientific motives of economy and generalisation lead us, then, to the theory of mathematical method which has just been sketched.

After what has just been said it is easy to see what must be thought about the intrinsic nature of propositions of pure mathematics. In pure mathematics we have never to discuss facts that are applicable to such and such an individual object; we need never know anything about the actual world. We are concerned exclusively with variables, that is to say, with any subject, about which hypotheses are made which may be fulfilled sometimes, but whose verification for such and such an object is only necessary for the *importance* of the deductions, and not for their truth. At first sight it might appear that everything would be arbitrary in such a science. But this is not so. It is necessary that the hypothesis *truly* implies the thesis. If we make the hypothesis that the hypothesis implies the thesis, we can only make deductions in the case when this new hypothesis truly implies the new thesis. Implication is a logical constant and cannot be dispensed with. Consequently we need *true* propositions about implication. If we took as premises propositions on implication which were not true, the consequences which would appear to flow from them would not be truly implied by the premises, so that we would not obtain even a hypothetical proof. This necessity for *true* premises emphasises a distinction of the first importance, that is to say the distinction between a premise and a hypothesis. When we say 'Socrates is a man, *therefore* Socrates is mortal', the proposition 'Socrates is a man' is a *premise*; but when we say: '*If* Socrates is a man, *then* Socrates is mortal', the proposition 'Socrates is a man' is only a hypothesis. Similarly when I say: 'If from p we deduce q and from q we deduce r, then from p we deduce r', the proposition 'From p we deduce q and from q we deduce r' is a hypothesis, but the whole proposition is not a hypothesis, since I affirm it, and, in fact, it is true. This proposition is a rule of deduction, and the rules of deduction have a twofold use in mathematics: both as premises and as a method of obtaining consequences of the premises. Now, if the rules of deduction were not true, the consequences that would be obtained by using them would not truly be consequences, so that we should not have even a correct deduction setting out from a false premise. It is this twofold use of the rules of deduction which differentiates the foundations of mathematics from the later parts. In the later parts, we use the same rules of deduction to deduce, but we no longer use them immediately as premises. Consequently, in the later parts, the immediate premises may be false without the deductions being logically incorrect, but, in the foundations, the deductions will be incorrect if the premises are not true. It is necessary to be clear about this point, for otherwise the part of arbitrariness and of hypothesis might appear greater than it is in reality.

Mathematics, therefore, is wholly composed of propositions which only contain variables and logical constants, that is to say, purely formal propositions – for the logical constants are those which constitute form. It is remarkable that we have the power of knowing such propositions. The consequences of the analysis of mathematical knowledge are not without interest for the theory of knowledge. In the first place it is to be remarked, in opposition to empirical theories, that mathematical knowledge needs premises which are not based on the data of sense. Every general proposition goes beyond the limits of knowledge obtained through the senses, which is wholly restricted to what is individual. If we say that the extension of the given case to the general is effected by means of induction, we are forced to admit that induction itself is not proved by means of experience. Whatever may be the exact formulation of the fundamental principle of induction, it is evident that in the first place this principle is general, and in the second place that it cannot, without a vicious circle, be itself demonstrated by induction.

It is to be supposed that the principle of induction can be formulated more or less in the following way. If we are given the fact that any two properties occur together in a certain number of cases, it is more probable that a new case which possesses one of these properties will possess the other than it would be if we had not such a datum. I do not say that this is a satisfactory formulation of the principle of induction; I only say that the principle of induction must be like this in so far as it must be an absolutely general principle which contains the notion of probability. Now it is evident that sense-experience cannot demonstrate such a principle, and cannot even make it probable; for it is only in virtue of the principle itself that the fact that it has often been successful gives grounds for the belief that it will probably be successful in the future. Hence inductive knowledge, like all knowledge which is obtained by reasoning, needs logical principles which are *a priori* and universal. By formulating the principle of induction, we transform every induction into a deduction; induction is nothing else than a deduction which uses a certain premise, namely the principle of induction.

In so far as it is primitive and undemonstrated, human knowledge is thus divided into two kinds: knowledge of particular facts, which alone allows us to affirm existence, and knowledge of logical truth, which alone allows us to reason about data. In science and in daily life the two kinds of knowledge are intermixed: the propositions which are affirmed are obtained from particular premises by means of logical principles. In pure perception we only find knowledge of particular facts. In pure mathematics one finds only logical truths. In order that such a knowledge be possible, it is necessary that there should be self-evident logical truths, that is to say, truths which are known without demonstration. These are the truths which are the premises of pure mathematics as well as of the deductive elements in every demonstration on any subject whatever.

It is, then, possible to make assertions, not only about cases which we have been able to observe, but about all actual or possible cases. The existence of assertions of this kind and their necessity for almost all pieces of knowledge which are said to be founded on experience shows that traditional empiricism is in error and that there is *a priori* and universal knowledge.

In spite of the fact that traditional empiricism is mistaken in its theory of knowledge, it must not be supposed that idealism is right. Idealism – at least every theory of knowledge which is derived from Kant – assumes that the universality of *a priori* truths comes from their property of expressing properties of the mind[1]: things appear to be thus because the nature of the

---

[1] It is possible that the true interpretation of Kant is less psychological than I supposed here; but the historical question has only a secondary importance for us in the present discussion.

appearance depends on the subject in the same way that, if we have blue spectacles, everything appears to be blue. The categories of Kant are the coloured spectacles of the mind; truths *a priori* are the false appearances produced by those spectacles. Besides, we must know that everybody has spectacles of the same kind and that the colour of the spectacles never changes. Kant did not deign to tell us how he knew this.

As soon as we take into account the consequences of Kant's hypothesis, it becomes evident that general and *a priori* truths must have the same objectivity, the same independence of the mind, that the particular facts of the physical world possess. In fact, if general truths only express psychological facts, we could not know that they would be constant from moment to moment or from person to person, and we could never use them legitimately to deduce a fact from another fact, since they would not connect facts but our ideas about the facts. Logic and mathematics force us, then, to admit a kind of realism in the scholastic sense, that is to say, to admit that there is a world of universals and of truths which do not bear directly on such and such a particular existence. This world of universals must *subsist*, although it cannot *exist* in the same sense as that in which particular data exist. We have immediate knowledge of an indefinite number of propositions about universals: this is an ultimate fact, as ultimate as sensation is. Pure mathematics – which is usually called 'logic' in its elementary parts – is the sum of everything that we can know, whether directly or by demonstration, about certain universals.

On the subject of self-evident truths it is necessary to avoid a misunderstanding. Self-evidence is a psychological property and is therefore subjective and variable. It is essential to knowledge, since all knowledge must be either self-evident or deduced from self-evident knowledge. But the order of knowledge which is obtained by starting from what is self-evident is not the same thing as the order of logical deduction, and we must not suppose that when we give such and such premises for a deductive system, we are of opinion that these premises constitute what is self-evident in the system. In the first place self-evidence has degrees: It is quite possible that the consequences are more evident than the premises. In the second place it may happen that we are certain of the truth of many of the consequences, but that the premises only appear probable, and that their probability is due to the fact that true consequences flow from them. In such a case, what we can be certain of is that the premises imply all the true consequences that it was wished to place in the deductive system. This remark has an application to the foundations of mathematics, since many of the ultimate premises are intrinsically less evident than many of the consequences which are deduced from them. Besides, if we lay too much stress on the self-evidence of the premises of a deductive system, we may be led to mistake the part played by intuition (not spatial but logical) in mathematics. The question of the part of logical intuition is a psychological question and it is not necessary, when constructing a deductive system, to have an opinion on it.

To sum up, we have seen, in the first place, that mathematical logic has resolved the problems of infinity and continuity, and that it has made possible a solid philosophy of space, time, and motion. In the second place, we have seen that pure mathematics can be defined as the class of propositions which are expressed exclusively in terms of variables and logical constants, that is to say as the class of purely formal propositions. In the third place, we have seen that the possibility of mathematical knowledge refutes both empiricism and idealism, since it shows that human knowledge is not wholly deduced from facts of sense, but that *a priori* knowledge can by no means be explained in a subjective or psychological manner.

15

Is Mathematics Purely Linguistic?

From the ms. now in the Bertrand Russell Archives, McMaster University. Published with the permission of the Bertrand Russell Archives.

If this question is to be asked intelligently, we must first define the two words 'mathematics' and 'linguistic'. To find a definition of 'mathematics' is no easy task. Let us therefore begin by defining the word 'linguistic'.

Let us begin by considering some instances of linguistic statements. The most obvious examples are those that occur in dictionaries. Sometimes, however, a dictionary will allow itself to deviate, as when Dr Johnson defines 'oats' as 'food for horses in England and men in Scotland'. He could not have pacified an indignant Scot by pretending that this remark was purely verbal. Definitions that are in fact not definitions are a stock form of wit. We are told, for instance, that an 'optimist' is 'a man who hopes to make a profit out of buying from a Scotchman and selling to a Jew'. This definition would have no point if we did not already know what an optimist is. Genuine definitions, unlike the above, assume that the word or phrase defined has not a previously known meaning. What they announce is a decision on the use of language. They say: 'I, the author, hereby announce that I shall, whenever I so desire, use a certain word or phrase A in place of a certain phrase B, and that, when I make this substitution, I shall consider that I have made no change in the significance of the sentence concerned.' A definition thus expresses a volition. If you want to disagree with it, you must disagree on ethical grounds, not by pretending that the definition is untrue. A definition is logically on a level with a translation, but it differs from a translation (at any rate where technical material is concerned) in being more under the control of the man making it. The statement '"chien" means "dog"', though linguistic, is one of fact, and is independent of anybody's volition. But when a man is inventing a new brand of mathematics, and requires new technical terms, his definitions depend upon his free choice; they can be appropriate or inappropriate, illuminating or confusing, but they cannot be true or false.

So much for definitions. Let us proceed to other forms of linguistic statements.

Consider such statements as 'Napoleon was Bonaparte' or 'Augustus was Octavian'. What does such a statement assert? Clearly not what (if anything) is asserted by 'Napoleon was Napoleon'. The latter is a statement which would never be made except in logic, whereas the former is one which might be made by a teacher of history. There are two things that it may mean: (1) 'Napoleon had another name, to wit, "Bonaparte"'; or (2) 'There was a man who had two names, to wit, "Napoleon" and "Bonaparte"'. There is an important difference between these two statements. (1) is about Napoleon, whereas (2) does not mention Napoleon. True, it mentions 'Napoleon', but 'Napoleon' is a word, not a man. The matter becomes clearer if we give names to words, instead of contenting ourselves with inverted commas. Let N be the name of the word 'Napoleon' and B the name of the word 'Bonaparte'. Then (1) says: 'N and B both named Napoleon', while (2) says: 'There was an entity such that N named it and B named it'. You can know this without knowing anything of Napoleon. You may find in an encyclopaedia: '*Bombastes*. See *Paracelsus*.' You thus learn such a proposition as (2), although both names may be new to you.

The above discussion is relevant to the discussion of identity. The law of identity is supposed to say 'A is A', but in fact it is never used in this form. If it were to be used in this form, it would need the following interpretation: 'There is a class of similar shapes, and the name of this class is "A". It is a convention of written language that two members of this class are to make the same contribution to any complex of shapes in which they may occur.' We used to be told that the Law of Identity was a law of thought, but it now appears that it is a convention of typography. Moreover it is a convention often deliberately abandoned; for example, Carnap, in his recent *Logical Foundations of Probability*, warns the reader that he uses the Greek letter π in two totally different senses.

The critical listener will have noted that in the above account of 'A is A' I spoke of 'the *same* contribution'. That is to say, I assumed another kind of identity than that of which I was speaking. It is not, in fact, in the form 'A is A' that identity occurs in ordinary speech. We may say 'All these murders were committed by the same man', or we can say 'Truman is the President of the United States' or 'Napoleon is Bonaparte'. Such statements *can* occur outside logic books.

We have already seen that 'Napoleon is Bonaparte' can be expressed in a way which does not use 'identity', by substituting 'the name "Bonaparte"' for 'Bonaparte'. Let us see whether this can be done in our other examples.

'A, B, and C were all murdered by the same man' can be interpreted as saying:

'There is an entity M such that M murdered A, M murdered B, and M murdered C'.

Here 'identity' is replaced by repetition of the letter M.

A similar elimination of 'identity' can be made in our other example. Put '$P(x)$' for 'x presides over the United States', where it is not yet assumed that only one man can do so. Then 'Truman is *the* President of the U.S.' may be expressed as:

$$P(\text{Truman}) : \phi x . \sim \phi(\text{Truman}) . \supset_{\phi x} . \sim P(x)$$

i.e. 'Truman has the property P, and, if x is any object and ϕ any property, then if x but not Truman has the property ϕ, it follows that x does not have the property P.'

Here, again, 'identity' has disappeared.

You may object that this is a trick, since in my translation I have to repeat the 'same' letter. This, however, is a mistake. Although, in fact, the same letter recurs, I do not have to say so. Moreover, what recurs is not the 'same' letter, but different instances of some letter. Take, again,

'A, B, and C were all murdered by the same man', which became:

'There is an M such that M murdered A, M murdered B, and M murdered C'. What is essential here is repetition of 'M'. But what do we mean by repetition of 'M'? We mean the occurrence of different members of the class which is 'M'. If I want to say:

'M occurs three times in the above sentence',

what I ought to say is:

'Three shapes occur in the above sentence, all of which are members of the class "M"'.

We cannot carry this further without embarking on an endless regress.

Thus it would seem that 'identity' can be eliminated from all statements in which it seems to occur. It has also appeared that some statements seeming to involve identity are linguistic, while others are not.

Consider next a different type of linguistic statement, e.g. 'no old maids are married'. We do not prove this by going over the census records one by one; we prove it by considering the meaning of words. By substituting the definition, the statement becomes:

'Whoever is old, female, and unmarried, is unmarried'.

This is an example of a general logical principle:

'If x has the two properties ϕ and ψ, x has the property ϕ'.

Or, more simply still,

'(p and q) implies p'.

This statement is of a sort that occurs in the premises of mathematics, when mathematics is deduced from logic. There is no valid ground for not calling it a mathematical statement. Every one would agree that the statement from which we started, namely 'no old maids are married', is a linguistic statement. It would seem, therefore, that '$p.q. \supset p$', which is its general form, is also linguistic. So far as it goes, this is an argument in favour of the view that mathematics is linguistic.

Let us take another linguistic statement, namely:

'If A is the husband of B, then B is the wife of A'.

We can define 'husband' in terms of 'wife', or 'wife' in terms of 'husband'. Either relation is the 'converse' of the other, and

IS MATHEMATICS PURELY LINGUISTIC?

the 'converse' of a relation R is that which holds between y and x whenever R holds between x and y. From this definition of 'converse', together with the definition:

'Wife = converse of husband' *Df*

our proposition follows. Here, again, our proposition differs from certain propositions of mathematical logic only by lack of generality.

From the above examples it is clear that linguistic propositions are of two sorts, those that depend upon vocabulary and those that depend upon syntax. 'Napoleon is Bonaparte' depends upon vocabulary, while 'unmarried women are unmarried' depends upon syntax. It is those that depend upon syntax that are akin to mathematical propositions, and that lend themselves to generalisation into propositions of logic.

What, exactly, is asserted by (say): 'A brown dog is a dog'? What must we know in order to know this? We need not know what is meant by the words 'brown' and 'dog', but we must know that they are class-words, and that, when juxtaposed, what is meant is their common part. We must also know what is meant by 'a' and by 'is a'. Thus all that we must know is syntactical. Moreover we are saying things *about* words or sentences. We are saying: 'If "x is a brown dog" is true, then "x is a dog" is true'. The fact that 'truth' has to be mentioned is characteristic of linguistic propositions of a certain sort. If I say 'that is a brown dog', there is no mention of 'truth'. In this case, given the English language, what I say is true (or false) in virtue of the character of the dog. And what I say expresses a thought which could be translated into any other language. The words are needed only to express the thought; they are (so to speak) transparent, and nothing is said about them. This is the ordinary everyday use of language.

But if I say: 'It is true that that dog is brown', I say something which, though implied by my former statement, is no longer about the dog, but about a sentence. Speaking generally, '"p" is true' is quite a different assertion from 'p'. As a rule, the only way of finding out that 'p' is true is to find out p. I know that 'that is a brown dog' is true because I can see that that is a brown dog. But I may know p without knowing '"p" is true', and vice versa. A man who knows no English can see that a dog is brown, but does not know that the sentence 'that is a brown dog' is true; on the other hand, he may hear an Englishman of high moral character pronouncing the words 'that is a brown dog', and will conclude that the sentence is true without knowing what it means.

I incline to think that, in all syntactical linguistic propositions, it is '"p" is true' rather than 'p' that occurs. I do not mean that we are concerned to *assert* that 'p' is true, but that we are concerned with this as a hypothesis. But let us now address ourselves to our second main question, and ask: What do we mean by 'mathematics'?

What is the definition of 'mathematics'? First of all, what do we mean by the question? We all know what mathematics is; it is what is called 'mathematics' in schools and universities. But one supposes, perhaps mistakenly, that those who organise curricula have had some reason to give the common name 'mathematics' to certain kinds of knowledge. In seeking a definition, we want to discover this reason. That is to say, we want to find some common character which will include all that is ordinarily called 'mathematics' and as little else as possible. In this sense I gave a definition of 'mathematics' in 1903 in the first sentence of *The Principles of Mathematics*, but the definition contained various errors, as I pointed out in the second edition of that book. Let us see whether we can do better.

Pythagoras, and Plato after him, had a theory of mathematics as charming as it was simple. Plato's theory was already less simple than that of Pythagoras, since he had to take account of geometry, which he believed not reducible to arithmetic. Pythagoras thought that mathematics is the study of numbers, and that each number is a separate eternal entity dwelling in a super-sensible heaven. When I was young I believed something like this; so did Frege to the end of his days. But study gradually dispelled this belief. In the first place much that is indubitably mathematics – for instance, topology – is not concerned with number. In the second place it turns out that arithmetic rests on logic; moreover the transition from logic to arithmetic is so gradual that no one can say where one begins and the other ends, so that we are compelled to regard mathematical logic and arithmetic as all one subject. In the third place – and this is the most serious matter – it turns out that numbers are nothing but a verbal convenience, and disappear when the propositions that seem to contain them are fully written out. To look for numbers in heaven is therefore as futile as to look for (say) 'etc'.

This last point is so important that I will illustrate it by translating '$1+1=2$'. I will not attempt a completely accurate translation; if you want that, you will find it in *110 of *Principia Mathematica*. Omitting some niceties, the proposition '$1+1=2$' can be interpreted by stages as follows.

We shall say that ϕ is a unit property if it has the two following properties: (1) there is an object a having the property ϕ; (2) whatever property f may be, and whatever object x may be, if a has the property f and x does not, then x does not have the property ϕ. We shall say that χ is a dual property if there is an object c such that there is an object d such that:

1. there is a property F belonging to c but not to d;
2. c has the property χ and d has the property χ;
3. whatever properties f and g may be, and whatever object x may be, if c has the property f and d has the property g and x has neither, then x does not have the property χ.

We can now enunciate '$1+1=2$' as follows: 'If ϕ and ψ are unit properties, and there is an object which has the property ϕ but not the property ψ, then "ϕ or ψ" is a dual property.'

It is a tribute to the giant intellects of school children that they grasp this great truth so readily.

We define '1' as the property of being a unit property and '2' as the property of being a dual property.

The point of this rigmarole is to show that '$1+1=2$' can be enunciated without mention of either '1' or '2'. The point may become clearer if we take an illustration. Suppose Mr A has one son and one daughter. It is required to prove that he has two children. We intend to state both premise and conclusion in a way not involving the words 'one' and 'two'.

We translate the above general statement by putting:

$\phi x . = . x$ is a son of Mr A,
$\psi x . = . x$ is a daughter of Mr A.

Then there is an object having the property ϕ, namely Mr A junior; whatever x may be, if it has some property that Mr A junior does not have, it is not Mr A junior, and therefore not a son of Mr A senior. This is what we mean by saying that 'being a son of Mr A' is a unit property. Similarly 'being a daughter of Mr A' is a unit property. Now consider the property 'being a son or daughter of Mr A', which we will call χ. There are objects, the son and daughter, of which (1) the son has the property of being male, which the daughter has not; (2) the son has the property χ and the daughter has the property χ; (3) if x is an object which lacks some property possessed by the son and also some property possessed by the daughter, then x is not a son or daughter of Mr A. It follows that χ is a dual property. In short (as Mr Micawber would say) a man who has one son and one daughter has two children.

We can now attempt a definition of 'mathematics'. You will have noticed that, when we set forth '$1 + 1 = 2$' explicitly, we do not mention any particular object or any particular property; we talk of 'any property' or 'any object', not of this or that property or object. That is to say, terms and properties are represented by *variables*. This is a necessary but not sufficient characteristic of mathematical and logical propositions. It is not a sufficient characteristic, because many propositions which possess it cannot be known to be true or false, except possibly in virtue of extra-logical evidence. Take (say) 'there are at least three objects in the world'. This can be stated as follows:

$(x, \psi, \chi, \theta)(\exists \phi, a, b, c) : \phi a . \phi b . \phi c : \psi a . \sim \psi x . \chi b . \sim \chi x . \theta c . \sim \theta x . \supset .$
$\sim \phi x .: (\exists f) . fa . \sim fb : (\exists g) . ga . \sim gc : (\exists h) . hb . \sim hc.$

There is no logical proof or disproof of this proposition; our

IS MATHEMATICS PURELY LINGUISTIC?

only reason for believing it is empirical. It is therefore not a proposition of mathematics or logic.

The further property needed to make a proposition one of mathematics or logic is difficult to define. It is the property traditionally expressed by saying that the propositions concerned are 'analytic' or 'logically necessary'. Or we may say that the propositions of logic or mathematics are 'true in virtue of their form'. If I say 'Socrates was wise', I say something substantial, which is known from history and cannot be known otherwise. But if I say 'Socrates was wise or not wise', I say something which requires no knowledge of history; its truth follows from the meanings of the words. What I say is an instance of the law of excluded middle, which says that, if p is any proposition, then we can assert 'p or not-p'. There are here two words which are not generalised; they are the words 'or' and 'not'. These are 'syntactical' words. These are, apart from variables, the only words that can occur in a proposition of logic or mathematics. But this only defines the propositions that can be *expressed* in mathematical or logical terms; it does not help us to know which of such propositions can be known to be *true*, which is what we now wish to ascertain.

Everything in mathematics can be deduced from a small number of premises. The premises may be chosen in a number of different ways. It is obvious that they must possess the defining properties of mathematical and logical propositions. We shall therefore simplify our problem by taking some very early proposition, such as might be made a premiss, and inquiring what it is that distinguishes it from propositions that can be known only empirically or not at all. Let us choose the law of excluded middle.

The law of excluded middle may be stated in various ways. We may say 'every proposition is either true or false'. We may say 'if "p" is any proposition, then either "p" or "not-p" is true'. Or we may (at least verbally) leave out the word 'true' and 'false', and say 'if "p" is any proposition, then p or not-p'. In every particular case, this last is the most natural form. We should give as instances of the law: 'It is raining or not raining', 'this number is a prime or not a prime', and so on. It is only in the general form that we feel inclined to bring in the word 'true'. The question of the occurrence or non-occurrence of the word 'true' is important, since, as I remarked before, it is quite a different matter to assert 'p' or to assert '"p" is true'. The latter is always linguistic; the former, in general, is not.

My own belief – though I say this with some hesitation – is that when words such as 'or' and 'not' come in, it is always necessary to bring in 'truth'. Let us concentrate on 'not'. Take such a statement as 'it is not raining'. This has not the direct application to fact that belongs to 'it is raining'. When we say 'it is not raining', the proposition 'it is raining' is first considered, and then rejected. 'Not-p' may be defined as '"p" is false'; it is, in fact, a statement about p in quotes. When we assert 'p or not-p', the 'or' must connect two propositions having (so to speak) the same syntactical status, therefore the 'p' also must be replaced by '"p" is true'. Thus the correct way to state the law of excluded middle becomes:

'"p" is true or "p" is false'.

We can now (assuming 'true' already defined) define 'false' as follows. Some among propositions are true; the remainder, by definition, are to be called 'false'. If the above is accepted, it is obvious that the law of excluded middle is purely verbal; it is a definition of 'false' or 'not' according to taste.

Mathematical propositions are 'true' in a certain sense, but not quite in the sense applicable to factual propositions. The proposition 'Queen Anne is dead' is true in virtue of a relation between the words and a certain non-verbal fact. Where such propositions are concerned, 'truth' is not a syntactical concept. But what fact ensures the truth of 'Queen Anne is dead or not dead'? No fact about Queen Anne: it is not a historical study of her reign that persuades me to accept this example of the law of excluded middle. There is, however, a fact which is relevant; it is a fact about the meanings of the words 'or' and 'not'. It is because this is the only relevant fact that mathematical propositions can be known without appeal to external observation. All mathematical proof consists merely in saying in other words

IS MATHEMATICS PURELY LINGUISTIC?

part or the whole of what is said in the premises. If, from a theorem A, you deduce a theorem B, it must be the case that B repeats A (or part of it) in other words. And the truth of A must result from the meanings of the words used in stating it.

We may say, as a definition: Mathematical and logical propositions are such as (*a*) apart from variables, contain only syntactical words, (*b*) can be seen to be true because of the meaning of the syntactical words they contain, or (alternatively) in virtue of their form. Something must be added about the definitions of 'syntax' and 'form'.

In every sentence, the words stand in certain relations to each other. These relations can be affirmed by other sentences, but not in the sentence itself. Take, for example, a subject-predicate sentence. In Latin and mathematical logic, this can be stated by mere juxtaposition of noun and adjective, putting the noun first. In English we use the word 'is'; we say 'Socrates is wise'. Here there are three words, and their relations are essential to the meaning of the sentence. We can become more explicit, and say: '"Wise" is a predicate applicable to Socrates'. But here we still have words interrelated in a manner essential to the meaning of the sentence. Whatever we do, we can never free ourselves from the necessity to take account of non-verbalised relations between words. When any such relation is verbalised, new non-verbalised relations take its place.

It is these non-verbalised relations that constitute syntax. Given any sentence, turn all the words in it into variables; what remains is the 'form' of the original sentence. We can always replace the original sentence by one in which the form is mentioned; this produces a sentence of a different form, containing a 'syntactical' word. We may say 'Socrates wise', meaning what in English is 'Socrates is wise'. We can turn 'Socrates' and 'wise' into variables, and arrive at the 'form' 'xP', which will be the common form of all subject-predicate propositions. Or we can, as in English, use the word 'is' to express the relation of subject and predicate. The word 'is' is a syntax-word, because it expresses the common 'form' of all our previous propositions 'xP'. Similarly we can take a dual

PHILOSOPHY OF LOGIC AND MATHEMATICS

relation, say 'Brutus killed Caesar'. Here the structure is unexpressed. We can generalise the 'form' by substituting variables; thus the form is expressed by 'xRy'. But if we want to *speak about* the form, and not merely to express it, we must start from 'Brutus had the relation *killing* to Caesar'. It is by generalising *this* that we are enabled to speak about relations, and not merely to use sentences in which they occur. Such words are 'syntactical', and are the only words, apart from variables, that can occur in mathematics or logic.

The above account of syntactical words is, perhaps, not applicable as it stands to such words as 'or' and 'not'. It is such words that characterise the calculus of propositions, in which we are not concerned with functions or with general propositions – i.e. '$(x).\phi x$' and '$(\exists x).\phi x$' do not occur. Everything in the calculus of propositions can be defined in terms of 'incompatibility'. We say that p and q are 'incompatible' if at least one of them is false. We write this '$p \mid q$'. The simplest proposition in the calculus is '$p \mid (p \mid p)$', which may be stated: 'p is incompatible with the incompatibility of p with itself'. This may be interpreted as either the law of excluded middle or the law of contradiction. It would seem that 'incompatibility' and its derivatives ('or', 'not', 'and', 'implies') must be added to syntactical concepts as above defined. They must also be called 'syntactical'.

We can now sum up this discussion. Our conclusion is that the propositions of logic and mathematics are purely linguistic, and that they are concerned with syntax. When a proposition 'p' seems to occur, what really occurs is '"p" is true'. All *applications* of mathematics depend upon the principle:

'"p" is true' implies 'p'.

All the propositions of mathematics and logic are assertions as to the correct use of a certain small number of words.

This conclusion, if valid, may be regarded as an epitaph on Pythagoras.

VI. APPENDIX
FOUR PAPERS BY HUGH MacCOLL

HUGH MacCOLL

The Scottish logician Hugh MacColl received his B.A. from the University of London and spent most of his life teaching mathematics in Boulogne. His major creative efforts came in two waves; first, in a series of papers on the calculus in the late 1870s, and then in a series of papers on symbolic logic, published in *Mind* from 1897 to 1905 and collected in *Symbolic Logic and its Applications* in 1906.

In logic, MacColl was one of the first to stipulate that the basic relation in logic is implication between propositions, and not class-inclusion. MacColl used the symbols τ, ι, ϵ, η, and θ to mean *true*, *false*, *certain*, *impossible*, and *variable*, and defined 'p implies q' as 'p and not q is impossible', anticipating Lewis's later definition of strict implication. The papers reprinted here include the sixth of the series 'Symbolic Reasoning', and a succession of notes from 1905 setting forth MacColl's views on the null class. These essays should be read in conjunction with chapter 4, above.

Symbolic Reasoning

First published in *Mind*, n.s. 14 (January 1905), pp. 74–81. Reprinted with the permission of the editor of *Mind*.

1. There is no question on which logicians are so divided as that of the 'Existential Import of Propositions'. When we make any affirmation A^B, or any[1] denial A^{-B}, do we, at the same time, implicitly assert that the subject A really exists? Do we assert that the predicate B really exists? Do the four technical propositions of the traditional formal logic, namely, 'Every (or all) A is B', 'No A is B', 'Some A is B', 'Some A is not B', necessarily imply the actual existence of the class A? Do they necessarily imply the actual existence of the class B? These are questions upon which logicians have expended a great deal of thought and no small amount of ink; yet they appear to be as far from coming to an agreement upon them as ever. A simple theory of the subject, a theory, to which they could all subscribe, should therefore be welcomed as a real boon. Such a theory I hope to be able to offer in what follows.

2. Let e_1, e_2, e_3, etc. (up to any number of individuals mentioned in our argument or investigation), denote our universe of *real existences*. Let o_1, o_2, o_3, etc., denote our universe of *non-existences*, that is to say, of unrealities, such as *centaurs, nectar, ambrosia, fairies*, with self-contradictions, such as *round squares, square circles, flat spheres*, etc., including, I fear, the non-Euclidean geometry of four dimensions and other hyperspatial geometries. Finally, let S_1, S_2, S_3, etc., denote our *Symbolic Universe*, or 'Universe of Discourse', composed of all things real or unreal that are named or expressed by words or other symbols in our argument or investigation. By this definition we assume our

---

[1] The symbol A^{-B} is here used as a convenient symbol for $(A^B)'$, the denial of the proposition A^B (see the *Athenaeum*, 5 September 1903).

Symbolic Universe (or 'Universe of discourse') to consist of our universe of realities, e_1, e_2, e_3, etc., together with our universe of unrealities, o_1, o_2, o_3, etc., *when both these enter into our argument*. But when our argument deals only with *realities*, then our Symbolic Universe S_1, S_2, S_3, etc., and our Universe of realities, e_1, e_2, e_3, etc., will be the same; there will be no universe of unrealities o_1, o_2, o_3, etc. Similarly, our Symbolic Universe may conceivably, but hardly ever in reality, coincide with our universe of unrealities.

3. Now, suppose we have a class A. The individuals, A_1, A_2, A_3, etc., compassing it must necessarily all belong to the *Symbolic* Universe S; but whether they all belong to the universe of *realities e*, or all to the universe of *unrealities o*, or some to the universe e and the rest to the universe o, depends upon the particular circumstances of our argument or investigation. When a class A belongs *wholly* to the universe e, or *wholly* to the universe o, we may call it a *pure* class; when it belongs *partly* to the class (or universe) e and *partly* to the class o, we may call it a *mixed* class. The *negative* class 'A (with a grave accent) consisting of the individuals 'A_1, 'A_2, 'A_3, etc., contains all the individuals of our symbolic universe which do not belong to the positive class A. Hence, the class 'e is synonymous with the class o; and the class 'o with the class e. The class 'A may be called the *complement* of the class A, because both together make up the Symbolic Universe.

4. The subject A of any affirmative proposition A^B, or of any denial A^{-B}, is always understood to denote *a single individual*. If A happens to be the name of a class, then, in any proposition A^B or A^{-B}, the subject A is understood to denote a certain known, or previously indicated, individual of the series A_1, A_2, A_3, etc., whose special name or number it is unnecessary to state. For example, suppose A denotes *American*, and B *barrister*, the proposition A^B will then assert that 'the *American* is a *barrister*'. It does not say *which* American out of the whole series A_1, A_2, A_3, etc., is referred to; that is supposed to be known. When it is necessary to state which, then, instead of A^B, we must write A_1^B, or A_2^B, or A_3^B, as the case may be.

5. Let S be any individual taken at random out of our Symbolic Universe S, and let a, a', b, b', etc., be synonymous respectively with S^A, S^{-A}, S^B, S^{-B}, etc. We then get the following self-evident or easily proved formulae, which we will name F_1, F_2, F_3, etc.

(1) A^S; (2) $(S^A)^{-\eta}$; (3) $a^{-\eta}$; (4) a^η;
(5) $(`A)^S$; (6) $(`S)^S$; (7) $(`A)^{-A} + (A \equiv S)$.

The formula F_6 looks somewhat paradoxical; but it can be easily proved. By our definitions (see §§ 2, 3), the symbol `S denotes an individual that does not belong to the class S. But, by definition, the class S denotes the *whole Symbolic Universe* (or 'universe of discourse') to which every individual (real, unreal, or self-contradictory) named in our argument *must* belong. Hence, `S is a self-contradiction. But, by our definition, all self-contradictions belong to the class 0. Hence `S must belong to the class 0. But, by definition, the Symbolic Universe S contains all the individuals $o_1$, $o_2$, $o_3$, etc., of the class 0, as well as all the individuals $e_1$, $e_2$, $e_3$, etc., which belong to the class of realities $e$. Hence, `S must belong to the class S. In other words, the formula $(`S)^S$, denoted by $F_6$, is always true. The preceding reasoning is a syllogism of the Barbara type, which may be expressed briefly as follows: 'Every `S is 0, and every 0 is S; therefore every `S is S'. The last formula $F_7$ asserts that an individual of the negative class `A does not belong to the positive class A, except when A is synonymous with S and therefore denotes the whole Symbolic Universe. This Symbolic Universe, or 'Universe of Discourse', may enlarge as the argument proceeds, seizing, appropriating, and firmly retaining every new entity (not excepting self-contradictory entities like `S) which we designate by a symbol. Suppose for example, that in the course of our argument we have had to speak of several classes, *pure* and *mixed* (see § 3), and that all the individuals of all these classes amount to 82, of which 80 belong to the class e, and 2 to the class 0. Then up till now, our Symbolic Universe S contains 82 individuals, so that we have

$$S = (S_1, S_2, \ldots S_{82}) = (e_1, e_2, \ldots e_{80}, o_1, o_2).$$

A fresh arrival 'S enters our Symbolic Universe, which immediately widens to make room for it; but the question has to be decided whether the stranger is to enter the class e or the class o, just as parents have to decide the sex of a fresh addition to their family before they know whether to call it *Eva* or *Oscar*. The question presents as little difficulty in the one case as in the other; the new comer 'S (or S_{83}) is immediately recognised as belonging to the class o, so that now we have

$$S = (S_1, S_2, \ldots S_{83}) = (e_1, e_2, \ldots e_{80}, o_1, o_2, o_3),$$

the newcomer 'S (or S_{83}) being synonymous with the newcomer o_3.

6. If every individual of a class A (whether a *pure* or a *mixed* class) belongs also to another class B; then, and then only, we say that 'Every (or all) A is B'. If this is not the case – if even a single A is excluded from the class B; then we say that 'Some A is not B'. If every individual in the class A be excluded from the class B; then, and then only, we say that 'No A is B'. If this is not the case – if a single individual of the class A belong also to the class B; then we say that 'Some A is B'. For example, let the class A consist of the five individuals S_1, S_2, S_3, S_4, S_5; let the class B consist of the eight individuals made up of the preceding five individuals together with the three S_6, S_7, S_8; and let the class C consist of the three S_7, S_8, S_9. More briefly expressed, let $A = (S_1, S_2, \ldots S_5)$; let $B = (S_1, S_2, \ldots S_8)$; and let $C = (S_7, S_8, S_9)$. Then, whether any of these three classes, A, B, C, be *pure* or *mixed* (see § 3), the following propositions follow necessarily from our data:

(1) Every (or all) A is B, (2) Some A is B,
(3) Some B is A, (4) Some B is not A,
(5) No A is C, (6) Some A is not C,
(7) No C is A, (8) Some C is not A,
(9) Some B is C, (10) Some B is not C.

Any of the three classes A, B, C may consist wholly of realities, or wholly of unrealities, or it may be a mixed class containing both; whatever hypothesis we take in that way, the preceding ten propositions are true. (See § 11.)

7. We may sum up briefly as follows: Firstly, when any symbol A denotes an *individual*; then, any intelligible statement $\phi(A)$, containing the symbol A, implies that the individual represented by A has a *symbolic* existence; but whether the statement $\phi(A)$ implies that the individual represented by A has a *real* existence depends upon the context. Secondly, when any symbol A denotes a *class*, then, any intelligible statement $\phi(A)$ containing the symbol A implies that the whole class A has a *symbolic* existence; but whether the statement $\phi(A)$ implies that the class A is *wholly real*, or *wholly unreal*, or *partly real and partly unreal*, depends upon the context.

8. For example, let M denote 'the *man* whom you see in the garden'; let U denote 'my *uncle*'; and let $\phi(M, U)$ denote the statement 'The *man* whom you see in the garden is my *uncle*'. In this case we generally have

$$\phi(M, U) : M^e\, U^e.$$

That is to say, the statement $\phi(M, U)$ would generally imply that both M and U really exist. Next, let B denote 'a *bear*', and let $\phi(M, B)$ denote the statement 'The *man* whom you see in the garden is really a *bear*'. Here we should generally have

$$\phi(M, B) : M^0\, B^e.$$

That is to say, the statement $\phi(M, B)$ would generally imply that B really exists, but that the individual M is imaginary – a mere optical illusion. Now take the statement $\phi'(M, B)$ which denies $\phi(M, B)$ and asserts that 'The *man* whom you see in the garden is *not* a *bear*'. Here we should generally have

$$\phi'(M, B) : M^e\, B^0.$$

That is to say, the denying statement $\phi'(M, B)$ would usually be understood to imply that M (the *man* seen in the garden) really exists, but that the particular *bear* spoken of is imaginary and non-existent. Lastly, take $\phi'(M, U)$ which denies $\phi(M, U)$ and asserts that 'The *man* whom you see in the garden is *not* my *uncle*'. Here we should generally say

$$\phi'(M, U) : M^e;$$

but not necessarily $\phi'(M, U):U^e$. That is to say, the denying statement $\phi'(M, U)$ would usually imply the real existence of the *man* M, but not necessarily the real existence of 'my *uncle*'; for the negative statement $\phi'(M, U)$ might be true even on the supposition that neither my father nor mother ever had a brother, so that the supposed uncle had never existed. Similarly, we may give examples of the implied existence or non-existence of *classes*, and show that as regards *real* and not mere *symbolic* existence, no absolute rule can be laid down; that, in each case, the conclusion depends upon the particular nature of the statement and upon the general context.

9. The preceding discussion seems to me to point to a serious and fundamental error in the commonly accepted systems of symbolic logic, founded on the Boolian principle of class-inclusion. These usually denote the class of individuals common to the classes A and B by the symbol AB, and they employ the symbol $(A = AB)$ to assert that the class A and the class AB are the same, every individual in either being also found in the other. Thus interpreted, they say, and say truly, that the statement of equivalence $(A = AB)$ is equivalent to the traditional 'All A is B', or 'Every A is B'. So far I agree with them. But when they define o (or any other symbol) as indicating non-existence, and then assert that the equivalence $(o = oA)$ is always true, whatever the class A may be, they appear to me to make an assertion which cannot easily be reconciled with their data or definitions. For suppose the class o to consist of the three unrealities o_1, o_2, o_3, and the class A to consist of o_3, e_1, e_2, e_3 (one unreality and three realities), the class oA common to both contains but one individual, the unreality o_3. We cannot here say that the class o, which contains three individuals, is the same as the class oA, which contains but one; neither can we say that every one of the three individuals o_1, o_2, o_3, which form the class o, is contained in the class A, which only contains one of them, namely, o_3. And, *a fortiori*, an *infinite* class (o_1, o_2, o_3, etc.), cannot be contained in a *finite* class oA, where $A = (A_1, A_2, \ldots A_m)$.

10. If in my system of logic my formula $(\eta = \eta A)$ asserted that

the *class* η and the *class* ηA contained exactly the same individuals, this formula would be open to exactly the same objections as the formula $(0 = 0A)$ just criticised. But my formula $(\eta = \eta A)$ does *not* assert this; it only asserts the truism expressed by the double implication $(\eta:\eta A)$ $(\eta A:\eta)$, namely, that it never happens that either of the two *statements* η and ηA is true while the other is false. The formula is equally valid in the form $(\eta_1 = \eta_2 A)$, whatever be the impossibilities η_1 and η_2, and whatever be the statement A. For, by a linguistic convention which I believe all logicians accept, any compound statement, say ABC, is considered *true* when, and only when, *all* its factors, A, B, and C, are true; but it is considered *false* if it has a *single false factor* A. Consequently, it must be *impossible* (or *always false*) if it has a single impossible factor η. Hence, $\eta_2 A$ is impossible because of the factor η_2. We may therefore denote $\eta_2 A$ by η_3 (impossibility No. 3), so that the formula $(\eta_1 = \eta_2 A)$ will then be equivalent to $(\eta_1 = \eta_3)$. Now, by definition.

$$(\eta_1 = \eta_3) = (\eta_1 : \eta_3)(\eta_3 : \eta_1) = (\eta'_1 \, \eta_3)^\eta (\eta_3 \, \eta'_1)^\eta.$$

But $\eta'_3 = \epsilon_1$, and $\eta'_1 = \epsilon_2$; for[1] the denial of any impossibility η_x is some certainty ϵ_y, so that the denial of η_3 is a certainty which we register as ϵ_1, and the denial of η_1 is another certainty which we register as ϵ_2. Hence, by substituting ϵ_1 for η'_3, and ϵ_2 for η'_1, we get

$$(\eta_1 = \eta_2 A) = (\eta_1 = \eta_3) = (\eta_1 \, \epsilon_1)^\eta (\eta_3 \, \epsilon_2)^\eta = \epsilon_3 \, \epsilon_4 = \epsilon_5.$$

11. Another disputed question which the preceding theory of the 'Existential Import of Propositions' appears to decide is the validity or non-validity of the four traditional syllogisms, Darapti, Felapton, Fesapo and Bramantip. Now, as I pointed out in *Mind*, July 1902, § 32, not one syllogism out of the whole nineteen is valid in its traditional form PQ∴R, as in this form it asserts without warrant that the two premises P and Q are

[1] The denial of a certainty is an impossibility, the denial of an impossibility is a certainty, and the denial of a variable is a variable. If the chance of A is a, the chance of A' is $1 - a$. When $a = 1$, then A is a certainty and A' an impossibility. When $a = 0$, then A is an impossibility and A' a certainty. When a is some fraction between 1 and 0, then $1 - a$ is also a fraction between 1 and 0, so that, in this case, A and A' are both variables.

both true. In this form therefore any syllogism is false whenever either P or Q is false. To render the syllogism valid, it should be written in the form PQ:R ('*If* P and Q are true, *then* R is true'). Thus written, if in any syllogism we substitute for P, Q, R its special premisses and conclusion, we shall find that PQ:R, which means PQR':η, is a formal certainty, whatever syllogism out of the nineteen we take as an example. Take Darapti, one of the four considered doubtful. Darapti, in its corrected or conditional form, says this '*If* every B is C, and every B is A, *then* some A is C.' This is supposed to fail when B is non-existent while A and C are existent but mutually exclusive. Let us see. Suppose

$$B = (o_1, o_2, o_3), \quad C = (e_1, e_2, e_3), \quad A = (e_4, e_5, e_6).$$

Here we have

$$P = \text{Every B is C} = \eta_1$$
$$Q = \text{Every B is A} = \eta_2$$
$$R = \text{Some A is C} = \eta_3,$$

three statements each of which contradicts our data, since, by our data in this case, the three classes A, B, C are mutually exclusive (see § 6). Hence, in this case, we have

$$(PQ:R) = (\eta_1 \eta_2 : \eta_3) = (\eta_4 : \eta_3) = (\eta_4 \eta'_3)^\eta = \epsilon_1;$$

so that Darapti, in its corrected form PQ:R, does *not* fail in the case supposed.

12. The fallacious reasoning by which the Boolian logicians have arrived at the conclusion that Darapti, even in its corrected form PQ:R, is not valid, is founded on the assumption that their definitions of their symbols lead to the conclusion that the statement (o = oA) is a formal certainty; whereas, consistently with their definitions, this statement may be either true or false. For example, in the case $B^o A^e$, given in § 11, the statement (o = oA) is false.

13. It is curious that, by fallacious reasoning of a totally different kind, I formerly arrived at the same erroneous conclusion as the Boolian logicians about Darapti and the other

three doubtful syllogisms. Finding, firstly, that the implication of the second degree

$$(b:c)(b:a):(a:c')'$$

which, I may denote by F(a, b, c), expresses Darapti on the assumption that the propositions a, b, c have all three the same subject, namely, *an individual taken at random out of our 'universe of discourse'*; and finding, secondly, that this formula, considered as a *general* formula, with no necessary reference to Darapti or any other syllogism, fails in the case $b^n(ac)^n$, I concluded, a little too hastily, that Darapti must also fail in this case. In this I overlooked the fact that, though the case of failure $b^n(ac)^n$ may arise in the *general* formula F(a, b, c) when a, b, c are understood to be wholly *unrestricted*, the case need not arise, and, as a matter of fact, cannot arise when the propositions a, b, c are subject to the restrictions which render F(a, b, c) equivalent to Darapti. For these restrictions necessarily imply $a^{-n}\ b^{-n}\ c^{-n}$ (see § 5, Formulae 2, 3).

14. Bearing upon this and similar pitfalls which waylay the too hasty investigator, in whatever branch of science, when he ventures to stretch his formulae beyond their proper limits, the following rules and cautions may be found useful. Let ϕ_u denote any formula $\phi(x, y, z,$ etc.$)$ when the variables, x, y, z, etc., have an *unrestricted* (or very wide) range of values; and let ϕ_r denote the same formula when the variables have a *restricted* range (or a narrower range within the same limits). Then, employing the symbol ϕ^ϵ to assert that ϕ is true for *all* admissible values of its constituents, x, y, z, etc., we have the true formula $\phi_u^\epsilon : \phi_r^\epsilon$; but *we have no right to assume the converse formula $\phi_r^\epsilon : \phi_u^\epsilon$, nor its equivalent, the formula $\phi_u^{-\epsilon} : \phi_r^{-\epsilon}$*. The assumption $\phi_r^\epsilon : \phi_u^\epsilon$ is the common fallacy in scientific researches of a too hasty induction, which erroneously supposes that the validity[1] of ϕ_r implies the validity of ϕ_u. The assumption $\phi_u^{-\epsilon} : \phi_r^{-\epsilon}$ which erroneously supposes that the non-validity of ϕ_u implies the non-validity of ϕ_r, is the fallacy which formerly led me into the error referred to in § 13.

[1] Any formula $\phi(x, y, z,$ etc.$)$ is called *valid* when we have ϕ^ϵ; that is to say, when the formula is true whatever values, within the limits of our data, we assign to the variables x, y, z, etc. The statement $\phi^{-\epsilon}$, that ϕ is *not* valid, does not imply ϕ^η, that it is *never* true.

Three Notes from 'Mind'

First published in April, July and October 1905, pp. 295–6, 401–2 and 578–9.

1 APRIL: EXISTENTIAL IMPORT

May I ask the Boolian logicians who still maintain that their formula $(0A = 0)$ is necessarily true, whatever the class A may be, to point out the error (if error they find) in the following reasoning?

According to their symbolic conventions, the statement $(XA = X)$ asserts that 'Every X is A', whatever X and A may represent. By their conventions also the symbol 0 represents non-existence. Let A represent *existent*. It follows that the statement $(0A = 0)$ asserts 'Every non-existence is existent', an assertion which is self-contradictory. Hence the statement $(0A = 0)$ is not always true for all values (i.e. meanings) of A.

Of course, the formula $(0A = 0)$ holds good in mathematics for every number or ratio A; as, for example, $(0 \times 2 = 0)$. But then, in mathematics $(0 \times 2 = 0)$ does *not* assert 'Every 0 is 2'.

2 JULY: THE EXISTENTIAL IMPORT OF PROPOSITIONS
(Reply to chapter 4 above)

Mr Russell has very kindly and courteously sent me a proof of the above, so that logicians might, in the same number of *Mind*, have an opportunity of reading his criticism side by side with any comments I might desire to make. My comments shall be brief. With much of what Mr Russell says in his able and interesting dissection of the question at issue I agree; but not with all. That the word *existence*, like many others, has various meanings is quite true; but I cannot admit that any of these 'lies wholly outside Symbolic Logic'. Symbolic Logic has a right to occupy itself with any question whatever on which it can throw any light. As regards Existential Import, the one important point on which I appear to differ from all other symbolists is the following. The null class o, which they define as containing no members, and which I, for convenience of symbolic operations, define as consisting of the null or unreal members, o_1, o_2, o_3, etc., is understood by them to be *contained in every class*, real or unreal; whereas I consider it to be *excluded from every real class*. Their convention of universal inclusion leads to awkward and, I think, needless paradoxes, as, for example, that 'Every round square is a triangle', because round squares form a *null* class, which, by them, is understood to be *contained in every class*. My convention leads, in this case, to the directly opposite conclusion, namely, that 'No round square is a triangle', because I hold that every purely *unreal* class, such as the class of round squares, is necessarily excluded from every purely *real* class, such as the class of figures called triangles.

I may mention, as a fact not wholly irrelevant, that it was in the actual application of my symbolic system to concrete problems that I found it absolutely necessary to label realities and unrealities by special symbols e and o, and to break up the latter class into separate individuals, o_1, o_2, o_3, etc., just as I break up the former into separate individuals, e_1, e_2, e_3, etc. It is a vital principle in the evolution of any effective symbolic system that we should modify, and, whenever possible, simplify our notation, in order to adapt it to the varying needs of different classes of problems. It is this elastic adaptability to circumstances – this readiness to change the meaning of any symbol (not excepting *zero*), and even of any conventional arrangement of symbols, whenever it suits the purpose of the investigation – that enables my symbolic system to solve certain classes of problems (especially in mathematics) which lie entirely beyond the reach of any other symbolic system within my knowledge. In saying this I do not mean in any way to suggest that other symbolic systems may not have the advantage over mine in regard to other classes of problems which I have never studied. Mr Russell's system in particular seems to be specially constructed to deal with problems which lie altogether out of the line of my researches. Different kinds of work require different kinds of instruments.

The following arrived too late to be aded to the article on 'Symbolic Reasoning':

[My statement in § 3 (of 'Symbolic Reasoning'), that 'if any two classes X and Y are mutually exclusive, the complementary classes 'X and 'Y overlap', requires qualification. I should have said 'if any two *non-complementary* classes, etc.' This I discovered symbolically as follows; though, of course, it may be proved more briefly. Let ϕ denote the *unqualified* statement. We get

$$\phi = (xy)^\eta : (x'y')^{-\eta} = (xy)^\eta (x'y')^\eta : \eta$$
$$= (x:y')(y':x) : \eta = (x=y') : \eta = (x=y')^\eta.$$

Thus, ϕ is equivalent to the statement that *the class* X *cannot be the complement of the class* Y, a statement which only holds good when X and Y are understood throughout to be *non-complementary*.]

3 OCTOBER: THE EXISTENTIAL IMPORT OF PROPOSITIONS

My reply to Mr Russell in the last number of *Mind* will also, on all essential points, serve as an answer to Mr Shearman's note in the same number. Mr Shearman, like most symbolists, maintains that 'it is not self-contradictory to say $(0 \prec A)$, whether A stands for "existent" or for any other term'. Now, consider the formula $AB \prec A$, which I believe all Boolians accept as valid for all values of A and B. It asserts that the class AB is always wholly contained in the class A. Let the classes A and B be both real but mutually exclusive. By our data, the class A, consisting of the individuals A_1, A_2, etc., really exists; so does the class B consisting of the individuals B_1, B_2, etc., but the class AB, consisting of the individuals $(AB)_1$, $(AB)_2$, etc., supposed to be common to A and B, has no real existence; it is an unreal class, so that the unreal individuals composing it may be denoted by 0_1, 0_2, etc. Can we consistently assert, as the formula $AB \prec A$ (or its equivalent in this case o ≺A) asserts, that the *unreal* (and therefore non-existent) individuals o_1, o_2, etc., are contained in the class of *real* individuals A_1, A_2, etc.? It is hardly an answer to say that the symbol o, as logicians usually define it, does not denote an unreal class made up of unreal members, as I define it, but a null or empty class containing no members; for is not a null class containing no members logically equivalent to an unreal class made up of unreal members? As I said in my reply to Mr Russell, the crucial point which here separates me, I believe, from all other symbolists is that I regard the class o, whether empty or made up of unrealities, as necessarily *excluded from every real class*; whereas they all regard it as *contained in every class whether real or not*.

Mr Shearman says that in the note which he criticises I confuse the term 'existent' with the existence of things denoted by the term, and the term o with the non-existence of things denoted by it. A little further on, he says – and if he will read Sections 11 and 12 of my article in the number of *Mind* containing his note, he will find that in this I quite agree with him – that 'the presence of this term "existent" does not imply the existence of things denoted by the term'. Now, is it not curious that the confusion of ideas which Mr Shearman imagines he finds in my note in regard to the words 'existent' and 'non-existent' is precisely the defect which I think I find in his note and in the reasoning of other symbolists? How is this? The explanation from my point of view is, that the confusion is solely on their side, and that it arises from the fact that they (like myself formerly) make no *symbolic* distinction between *realities* and *unrealities*, which I now respectively represent by the symbols *e* and o. With them, 'existence' means simply existence in the Universe of Discourse, whether the individuals composing that universe be real or unreal; and the symbol o, as they understand it, merely denotes *absence* from that universe. With me, the symbol *e* denotes *realities*, and o denotes *unrealities*, both of which may, or may not, co-exist in the Universe of Discourse or Symbolic Universe, S. Absence from the Universe of Discourse I hold to be illogical. Once anything (real or unreal) is spoken of, it must, from that fact alone, belong to the Symbolic Universe S, though not necessarily to the universe of realities e.

I cannot see the relevancy of Mr Shearman's argument commencing with the statement that 'with two terms o and "existent" the universe of discourse is necessarily divided into four compartments'. Even if the classes corresponding to these four compartments were all mutually exclusive, as he seems erroneously to assume, his criticism in this paragraph would not touch the principle of my note. The argument of my note, and my argument still, is that, since the statement $(XA = X)$, or its equivalent $(X \prec A)$, is understood by Boolian logicians to assert that 'Every individual of the class X is also an individual of the class A', consistency requires that the statement $(oe = o)$, or its equivalent $(o \prec e)$, shall similarly assert that 'Every individual of the class o is also an individual of the class e'; and that this being a self-contradiction, the formula $(oA = o)$ or $(o \prec A)$ fails when $A = e$ ('existent').

The following is a point of some importance. Let A and B be any two classes; let S be an individual taken at random from our universe of discourse; and let (AB), within brackets, denote the class of individuals common to A and B. So long as A and B are real and not mutually exclusive, we have

$$S^A S^B = S^{(AB)} = \theta.$$

But when A and B are real but *mutually exclusive*, the class (AB) is *unreal*, so that in this case we have

$$S^A S^B = \eta, \quad \text{but} \quad S^{(AB)} = S^0 = \theta.$$

Thus, $S^A S^B$ and $S^{(AB)}$ are equivalent when A and B are real and not mutually exclusive; but they are *not* equivalent when A and B are real and mutually exclusive.

In my *general* logic, or logic of *statements*, the implication $(AB:A)$ – which is *not* (as some have supposed) equivalent to the Boolian $(AB \prec A)$ – is always true; for by definition we get

$$AB:A = (AB \cdot A')_\eta = (AA' \cdot B)_\eta = (\eta B)_\eta = e.$$

Similarly may be proved the truth of my formula $(\eta:A)$, which is *not* equivalent to the Boolian ($0 \prec A$). A little consideration will show that though the implication ($\eta : A$) is valid, the implication ($Q^\eta : Q^A$) is not. The latter fails both in the case $Q^\eta A^\epsilon$ and in the case $Q^\eta A^\theta$. In the first case, putting $Q = \eta$ and $A = \epsilon$, we get

$$Q^\eta : Q^A = \eta^\eta : \eta^\epsilon = \epsilon : \eta = (\epsilon \eta')^\eta = (\epsilon \epsilon)^\eta = \eta;$$

and in the second case, putting $Q = \eta$, $A = \theta$, we get

$$Q^\eta : Q^A = \eta^\eta : \eta^\theta = \epsilon : \eta = \eta, \quad \text{as before.}$$

The difference between my symbol of implication (:) and the usual symbol of class inclusion ($\prec$) will appear from the fact that the statements $\eta : \epsilon$ and $\eta : \theta$ are both true, while the statement $\eta \prec \epsilon$ and $\eta \prec \theta$ are both false. For example, $\eta \prec \epsilon$ asserts that every *impossibility* is a *certainty*, which is absurd; whereas $\eta : \epsilon$ only asserts $(\eta \epsilon')^\eta$, which is self-evident.

VII
BIBLIOGRAPHY

A. HISTORICAL BACKGROUND

Includes major developments in foundational studies before *Principia Mathematica* and works before 1910 referred to in the essays and introductions in this book.

1847 Boole, George.
The Mathematical Analysis of Logic (London and Cambridge).

1854 Boole, George.
An Investigation of the Laws of Thought (London).

1870 Peirce, Charles Sanders.
Description of a notation for the logic of relatives, resulting from an amplification of the conceptions of Boole's calculus of logic, *Memoirs of the American Academy of Arts and Sciences*, **9**, 317–78.

1872 Dedekind, Richard.
Stetigkeit und irrationale Zahlen (Braunschweig).

1874 Cantor, Georg.
Uber eine Eigenschaft des Inbegriffes aller reellen algebraischen Zahlen, *Journal für die reine und angewandte Mathematik*, **77**, 258–62.

1877 Schröder, Ernest. *Der Operationskreis des Logikkalkuls* (Leipzig).

1878 Cantor, Georg.
Eine Beitrag zur Mannigfaltigkeitslehre, *Journal für die reine und angewandte Mathematik*, **84**, 242–58.

1879 Frege, Gottlob.
Begriffschrift, eine der arithmetischen nachgebildete Formelsprache des reinen Denkens (Halle).

1880 Peirce, Charles Sanders.
On the algebra of logic, *American Journal of Mathematics*, **3**, 15–57.

1883 Bradley, F. H.
The Principles of Logic (Oxford).
Cantor, Georg.
Ueber unendliche, lineare Punktmannichfaltigkeiten, *Mathematische Annalen*, **21**, 545–591.

1884 Frege, Gottlob.
Die Grundlagen der Arithmetik, eine logisch-mathematische Untersuchung über den Begriff der Zahl (Breslau).
Weierstrass, Karl.
Zur Theorie der aus n Haupteinheiten gebildeten complexen Grössen. *Nachrichten von der Königlichen Gesellschaft der Wissenschaften zu Göttingen*, 395–419. Weierstrass published little and his work became known mainly through his pupils. In the *Principles of Mathematics*, Sec. 268, Russell quotes from Otto Stolz, *Vorlesungen über allgemeine Arithmetik* (2 parts, Leipzig 1885–1886) concerning Weierstrass.

1887 Cantor, Georg.
Mitteilungen zur Lehre vom Transfiniten, *Zeitschrift für Philosophie und philosophische Kritik*, n.s. **91**, 81–125, 252–70.

1888 Cantor, Georg.
Ibid. **92**, 240–65.
Dedekind, Richard.
Was sind und was sollen die Zahlen? (Brunswick).

1889 Peano, Giuseppe.
Arithmetices principia, nova methodo exposita (Turin).

1890 Cantor, Georg.
Uber eine elementare Frage der Mannigfaltigkeitslehre. *Jahresbericht der Deutschen Mathematiker-Vereinigung*, **I**, 75–8.
Schröder, Ernest. *Vorlesungen über die Algebra der Logik*, I (Leipzig).

1891 Frege, Gottlob.
Function und Begriff. Vortag gehalten in der Sitzung vom 9. Januar 1891 der Jenaischen Gesellschaft für Medicin und Naturwissenschaft.
Peano, Giuseppe.
(a) Principii di logica matematica. *Rivista di Matematica*, **1**, 1–10.
(b) Sul concetto di numero. *Ibid.* 87–102, 256–67.
Schröder, Ernest.
Vorlesungen über die Algebra der Logik, II (Leipzig).

1892 Frege, Gottlob.
(a) Uber Begriff und Gegenstand. *Vierteljahrschrift fur Wissenschaftliche Philosophie.*
(b) Uber Sinn und Bedeutung. *Zeitschrift für Philosophie und philosophische Kritik*, n.s. **100**, 25–50.

1893 Frege, Gottlob.
Grundgesetze der Arithmetik, begriffsschriftlich abgeleitet, I (Jena).

1894 Peano, Giuseppe.
Notations de logique mathématique. Introduction au Formulaire de mathématique (Turin).

1895 Cantor, Georg.
Beiträge zur Begrundung der transfiniten Mengenlehre (Erster Artikel). *Mathematische Annalen*, **46**, 481–512.
Peano, Giuseppe.
Review of Frege: *A* 1893, *Revista di Matematica*, **5**, 122–128.
Schröder, Ernest.
Vorlesungen über der Algebra der Logik, III (Leipzig).

1896 Burali-Forti, Cesare.
Le classi finite, *Atti dell'Accademia di Torino*, **32**, 34–52.

1897 Burali-Forti, Cesare.
Una questione sui numeri transfiniti, *Rendiconti del Circolo matematico di Palermo*, **11**, 154–64.
Cantor, Georg.
Beitrage zur Begrundung der transfiniten Mengenlehre (Zweiter Artikel), *Mathematische Annalen*, **49**, 207–46.

1898 Peano, Giuseppe.
Formulaire de Mathématiques, II (Turin).
Whitehead, A. N.
A Treatise of Universal Algebra, I (Cambridge).

1899 Cantor, Georg.
(a) Letter to Richard Dedekind, 28 July 1899; in Georg Cantor, *Gesammelte Abhandlungen mathematischen und philosophischen Inhalts* (Olms, Hildesheim, 1932), 443–47.
(b) Letter to Dedekind, 31 August 1899. In *Gesammelte Abhandlungen*, 448.
Couturat, Louis.
La logique mathématique de M. Peano, *Revue de Métaphysique et de Morale*, **7**, 616–646.
Meinong, Alexius.
Uber Gegendstände höherer

A. HISTORICAL BACKGROUND

Ordnung und deren Verhaltnis zur inneren Wahrnehmung, *Zeitschrift für Psychologie und Physiologie der Sinnesorgane*, **21**, 182–272.
Moore, G. E.
The nature of judgment, *Mind*, n.s. **8**, 176–93.

1900 Moore, G. E.
(a) Identity, *Proceedings of the Aristotelian Society*, v. 1, pp. 103–27.
(b) Necessity, *Mind*, n.s. **9**, 288–304.

1902 Frege, Gottlob.
Letter to Russell. Printed in *From Frege to Gödel: A Source Book in Mathematical Logic*, ed. J. van Heijenoort (Cambridge, Harvard University Press, 1967), 127–8.
Meinong, Alexius.
Uber Annahmen (Leipzig).
Whitehead, A. N.
On cardinal numbers, *American Journal of Mathematics*, **24**, 267–93.

1903 Frege, Gottlob.
Grundgesetze der Arithmetik begriffsschriftlich abgeleitet, II (Pohle, Jena).
Keyser, C. J.
Concerning the axiom of infinity and mathematical induction, *Bulletin of the American Mathematical Society*, **9**, 424–34.
Moore, G. E.
(a) Experience and empiricism, *Proceedings of the Aristotelian Society*, **3** (1902–3), 80–95.
(b) The refutation of idealism, *Mind*, n.s. **12**, 433–53.

1904 Bôcher, Maxime.
The Fundamental Conceptions and Methods of Mathematics, *Bulletin of the American Mathematical Society*, **11**, 115–135.
Couturat, Louis.
Les principes des mathématiques, *Revue de Métaphysique et de Morale*, **12**, 19–50, 211–40, 664–98, 810–844.
Hardy, G. H.
A theorem concerning the infinite cardinal numbers, *Quarterly Journal of Pure and Applied Mathematics*, **35**, 87–94.
Hilbert, David.
Uber die Grundlagen der Logik und der Arithmetik, *Verhandlungen des Dritten Internationalen Mathematiker-Kongresses in Heidelberg vom 8. bis 13. August 1904* (Teubner, Leipzig, 1905).
Huntington, E. V.
Sets of independent postulates for the algebra of logic, *Transactions of the American Mathematical Society*, **5**, 288–309.
Jourdain, P. E. B.
(a) On the transfinite cardinal numbers of well-ordered aggregates, *Philosophical Magazine*, series 6, 61–75.
(b) On transfinite cardinal numbers of the ordinal form, *Ibid.* series 9, 42–56.
Keyser, C. J.
On the axiom of infinity, *Hibbert Journal*, **2**, 532–52.
Meinong, Alexius, and others, *Untersuchungen zur Gegenstandstheorie und Psychologie* (Leipzig).
Zermelo, Ernst.
Beweis, dass jede Menge wohlgeordnet werden kann, *Mathematische Annalen*, **59**, 514–16.

1905 Borel, Emile.
Quelques remarques sur les principes de la théorie des

ensembles, *Mathematische Annalen*, **60**, 194–95.
Boutroux, P.
Correspondance mathématique et relation logique, *Revue de Métaphysique et de Morale*, **13**, 621–37.
Couturat, Louis.
(*a*) *L'algebra de la logique* (Paris)
(*b*) *Les principes des mathématiques*, avec un appendice sur la philosophie des mathématiques de Kant (Paris).
Hilbert, David.
On the foundations of logic and arithmetic, *The Monist*, **15**, 338–52. Translation of Hilbert, 1904.
Hobson, E. W.
On the general theory of transfinite numbers and order types, *Proceedings of the London Mathematical Society*, series 2, **5**, 170–88.
Jourdain, P. E. B.
On a proof that every aggregate can be well-ordered, *Mathematische Annalen*, **60**, 465–470.
König, Julius.
(*a*) Zum Kontinuum-Problem, *Mathematische Annalen*, **60**, 177–80. Berichtungen, 462.
(*b*) Uber die Grundlagen der Mengenlehre und das Kontinuum-problem, *Ibid.* 156–60.
MacColl, Hugh.
(*a*) Symbolic reasoning, VI, *Mind*, n.s. **14**, 74–81.
(*b*) Note to *Mind*, n.s. **14**, 295–6.
(*c*) Note to *Mind*, n.s. **14**, 401–402.
(*d*) Note to *Mind*, n.s. **14**, 578–80.
Richard, Jules.
Les principes des mathématiques et le problème des ensembles, *Revue générale des sciences pures et appliquées*, **16**, 541.

1906 Couturat, Louis.
Pour la logistique (Réponse à M. Poincaré), *Revue de Métaphysique et de Morale*, **14**, 208–250.
Dixon, A. C.
On 'well-ordered' aggregates, *Proceedings of the London Mathematical Society*, series 2, **4**, 18–20.
Hobson, E. W.
On the arithmetic continuum, *Ibid.* 21–8.
Meinong, Alexius.
Uber die Erfahrungsgrundlagen unseres Wissens (Berlin).
Poincaré, Henri.
Les mathématiques et la logique, *Revue de Métaphysique et de Morale*, **14**, 17–34, 294–317, 866–8.

1907 Brouwer, L. E. J.
Over de grondslagen der wiskunde (Maas and van Suchtelen, Amsterdam and Leipzig; Noordhoff, Groningen).
Meinong, Alexius.
Uber die Stellung der Gegendstandstheorie im System der Wissenschaften (Leipzig).

1908 Brouwer, L. E. J.
De onbetrouwbaarheid der logische principes, *Tijdschrift voor wijsbegeerte*, **2**, 152–8.
Grelling, Kurt and Leonard Nelson.
Bemerkungen zu den Paradoxien von Russell und Burali-Forti. Bemerkungen zur Vorstehenden Abhandlung von Gerhard Hessenberg, *Abhandlung Fries-Schule*, n.s. **2**, 300–34.
Hausdorff, Felix.
Grundzuge einer Theorie der geordneten Mengen, *Mathe-*

B. RUSSELL'S WRITINGS ON LOGIC

matische Annalen, **65**, 435–505.
Zermelo, Ernst.
(*a*) Neuer Beweis für die Moglichkeit einer Wohlordnung. *Mathematische Annalen*, **65**, 107–28.
(*b*) Untersuchungen über die Grundlagen der Mengenlehre 1, *Ibid.* pp. 261–81.
(*c*) Ueber die Grundlagen der Arithmetik. *Atti del IV Congresso Internazionale dei matematici, Roma 6–11 Aprile 1908* (Accademia dei Lincei, Rome 1909), **2**, 8–11.

1909 Poincaré, Henri. La logique de l'infini, *Revue de métaphysique et de Morale*, **17**, 451–82.
Zermelo, Ernst.
Sur les ensembles finis et le principe de l'induction complète. *Acta mathematica*, **32**, 183–93.

1911 Brentano, Franz.

Psychologie vom Empirischen Standpunkt, 2nd ed. (Leipzig).

Frege 1879, parts of Peano 1889, Burali-Forti 1897, Cantor 1899, Frege 1902, Hilbert 1904, Zermelo 1905, Richard 1905, Konig 1905*b*, Zermelo 1908*a*, and 1908*b*, are available in English in *From Frege to Gödel: A Source Book in Mathematical Logic*, ed J. van Heijenoort, Cambridge: Harvard University Press, 1967.
Frege 1884 is available in English translation by J. L. Austin, Oxford: Basil Blackwell, 1950, and one fifth of Frege 1893 is available in English translation by Montgomery Furth, Berkeley and Los Angeles: University of California Press, 1964.

B. RUSSELL'S WRITINGS ON LOGIC

Compiled by Kenneth Blackwell. Includes all known works, published and unpublished, by Russell on subjects in logic. 'Logic' has been broadly construed, but works that are clearly epistemology, ethics, etc. have been excluded. Books published in a given year are listed at the beginning of the year. Articles are listed chronologically within the year; if exact date of publication or writing is not known, they are listed at the end of the probable year of composition. Several unsigned reviews have been included. The evidence for Russell's authorship is considered overwhelming, but has not been set out here. It is available in the Bertrand Russell Archives, as are copies of all items in the following list. To the list should be added a large quantity of material preparatory to *The Principles of Mathematics* and *Principia Mathematica*, now in the possession of the Bertrand Russell Archives, McMaster University.

1896 (*a*) The logic of geometry, *Mind*, n.s. **5**, 1–23.
(*b*) The *a priori* in geometry, *Proceedings of the Aristotelian Society*, o.s. **3** (1895–6), 97–112.
1897 (*a*) *An Essay on the Foundations of Geometry*. London: Cambridge University Press. Revised edition in French as *Essai sur les fondements de la Géométrie*, Paris: Gauthier-Villars, 1901.

(b) Review of L. Couturat's *De l'Infini mathématique*, *Mind*, n.s. **6**, 112–19.

(c) On the relations of number and quantity, *Mind*, n.s. **6**, 326–41.

1898 (a) Les Axiomes propres à Euclide. Sont-ils Empiriques? *Revue de Métaphysique et de Morale*, **6**, 759–76.

1899 (a) The Classification of Relations. Unpublished ms. in Russell Archives. 20 pp. January 1899.

(b) Review of A. Meinong's *Uber die Bedeutung des Weberschen Gesetzes*, *Mind*, n.s. **8**, 251–6.

(c) Sur les axiomes de la géométrie, *Revue de Métaphysique et de Morale*, **7**, 684–707.

1900 (a) *A Critical Exposition of the Philosophy of Leibniz, with an Appendix of Leading Passages*. London: Cambridge University Press. (2nd ed., with new preface, London: George Allen and Unwin, 1937.)

(b) Necessity and Possibility. Unpublished ms. in the Russell Archives. 33 pp. [c. 1900.]

1901 (a) L'idée de l'ordre et la position absolue dans l'espace et dans le temps, *1st International Congress of Philosophy, Paris, 1900*. Paris: Colin. III, 241–77.

(b) Sur la logique des relations avec des applications à la théorie des séries, *Revue de Mathématiques* (Turin), **7**, 115–148. (Reprinted in *Logic and Knowledge* (1956). This is the first article Russell wrote after encountering Peano.)

(c) On the notion of order, *Mind*, n.s. **10**, 30–51.

(d) Is position in time and space absolute or relative? *Mind*, n.s. **10**, 293–317.

(e) Recent work on the principles of mathematics, *International Monthly*, **4**, 83–101. (Reprinted as 'Mathematics and the Metaphysicians' with six footnotes added in 1917, in *Mysticism and Logic* (1918).)

(f) Recent Italian Work on the Foundations of Mathematics. Unpublished ms. in the Russell Archives. 28 pp. [Possibly 1900.]

1902 (a) Geometry, Non-Euclidean. *The New Volumes of the Encyclopaedia Britannica*. London: Black; New York: Encyclopaedia Britannica. 10th ed., IV, 664–74.

(b) On finite and infinite cardinal numbers [Section III of *On Cardinal Numbers* by A. N. Whitehead], *American Journal of Mathematics*, **24**, 378–83.

(c) Théorie générale des séries bien-ordonnées, *Revue de Mathématiques* (Turin), **8**, 12–43.

(d) Letter to Frege. In *From Frege to Gödel*, ed. J. van Heijenoort. Cambridge, Mass.: Harvard University Press, 1967. Pp. 124–5.

1903 (a) *The Principles of Mathematics*. London: Cambridge University Press. (2nd ed with new Introduction, London: George Allen and Unwin, 1937; New York: Norton, 1938.)

(b) Review of K. Geissler's *Die Grundsätze und das Wesen des Unendlichen in der Mathematik und Philosophie*, *Mind*, n.s. **12**, 267–9.

1904 (a) Meinong's theory of com-

B. RUSSELL'S WRITINGS ON LOGIC

plexes and assumptions, *Mind*, n.s. **13**, 204–19; 336–54; 509–524. (Reprinted in this volume, chapter 1.)
(*b*) The axiom of infinity, *Hibbert Journal*, **2**, 809–12. (Reprinted in this volume, chapter 11.)
(*c*) Non-Euclidean geometry, *The Athenaeum*, no. 4018, 29 October, 592–593.
(*d*) On Functions, Classes and Relations. Unpublished ms. in the Russell Archives. 18 pp. 1904.
(*e*) On Meaning and Denotation. Unpublished ms. in the Russell Archives. 100 pp. [Possibly 1905.]
(*f*) Points about Denoting. Unpublished ms. in the Russell Archives. 17 pp. [Possibly 1905.]
(*g*) On the Meaning and Denotation of Phrases. Unpublished ms. in the Russell Archives. 24 pp. [Possibly 1905.]

1905 (*a*) The existential import of propositions, *Mind*, n.s. **14**, 398–401. (Reprinted in this volume, chapter 4.)
(*b*) Review of H. Poincaré's *Science and Hypothesis*, *Mind*, n.s. **14**, 412–18. See also Russell's reply to Poincaré's criticism of this review, in *Mind*, n.s. **15** (1906), 141–3.
(*c*) On denoting, *Mind*, n.s. **14**, 479–93. (Reprinted in *Logic and Knowledge* (1956) and in this volume, chapter 5.)
(*d*) Review of A. Meinong's *Untersuchungen zur Gegenstandstheorie und Psychologie*, *Mind*, n.s. **14**, 530–8. (Reprinted in this volume, chapter 2.)

(*e*) Sur la relation des mathématiques à la logistique, *Revue de Métaphysique et de Morale*, **13**, 906–17. (Reprinted in English in this volume, chapter 12.)
(*f*) On Fundamentals. Unpublished ms. in the Russell Archives. 40 pp. Begun 7 June 1905. Russell also noted: 'Pp. 18ff. contain the reasons for the new theory of denoting.'
(*g*) On Substitution. Unpublished ms. in the Russell Archives. 13 pp. Dec. 1905.

1906 (*a*) On some difficulties in the theory of transfinite numbers and order types, *Proceedings of the London Mathematical Society*, series 2, **4**, 29–53. (Reprinted in this volume, chapter 7.)
(*b*) On the substitutional theory of classes and relations. Read before the London Mathematical Society in April 1906. Ms. in the Russell Archives. 45 pp. (First published in this volume, chapter 8.)
(*c*) The theory of implication, *American Journal of Mathematics*, **28**, 159–202.
(*d*) Review of H. MacColl's *Symbolic Logic and its Applications*, *Mind*, n.s. **15**, 255–60. Another review, unsigned but verified as Russell's, is in *The Athenaeum*, no. 4092: 31 March, 396–7.
(*e*) On Substitution. Unpublished ms. in the Bertrand Russell Archives. April–May 1906. 146 pp.
(*f*) Review of A. Meinong's *Ueber die Erfahrungsgrundlagen unseres Wissens*, *Mind*, n.s. **15**, 412–15.

(g) Les paradoxes de la logique, *Revue de Métaphysique et de Morale*, **14**, 627–50. English ms. in the Russell Archives, titled 'On "Insolubilia" and their Solution by Symbolic Logic'. 44 pp. (Reprinted in this volume, chapter 9.)
(h) The paradox of the liar. Unpublished ms. in the Russell Archives. Sept. 1906. 120 pp. Marginal corrections dated June 1907.
(i) The nature of truth, *Mind*, n.s. **15**, 528–33.

1907 (a) On the nature of truth, *Proceedings of the Aristotelian Society*, n.s. **7**, 1906–7, 28–49. Parts I and II only reprinted in *Philosophical Essays* (1910).
(b) The Regressive Method of Discovering the Premises of Mathematics. Read to the Cambridge Mathematical Club, 9 March 1907. Ms. in the Russell Archives. (First published in this volume, chapter 13.)
(c) The study of mathematics, *New Quarterly*, **1**, 29–44. (Reprinted in *Philosophical Essays* (1910) and *Mysticism and Logic* (1918).)
(d) Review of A. Meinong's *Uber die Stellung der Gegendstandstheorie im System der Wissenschaften*, *Mind*, n.s. **16**, 436–439. (Reprinted in this volume, chapter 3.)

1908 (a) Transatlantic 'truth', *Albany Review*, **2**, 393–410. (Reprinted in *Philosophical Essays* (1910).)
(b) 'If' and 'Imply', *Mind*, n.s. **17**, 300–1.
(c) Mr Haldane on infinity, *Mind*, n.s. **17**, 238–42.
(d) Mathematical logic as based on the theory of types, *American Journal of Mathematics*, **30**, 222–62. (Reprinted in *Logic and Knowledge* (1956).)
(e) Review of L. Bloch's *La Philosophie de Newton*, *Nature*, **78**, 99–100. Unsigned, but verified as Russell's.

1909 (a) Pragmatism, *Edinburgh Review*, **209**, 363–88.
(b) Review of A. Reymond's *Logique et Mathématiques*, *Mind*, n.s. **18**, 299–301.
(c) Review of Paul Carus's *The Foundations of Mathematics*, *Mathematical Gazette*, **5**, 103–4. (Reprinted in *The Monist*, **20**, 1910, 64–5.)

1910 (a) *Principia Mathematica*, vol. I. With A. N. Whitehead. London: Cambridge University Press. 2nd edition, with new introduction (by Russell), 1925.
(b) *Philosophical Essays*. London: Longmans Green, 1910. (2nd ed. with some changes of contents, London: George Allen and Unwin, 1966; New York: Simon and Schuster, 1966.)
(c) La Théorie des types logiques. *Revue de Métaphysique et de Morale*, **18**, 263–301. English ms. in the Russell Archives titled 'The Theory of Logical Types'. (Reprinted in this volume, Chapter 10.)
(d) Some explanations in reply to Mr Bradley, *Mind*, n.s. **19**, 373–8.
(e) Review of G. Mannoury's *Methodologisches und Philosophisches zur Elementar-Mathematik*, *Mind*, n.s. **19**, 438–9.

1911 (a) Le réalisme analytique,

Bulletin de la Société Française de Philosophie, **11**, 55–82.
(*b*) L'importance philosophique de la logistique, *Revue de Métaphysique et de Morale*, **19**, 281–91. English translation in *The Monist*, **23**, 1913, 481–93. (Reprinted in this volume, chapter 14.)
(*c*) Sur les axiomes de l'infini et du transfini, *Société mathématique de France. Comptes rendus des Séances de 1911*, no. 2, 22–35.

1912 (*a*) *Principia Mathematica*, vol. II. With A. N. Whitehead. London: Cambridge University Press. 2nd edition, 1927.
(*b*) *The Problems of Philosophy*. London: Williams and Norgate (Home University Library).
(*c*) On the relation of universals and particulars, *Proceedings of the Aristotelian Society*, n.s. **12**, 1911–12, 1–24. Reprinted in *Logic and Knowledge* (1956).
(*d*) Review of C. Mercier's *A New Logic*, *The Nation* (Lond.), **10**, 23 Mar., 1029–30. Unsigned.
(*e*) Review of F. C. S. Schiller's *Formal Logic*, *The Nation* (Lond.), **11**, 18 May, 258–9.
(*f*) Review of H. S. Macran's *Hegel's Doctrine of Formal Logic*, *The Nation* (Lond.), **11**, 17 Aug., 739–40. Unsigned.
(*g*) Réponse à M. Koyré. *Revue de Métaphysique et de Morale*, **20**, 725–6. Reply to Koyré's 'Sur les nombres de M. Russell' on pp. 722–4.

1913 (*a*) *Principia Mathematica*, vol. III. With A. N. Whitehead. London: Cambridge University Press. 2nd edition, 1927.

1914 (*a*) *Our Knowledge of the External World*. Chicago and London: Open Court. 2nd ed., with revisions, London: George Allen & Unwin, 1926; with new preface and slightly different revisions, New York: Norton, 1929.
(*b*) Review of A. Ruge, *et al.*, *Encyclopaedia of the Philosophical Sciences: vol. I, Logic*. *The Nation* (Lond.), **14**, 771–2.
(*c*) Preface to Henri Poincaré's *Science and Method*. London: Nelson, 1914.
(*d*) Mysticism and logic, *Hibbert Journal*, **12**, 780–803. Reprinted in *Mysticism and Logic* (1918).
(*e*) *Scientific Method in Philosophy*. London: Oxford University Press. 25 pp. Reprinted in *Mysticism and Logic* (1918).

1918 (*a*) *Mysticism and Logic, and other Essays*. Longmans Green.
(*b*) The philosophy of logical atomism, *The Monist*, **28**, 495–527; **29**, 1919, 33–63, 190–222, 344–80. Lectures delivered in London in 1918. (Reprinted in *Logic and Knowledge* (1956).)

1919 (*a*) *Introduction to Mathematical Philosophy*. London: George Allen & Unwin; New York: Macmillan.
(*b*) Review of J. Dewey's *Essays in Experimental Logic*, *Journal of Philosophy*, **16**, 5–26.
(*c*) Note on C. D. Broad's ['A general notation for the Logic of Relations'], *Mind*, n.s. **28**, 124.
(*d*) On propositions: what they are and how they mean, *Proceedings of the Aristotelian Society*, supp. vol. II, 1–43. Reprinted in *Logic and Knowledge* (1956).
(*e*) A microcosm of British philosophy [review of *Pro-*

ceedings of the Aristotelian Society, 1918–19], *The Athenaeum*, no. 4671, 7 Nov., 1149–50.

1920 (*a*) Review of B. Bosanquet's *Implication and Linear Inference*, *The Nation* (Lond.), **26**, 27 Mar., 898, 900. Unsigned. Another signed 'B.R.', appeared in *The Athenaeum*, no. 4694, 16 April 1920, 514–15.
(*b*) Mathematical philosophy, *Science Progress*, **15**, 101.
(*c*) The meaning of 'meaning'. [Symposium: F. C. S. Schiller, Bertrand Russell, H. H. Joachim.] *Mind*, n.s. **29**, 398–404 (Russell's contribution).

1922 (*a*) Introduction to Ludwig Wittgenstein's *Tractatus Logico-Philosophicus*. London: Kegan Paul, Trench & Trubner; New York: Harcourt, Brace. Written in early 1920.
(*b*) Review of J. M. Keynes's *A Treatise on Probability*, *Mathematical Gazette*, **11**, 119–25.

1923 (*a*) Vagueness, *Australasian Journal of Psychology and Philosophy*, **1**, 84–92.
(*b*) Review of C. K. Ogden and I. A. Richards' *The Meaning of Meaning*, *The Nation and The Athenaeum*, **33**, 87–8.
(*c*) Review of Hu Shih's *The Development of the Logical Method in Ancient China*, *The Nation and The Athenaeum*, **33**, 778–9.
(*d*) Truth-Functions and Meaning-Functions. Unpublished ms. in the Russell Archives. 5 pp. [c. 1923.]

1924 (*a*) Logical Atomism. *Contemporary British Philosophy: Personal Statements*. First series. London: George Allen & Unwin; New York: Macmillan. Pp. 356–83.
(*b*) Philosophy in the twentieth century. *The Dial*, **77**, 271–90. (Reprinted in *Sceptical Essays*.)
(*c*) Preface [in French] to J. Nicod's *La Géométrie dans le Monde Sensible* [Paris: Alcan, 1924]. *Revue Philosophique*, **98**: Nov.–Dec., 450–4. (Reprinted (in English) in Nicod's *Foundations of Geometry and Induction* (London: Kegan Paul, Trench & Trubner; New York: Harcourt, Brace, 1930) and Nicod's *Geometry and Induction* (London: Routledge and Kegan Paul; Berkeley: University of Calif., 1970).)

1925 (*a*) Second edition of *Principia Mathematica*, vol. I. The new Introduction and three appendices to vol. I are wholly due to Russell.

1926 (*a*) Review of Ogden and Richards' *The Meaning of Meaning*, *The Dial*, **81**, 114–21.

1927 (*a*) *The Analysis of Matter*. London: Kegan Paul, Trench & Trubner, New York: Harcourt, Brace.
(*b*) *An Outline of Philosophy*. London: George Allen & Unwin; New York: Norton (under the title of *Philosophy*). Especially ch. XXIV, Truth and Falsehood, and ch. XXV, The Validity of Inference.

1930 (*a*) Heads or tails, *Atlantic Monthly*, **146**, 163–70.

1931 (*a*) Review of F. P. Ramsey's *Foundations of Mathematics and other Logical Essays*, *Mind*, n.s. **46**, 476–82.

1932 (*a*) Review of Ramsey's *The Foundations of Mathematics*, *Philosophy*, **7**, 84–6.

1936 (*a*) On order in time, *Proceedings of the Cambridge Philosophical Society*, **32**, 216–28.

(b) Review of A. J. Ayer's *Language, Truth and Logic*, London Mercury, **33**, 541–3.
(c) Review of John Laird's *Recent Philosophy*, The Listener, **16**, 14 Oct., supp. p. iii.

1937 (a) New introduction to 2nd edition of *The Principles of Mathematics*.

1938 (a) The relevance of psychology to logic, *Proceedings of the Aristotelian Society*, supp. vol. XVII, 42–53.
(b) On the Importance of Logical Form. *International Encyclopaedia of Unified Science*. Ed. O. Neurath, R. Carnap and C. W. Morris. Chicago: University of Chicago: **I** (no. 1), 39–41.

1939 (a) Dewey's New Logic. In *The Philosophy of John Dewey*. Ed. P. A. Schilpp. Evanston and Chicago: Northwestern University. Pp. 135–56.

1940 (a) *An Inquiry into Meaning and Truth*. New York: Norton; London: George Allen & Unwin.

1944 (a) Reply to Criticisms. *The Philosophy of Bertrand Russell*. Ed. P. A. Schilpp. Evanston and Chicago: Northwestern University. Pp. 681–741.

1945 (a) *A History of Western Philosophy*. New York: Simon and Schuster, 1945; London: George Allen & Unwin, 1946. Especially ch. XXXI, The Philosophy of Logical Analysis.
(b) Logical positivism, *Polemic*, no. 1, 6–13.

1946 (a) The problem of universals, *Polemic*, no. 2, 21–35.
(b) My Own Philosophy. Unpublished ms. in the Russell Archives. 27 pp. [1946.]

1947 (a) Review of A. J. Ayer's *Language, Truth and Logic*, 2nd edition. *Horizon*, **15**, 71–2.
(b) Logical analysis, *The Listener*, **37**, 3 April, 500. (Reprinted as 'A Plea for Clear Thinking' in *Portraits from Memory*.)

1948 (a) *Human Knowledge: Its Scope and Limits*. London: George Allen & Unwin; New York: Simon and Schuster. Especially Part II: Language, and Part V: Probability.
(b) Whitehead and *Principia Mathematica*, Mind, **57**, 137–8.

circa 1951 (a) Is Mathematics Purely Linguistic? Ms. in the Russell Archives. 22 pp. (First published in this volume, chapter 15.)

1953 (a) The cult of 'Common Usage', *British Journal for the Philosophy of Science*, **3**, 103–7. (Reprinted in *Portraits from Memory*.)

1954 (a) Review of A. J. Ayer's *Philosophical Essays*, The Observer, 8 Aug., 7.

1955 (a) My Debt to German Learning. Unpublished ms. in the Russell Archives. 5 pp. Sept. 1955.

1956 (a) *Logic and Knowledge*. Ed. R. C. Marsh. London: George Allen & Unwin.
(b) Review of J. O. Urmson's *Philosophical Analysis*, Hibbert Journal, **54**, 320–9. (Reprinted in *My Philosophical Development* (1959).)

1957 (a) The pursuit of truth, *London Calling*, no. 910; 11 April, 14. (Reprinted in *Fact and Fiction*. London: George Allen & Unwin, 1961; New York: Simon and Schuster, 1962.)

(b) Review of G. F. Warnock's 'Metaphysics in Logic', *Journal of Philosophy*, **54**, 225–30. (Reprinted in *My Philosophical Development* (1959).)

(c) Mr Strawson on Referring, *Mind*, n.s. **66**, 385–9. (Reprinted in *My Philosophical Development* (1959) and in this volume, chapter 6.)

1958 (a) Mathematical infinity, *Mind*, **67**, 385.

1959 (a) *My Philosophical Development*. London: George Allen & Unwin; New York: Simon and Schuster.

(b) Introduction to Ernest Gellner's *'Words and Things'*. London: Gollancz, 1959; Penguin Books, 1968.

1960 (a) Notes on *Philosophy*, January 1960. *Philosophy*, **35**, April, 146–7.

1961 (a) Preface to J. Nicod's *Le Problème logique de l'induction*. Paris: Presses Universitaires de France. Reprinted (in English) in J. Nicod, *Geometry and Induction*.

1965 (a) Letters to Meinong. *Philosophenbriefe aus der Wissenschaftlichen Korrespondenz von Alexius Meinong*. Ed. R. Kindinger. Graz: Akademische Druck-u. Verlagsanstalt.

1967 (a) The Autobiography of *Bertrand Russell*. 3 vols. London: George Allen & Unwin, 1967–9; Boston: Atlantic – Little, Brown, 1967–8; New York: Simon and Schuster, 1969. Especially the appendices for correspondence with such philosophers as Bradley, James, Moore, Wittgenstein, Quine and Ayer.

(b) False and true, *The Observer*, 12 March, 33. A letter correcting the statement in his *Autobiography*, vol. 1, of the paradox involving 'The statement on the other side of this piece of paper is false'.

1969 (a) Blurb for G. Spencer Brown's *Laws of Form*. London: George Allen & Unwin, 1969. The blurb, which shows Russell's continuing interest in mathematical topics, is: 'In this book Mr Spencer Brown has succeeded in doing what, in mathematics, is very rare indeed. He has revealed a new calculus, of great power and simplicity. I congratulate him.'

1971 (a) Addendum to my 'Reply to Criticisms'. Ed. P. A. Schilpp. *The Philosophy of Bertrand Russell*. 4th ed. La Salle: Open Court. Pp. xvii–xx.

C. SECONDARY MATERIAL

The difficulty in compiling a secondary source bibliography for Russell lies in keeping it from ballooning into a bibliography of twentieth century analytic philosophy. This bibliography is highly selective, and limits itself to material relating to the topics of this book. The five sections correspond to the five sections of this book.

I. GENERAL

1944 Schilpp, Paul Arthur (ed.). *The Philosophy of Bertrand Russell*. Chicago: Northwestern University.) In this volume especially:

Weitz, Morris.

C. SECONDARY MATERIAL

Analysis and the Unity of Russell's Philosophy, 57–121.
Russell, Bertrand.
My Mental Development, 3–20.

1959 Russell, Bertrand.
My Philosophical Development.
London: George Allen & Unwin.

1963 Nidditch, P.
Peano and the recognition of Frege, *Mind*, n.s. **72**, 102–10.

1966 Quine, Willard Van Orman.
Russell's ontological development. *Journal of Philosophy* **63**, 657–67.

1967 Russell, Bertrand.
Autobiography I, 1872–1914.
Boston: Little, Brown, and Co.
Schoenman, R. (ed.).
Bertrand Russell: Philosopher of the Century. London: George Allen & Unwin.
Pears, D. F.
Bertrand Russell and the British Tradition in Philosophy. London: Fontana/Collins; New York: Random House.

1969 Clack, Robert J.
Bertrand Russell's Philosophy of Language. The Hague; Martinus Nijoff.

1970 Klemke, E. D. (ed.).
Essays on Bertrand Russell. Urbana: University of Illinois Press.

1971 Ayer, A. J.
Russell and Moore: The Analytical Heritage. London: Macmillan; Cambridge: Harvard University Press.

1972 Grattan-Guinness, Ivor.
Bertrand Russell on his paradox and the multiplicative axiom. An unpublished letter to Philip Jourdain 1906, *Journal of Philosophical Logic*, **1**, 103–10.
Jager, Ronald.
The Development of Bertrand Russell's Philosophy. London: George Allen & Unwin.
Pears, D. F. (ed.).
Bertrand Russell: A Collection of Critical Essays. New York: Doubleday and Co.

II. RUSSELL'S CRITIQUE OF MEINONG

1932 Ryle, Gilbert.
Systematically misleading expressions, *Proceedings of the Aristotelian Society*, **32** (1931–1932), 139–170.

1933 Findlay, J. N.
Meinong's Theory of Objects.
Oxford: Clarendon Press.

1960 Chisholm, Rodrick C. (ed.).
Realism and the Background of Phenomenology. Glencoe: The Free Press.

1967 Bergmann, Gustav.
Realism: A Critique of Brentano and Meinong. Madison: University of Wisconsin Press.
Linsky, Leonard.
Referring. Ch. II. London: Routledge and Kegan Paul.
Suter, Ronald.
Russell's criticisms of Meinong in 'On Denoting', *Philosophy and Phenomenological Research.* **18**, 512–16.

1970 Gram, M. S.
Ontology and the Theory of Descriptions. Section I. In E. D. Klemke, *Essays on Bertrand Russell.* Pp. 118–146.

III. DESCRIPTIONS AND EXISTENCE

1933 Reeves, J. W.
The origin and consequences of the theory of descriptions, *Proceedings of the Aristotelian Society*, **34** (1932–3), 211–30.

1936 Kneale, W.
Is existence a predicate? *Proceedings of the Aristotelian Society*, suppl., **15**, 154–74.
Moore, G. E.
Is existence a predicate? *Ibid.* 175–88.

1939 Quine, Willard Van Orman.
Designation and existence, *Journal of Philosophy*, **36**, 701–709.

1944 Moore, G. E.
Russell's Theory of Descriptions. In *The Philosophy of Bertrand Russell*, ed. P. A. Schilpp, 177–225.

1948 Hallden, Soren.
Certain problems connected with the definition of identity and of definite descriptions given in *Principia Mathematica*, *Analysis*, **9**, 29–33.
Quine, Willard Van Orman.
On what there is, *Review of Metaphysics*, **2**, 115–35.
Smullyan, A. F.
Modality and description, *Journal of Symbolic Logic*, **13**, 31–7.

1950 Geach, P. T.
(*a*) Russell's Theory of Descriptions, *Analysis*, **10**, 84–88.
(*b*) Russell's Analysis of Existence, *Analysis*, **11**, 124–31.
Strawson, P. F.
On Referring, *Mind*, n.s. **59**, 320–44.

1951 Donagan, Alan.
Recent Criticisms of Russell's Analysis of Existence, *Analysis*, **12**, 132–7.

1952 Martin, Richard M.
On the Berkeley–Russell theory of proper names, *Philosophy and Phenomenological Research*, **13**, 221–31.
Pap, Arthur.
Logic, existence, and the theory of descriptions, *Analysis*, **13**, 97–111.

1953 Wilson, N. L.
(*a*) Description and designation, *Journal of Philosophy*, **50**, 369–83.
(*b*) In defense of proper names against descriptions, *Philosophical Studies*, **4**, 72–8.

1954 Butler, R. J.
The scaffolding of Russell's theory of descriptions, *Philosophical Review*, **63**, 350–64.
Sellars, Wilfrid.
Presupposing, *Philosophical Review*, **63**, 197–215.
Strawson, P. F.
A Reply to Mr Sellars, *Philosophical Review*, **63**, 216–231.

1956 Leonard, Henry.
The logic of existence, *Philosophical Studies*, **7**, 49–64.

1957 Hochberg, Herbert.
Descriptions, scope, and identity, *Analysis*, **18**, 20–2.

1958 Searle, John.
Russell's objections to Frege's theory of sense and reference, *Analysis*, **18**, 137–42.

1959 Geach, P. T.
Russell on meaning and denoting, *Analysis*, **19**, 69–72.
Hailperin, Theodore, and Leblanc, Hughes.
Nondesignating singular terms,

C. SECONDARY MATERIAL

Philosophical Review, **68**, 239–243.
Hintikka, Jaakko.
Existential presuppositions and existential commitment, *Journal of Philosophy*, **63**, 125–137.
Rescher, Nicholas.
On the logic of existence and denotation, *Philosophical Review*, **68**, 157–80.
1960 Jager, Ronald.
Russell's denoting complex, *Analysis*, **20**, 53–62.
Lejewsky, Czeslaw.
A re-examination of Russell's theory of descriptions, *Philosophy*, **35**, 14–29.
1962 Linsky, Leonard.
Reference and referents, in *Philosophy and Ordinary Language*, ed. C. Caton. Urbana: University of Illinois Press.
1964 Kalish, D. and Montague, R.
Remarks on descriptions and natural deduction I, *Archiv fur mathematische Logik und Grundlagenforschung*, **3**, 50–64.
1965 Prior, A. N.
Existence in Leśniewski and Russell in *Formal Systems and Recursive Functions* (Amsterdam), 149–55.
1966 Linsky, Leonard.
Substitutivity and descriptions, *Journal of Philosophy*, **58**, 673–84.

1967 Ayer, A. J.
An appraisal of Bertrand Russell's Philosophy. In *Bertrand Russell: Philosopher of the Century*, ed. R. Schoenman, pp. 167–78.
Linsky, Leonard.
Referring. Chap. IV. London, Routledge and Kegan Paul.
1968 Cassin, Christine.
Bertrand Russell's theory of descriptions (1903–1919). Dissertation, Florida State University.
1970 Cassin, Chrystine E.
(*a*) Russell's discussion of meaning and denotation. In E. D. Klemke, *Essays on Bertrand Russell*, 256–72.
(*b*) Russell's distinction between the primary and secondary occurrence of definite descriptions, *Ibid.* 273–84.
Hochberg, Herbert.
Strawson, Russell, and the King of France, *Ibid.* 309–41.
Jacobson, Arthur.
Russell and Strawson on referring, *Ibid.* 285–308.
Kaplan, David.
What is Russell's Theory of Descriptions? in *Physics, Logic, and History*, pp. 277–96, ed. W. Yourgrau and Allen D. Breck. New York: Plenum Press.

IV. CLASSES AND THE PARADOXES

1909 Poincaré, Henri.
La logique de l'infini, *Revue de Métaphysique et de Morale*, **17**, 451–82.
1914 König, Julius.
Neue Grundlagen der Logik, Arithmetik, und Mengenlehre (Leipzig), p. 155.

1921 Chwistek, Leon.
Antynomje logiki formalng (Antinomies of formal logic), *Przeglad Filozoficzny*, **24**, 164–171. Reprinted in *Polish Logic*, ed. Storrs McCall. Oxford, 1967.

BIBLIOGRAPHY

1922 Chwistek, Leon.
Zasady czysteg teerzi typow (The principles of a simple theory of types), *Przeglad Filozoficzny*, **25**.

1923 Fraenkel, A.
Einleitung in die Mengenlehre (Berlin), pp. 183 ff.

1924 Chwistek, Leon.
The theory of constructive types, *Bocznik Polskiege Towarzystma Matematycznego* (Year Book of the Polish Mathematical Society), **2**, 9–48.

1925 Ramsey, F. P.
The foundations of mathematics, *Proceedings of the London Mathematical Society*, series 2, **25**, 338–84.

1926 Langer, S. K.
Confusion of symbols and confusion of logical types, *Mind*, n.s. **35**, 222–9.

1928 Hilbert, D. and Ackermann, W. *Grundzüge der Theoretischen Logik* (Berlin-Göttingen-Heidelberg), pp. 114–15.
Weiss, Paul.
The theory of types, *Mind*, n.s. **37**, 338–48.

1930 Hahn, Hans.
Uberflüssige Wesenheiten (Vienna).

1931 Joergensen, Joergen.
A Treatise of Formal Logic (Copenhagen), III, ch. 12.

1934 Black, Max.
The Nature of Mathematics (Part I – Logistic) London.

1936 Quine, Willard Van Orman.
On the axiom of reducibility, *Mind*, n.s. **45**, 498–500.

1937 Quine, Willard Van Orman.
New foundations for mathematical logic, *American Mathematical Monthly*, **44**, 70–80.

1938 Fitch, Frederick.
The consistency of the ramified *Principia*, *Journal of Symbolic Logic*, **3**, 140–50.
Quine, Willard Van Orman.
On the theory of types, *Ibid*. 125–39.

1940 Church, Alonzo.
A formulation of the simple theory of types, *Journal of Symbolic Logic*, **5**, 56–68.

1941 Quine, Willard Van Orman.
Whitehead and the rise of modern logic, in *The Philosophy of Alfred North Whitehead*, pp. 125–64, ed. P. A. Schilpp (La Salle: Open Court).

1944 Black, Max.
Russell's philosophy of language, in *The Philosophy of Bertrand Russell*, ed. P. A. Schilpp, pp. 227–56.
Gödel, Kurt.
Russell's mathematical logic, *Ibid*. 123–54.

1948 Turing, A. M.
Practical forms of type theory, *Journal of Symbolic Logic*, **13**, 80–94.

1949 Henkin, Leon.
Completeness in the theory of types, *Journal of Symbolic Logic*, **14**, 159–66.

1950 Copi, Irving.
The inconsistency or redundancy of *Principia Mathematica*, *Philosophy and Phenomenological Research*, **11**, 190–9.
Shearn, Martin.
Whitehead and Russell's theory of types – a reply, *Analysis*, **11**, 45–8.
Smart, J. J. C.
Whitehead and Russell's theory of types, *Analysis*, **10**, 93–6.

1951 Myhill, John.
Report of some investigations concerning the consistency of

C. SECONDARY MATERIAL

the axiom of reducibility, *Journal of Symbolic Logic*, **16**, 35–42.
Smart, J. J. C.
The theory of types again, *Analysis*, **11**, 31–7.
1958 Borkowski, Ludwig.
Reduction of arithmetic to logic based on the theory of types, *Studia Logica*, **8**, 283–95.
1960 Schutte, Karl.
Syntactical and semantical properties of simple type theory, *Journal of Symbolic Logic*, **25**, 305–26.
1963 Peters, Franz.
Russell on class theory. *Synthèse*, **15**, 327–35.
Sommers, Fred.
Types and ontology, *Philosophical Review*, **72**, 327–63.
Sellars, Wilfrid.
Classes as abstract entities and the Russell paradox. *Review of Metaphysics*, **17**, 67–90.
1971 Copi, Irving.
The Theory of Logical Types. London: George Allen & Unwin.

V. PHILOSOPHY OF LOGIC AND MATHEMATICS

Includes works in the logicist tradition after Russell, and major technical results about the *Principia* system.

1904 Wilson, Edwin B.
Review of *Principles of Mathematics*, *Bulletin of the American Mathematical Society*, **11**, 74–93.
1912 Shaw, James B.
Review of *Principia Mathematica*, *Bulletin of the American Mathematical Society*, **18**, 386–411.
1915 Lowenheim, L.
Uber Möglichkeiten im Relativkalkul, *Mathematische Annalen*, **76**, 447–470.
1918 Weyl, Hermann.
Das Kontinuum (Leipzig).
1920 Skolem, Thoralf.
Logisch-kombinatorische Untersuchungen über die Erfullbarkeit oder Beweisbarkeit mathematischer Sätze nebst einem Theoreme uber dichte Mengen, *Videnskapsselskapets skrifter, I Matematisk-naturevidenskabelig klasse*, no. 4.
1921 Wittgenstein, Ludwig.
Tractatus-Logico-Philosophicus. *Annalen der Naturphilosophie*. Eng. translation by C. K. Ogden. London: Routledge and Kegan Paul, 1922.
1925 Ramsey, F. P.
The foundations of mathematics, *Proceedings of the London Mathematical Society*, series 2, **25**, 338–84.
1926 Ramsey, F. P.
Mathematical logic, *Mathematical Gazette*, **13**, 185–94.
1927 Russell, Bertrand.
Introduction to *Principia Mathematica*, 2nd ed. London: Cambridge University Press.
1928 Carnap, Rudolph.
Die Logische Aufbau der Welt (Berlin).
Church, Alonzo.
Review of *Principia Mathematica* vols. ii and iii, *Bulletin of the American Mathematical Society*, **34**, 237–40.
Skolem, Thoralf.
Uber die Mathematische Logik, *Norsk Matematisk Tidsskrift*, **10**, 125–42.
1929 Carnap, Rudolph.
Abriss der Logistik (Wien).

BIBLIOGRAPHY

1930 Gödel, Kurt.
Die Vollstandigkeit der Axiome des logischen Funktionenkalküls, *Monatshefte für Mathematik und Physik*, **37**, 349–60.

1931 Carnap, Rudolf.
The logicist foundations of mathematics, *Erkenntnis*, 1931; in English in Pears' *Bertrand Russell*, pp. 175–91.

Gödel, Kurt.
Uber formal unentscheidbare Sätze der *Principia Mathematica* und verwandter Systeme I, *Ibid.* **38**, 173–98.

1934 Nelson, E. J.
Whitehead and Russell's theory of deduction as a non-mathematical science, *Bulletin of the American Mathematical Society*, **40**, 478–86.

1936 Church, Alonzo.
A note on the Entscheidungsproblem, *Journal of Symbolic Logic*, **1**, 40–41, 101–2.

1956 Hochberg, Herbert.
Peano, Russell, and logicism, *Analysis*, **16**, 118–20.

1960 Church, Alonzo.
Mathematics and Logic. In *Logic, Methodology, and Philosophy of Science. Proceedings of the 1960 International Congress*, ed. E. Nagel, P. Suppes, and A. Tarski. Stanford: Stanford University Press.

1962 Henkin, Leon.
Are logic and mathematics identical? *Science*, **138**, 788–794.

1965 Wang, Hao.
Russell and his logic. *Ratio*, **7**, 1–34.

1967 Prior, A. N.
Russell, Bertrand Arthur William; Logic and mathematics. Article in *Encyclopedia of Philosophy*, ed. Paul Edwards. New York: Random House.

Putnam, Hilary.
The Thesis that Mathematics is Logic. In R. Schoenman, *Bertrand Russell: Philosopher of the Century*, pp. 273–303.

1970 Hochberg, Herbert.
Russell's Reduction of Arithmetic to Logic. In E. D. Klemke, *Essays on Bertrand Russell*, pp. 396–415.

Pollock, John L.
On Logicism, *Ibid.* 388–95.

1972 Chihara, Charles S.
Russell's Theory of Types. In Pears, *Bertrand Russell*, pp. 245–89.

Kreisel, George.
Bertrand Russell's Logic. In Pears, *Bertrand Russell*, pp. 168–74.

INDEX

acquaintance, 103, 119, 224–5
act, content and object, 33–4, 38–9, 49, 55–6, 60, 64
adequacy, 51–2
affirmation and denial, 41, 75–6
ambiguity, 218–19, 229–30
Amseder, 79–88, 107
assumptions (*Annahmen*), 23, 39, 42–4
Avenarius, 88
awareness, 65–6
axiom: of choice (multiplicative axiom, Zermelo's axiom), 15, 135–6, 156–64, 210
 of infinity, 253–9
 of reducibility, 240–44, 248–50
axiomatic set theory, 130

being, 17, 49
belief, 21, 36–8, 56, 74–5
Benussi, V., 87–8
Bernays, P., 130
Bernstein, F., 139
Berry, G. G., 128, 143, 210
Bôcher, M., 130–1, 167, 280
Boole, G., 313–22
Boutroux, P., 14, 254, 260, 262–8
Boyle, R., 280
Bradley, F. H., 105

Cantor, G., 12, 127–8, 138–9, 143, 146, 148, 154, 160, 163–4, 175, 182–3, 186, 195–8, 213–14, 284–6
Cantor's paradox (paradox of the greatest cardinal), 126, 129, 138
Carnap, R., 255, 297
certainty of logic, 194, 272–83, 299
class, 99, 128–9, 136–7, 170–71, 192, 199–200, 243–50
complex, 24, 27, 50, 55, 61, 66–7, 70, 83, 223, 225
contextual definition, 201
content, 23–4

Dedekind, R., 151, 258
diversity (and negation), 40
Dixon, A., 184

egocentricity, 121, 126

Epimenides paradox, 129, 132–3, 196–198, 204, 227
Euclid, 273
excluded middle, 207–9, 303–6
existence, 24, 93, 95, 100–2
existence *vs.* subsistence, 29, 31, 37–8, 60, 76, 78–80, 107, 293
existence presuppositions, 95
existential import, 95, 98–102
expression (and indication), 62
extension (*vs.* intension), 137, 262–3, 268, 294–8

facts, 75–6, 213
Flew, A., 120
Frankel, A., 130
Frankl, W., 88
free logic, 11, 95
Frege, G., 11–12, 21, 23, 44, 64, 81, 84, 95–6, 104, 108, 149, 171, 244, 254, 278, 280, 284, 300
functional hierarchy, 238–9
functions, 260–3

Gegenstandstheorie, 27–9, 89
geometry, 91–2
Graz school, 17
Grattan-Guinness, I., 13, 15, 129

Hardy, G., 156
Hilbert, D., 154
Hobbes, T., 33
Hobson, E., 33–6, 147–51, 156, 163, 180, 184
Human Knowledge, 121
Husserl, E., 254

ideal objects, 28
idealism, 64, 74, 149, 286, 292
identity, 110, 114, 118, 169, 217, 242, 296–8
identity of indiscernables, 242–3
immanent objects, 58–9, 63–7
implication (*vs.* inference), 18, 44–6
inference, 44–7
intuitionism, 132

343

INDEX

Jourdain, P. E. B., 129, 135, 142, 152, 284
judgment, 18, 23, 39, 42, 52, 61, 64, 70, 77, 79, 223-6

Kalish, D., 97
Kant, I., 77, 81, 292-3
Keyser, C., 253-6
knowledge, 60, 75, 292
König, J., 128, 184

Leibniz, G. W., Baron von, 192, 242-3, 285
Lewis, C. I., 307
Liel, W., 88
limitations of size approach, 130, 152
linguistic statements, 170, 295-8
Linsky, L., 97
logical priority, 25, 272-83

MacColl, H., 11, 14, 96-8, 98-102, 117, 307-22
Mach, E., 91
mathematical induction, 211-12
'Mathematical logic as based on the theory of types', 11, 215
mathematics, definition of, 300-3
matrix, 169, 234
meaning (and denotation), 100, 108, 111-13, 165
Meinong, A., 11, 13, 14, 17, 93, 96, 104, 107, 109, 110, 117
Moore, G. E., 21, 23, 37, 54, 64
Montague, R., 97
Müller-Lyer, 87
multiplicative axiom, *see* axiom of choice

necessity, 26, 45
'no classes' theory, 130, 154-6, 190, 193-6, 198, 202-6
nominalism, 130-1
null class, 99, 117-18, 309, 318
numbers: cardinal, 175-6, 202
    ordinal, 180-84

objects, 62
objects of higher order, 24
objectives, 54-62, 89
'On Denoting' (descriptions), 11, 13, 17, 19, 96-7
ontological argument, 81, 117
ontology, 17, 96, 133-4

Peano, G., 11, 12, 134, 169, 172, 190, 193, 198, 206, 232, 262, 263, 276-7, 284
perception, 21, 30-6, 87, 90, 223, 232
phenomenology, 18
Plato, 301, 306
Poincaré, H., 14, 15, 128-33, 192-8, 208-13, 215, 241, 251
predicative *vs*. non-predicative functions, 141, 237, 241
presentation, 23-4, 38, 49, 50, 55, 61, 64-70, 77, 89
primary and secondary occurrence, 114-16
Principia Mathematica, 11-16, 95, 131-2, 253-5, 301
Principles of Mathematics, 11-14, 17-18, 25, 27, 42, 96, 127, 193, 300
propositions, 18, 21, 22-3, 26, 34-5, 54, 76, 79, 92, 188, 204, 207, 230, 239
psychologism, 22, 58, 77, 254, 264
Pythagoras, 301, 306

Quine, W. V. O., 122, 130, 133, 134

Ramsey, F. P., 16
realism, 11, 96, 129, 286, 293
realistic thesis, 18
relations, 27-8, 49-53, 68-9, 70-2, 170, 174, 196, 306
Richard, J., 196-7, 209
round squares, 19, 79-81, 92, 100, 117
Russell's paradox, 12, 13, 128, 140, 199, 219

Saxinger, R., 88
Schröder, E., 139
Schumann, 29, 30
Schwarz, 88
Searle, J., 96
Sein (and So-Sein), 19, 79
sentences, 42
Shearman, 319-21
Smullyan, A. F., 97
Strawson, P. F., 120-6
substitutional theory, 11, 130-2, 155-9, 167-89, 261
syntax, 12, 304-6

theory of descriptions, 13, 14, 81, 86, 96, 129
theory of knowledge, 21-2, 36, 51, 58, 62-3, 78, 103
time, 31-2

INDEX

transcendent objects, 67, 74
truth and falsity, 56, 65, 72–6, 125, 221–8, 308
types, 12, 14–15, 176, 193, 201, 217, 234

Uber Annahmen, 77

value, 57, 88
vicious circles, 88, 196, 198, 204–9, 215–19, 222, 231, 249, 251
Von Neumann, J., 130

Weierstrauss, K., 284
Whitehead, A. N., 12, 15, 95, 131–2, 158, 253–4
William of Occam, 196
Wittgenstein, L., 15–16

Zeno, 286
Zermelo, E., 15, 130, 135–6, 142, 156–164, 199
'zigzag' theory, 130, 145–52, 193, 200